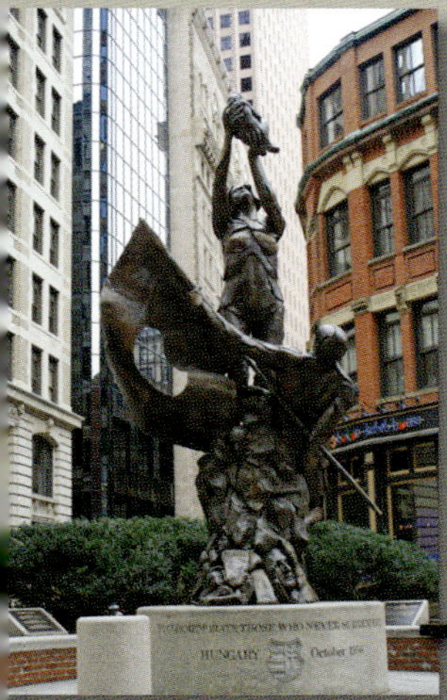

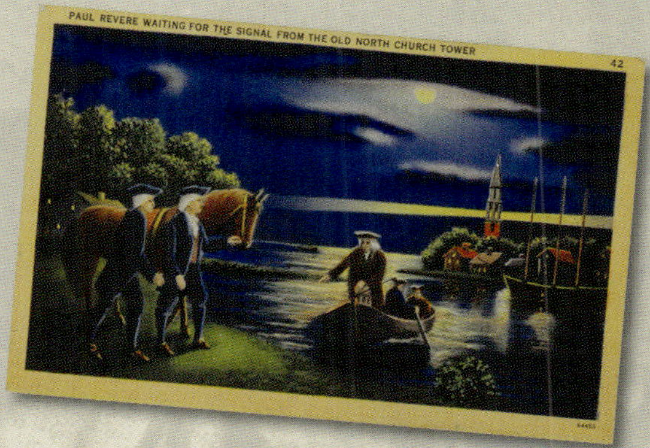

BOSTON

Past & Present

MARY L. MARTIN & E. ASHLEY ROONEY

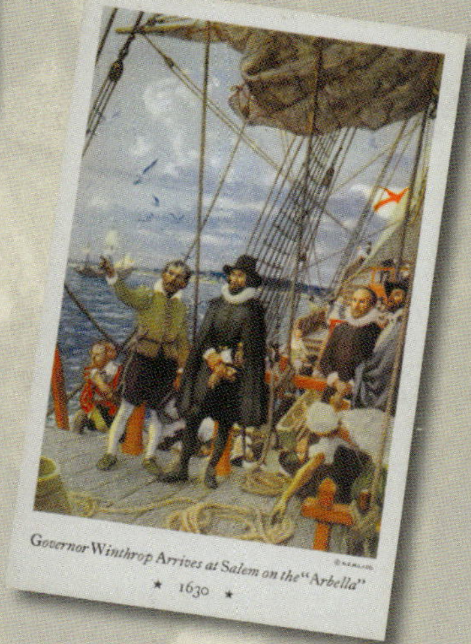

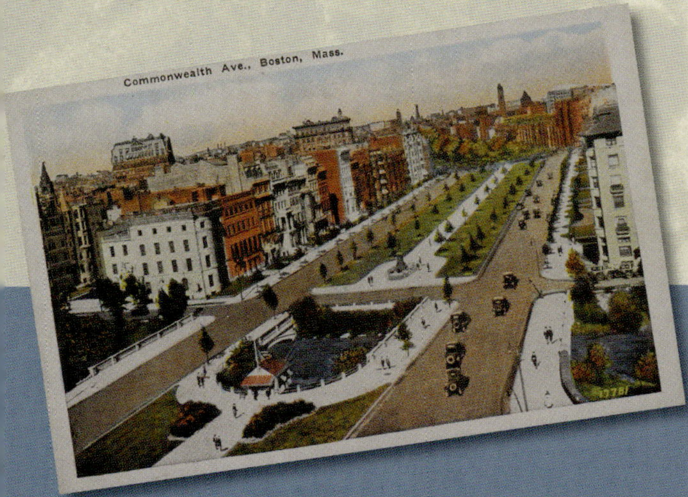

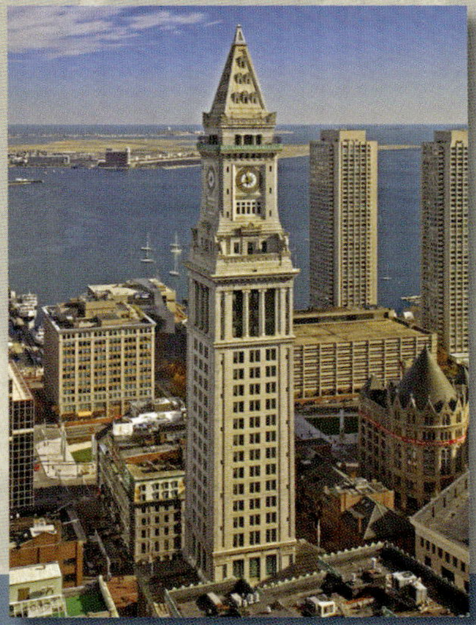

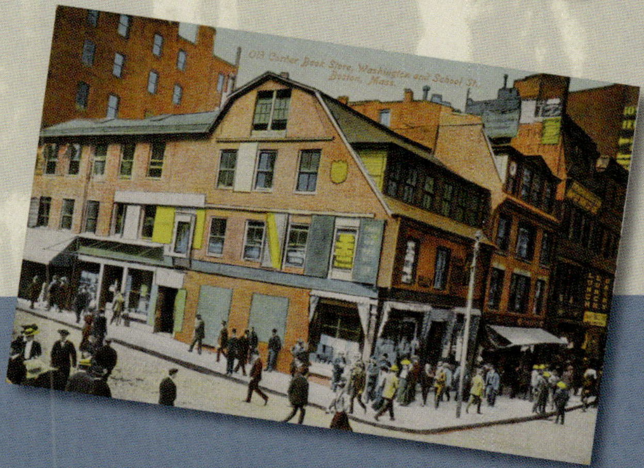

Schiffer Publishing Ltd
4880 Lower Valley Road Atglen, Pennsylvania 19310

Acknowledgments

D. Peter Lund played a major role in this book. He sorted, listened, photographed, and helped make sense of those narrow winding Boston streets. Paul Doherty took some wonderful photographs, and Mary Bicknell showed up at my door with some great references.

Images are from Mary L. Martin Postcards unless otherwise credited.

Other Schiffer Books by E. Ashley Rooney:
Waterfront Homes: from Castles to Cottages (2003)
Garden Ornaments: Pots, Pergolas, Pedestals and More (2003)
Old Barns – New Homes: A Showcase of Architectural Conversions (2004)
Spectacular Small Kitchens: Design Ideas for Urban Spaces (2005)
Retreats to Retirement: Dreams to Reality (2005)
Cliffhangers & Hillside Houses (2006)
Table Décor: Festive Occasions, Weddings, and Other Events (2006)
Lexington to Concord: The Road to Independence in Postcards (2007)
Berkshire Ghosts, Legends and Lore (2007)
Walls, Fences, and Gates (2007)
Shingle Style Houses: Past and Present (2007)
Green Residences for the 21st Century (2008)
Cambridge, Massachusetts, Past and Present (2008)
Washington, D.C. Ghosts, Legends, and Lore (2008)

Library of Congress Control Number: 2008924905

Title page credit: "Boston Skyline" ©Steve Sakata. Image from BigStockPhoto.com
Cover and Contents page photos: The Old State House stands proudly among Boston's twentieth century government buildings. *Courtesy of Paul E. Doherty*

Designed by John P. Cheek
Type set in Engravers Roman Bd BT/Zurich BT

ISBN:978-0-7643-3058-2
Printed in China

Published by Schiffer Publishing Ltd.
4880 Lower Valley Road
Atglen, PA 19310
Phone: (610) 593-1777; Fax: (610) 593-2002
E-mail: Info@schifferbooks.com

For the largest selection of fine reference books on this and related subjects, please visit our web site at **www.schifferbooks.com**
We are always looking for people to write books on new and related subjects. If you have an idea for a book please contact us at the above address.

This book may be purchased from the publisher.
Include $5.00 for shipping.
Please try your bookstore first.
You may write for a free catalog.

In Europe, Schiffer books are distributed by
Bushwood Books
6 Marksbury Ave.
Kew Gardens
Surrey TW9 4JF England
Phone: 44 (0) 20 8392-8585; Fax: 44 (0) 20 8392-9876
E-mail: info@bushwoodbooks.co.uk
Website: www.bushwoodbooks.co.uk
Free postage in the U.K., Europe; air mail at cost.

Contents

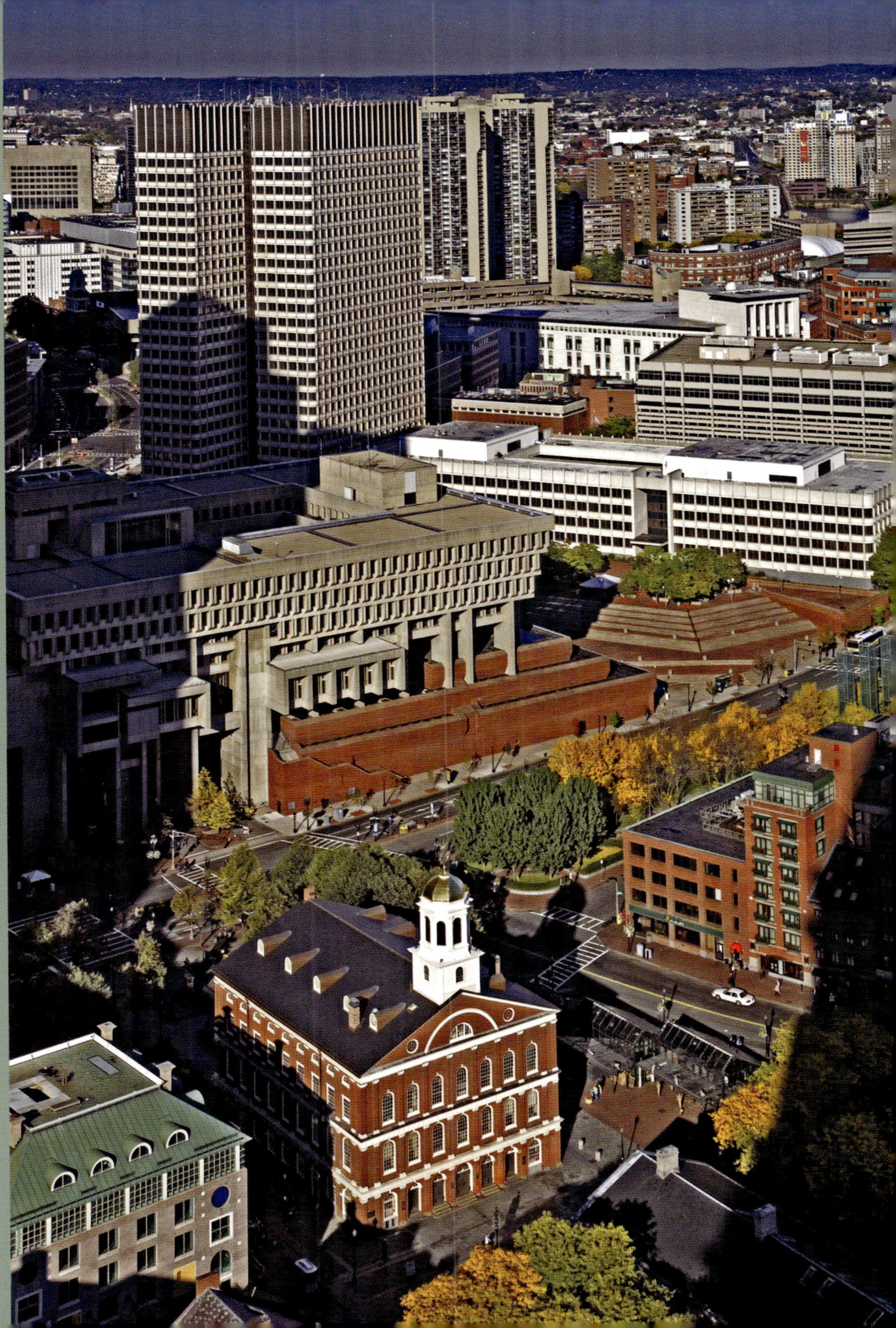

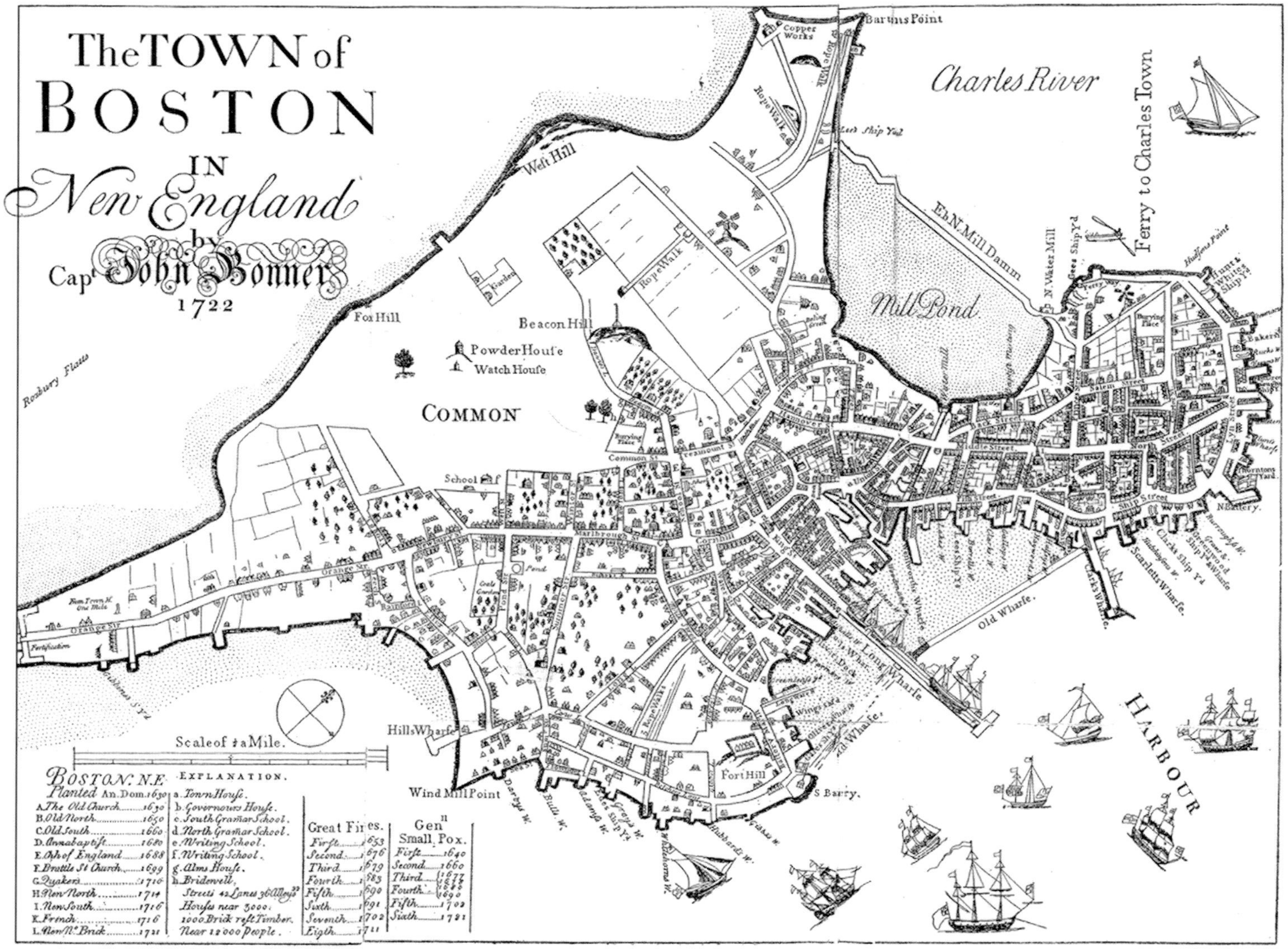
The TOWN of
BOSTON
IN
New England
by
Capt John Bonner
1722
Charles River
Ferry to Charles Town
Mill Pond
COMMON
Beacon Hill
Powder House
Watch House
Fox Hill
West Hill
Roxbury Flatts
Old Wharfe
Long Wharfe
HARBOUR
Fort Hill
Hills Wharfe
Wind Mill Point
Scale of ½ a Mile.
BOSTON N.E.
Planted An. Dom. 1630
A. The Old Church 1630
B. Old North 1650
C. Old South 1660
D. Annabaptist 1680
E. Chh of England 1688
F. Brattle St Church 1699
G. Quakers 1710
H. New North 1714
I. New South 1716
K. French 1716
L. New Nd Brick 1721
EXPLANATION.
a. Town House.
b. Governours House.
c. South Gramar School.
d. North Gramar School.
e. Writing School.
f. Writing School.
g. Alms House.
h. Bridewell.
Streets 42 Lanes 36 Alleys 22
Houses near 3000.
1000 Brick rest Timber.
Near 12000 People.
Great Fires.
First 1653
Second 1676
Third 1679
Fourth 1683
Fifth 1690
Sixth 1691
Seventh 1702
Eigth 1711
Genll Small Pox.
First 1640
Second 1660
Third 1677 1678
Fourth 1689 1690
Fifth 1702
Sixth 1721

Chapter 1

Boston History

The city is a beautiful one, and cannot fail, I should imagine, to impress all strangers very favourably. The private dwelling-houses are, for the most part, large and elegant; the shops extremely good; and the public buildings handsome. The State House is built upon the summit of a hill, which rises gradually at first, and afterwards by a steep ascent, almost from the water's edge. In front is a green enclosure, called the Common. The site is beautiful: and from the top there is a charming panoramic view of the whole town and neighbourhood. In addition to a variety of commodious offices, it contains two handsome chambers; in one the House of Representatives of the State hold their meetings: in the other, the Senate. Such proceedings as I saw here, were conducted with perfect gravity and decorum; and were certainly calculated to inspire attention and respect. –Charles Dickens, *American Notes*, 1842, Chapter 3

Boston, Massachusetts, was one of a number of towns (others being Cambridge, Charlestown, Watertown, and Roxbury) established by around a thousand English Puritan colonists of the Massachusetts Bay Colony under the leadership of governor John Winthrop. Like the Pilgrims, Puritans refused to accept the Church of England, but they were willing to remain members of it in order to attempt to purify it. When Charles I became the English king, his government's persecution of the Puritans increased, and many left the land of their birth.

John Winthrop and other Puritans had obtained a royal charter from King Charles I, in 1630, for the Massachusetts Bay Colony and pledged in the Cambridge Agreement to establish a new colony in New England. An ardent Puritan, John Winthrop believed fervently that the Anglican Church needed to be brought into a state of purity as it had been in the time of Christ.

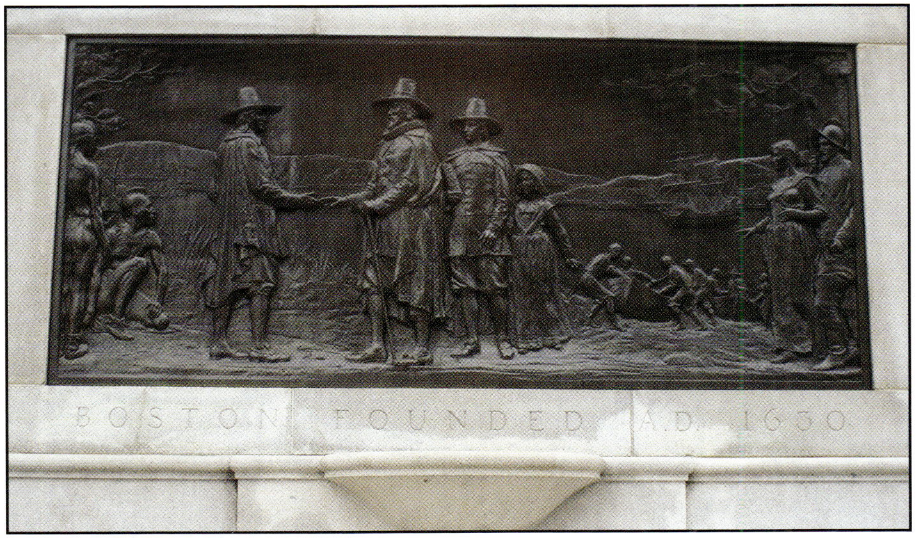

This plaque on the Boston Common shows Governor John Winthrop arriving at the Shawmut peninsula. *Courtesy of D. Peter Lund*

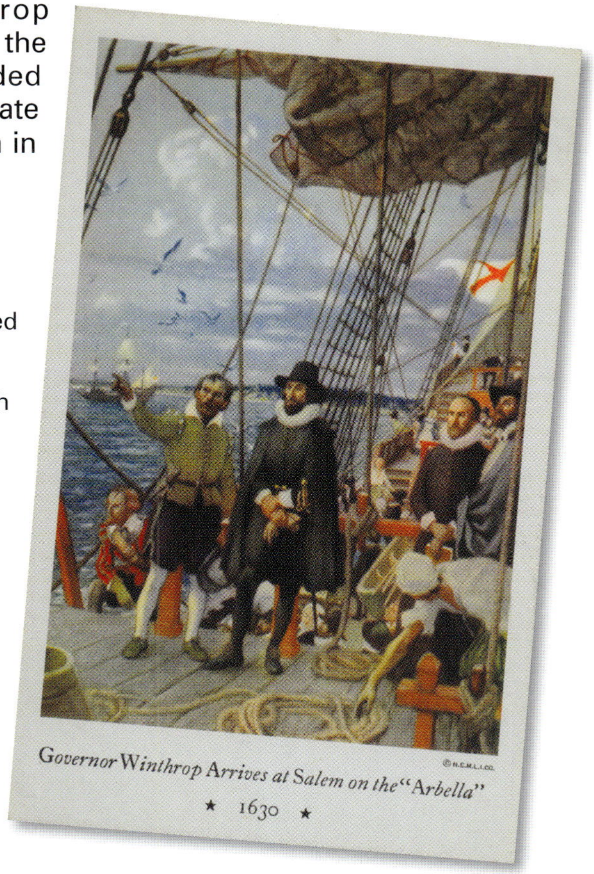

John Winthrop was elected the first Governor of Massachusetts, and the Deacon of the First Church of Boston.

Elected governor of Massachusetts by the company in London, Winthrop is famous for his "City on a Hill" sermon, made onboard the ship *Arbella* that brought him to the New World. In that sermon, he declared that the Puritan colonists immigrating to the New World were part of a special pact with God to create a holy community.

> *Consider that we shall be as a City upon a Hill, the eyes of all people are upon us; so that if we shall deal falsely with our God in this work we have undertaken and so cause him to withdraw his present help from us, we shall be made a story and a byword through the world.* –John Winthrop, *A Model of Christian Charity*

Unlike the Pilgrims who settled Plymouth, Massachusetts, in 1620, many Puritans had titles, property, and education; their leaders were well-educated scholars. Along with money, furniture, and other worldly goods, they brought with them a vision of the future. As John Winthrop stated, they wanted their new colony to be a biblical witness, a "city on a hill," and an example of biblical righteousness in church and state to be admired by the world.

Ten years after the Pilgrims landed at Plymouth, Winthrop and his fellow Puritans arrived at Salem, on June 22, 1630. During that summer many became ill and died. Winthrop traveled along the coast to Charleston, looking for a suitable site for a capital. There, Winthrop met the reclusive Rev. William Blaxton (modernized to Blackstone), the area's first English resident. Blackstone invited them to visit the Shawmut peninsula with its clear spring of water. The site provided potable water, good anchorage, and good defenses.

> *Boston...situation is very pleasant, being a peninsula hemmed on the south side by the Bay of Roxbury and on the north side with the Charles River, the marshes on the back side being not half a quarter of a mile over; so that a little fencing will secure their cattle from the wolves; it being a neck and bare of wood they are troubled with these great annoyances, wolves, rattlesnakes, and mosquitoes. This neck of land is not over four miles in compass, in form almost square, having on the south side a great broad hill [Fort Hill].... To the northwest is a high mountain with three little rising hills on the top of it, wherefore it is called the Tramount [Beacon Hill].* –As described by one of the earliest visitors, *State Street & Trust Company*, p. 7.

On September 17, 1630, Winthrop founded a town on the peninsula, which was surrounded by Massachusetts Bay and the Back Bay, an estuary of the Charles River. Originally it was called Trimountain, but the Puritans soon renamed it Boston after the town of Boston in Lincolnshire, England, from which several prominent colonists had emigrated. Two years later, the new town of Boston became the seat of government for the surrounding towns, including Roxbury, Charlestown, Newtowne (in 1638 Newtowne became Cambridge), and Dorchester.

The colonists faced a harsh New England winter, rocky soil, Native Americans, and other obstacles, but they planted fields, built houses, and cleared the forests. By 1634, they had purchased Boston Common as a public park and laid out space for a pasture, a training field, and an area for punishing lawbreakers. With its excellent harbor and abundant codfish, Boston became the leading commercial center in the region. By 1636, the colonists had collected and shipped to England enough beaver pelts to pay off their debt. They launched the first ship built in the New World, constructed Long Wharf projecting nearly a half mile into the bay in 1710, and created a millpond to drive gristmills and sawmills.

The Puritans lived in a world where church and state were one. They believed that religion and education were essential elements of a Christian community. In 1635, the Puritans founded America's first public school, Boston Latin School. By autumn 1636, six years after the Puritans' arrival, The Great and General Court selected Newtowne over Salem as the location for the colony's first college, named subsequently after John Harvard. Along with the Boston Latin School, it initiated Boston's reputation as an intellectual and educational center.

By 1640, more than twenty thousand immigrants had arrived in Boston and gone to places inland. Settlements grew into towns around the city, mills were built along the rivers for logging, fishing boats were constructed to catch cod and haddock, and animals grazed. Colonial Boston had a meetinghouse, market square, and thatched wooden houses with diamond-paned casement windows lining the narrow port-side streets. Their shipyards were soon building American-made vessels that transported lumber, salted fish, and furs back to England.

Although the Puritans had left England to pursue religious freedom, they were loath to offer the same freedom to others. Ironically, Blackstone left the area because of the harsh, intolerant Puritan society. A young English clergyman, Roger Williams, arrived from England and preached revolutionary doctrines. Before he was exiled, he left Boston and founded the state of Rhode Island. Soon thereafter, the

Boston colony charged Anne Hutchinson with heretical thinking and traducing the ministers. She was tried in Cambridge in 1637, excommunicated for not conforming to the Puritan ways, and banished from the colony. On June 1, 1660, Quaker preacher Mary Dyer was hanged on Boston Common for repeatedly defying a law banning Quakers from the colony. Until 1664, only Puritan church members could be Massachusetts citizens. The Salem Witch Trials marked the end of the seventeenth century.

In 1674, approximately 1,500 families lived in Boston. By 1675, Boston had 4,000 residents, which grew to 15,520 by 1765.

Rebellious Stirrings

By the early eighteenth century, two-story Georgian-style buildings were replacing the earlier houses in Boston. Some local residents were importing china, silver, and cabinetwork and hoping to have their portraits painted. Numerous New England merchants and ship owners were beginning to accumulate fortunes along with associated accouterments, such as fine houses, gardens, servants, and carriages. The shipyards were expanding and foreign and domestic trade was growing at the proliferating waterfront docks. Three days a week, local farmers and fishermen sold their goods at a large public market. Boston was becoming a major city.

Boston citizens, however, were determined to remain independent and prevent the British government from meddling in their affairs. During the final decades of the seventeenth century, King Charles II nullified the Massachusetts Bay Charter, putting the colony under control of his throne. Charles' successor, James II, appointed Edmund Andros governor of the Dominion of New England, which comprised Massachusetts (including Maine), Plymouth Colony, Rhode Island, Connecticut, and New Hampshire. Boston became his capital, and the colony's self-government came to a halt. Andros so angered the colonists that once King William and Queen Mary assumed the British throne, the colonists rioted and ran him out of town. In 1691, William and Mary of England granted a new charter to the colony, combining it with the Plymouth colony and recognizing a bicameral legislature.

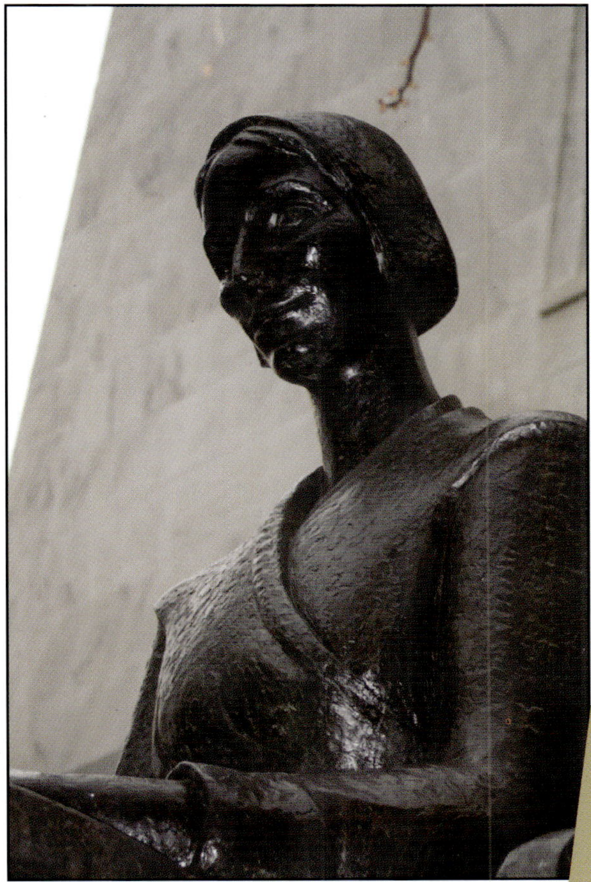

A Puritan turned Quaker, Mary Dyer was hanged on the Common for repeatedly defying a law banning Quakers from the colony. She is one of the four executed Quakers known as the Boston martyrs. This bronze statue by Quaker sculptor Sylvia Shaw Judson is in front of the Massachusetts State House. *Courtesy of D. Peter Lund*

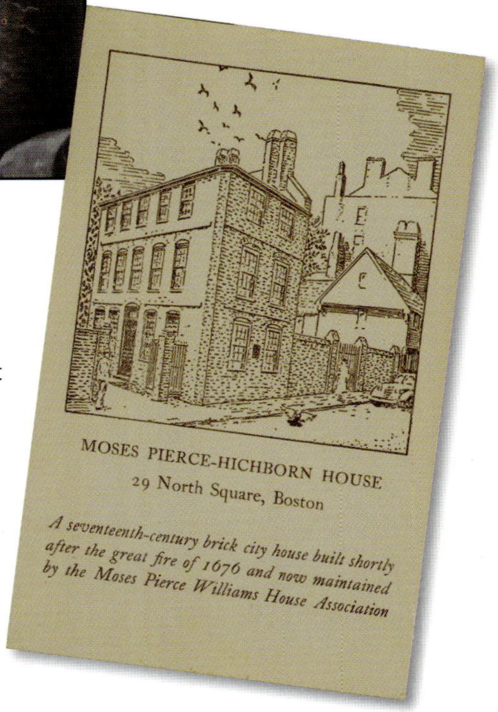

Moses Pierce, a glazier, built this house in 1711 on Clark Square.

By this time, England and France were vying for control of North America. France claimed most of North America west of the Appalachian Mountains. The English had settled in the south or New England and along the seaboard. With their insatiable appetite for territorial expansion, the English colonists rapidly pushed westward, where they acquired land and established frontier communities. They took saws and axes to the wilderness, cutting down the great forests, planting fields, and establishing themselves as farmers on land purchased or taken from the Indians. The Indians, who had lived in the region for generations, were largely overlooked, except for their value as allies in war. After many years of war, the British were awarded all of North America east of the Mississippi, other than New Orleans, in the Treaty of Paris, February 10, 1763.

The British victory was costly. Because the results of the French and Indian War benefited the colonies, King George III and his government began to tax their American possessions as a way of recouping their war costs. They instituted the Stamp Act (a tax on newspapers, legal documents) in 1765 and the Townshend Acts, which taxed common imports such as lead, paper, and tea in 1767. Although the citizens of Massachusetts considered themselves British, they were incensed about the repressive taxes imposed by the English Parliament. The colonists claimed they had no obligation to pay taxes imposed by a Parliament in which they had no representation.

No Taxation Without Representation

Led by Samuel Adams and the Sons of Liberty of Boston, they turned to smuggling and boycotting British goods.

The Stamp Act was repealed, but in response to the colonists' anger, Britain sent troops to Boston to protect their commissioners. Using soldiers, tax collectors, and other officials, Britain hoped to regain authority over the "provincials" or "Yankees," who were beginning to rebel against Parliamentary control. Bostonians often jeered the soldiers and threw stones or snowballs. On March 5, 1770, the situation reached a crisis point: shots were fired, and five Americans fell in what is known as "The Boston Massacre."

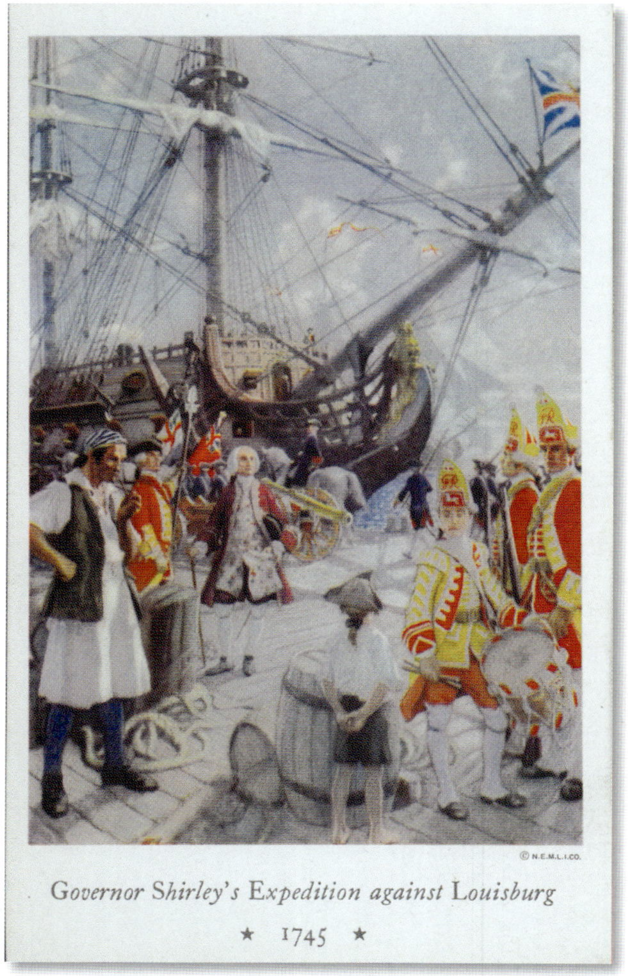

Based in Louisburg, Nova Scotia, French privateers preyed on New England fishermen working the Grand Banks. In 1745, Massachusetts Governor Shirley, promoted the successful expedition against Louisburg as part of the war with France and forced its surrender.

In 1773, the British Parliament passed the Tea Act, which led to the Boston Tea Party. On December 16, 1773, angry colonists thinly disguised as Indians boarded the East India Company's ships and dumped crates of tea into Boston Harbor. For weeks later, tea washed up on the Boston beaches. Angered by the Boston Tea Party, British leaders passed a series of repressive acts, closed Boston Harbor in 1774, and appointed General Thomas Gage to establish order in the unruly colonies.

The colonists responded with petitions, protests, and demonstrations. In Massachusetts, John Hancock, Sam Adams, and others clamored for the right to run their own affairs. The gun was cocked for an historic conflict that would divide English-speaking people one from another and see the emergence of the American republic.

In those days, Boston was a prosperous maritime community. Many residents wanted the freedom to govern themselves. That fall, the provincial Congress of Massachusetts created a Committee of Safety, collected gunpowder and weapons, and revived the old New England training bands. All men between the ages of 16 and 50 were asked to enlist themselves in the militia. Older men were organized into a group called the alarm list. The Provincial Congress also recommended that one quarter of the militia be organized in minute companies ready to march at the shortest notice.

Throughout the winter of 1774-1775, the colonists prepared for the coming confrontation with the British. They hid arms and supplies, trained militia, and organized their defenses. Some veterans of the French and Indian war served as drill leaders. Their "militia" had little in the way of uniforms or military arms; they were armed citizen soldiers preparing for war.

Tensions were high in the Massachusetts Bay Colony by springtime. Colonists were clamoring for the right to run their own affairs, some going as far as to call for independence from the mother country. On April 18, 1775, the military governor of Massachusetts, General Thomas Gage, decided to send British troops to capture Samuel Adams and John Hancock, prominent leaders in the colonial cause, who were purported to be in Lexington. Following their capture, the troops were then to march to Concord and destroy the military supplies stored there. Word of General Gage's intentions reached the patriots, prompting them to sound the alarm. Paul Revere and his cohorts arranged for a signal. Should the British regulars move out by land over Boston Neck, one lantern was to be hung from the steeple of the North Church, Boston's tallest building at that time. If by sea, across the river, two lanterns were to be hung.

That night the British crossed the river (two if by sea) and then waded through the swamps of East Cambridge. Through the dark night, the cold, wet British soldiers marched toward Lexington along what is now Massachusetts Avenue. As the British were being rowed to the opposite shore that night of April 18, 1775, Revere set off for Lexington (a ride of nearly thirteen miles) to warn Hancock and Adams about the British movement. Having left Boston by the land route, William Dawes joined him, and they and other riders roused the town leaders and militia commanders throughout the area that night. Their mission was to alert the militia along the route. "The regulars are coming out," was their cry. In the riders' wake, there erupted the peeling of meetinghouse bells, the beating of drums, and the firing of muskets– all warning of the approaching danger and calling the local militias to action.

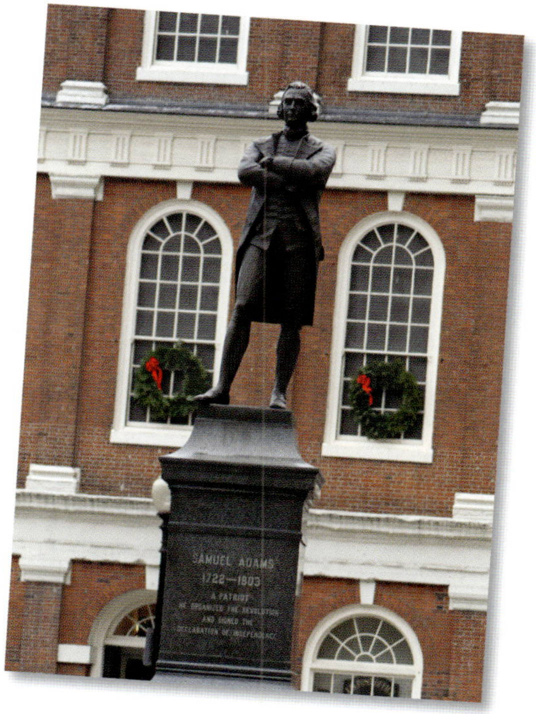

Anne Whitney, the sculptor of this bronze statue of Samuel Adams, portrayed him as he is supposed to have appeared just after demanding that Governor Hutchinson remove the British troops from Boston after the Boston Massacre. Erected in 1880, the statue now stands adjacent to Faneuil Hall on Congress Street. *Courtesy of D. Peter Lund*

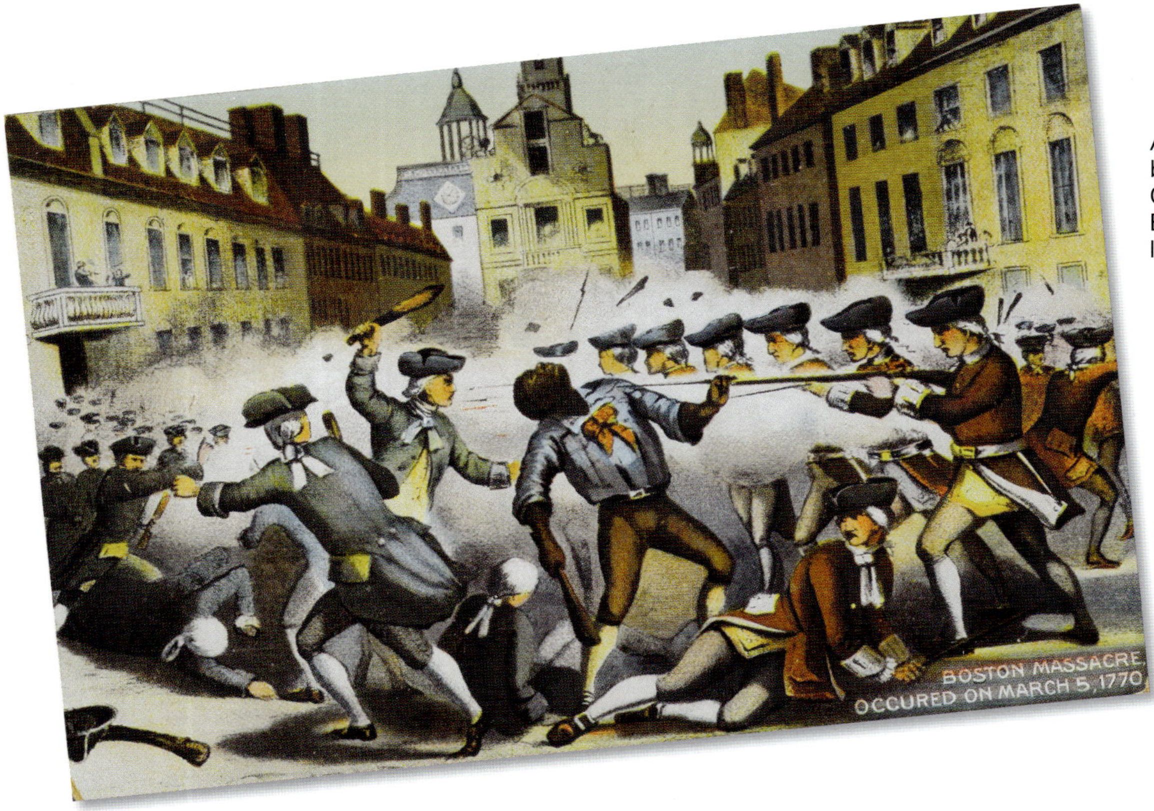

A circle of cobblestones below the balcony on the eastern facade of the Old State House marks the site of the Boston Massacre, one of the events leading to the American Revolution.

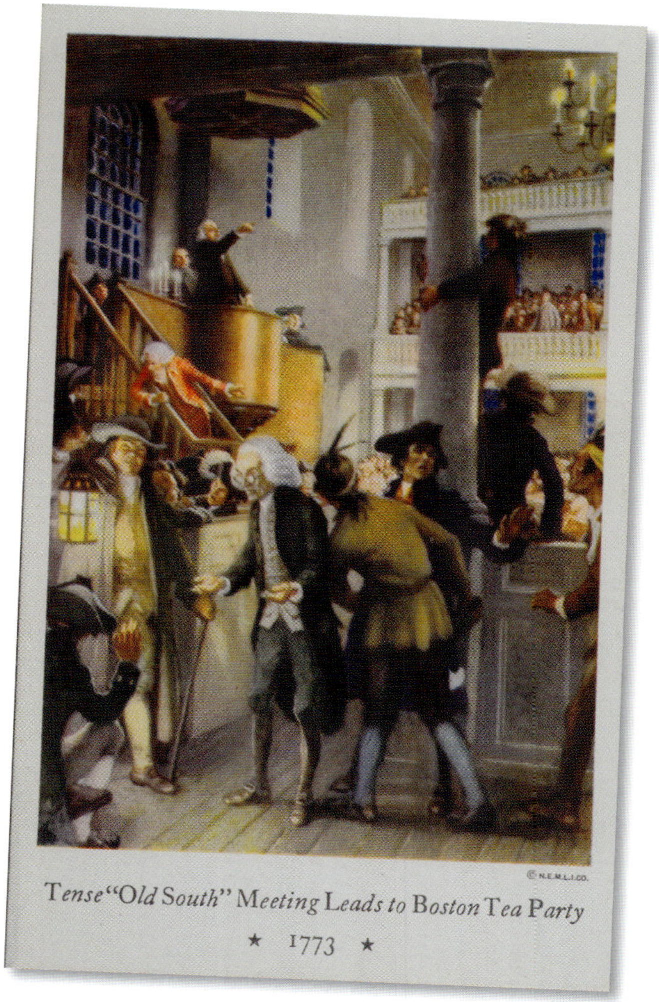

American colonists protested against Great Britain's repressive measures by destroying many crates of tea on ships in Boston Harbor.

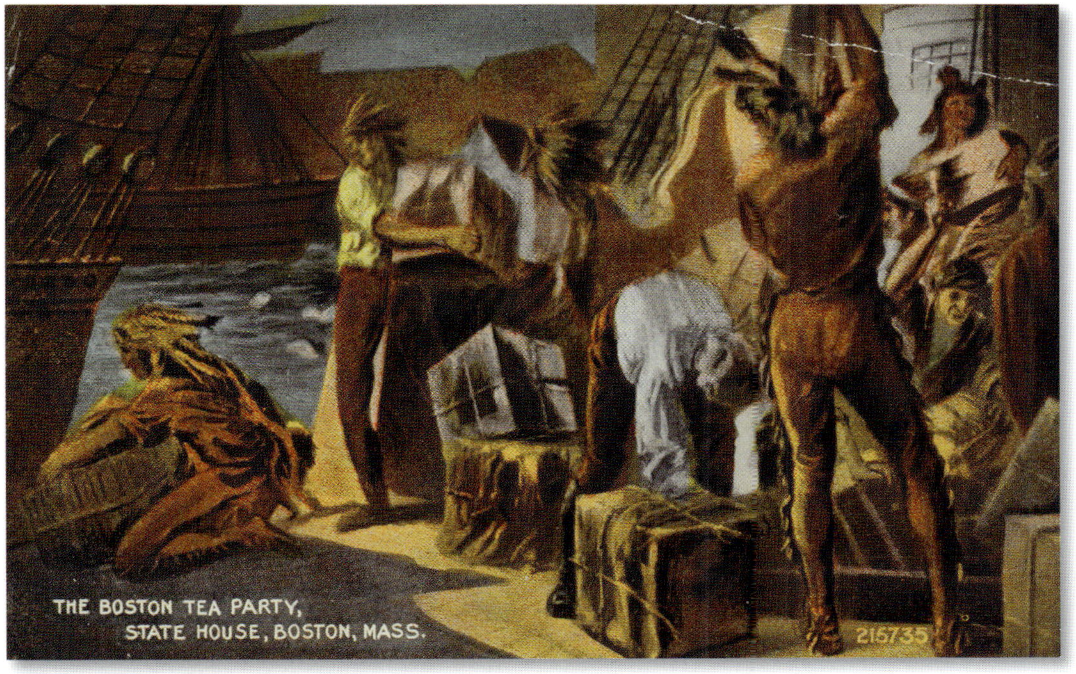

The Boston Tea Party, Thursday, December 16, 1773, helped spark the American Revolution.

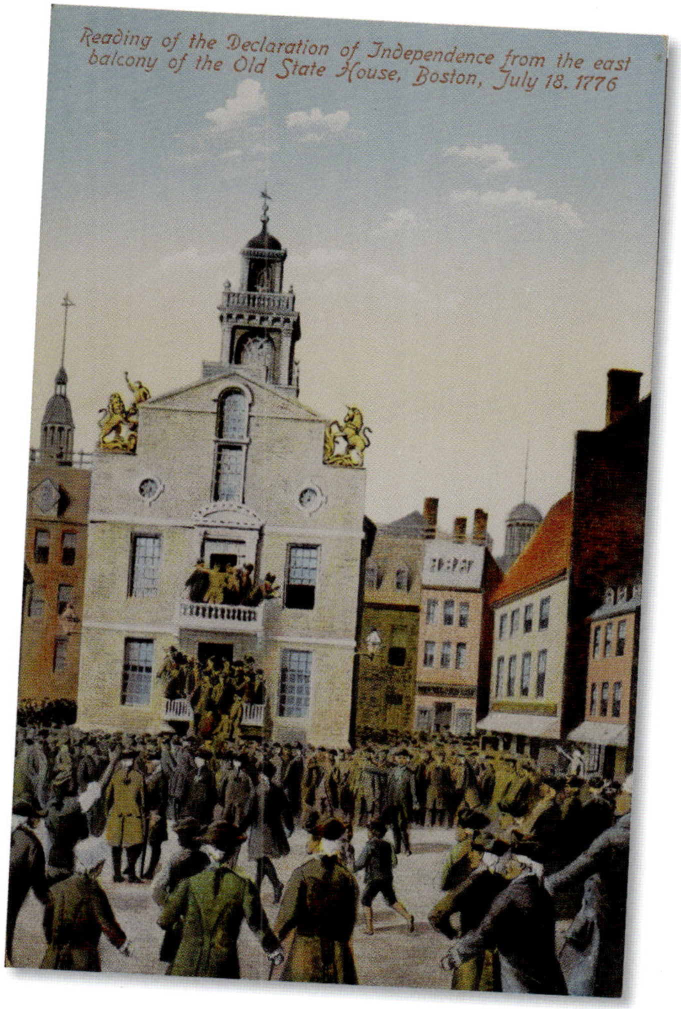

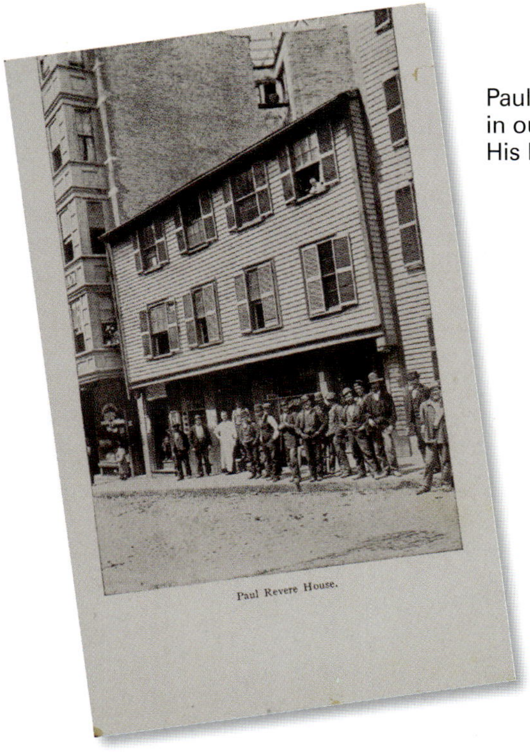

Paul Revere played a major role in our War for Independence. His house still stands.

On July 18, 1776, the Declaration of Independence was read from the balcony of the Old State House.

"A Glorious Morning for America"

Colonial militia dressed in their own clothing. They had long hair worn straight or pulled back in a ponytail or queue beneath large, weather-beaten, floppy brimmed hats. Although they had a ragtag look about them, these farmers and artisans were ready to use their weapons to defend their homes and their way of life. All night, bells rang, dogs barked, candles were lit, muskets were loaded as the colonists prepared for the next day.

The British had approximately 700 select soldiers. They were all precision, glitter, and polish, the most formidable fighting force of the era. There was no way that these exuberant, undisciplined, and untrained colonials could defeat them. Their scarlet coats shining, their bayonets gleaming, the British regulars marched down the road with practiced precision. In the dank early dawn, they marched on to the Lexington Common, forcing the local militia back. Women and children huddled behind the doorways and peered through windows of the several houses surrounding the green.

A single shot was fired – British or American, no one knows. But with it – the American Revolution began. Eight dead Americans were left on the green as the triumphant British marched on to Concord and the battle at the bridge. The first blood had been shed. Concord, Massachusetts, is renowned as the site of the battle of the bridge, where the Americans first fought back. These first two battles on April 19, 1775, marked the beginning of the American War for Independence.

The Battle of Bunker Hill took place on June 17, 1775, as part of the Siege of Boston. Although the British forced the Americans from the Charlestown peninsula, they lost 1,054 men, many of whom were officers. Initially characterized as an American defeat, the Battle of Bunker Hill is now considered a heroic stand against oppressive forces. Following that battle, Boston remained under British control for almost a year. In March 1776, George Washington masterminded an attack that forced the British to evacuate Boston. Many local Anglicans left with them.

After the remaining colonies declared their independence from Great Britain, the Declaration of Independence was signed on July 4, 1776. Boston's John Hancock was the first to sign it. The American War for Independence came to an end in 1781.

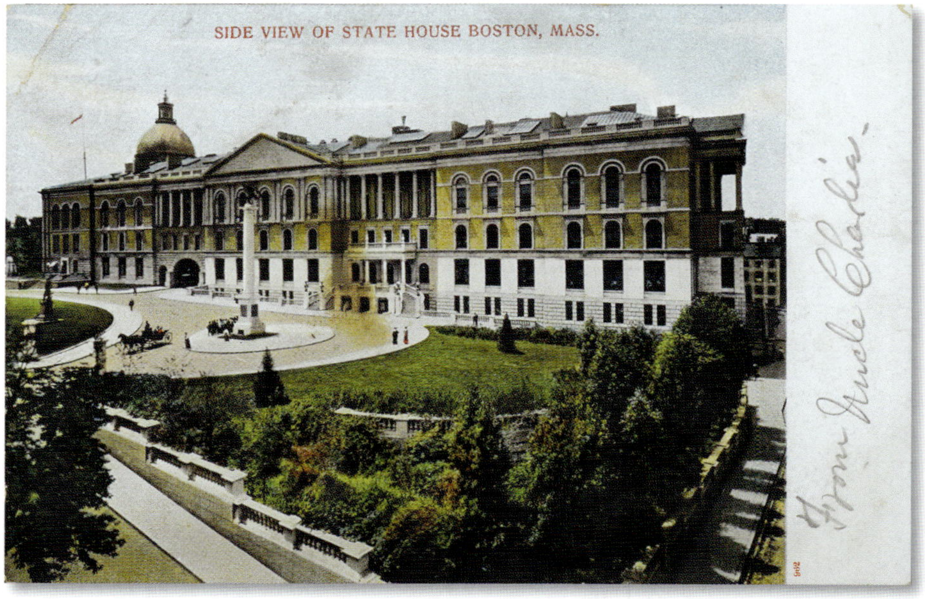

Built between 1795 and 1797 on Beacon Hill, the Massachusetts State House overlooks the Boston Common.

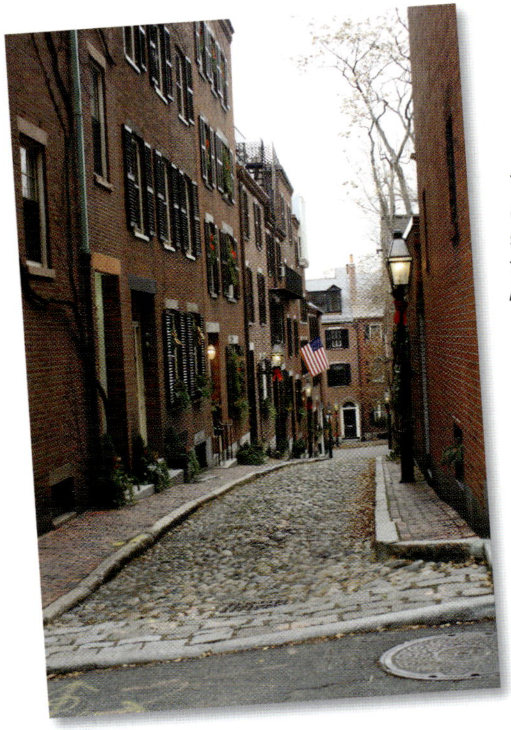

The narrow lanes were often paved with cobblestones brought up from the beaches. *Courtesy of D. Peter Lund*

The Nineteenth Century

The original colonial settlement grew quickly after the Revolution. Residents squeezed new houses between older dwellings on the available land. The garden plots and farms disappeared, and narrow crooked alleys meandered between the houses. In the newer areas, the streets were paved with cobblestones and lit by public streetlights. A lamplighter filled them with whale oil and lit them each evening.

By the end of the eighteenth century, Boston was a crowded colonial seaport with a booming economy. Although the Revolutionary War and then the War of 1812 had curtailed American shipping, sharp Yankee traders entered the rich China, India, and spice island trades, trading cloth, copper, and iron nails for Pacific Northwest furs, which they then traded for Chinese silks, china, spices, and tea. One enterprising merchant even sold ice to the West Indies. The shippers and merchants prospered as did all the associated trades. Boston homes still display Chinese porcelain brought home from these early trips.

Massachusetts had plentiful waterpower, skilled labor, and available capital. In 1814, Francis Cabot Lowell set up his power loom in Waltham, and the textile industry, which transformed many Massachusetts cities into major manufacturing centers, began. Farmers left their fields to enter manufacturing; young women left their homes to find jobs in the textile factories.

Adjacent to Boston was Cambridge with the oldest university in the country. Many scholars and their families came to learn there and then stayed on in this dynamic area. Many made their fortunes in the seafaring trade. Others began profitable textile mills. Many were involved in politics, which is certainly appropriate, given the history of our War for Independence. Two members of the Adams family (both local residents) were elected to the presidency: John Adams (1797-1801) and his son John Quincy Adams (1825-1829). Many of the Brahmin families claim hereditary and cultural descent from Boston's founding fathers, while others entered the New England "aristocracy" during the nineteenth century through their profits from commerce and trade or by marrying into established Brahmin families.

Capitalism as we know it today was still very much in its infancy. Although most people still lived on small farms, New England developed a relatively diverse economy with many small mills and shops. Over the next several decades, the labor force grew as people left the farms for the city, and more immigrants arrived in Boston. As manufacturing enterprises grew, Boston prospered in the early nineteenth century. Improved roads, new bridges, and canals linking cities and towns stimulated the economy further. To provide housing for its burgeoning population, Boston embarked on ambitious land-filling projects.

In 1822, Boston became a city of approximately 43,000 residents. By 1830, Boston 's population was approximately 60,000. The Irish had been immigrating to Boston ever since the mid-seventeenth century. By the late 1820s and 1830s, the number of Irish immigrating to Boston increased significantly. Thousands of poor and often illiterate Irish immigrants driven from their homeland by the potato famine began arriving in the 1840s. Most settled in the vermin-infested tenements in the city, where raw sewage and garbage littered the streets. Confronting them were signs " No Irish need apply." Disease carried off large numbers of children and women. One hundred years later, the Irish were a major force in Boston. A future president came from their ranks.

Conversely, Boston residents had a great interest in the social, moral, and political questions of the day. One of the major issues was the question of slavery. Boston was the center of the antislavery movement and the home of many fervid abolitionists.

Boston's second mayor, Josiah Quincy, "began to level and fill the original peninsula" and built Quincy Market. Today, Custom House, many of the Atlantic Avenue warehouses, and much of State Street, the financial section of the city, are sited where Town Cove once was.

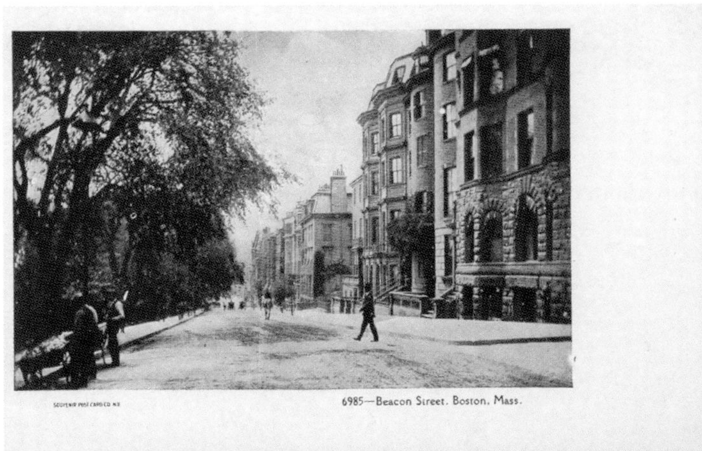

During Boston's Federal period 1775-1837, freestanding wooden buildings gave way to rows of brick houses, often attached, lining the new straight streets.

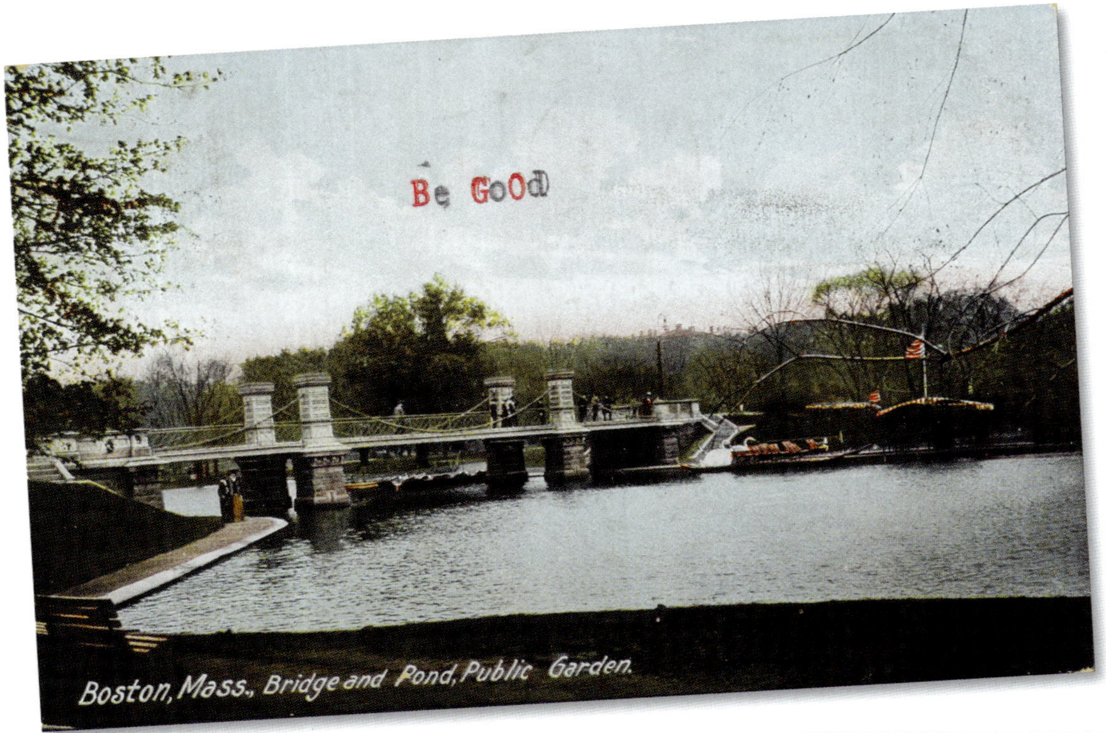

The Public Garden, the first public botanical garden in the nation, was established in 1837.

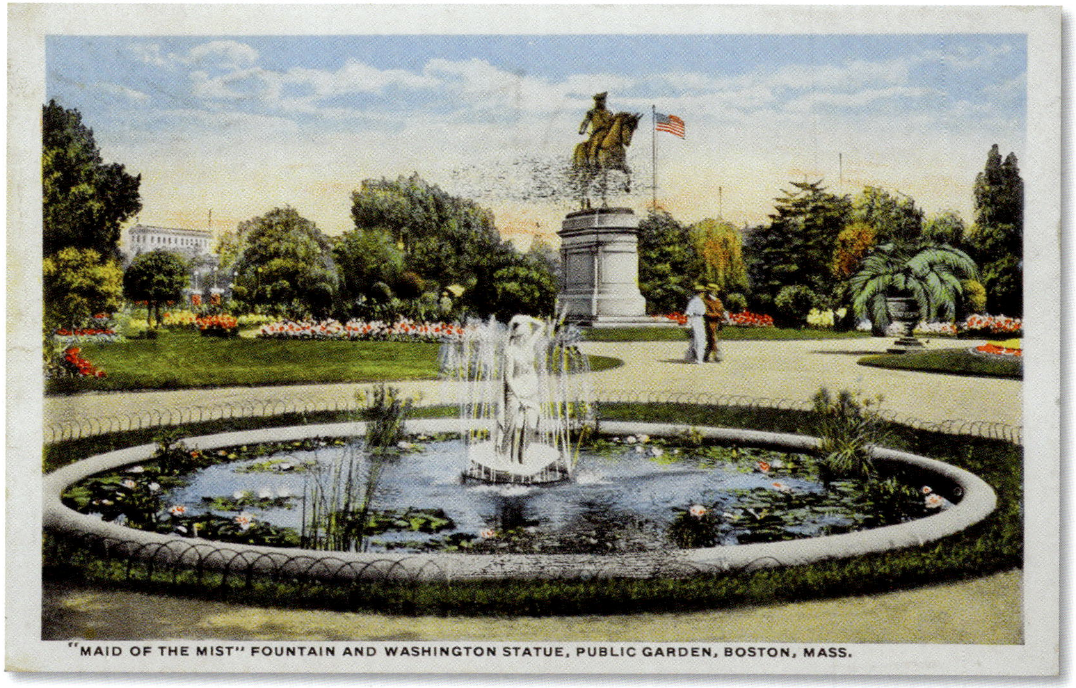

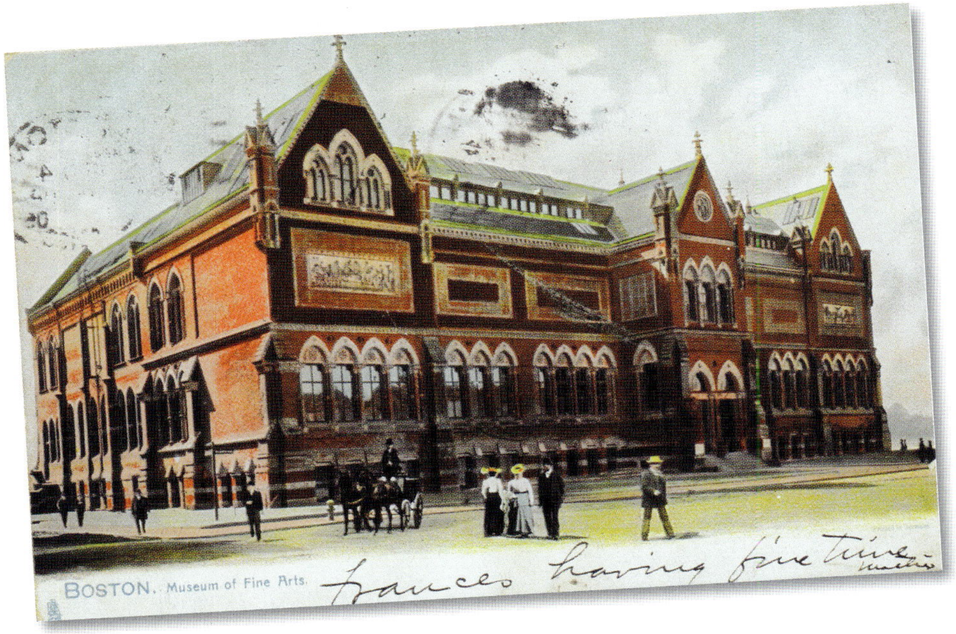

Boston quickly outgrew its first Museum of Fine Arts built in 1876.

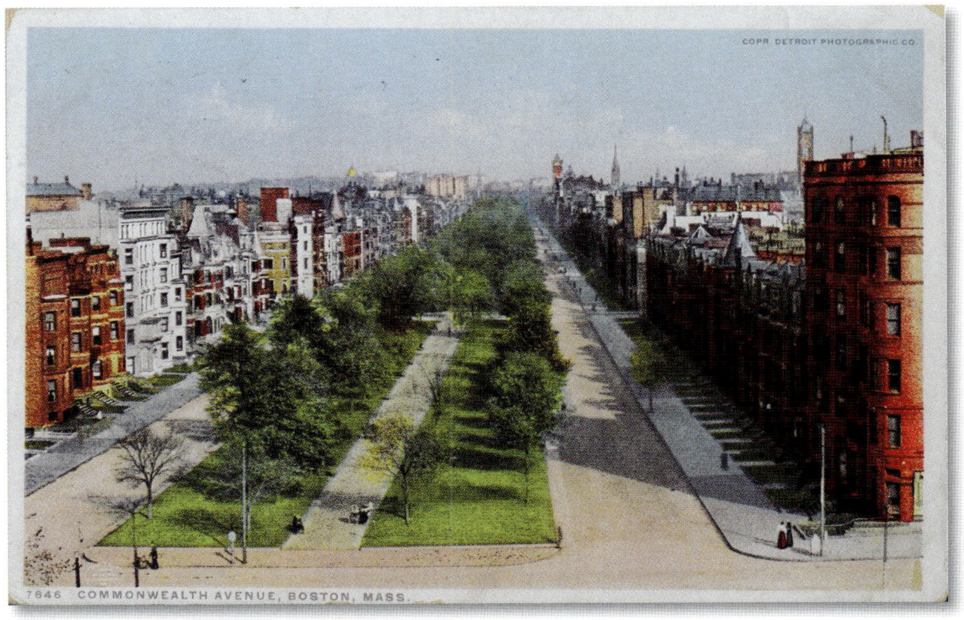

Back Bay was laid out, following a French model.

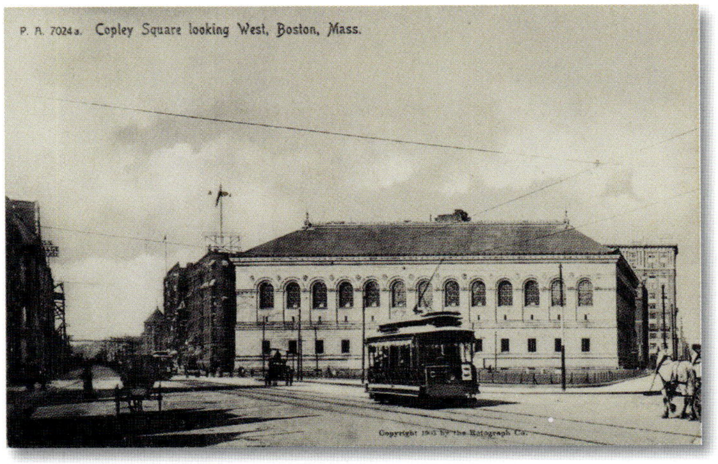

Boston city officials established the Boston Public Library by a city ordinance in 1852. Designed by Charles McKim, it is considered one of the most beautiful buildings in the nation.

By mid-century, the face of Boston was changing radically. The hills on the Shawmut peninsula were leveled, and the mud flats filled. The land reclamation of Back Bay began, and the old water line disappeared. Land values increased swiftly, making these ventures profitable. The only traces of this work are in the names (Mount Vernon Street) and in the narrow crooked North End streets, which have kept their original circuitous routes that allowed them to avoid the hills.

One of the major institutions in Boston has always been education. Although those strong-minded Puritans lacked many of the niceties that they were accustomed to in England, they fervently believed in the importance of education. In 1636, only six years after their arrival, after all, they founded Harvard, which is acknowledged as the oldest institution of higher learning in the United States. In 1807, The Boston Athenaeum was organized to promote literary and scientific learning. Thinkers, writers, political leaders, and reformers were attracted to Boston and its environs. Thoreau, Longfellow, Emerson, Hawthorne, Alcott, and Henry James were just some of the famous authors. Some of America's leading abolitionists found a home here, and the city played an active role in the Underground Railroad. Massachusetts's soldiers were among the first to volunteer for the Civil War.

From 1844 to 1854, Boston led the nation in foreign trade. The great merchant fleets still operated under sail, but the demand for speed brought in the "clipper" ship. By 1849, Boston ships were dispatching hopeful gold miners and goods to San Francisco, and those in the shipping industry recognized great profits.

Boston manufacturers found the Civil War to be lucrative as they produced weapons, shoes, blankets, and other war materials. Other Bostonians found their calling in railroads, textiles, or banking. The advent of new machines and technologies replaced manual labor, speeded up production, and created factory workers. Boston's immigrant labor and new industrial technology helped build the textile businesses, the boot and shoe, piano and organ, and machinery factories. Boston innovators played a major role in the development of the telephone industry and even placed the banana in grocery stores. The Boston Public Library, colleges such as Boston University and MIT, cultural institutions, and hospitals were a result of the new mercantile wealth and the philanthropy of public-minded citizens.

In 1872, a massive fire in downtown Boston destroyed approximately 770 commercial buildings. As part of the post-fire reconstruction, several streets in downtown Boston were widened. Most of the rubble and building ruins were dumped in the harbor to fill in Atlantic Avenue. The city began to add large suburban areas such as Charlestown and Dorchester and to develop a park system and a modern sewer system. By 1875, 347,000 persons lived in Boston, and the city remained a leading commercial center for the processing of wool and the manufacture of clothing, textiles, shoes, and leather goods.

As the railroad grew in importance during the mid-nineteenth century, wealthy Boston residents used it to escape from the city during the heat of summer. Although the Industrial Revolution meant increasing wealth, the Victorians wished their homes to be a haven from the increasingly disease- and crime-ridden cities. Once the railroad came into its own, it was possible to hold a well paying job in the city and to raise a family far away from its harmful influence. The marked improvement in service resulted in more families moving to a semi rural environment, where the air and water were pristine and the head of household could commute to the city.

During the nineteenth century, successive waves of immigrants found homes in the port town with its variety of neighborhoods. In the first half of the nineteenth century, most of the immigrants came from England, Scotland, Ireland, and northern parts of France and Germany. Beginning in the 1880s, the newcomers began coming from southern and eastern Europe – Italy, Poland, Greece and Russia. By 1880, the US Census found that there were 362,839 residents in all Boston. In 1920, the population had grown to 750,000.

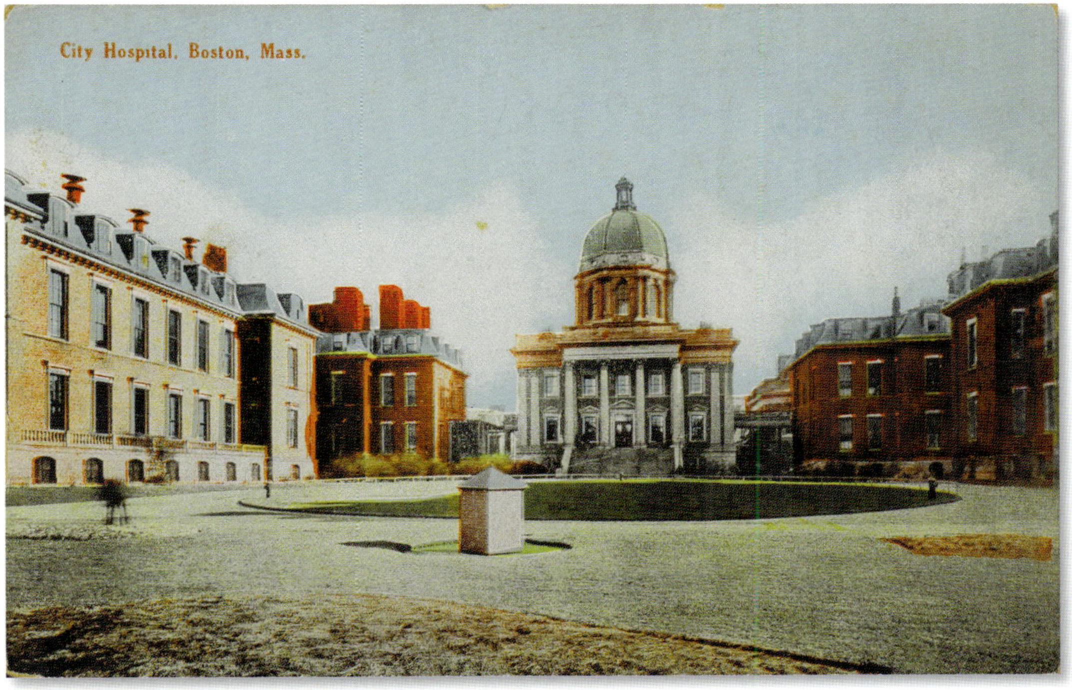

Opened in 1864, Boston City Hospital was the first municipal hospital established in the United States. The original buildings overlooked a large open forecourt; mansard-roofed pavilions flanked the domed administration building.

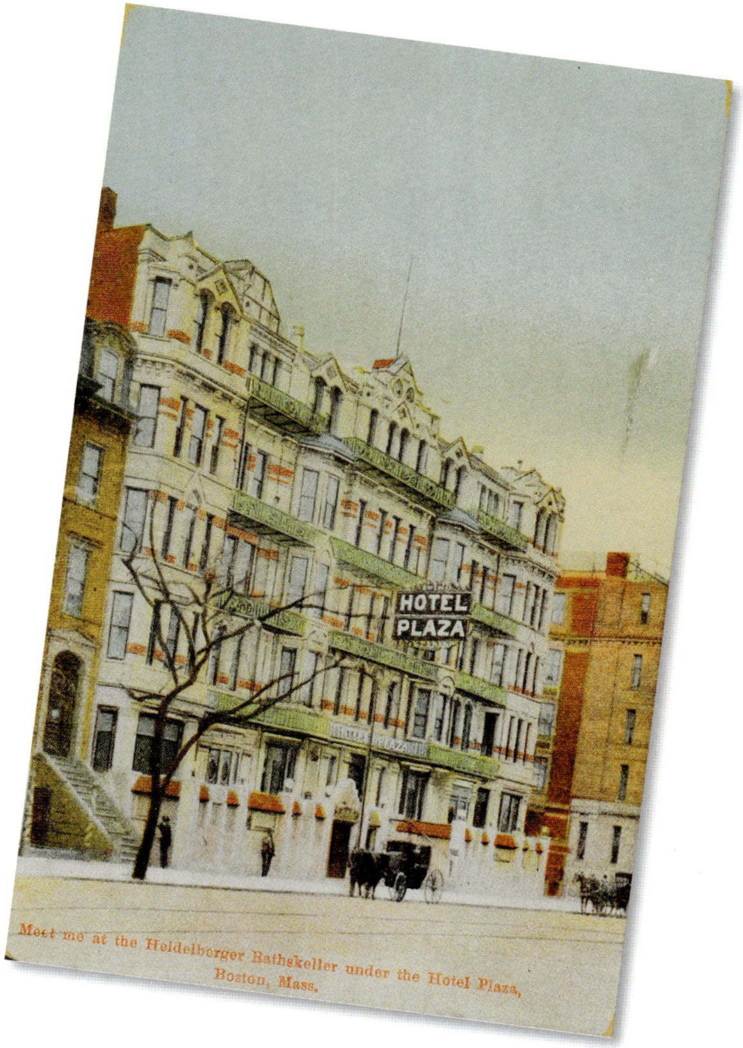

New upscale neighborhoods were developed.

Boston and its Beliefs

Boston and its historic sites are our American heritage. Here, our forebears established many of the great intellectual, political, and educational tenets that form the backbone of our culture. When he witnessed first shots fired in Lexington, Sam Adams, ever the propagandist, said, "Oh what a glorious morning for America."

Boston takes its historical role seriously. Its 2.5–mile Freedom Trail leads visitors to sixteen nationally significant sites. Each one – whether they are churches, meeting houses, burying grounds – are part of our history. They tell the story of the American Revolution and those early patriots who believed that people had the right to "life, liberty, and the pursuit of happiness."

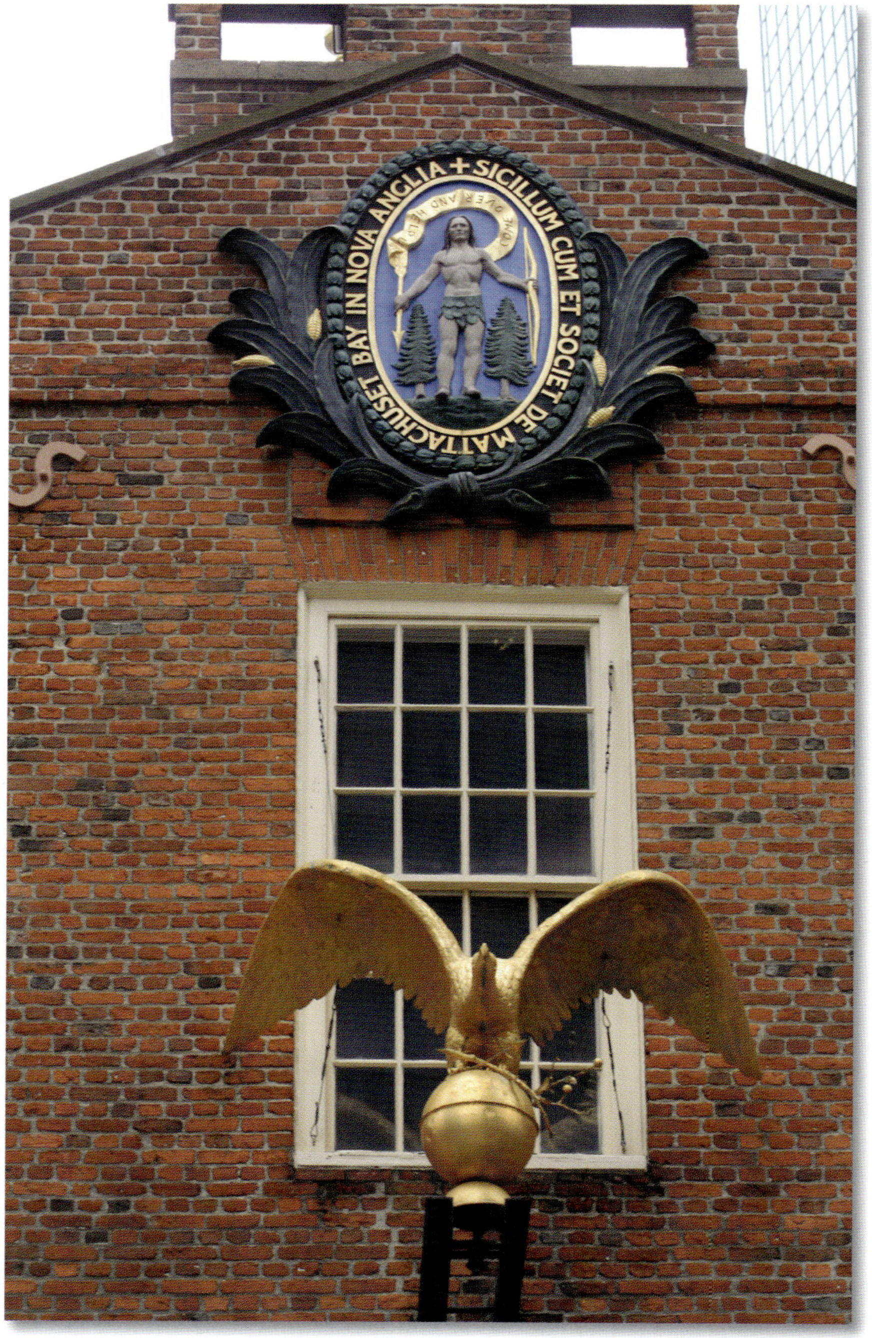

Built in 1713, the Old State House is the oldest surviving public building in Boston, and the seat of the first elected legislature in the New World. A unicorn and a lion, symbols of the royal government in London, are on its east side. The originals were burned in a bonfire in 1776 when the Declaration of Independence was read from the balcony. When the Boston Historical Society restored the building to its historical appearance in 1882, they were returned to their original place. The American eagle was added -- appropriately on the west side -- at that time. *Courtesy of D. Peter Lund*

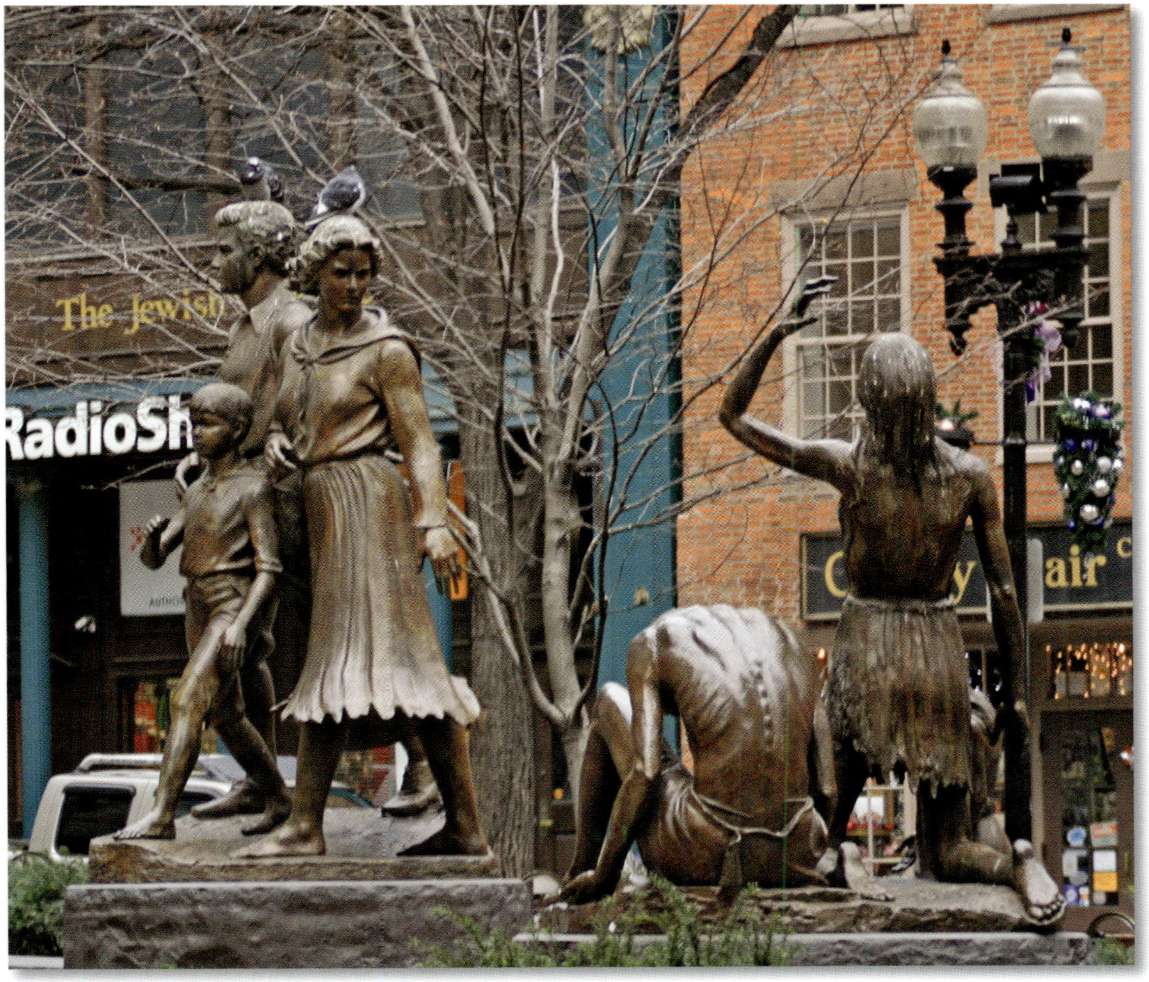

One hundred and fifty years ago, Irish immigrants fled their homeland to escape a five-year potato famine. Most settled in the city and struggled to make a life. Twin sculptures by artist Robert Shure and eight narrative plaques depict their struggle to succeed in America. *Courtesy of D. Peter Lund*

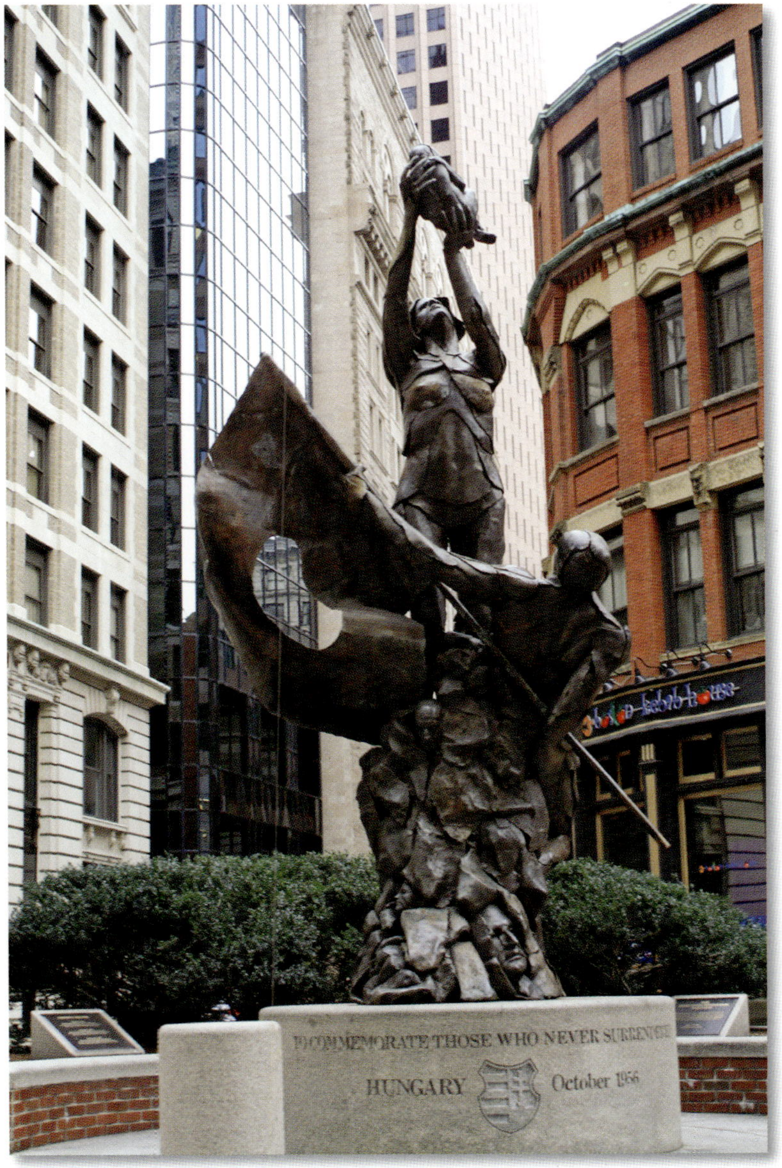

On October 23, 1956, Hungarian students revolted against communist occupation. Thousands died, and hundreds of thousands of intellectuals, artists, and supporters of democracy fled the country, to ports including Boston. In Boston's Liberty Square can be found Gyuri Hollosy's memorial to the fallen heroes of the Hungarian Revolution. *Courtesy of D. Peter Lund*

General prosperity and the citizens' devotion to public service and pursuit of culture combined to make the nineteenth century a true golden age. If Boston was not the center of the universe, which some believed, it was certainly the "Athens of America." It had more statesmen, educators, and literary figures than any other American city. The *Atlantic Monthly,* which published such writers as Hawthorne, Thoreau, Twain, and Harte, symbolized its literary supremacy. The Museum of Fine Arts, and the Opera House were opened and the Boston Symphony Orchestra performed. Boston had the first subway in the United States, the "T."

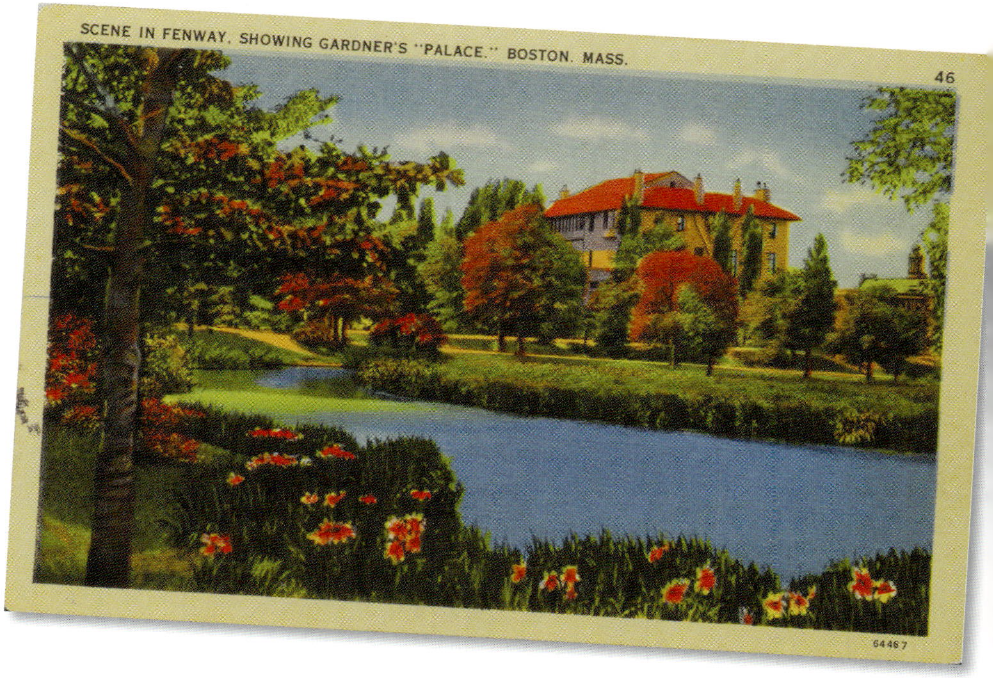

One of the loveliest is the Isabella Stewart Gardner museum, a four-story Italian palace filled with treasures and flowers.

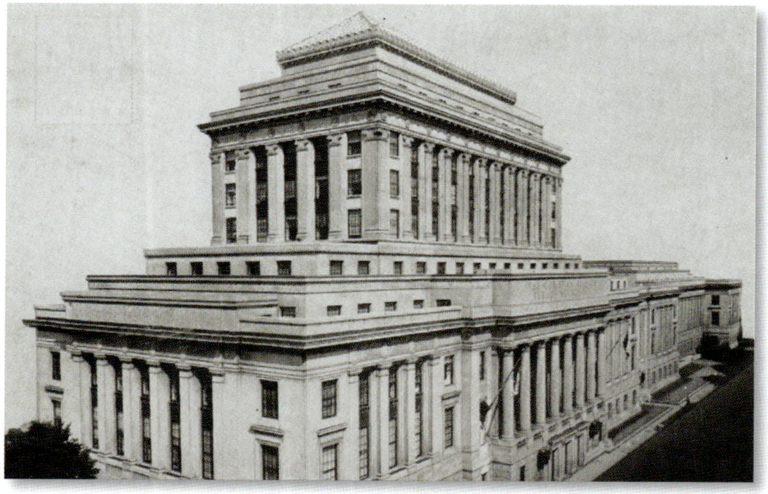

By the nineteenth century, Boston had many beautiful buildings.

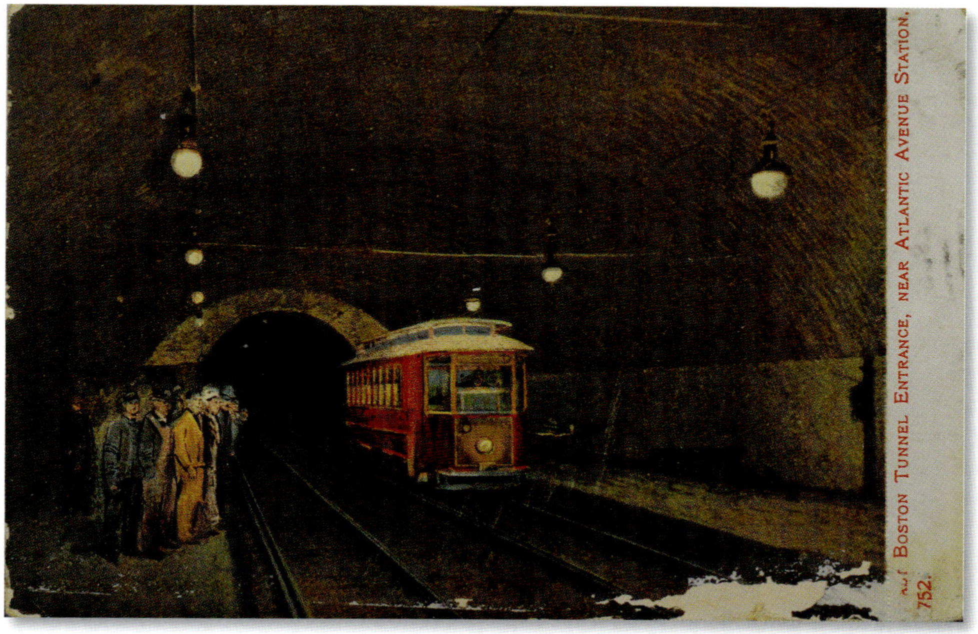

Boston's subway system is the oldest in the country.

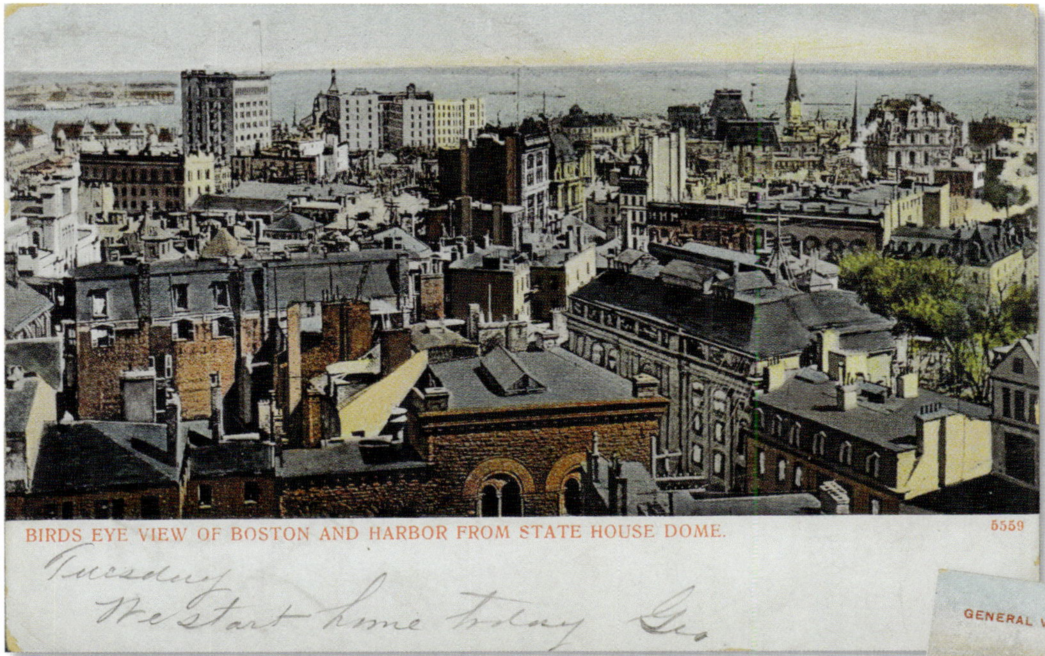

Birdseye view of Boston and the harbor from the State House.

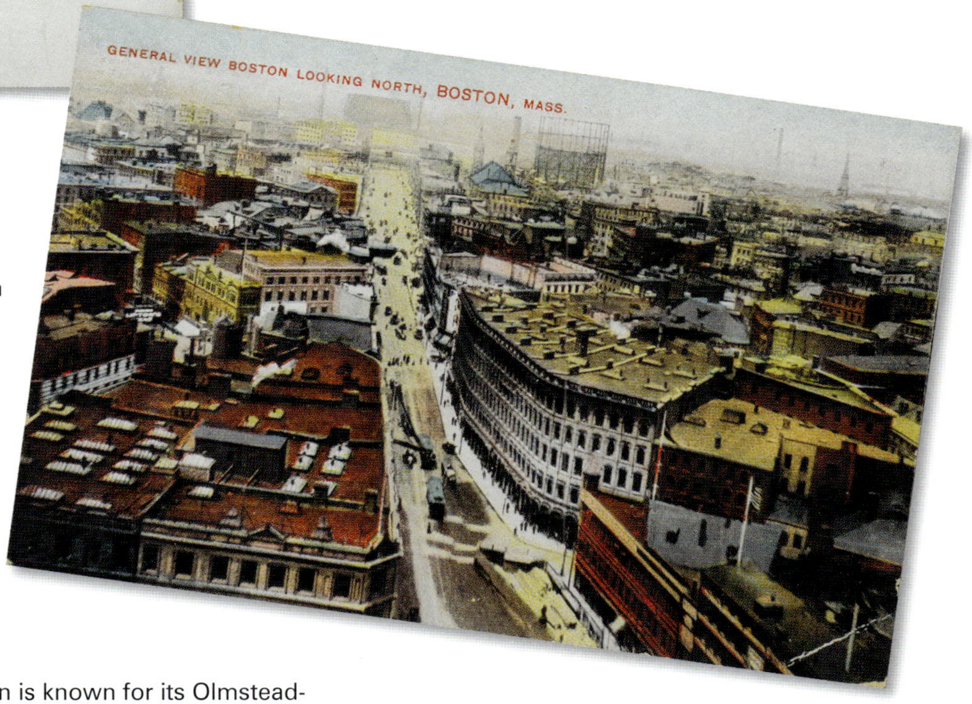

General view of Boston looking south.

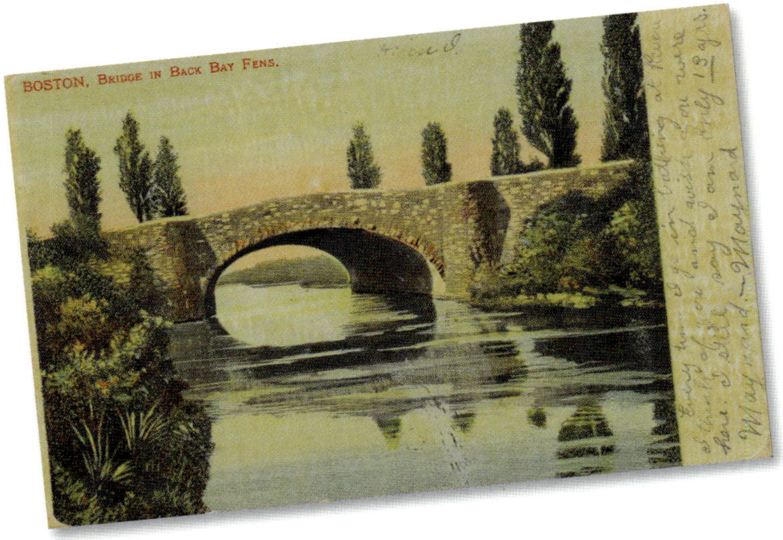

Boston is known for its Olmstead-designed park system linked together by parkways and waterways.

The 20th Century

Today's Boston is a city that sees the future and applies a rare combination of innovation and experience to transform challenges into opportunities. –Thomas M. Menino, Mayor, City of Boston

In 1900, the port of Boston was considered the second ranking port in the nation (Bunting, p. 17). But it, like Boston's manufacturing industries, began to decline during the early twentieth century. The once thriving factories and mills, which had produced more than one-third of the nation's woven goods and about half the boots and shoes produced in the nation, had become old and obsolete. The tenements were aging and decaying. Many businesses closed and relocated to the south. Prosperity continued, however, with the development of service industries, banking and finance, retailing, and wholesaling.

Boston suffered with the rest of the nation during the Great Depression. Its textile and shoe manufacturing industries went elsewhere. With the outbreak of World War II, factories were retooled for the war effort, and people went back to work on the production lines.

By the 1950s, fishing and farming were declining in the state, but the Boston area emerged as a leader in the fledgling computer and high-tech industries. MIT graduates and others created and staffed many of these new companies. As always, its citizens played a major role in politics. During this century, two presidents came from Massachusetts: John F. Kennedy and George H. W. Bush.

Boston began building steel and glass buildings thrusting skywards. The Prudential Insurance Company tower in 1961 and then the John Hancock Tower in 1973 led the way. City officials tore down Scollay Square and, with federal help, built Government Center. By 1976, the restored Quincy Market reopened, encouraging more tourists to visit Boston. The city's hospitals were world renown, and its financiers developed an international reputation.

As its 400th anniversary approaches, Greater Boston finds itself with a worldwide reputation. Its educational, medical, financial and service industries continue to expand. Tourism is a major factor in this historic city, and its skyline is continually reaching upward while it retains the buildings from its rich architectural past.

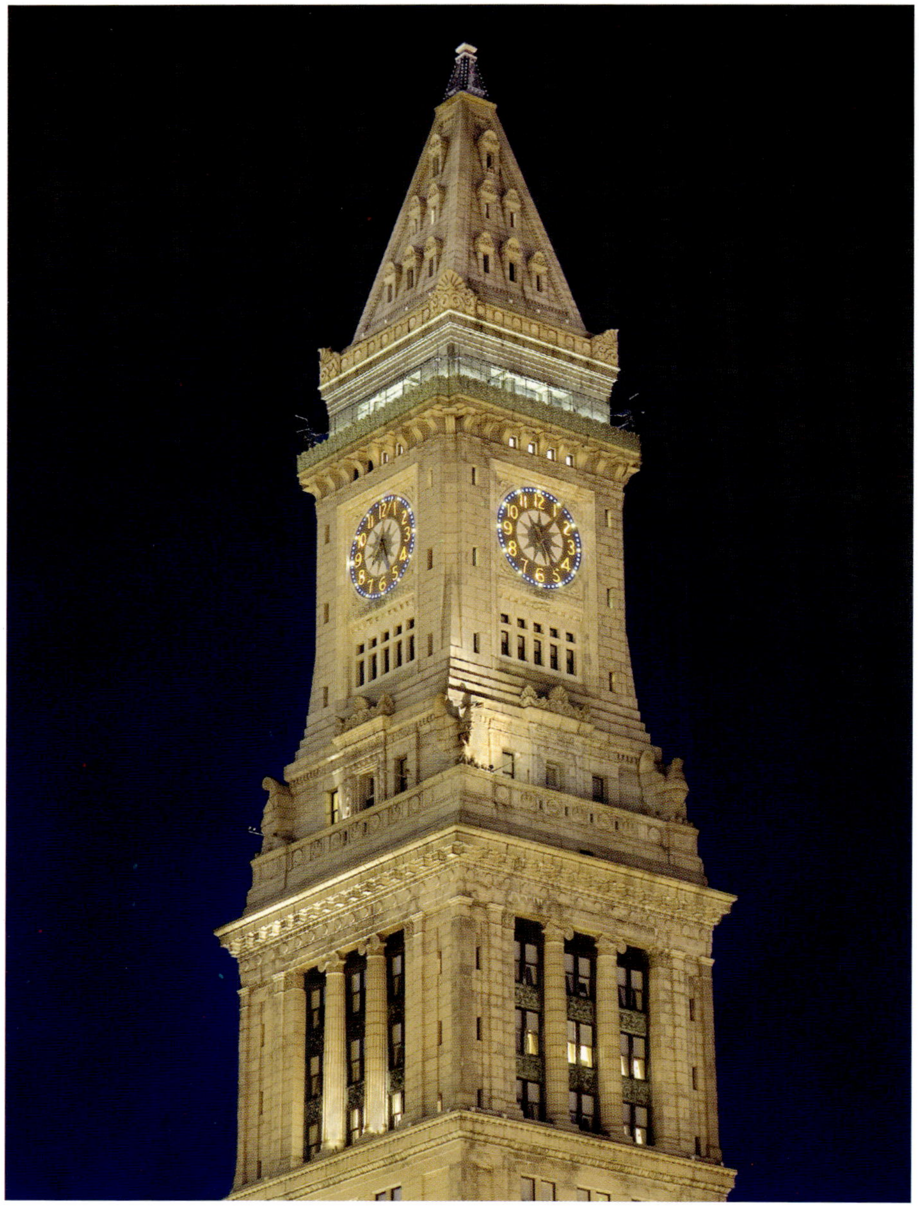

The Custom House tower is a later addition. *Courtesy of Paul E. Doherty*

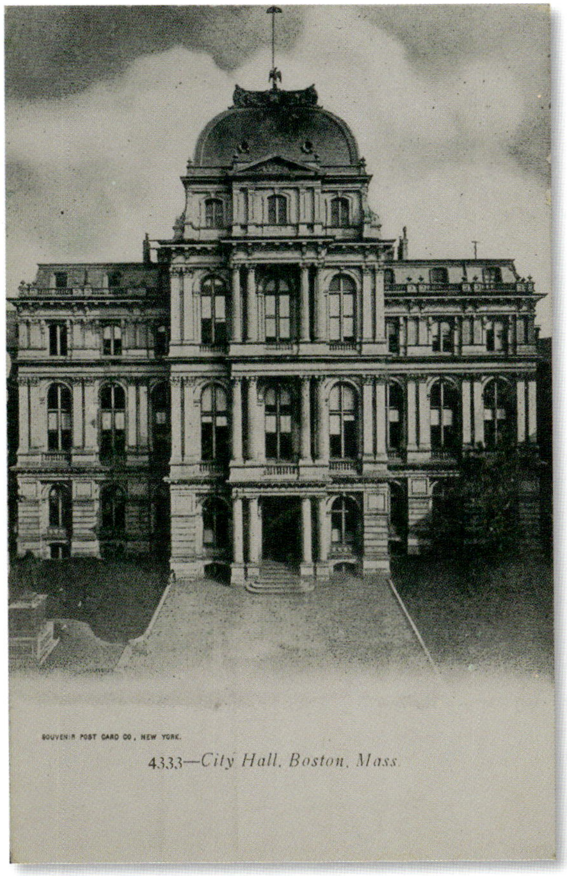

Built in 1862-1865, Boston's Old City Hall was refashioned into a commercial building when Government Center was built. The American Institute of Architects commended this innovative idea of rehabilitating a public building for a new use, which allows us to preserve the energy used to make them originally and prevents unnecessary disruption of a neighborhood. By remodeling, the building can remain in place, mellowing with time.

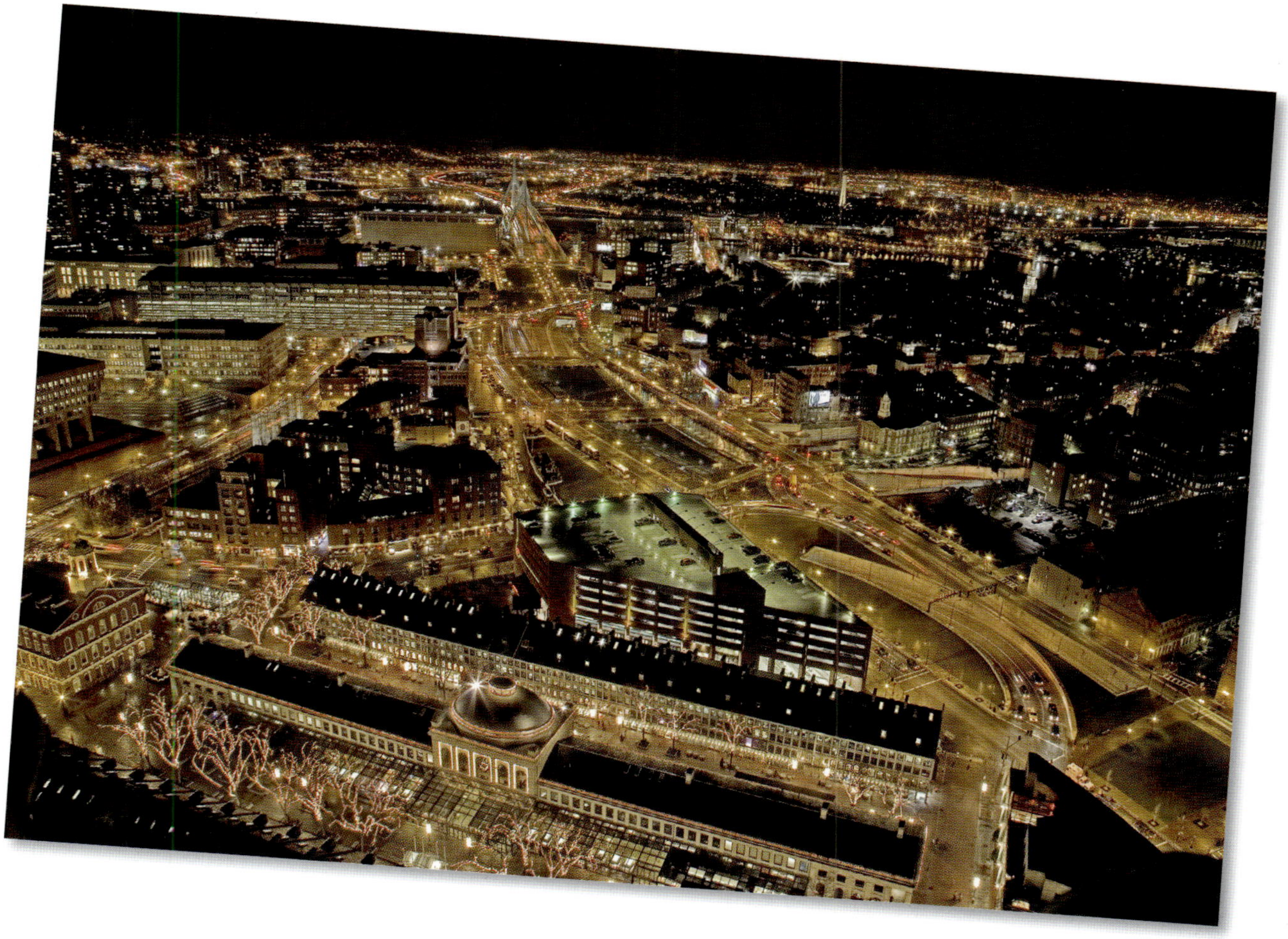

Beginning in 1991, Boston began the Big Dig, a multibillion-dollar project that rerouted the Central Artery (Interstate 93), the chief controlled-access highway through the heart of the city into a 3.5 mile (5.6km) tunnel under the city. Interstate 93, which runs through the city, can be seen here in this spider web of roads and highways. The new Leonard P. Zakim Bunker Hill Bridge is in the distance. To the right is Bunker Hill Monument, and the dark area in the foreground is the North End. To the left can be seen Quincy Market and Faneuil Hall. *Courtesy of Paul E. Doherty*

Chapter 2

Central Boston

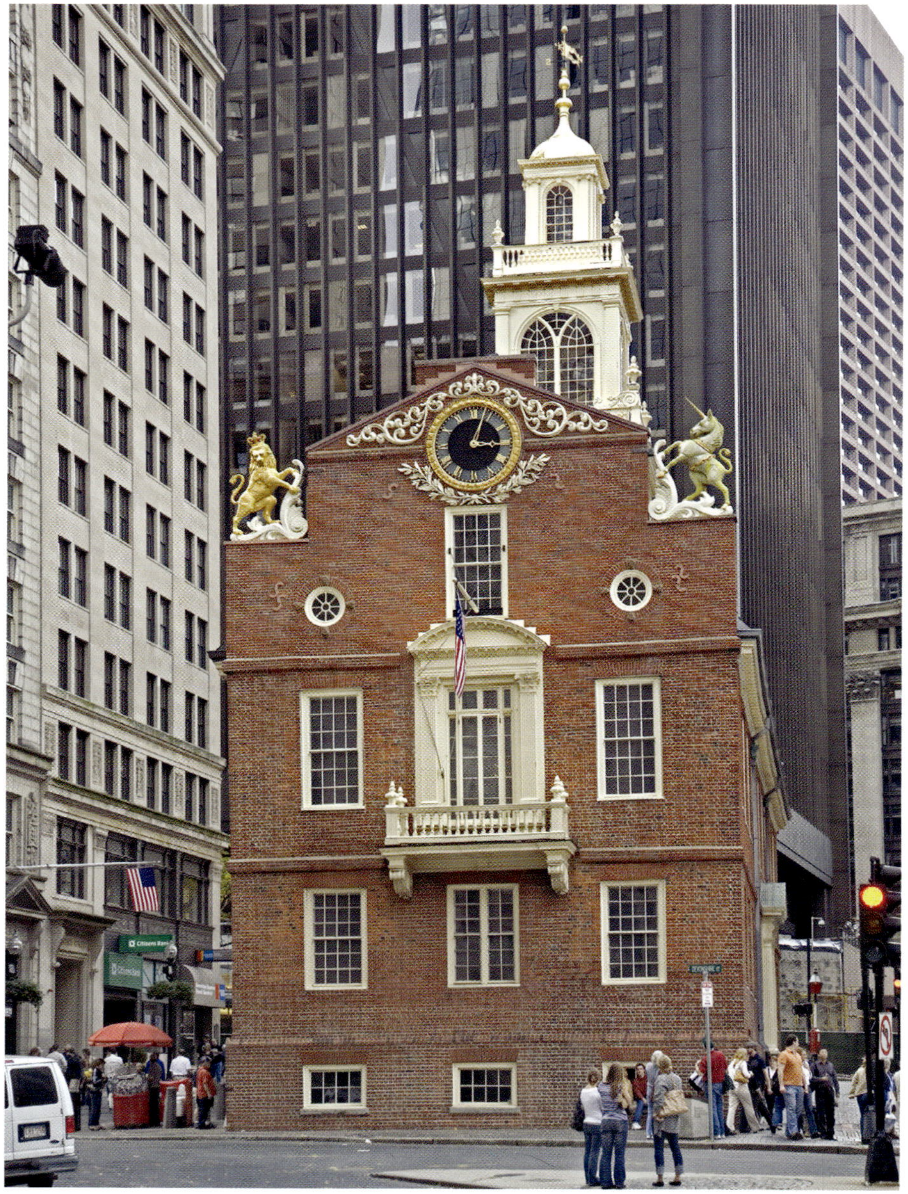

The contrast between the elegant Old State House (206 Washington Street) and the post-modernist buildings surrounding it is striking. This historical site is Boston's oldest surviving public building. Called the "Georgian Jewel," it opened as the site of provincial government in 1713. In 1747, a fire destroyed its interior and part of the brick walls. The present graceful red brick building has a gambrel roof decorated by the reinstalled pre-revolutionary symbols of a gold unicorn and lion. This building was the setting for many stirring speeches and debates by dedicated patriots against the British crown. *Courtesy of Paul E. Doherty*

Old State House

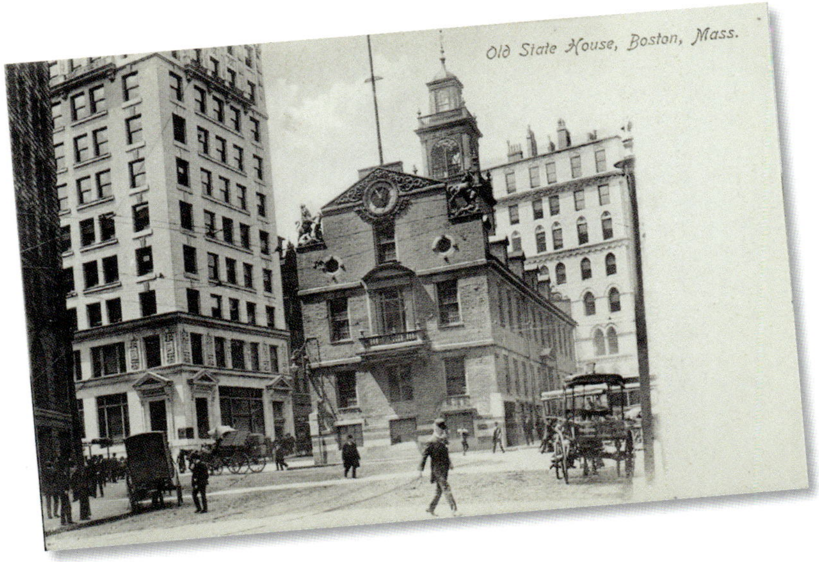

Old State House, Boston, Mass.

In front of the Old State House, a circle of cobblestones commemorates the Boston Massacre. At this site on March 5, 1770, the friction between the colonists and British soldiers erupted into violence. An angry crowd of colonists hurled snowballs, rocks, clubs, and insults at the soldiers, who in turn, fired into the crowd and killed five colonists. Samuel Adams and other patriots called the event a "massacre." Seven of the British soldiers were later tried for murder. John Adams represented them in court: five were acquitted, two found guilty of manslaughter. Today, a circle of paving stones marks the spot of the massacre.

As the center of political life in the colonies, the Old State House has been called one of the most important public buildings in early America. A Merchant's Exchange occupied the first floor, and John Hancock and others rented the basement for warehouse space. The Council Chamber of the Royal Governor was located upstairs at the east end of the building.

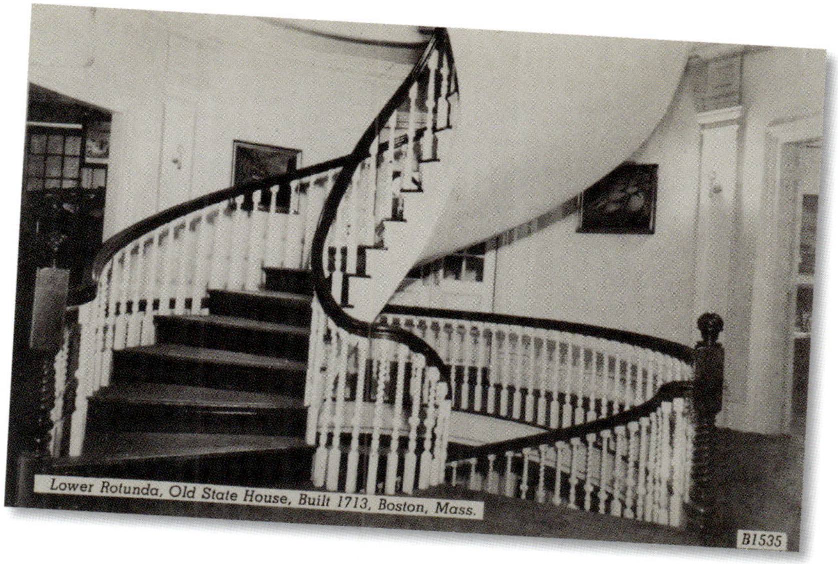

Lower Rotunda, Old State House, Built 1713, Boston, Mass. B1535

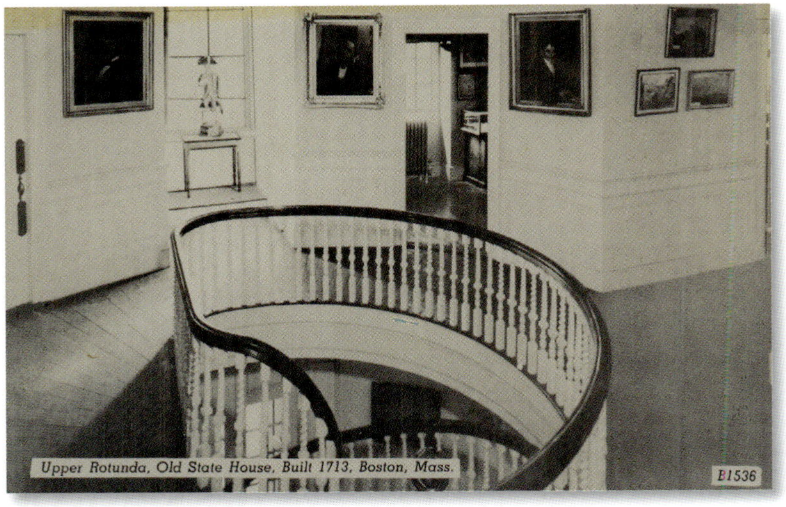

Upper Rotunda, Old State House, Built 1713, Boston, Mass. B1536

The Massachusetts Assembly, one of the most independent of the colonial legislatures, met in the central area of the second floor. In 1766, citizens could hear their elected officials debate the popular issues of the day from a visitors' gallery, which no longer exists.

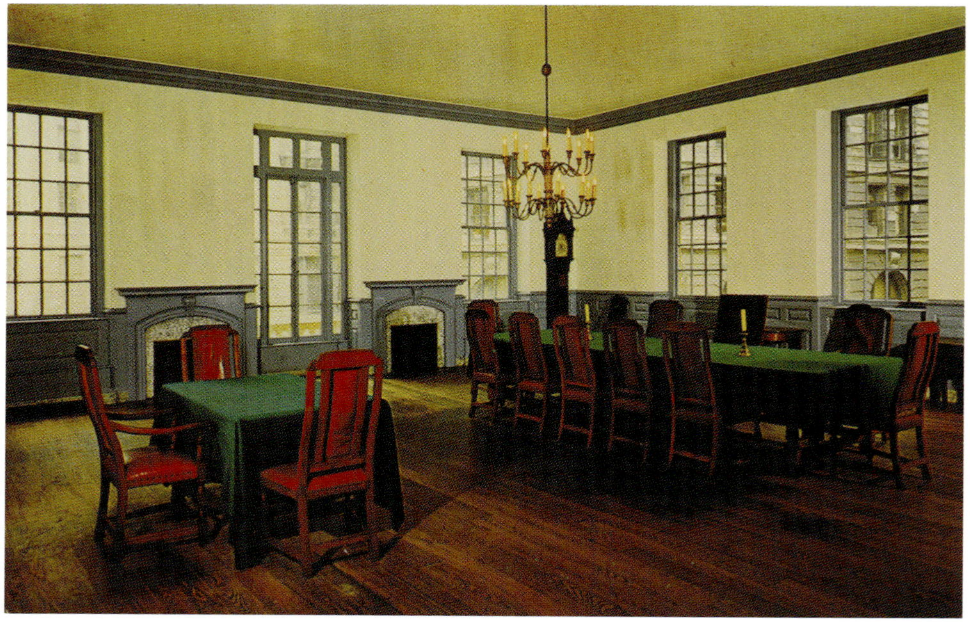

The Massachusetts Supreme Judicial Court, the longest seated court in the nation, met here for many years and was responsible for the ruling decisions in many early landmark trials. This Court helped draft the Massachusetts Constitution, upon which the United States Constitution is based. Official proclamations were read from the Old State House balcony, on the east side of the building, looking down State (formerly King) Street. On July 18, 1776, the ecstatic citizens of Boston heard the Declaration of Independence proclaimed from the balcony. In their patriotic fervor, they removed and burned the British lion and unicorn that resided on the roof. When they were replaced in 1882, a gilded eagle was added.

The Old State House continued as the seat of Massachusetts's government until the governor, state legislature, and other state officials moved to the New State House on Beacon Hill in 1798. From 1830 to 1841, the building was used as Boston's City Hall but then returned to commercial use. During the mid-nineteenth century, the building began to deteriorate. In the late nineteenth century, a group of determined citizens began efforts to save the building. Today, the Old State House houses the Boston Historical Society, its museum, and a gift shop. A site within the Boston National Historical Park, it is known as "the most important public building in American history prior to the Declaration of Independence" (Harris, p. 201).

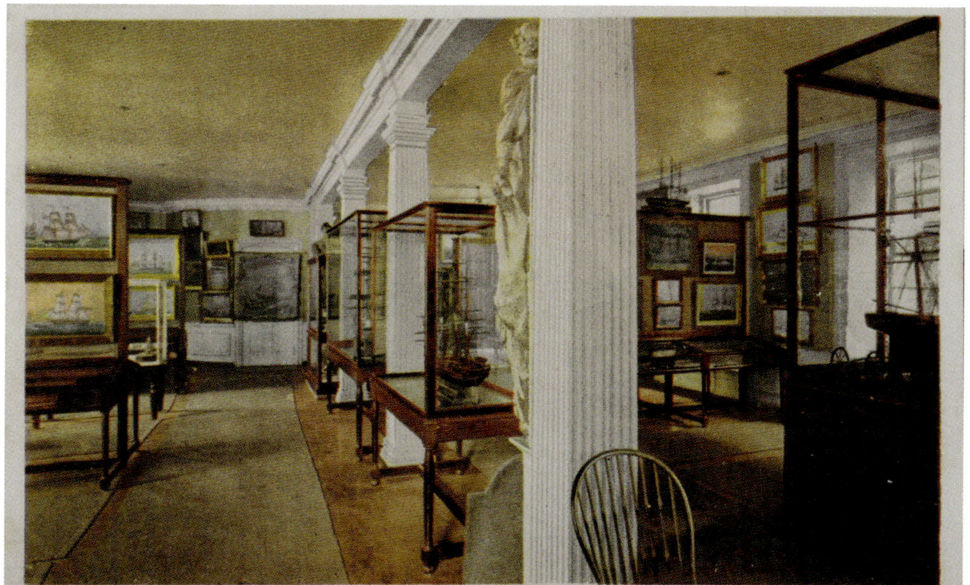

D 70141 ROBERT KEAYNE HALL, OLD STATE HOUSE, BOSTON, MASS.

COPR. DETROIT PUBLISHING CO.

Faneuil Hall

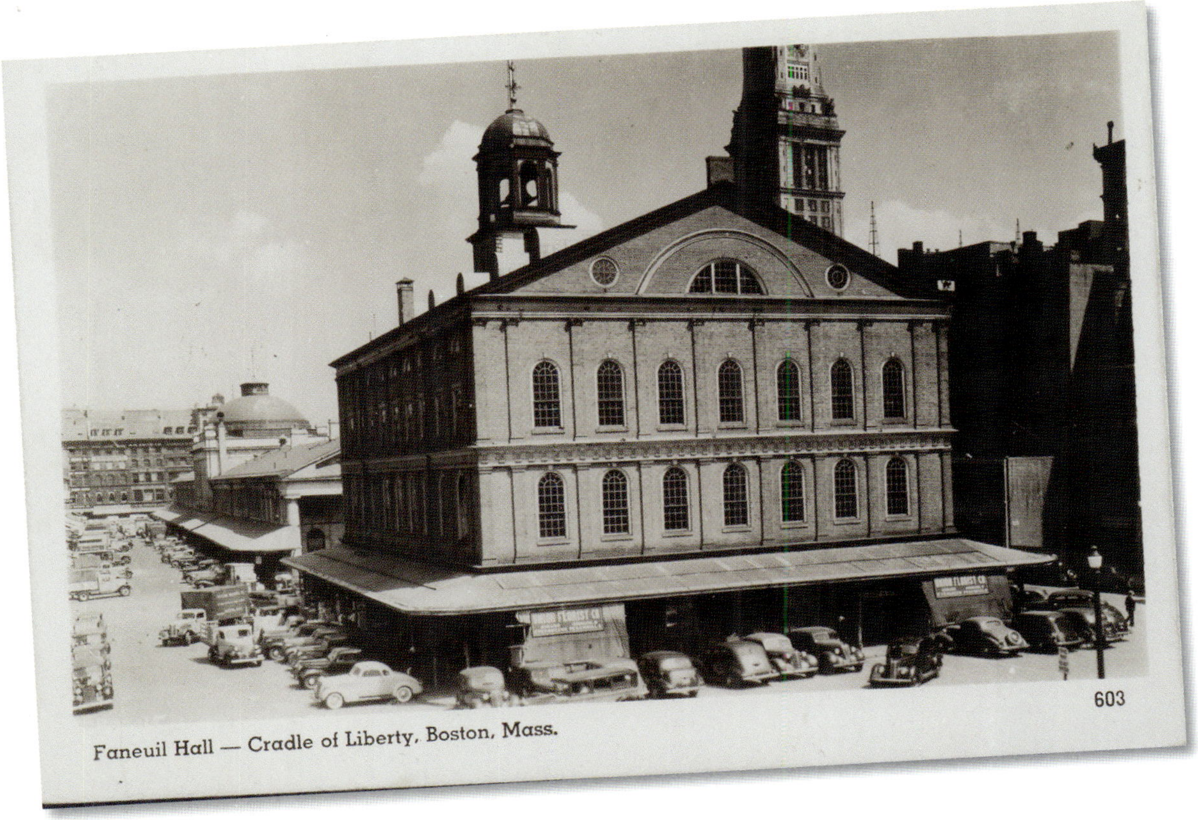

Peter Faneuil, a Huguenot merchant, gave the red brick Faneuil Hall to Boston as a forum for discussing issues of the day. Constructed by John Smibert in 1740-1742, it had assembly rooms above and an open market below – much like European market buildings. In 1806, Charles Bulfinch, enlarged the Georgian style building, doubling its space and adding a third floor.

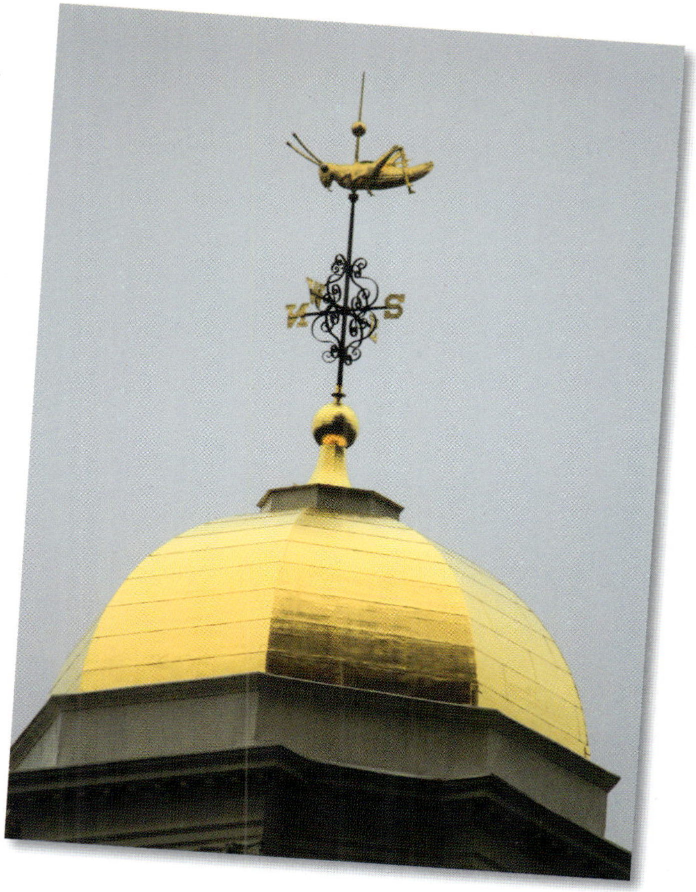

Silversmith Shem Drowne created the gilded grasshopper weathervane on top of the building in 1742. He modeled it on the London Royal Exchange grasshopper weathervane, thus associating the new building with one of the great Old World financial centers. The thirty-eight pound grasshopper is fifty-two inches long. Made of solid copper covered with gold leaf, it has glass eyes, which are said to have begun life as doorknobs. *Courtesy of D. Peter Lund*

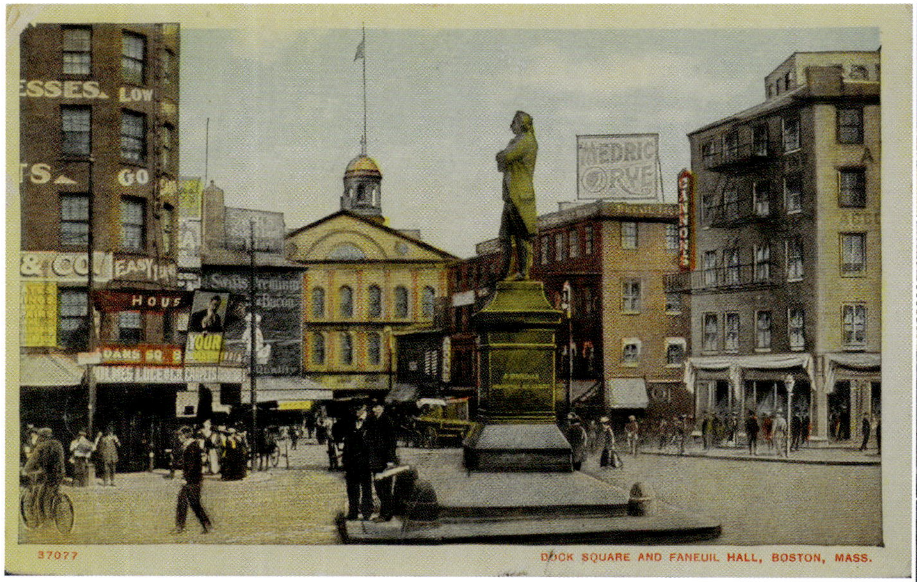

The statue of Samuel Adams stands proudly.

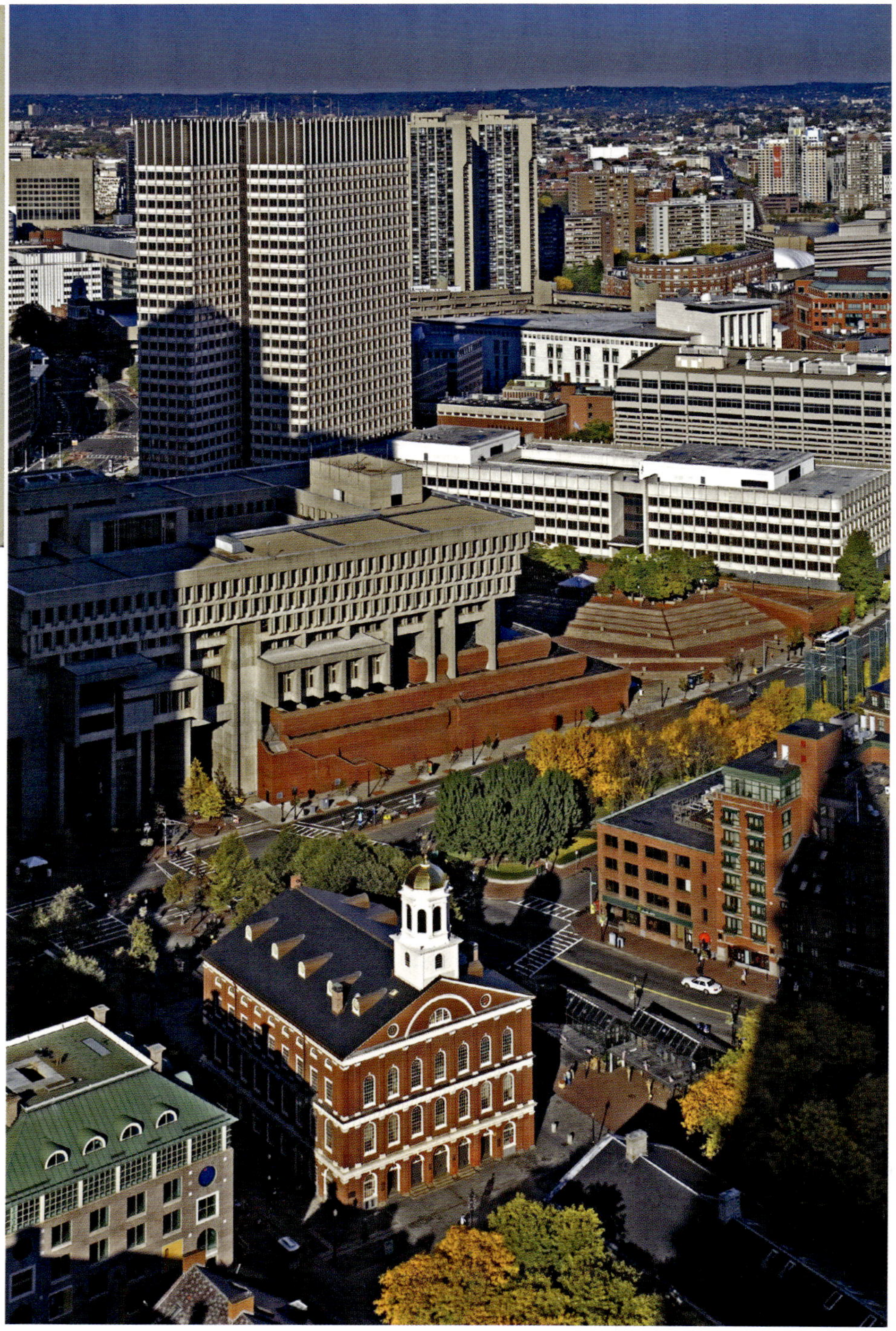

Faneuil Hall and one end of Quincy Market can be seen in the foreground. The monumental Boston City Hall was built from 1963-1968. Behind it lies the brick and concrete Government Center built on old Scollay Square. *Courtesy of Paul E. Doherty*

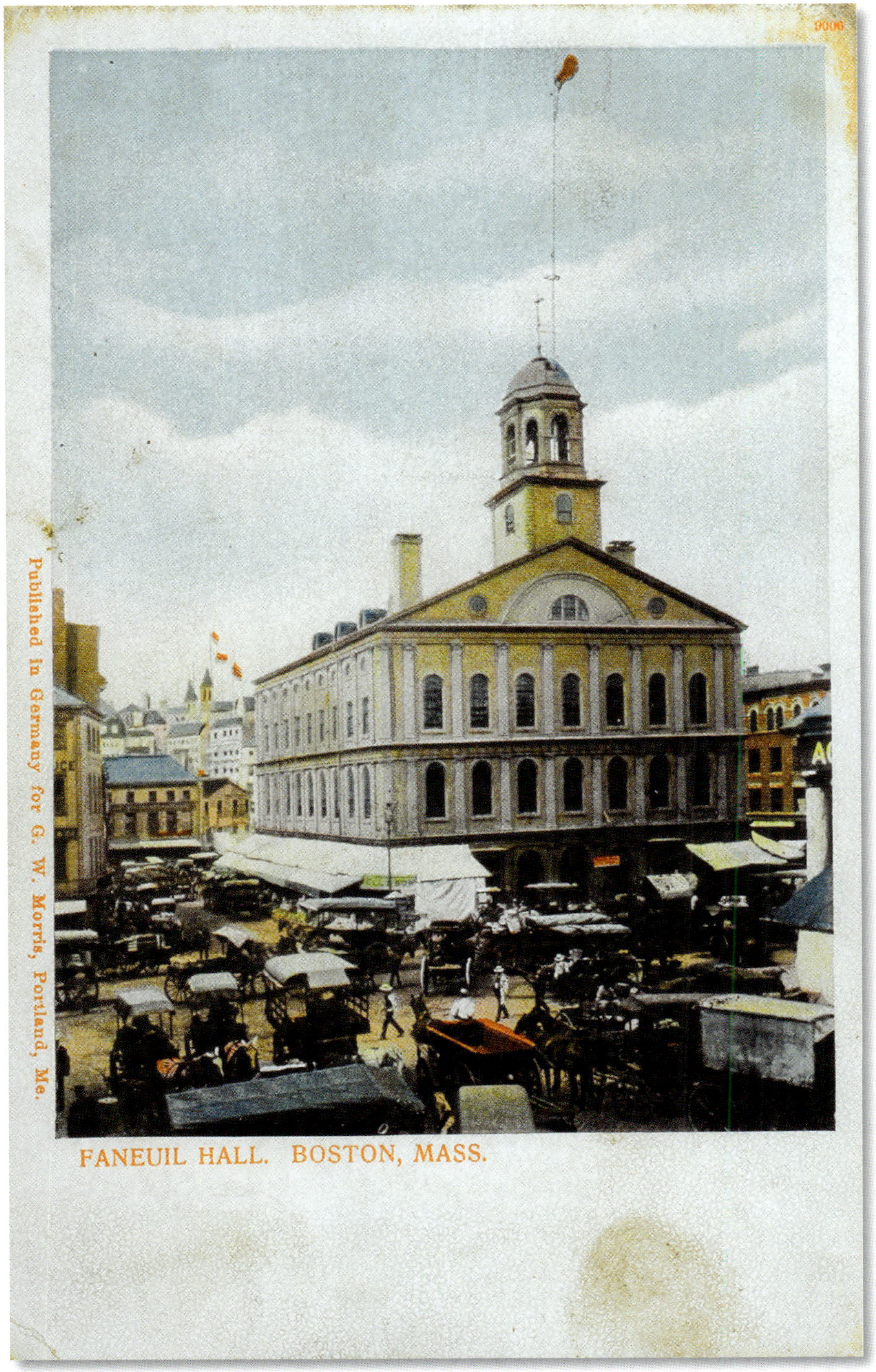

A U.S. National Historical Landmark and on the National Register of Historic Places, Faneuil Hall is also known as the "Cradle of Liberty." During the American Revolution, Samuel Adams, John Hancock, and James Otis gave speeches there. In later centuries, abolitionists and others delivered fiery orations there. During the eighteenth and nineteenth centuries, Faneuil Hall was a bustling produce, meat, and fish market.

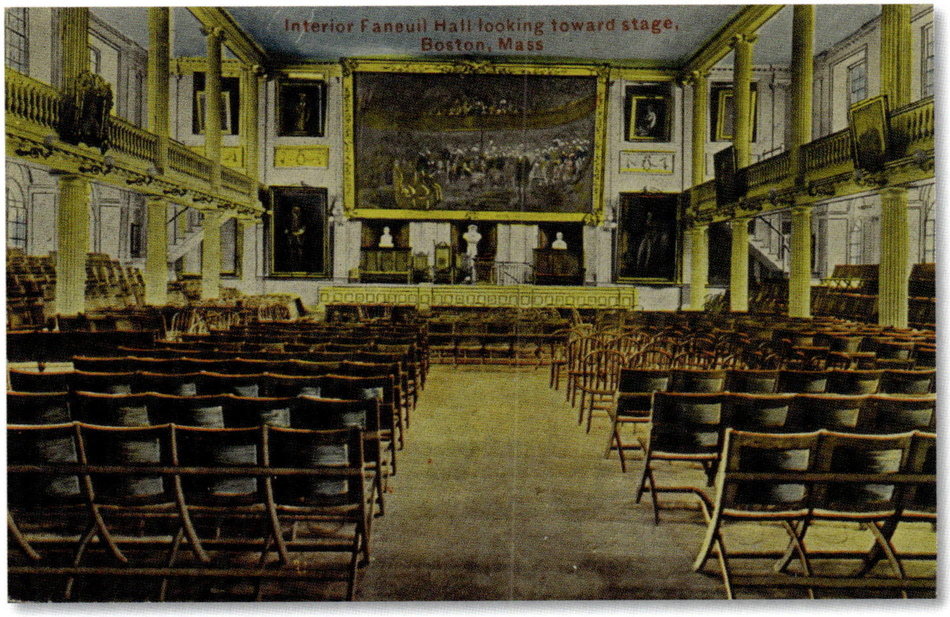

When Boston was incorporated as a city in 1822, the use of Faneuil Hall as the government meeting place came to an end. Over the years, it and surrounding buildings fell into disrepair until Benjamin Thompson & Associates restored them in the 1970s. Today, Faneuil Hall Marketplace, which includes North and South Markets and refurbished warehouses, is a lively emporium loaded with restaurants and stores. Jugglers, mime artists, musicians, and magicians perform throughout the attractive and traffic-free cobblestone marketplace.

In 1826, Josiah Quincy began Boston's first urban renewal with the reclamation of the waterfront. His plan called for filling in the tidal flats, demolishing the old buildings, and building six, granite-paved streets lined with granite warehouses. Named for him, the 555-foot Quincy Market was built on this reclaimed land in 1824-1826.

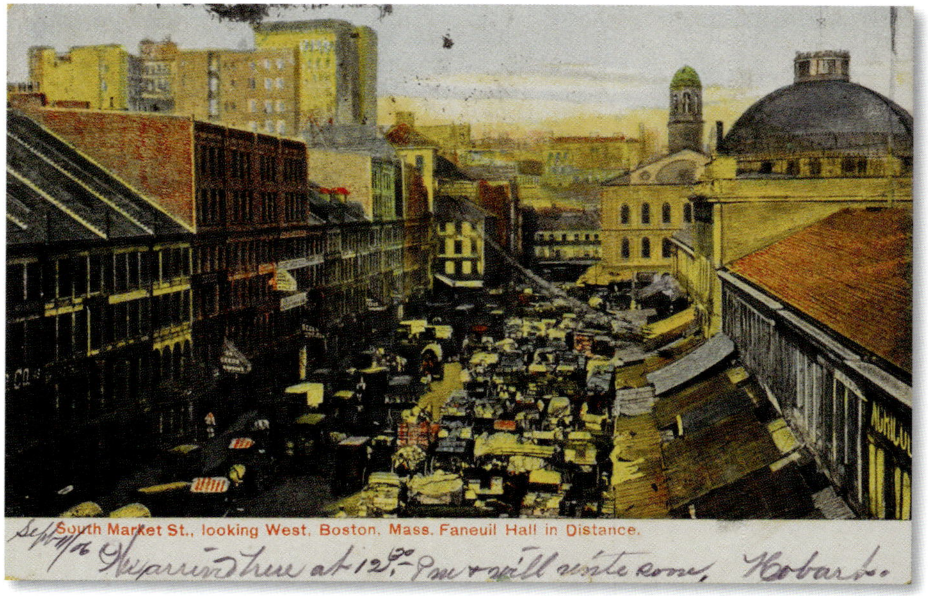

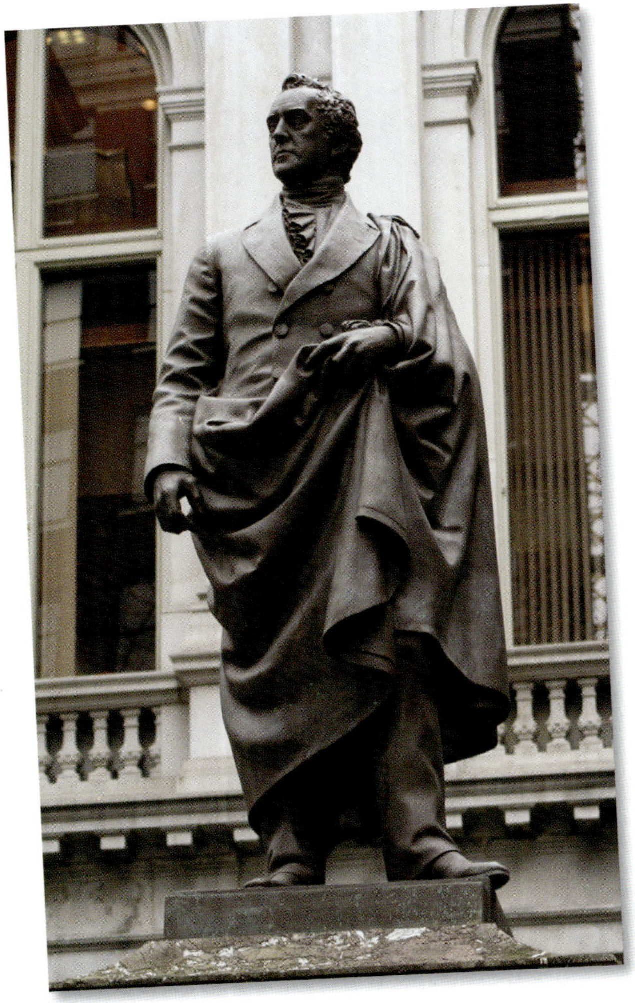

Josiah Quincy, the second Mayor of Boston, served six consecutive, one-year terms from 1823-1828. During his tenure, he was responsible for the development that expanded the produce and meat markets in Faneuil Hall into three new buildings known as the Quincy Markets. Thomas Ball designed this 1879 statue.

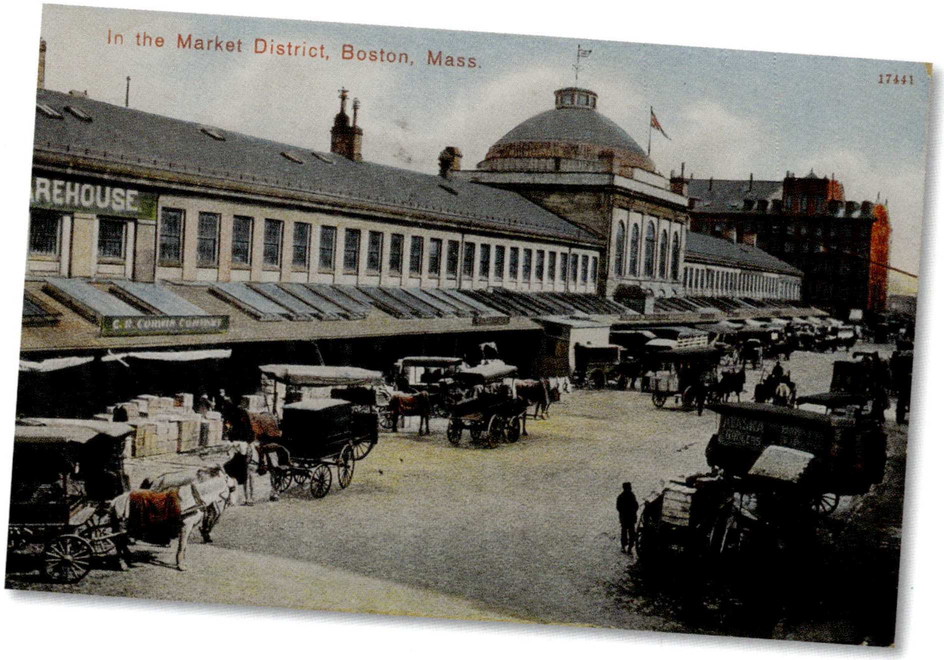

Planned as an extension to the first Faneuil Hall Market, this market with its distinguished copper dome and cupola attracted resident and store owners, who came here to buy from farmers, bakers, fishmongers, and artisans.

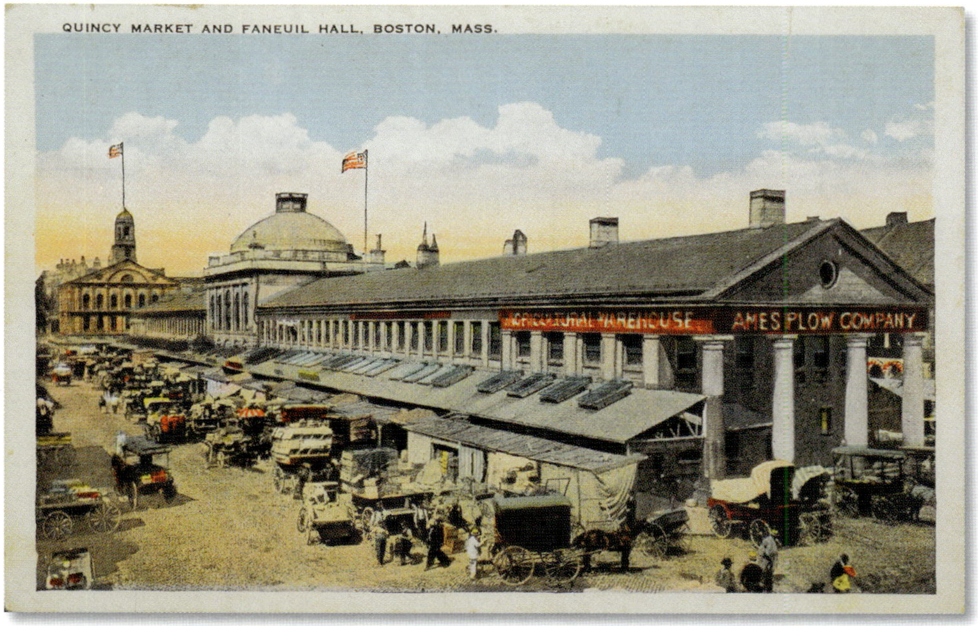

Architect Alexander Parris designed the rectangular granite warehouse for grain and other foodstuffs in a Greek revival style. At the time of construction, the facade's four Doric columns were the largest single pieces of granite ever to be quarried in the United States.

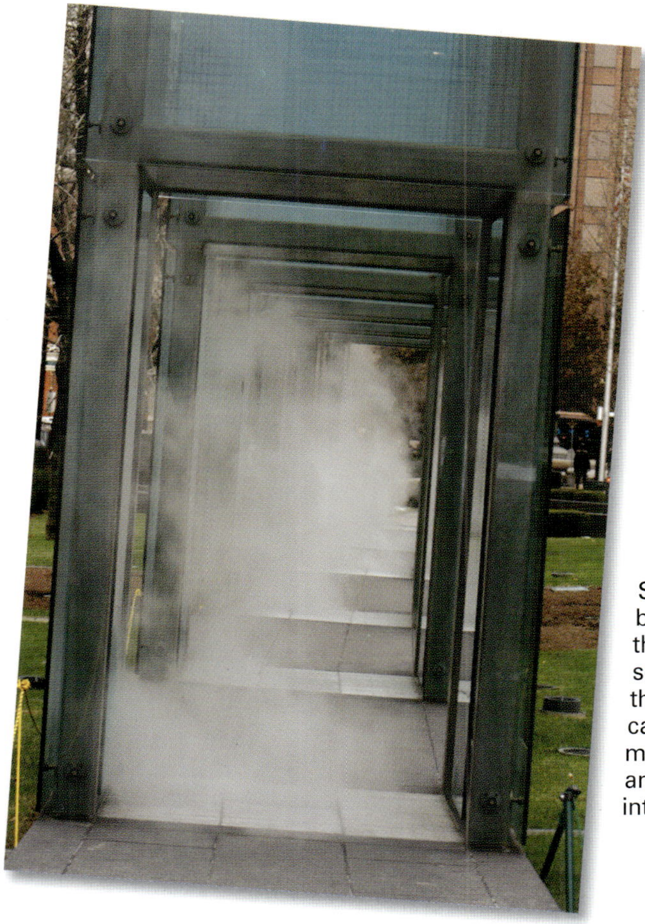

Six million numbers are etched into the glass to represent those killed in the Holocaust. You can walk into the monument as our ancestors walked into the camps.

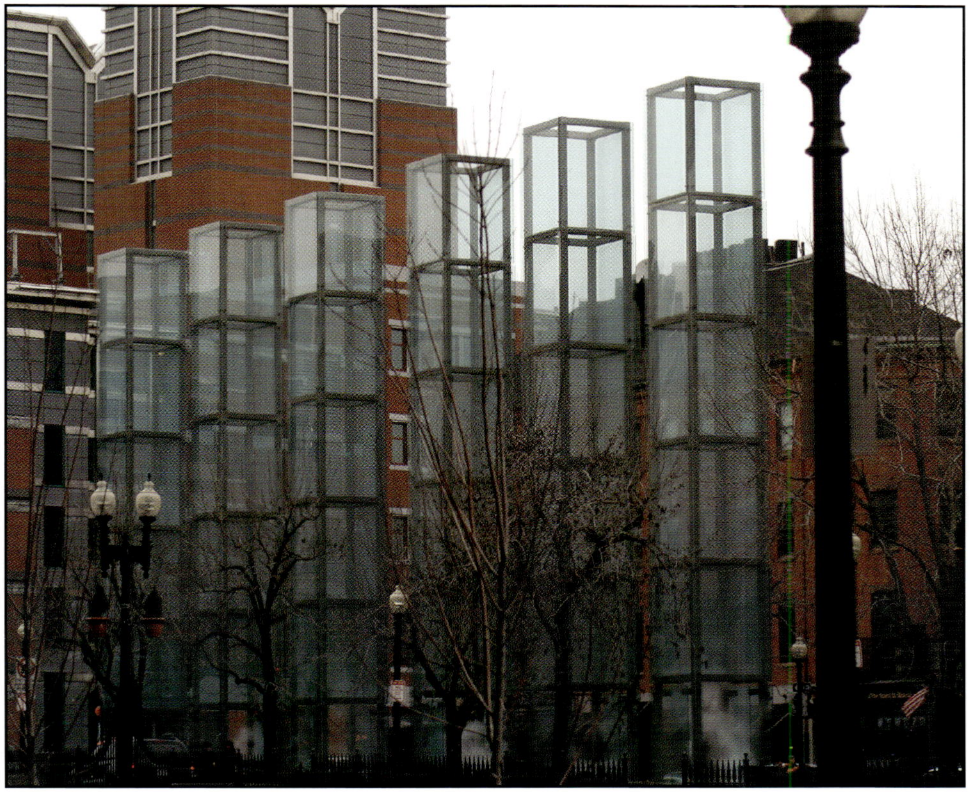

The New England Holocaust Memorial has six, smoke-filled 54-foot glass towers, representing the major Nazi concentration camps. Each tower is illuminated from the top and bottom.

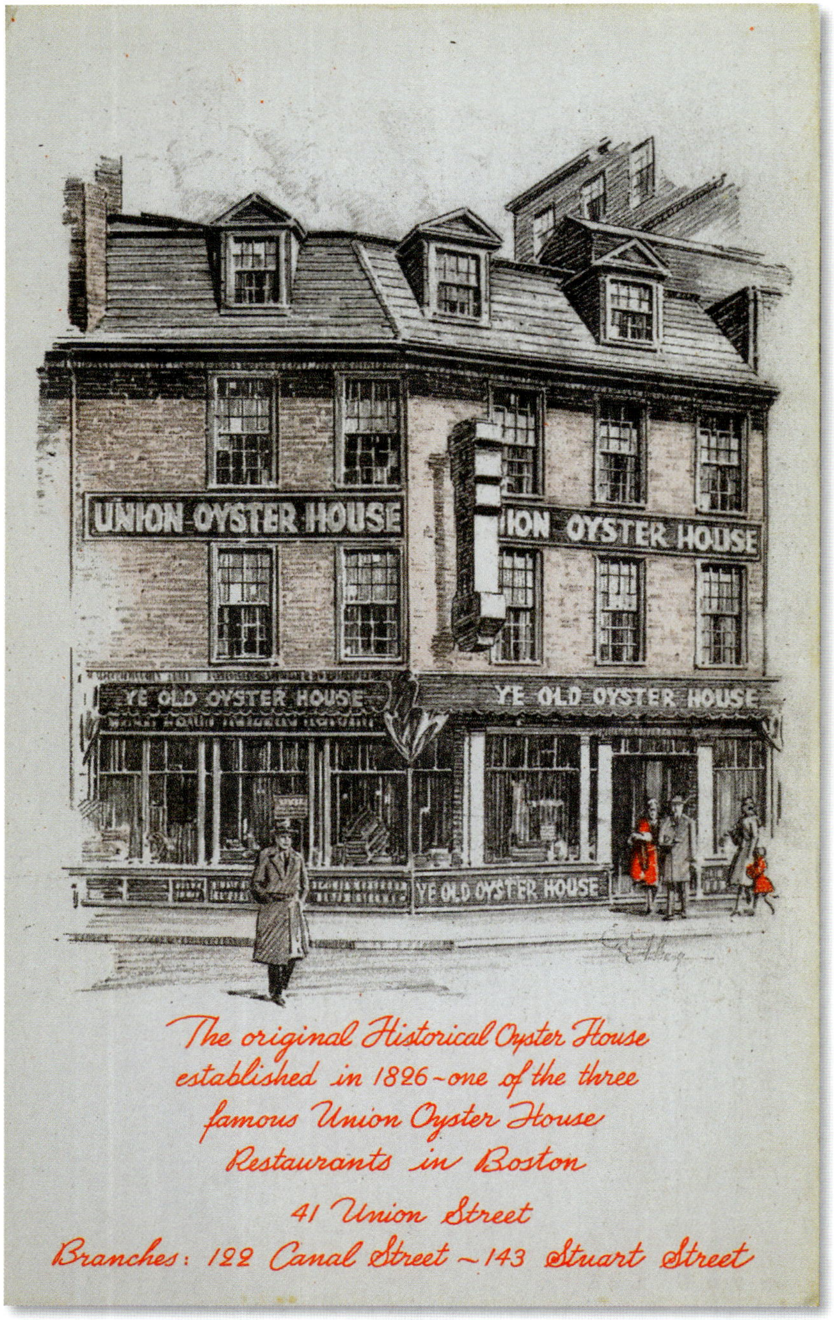

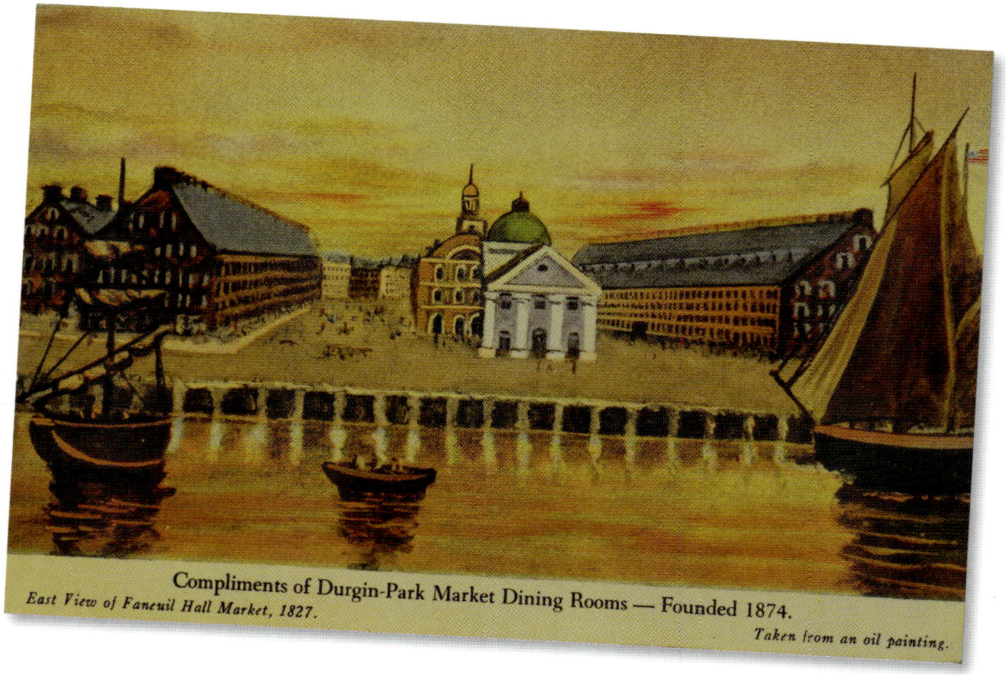

Durgin Park restaurant is a Boston institution. Famous for its snippy staff, it serves those New England dishes that no one else cooks, e.g., Indian pudding, baked beans, and baked scrod.

Union Oyster House has been serving diners since 1826, which makes it the oldest continuously operating restaurant in the nation. Originally, the building was a dry goods store. Daniel Webster used to frequent here, consuming a tumbler of brandy and water with each plate of half-dozen oysters. The historians say he rarely had less than six plates. That's a lot of brandy! Toothpicks made their first public appearance here.

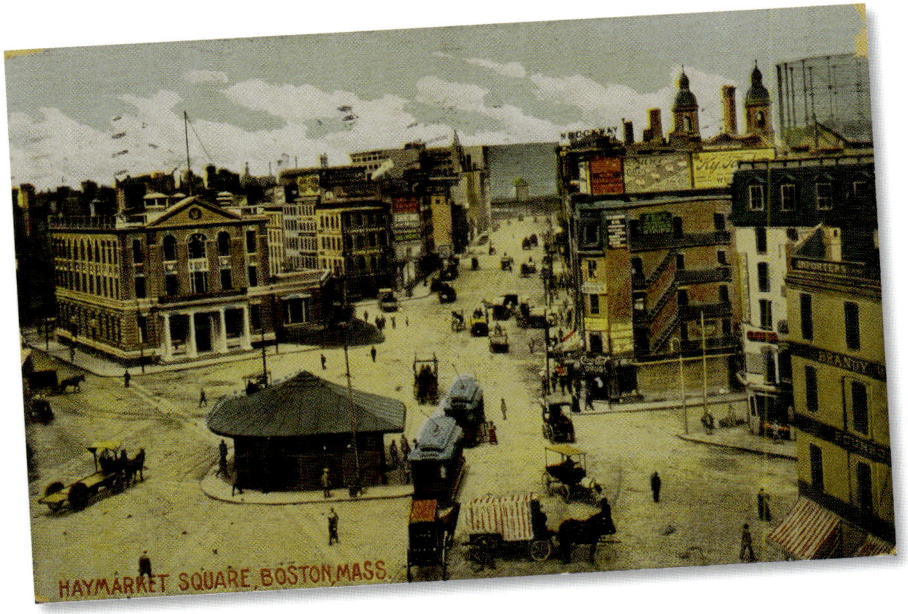

Haymarket Square is an area noted for its old style open-air markets. Originating at the turn of the century, the market is predominantly Italian. This market has become smaller as Boston has grown.

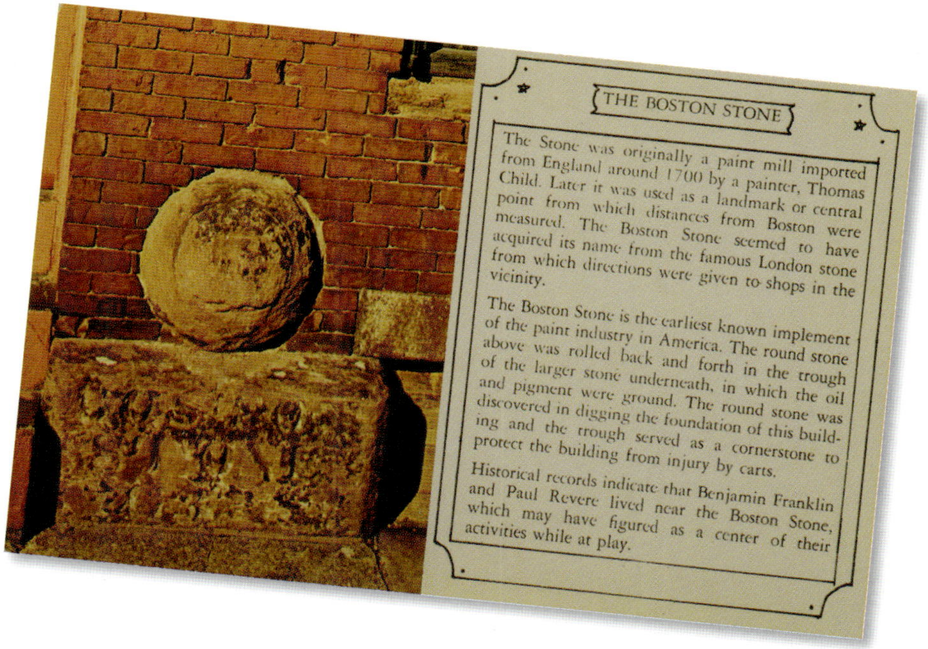

Imported from England in the seventeenth century, the Boston Stone (9 Marshall Street) was originally used for grinding substances that became pigments in paint. Researchers say that for many years, surveyors used the stone as a starting point because it was close to the center of town.

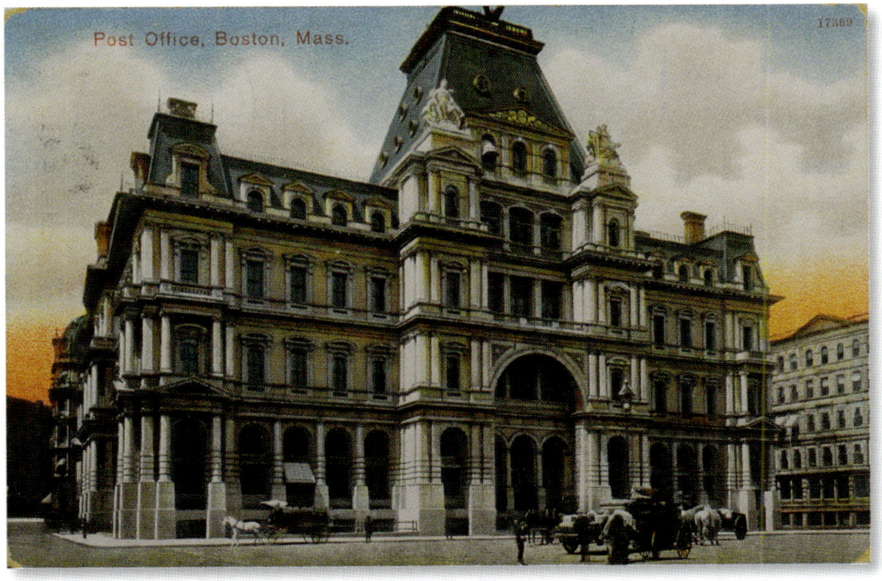

On December 25, 1868, the *New York Times* reported that the federal authorities "had decided upon the general plan of the new Post Office building to be erected in this city. The edifice will be of the Renaissant style of the modern French school. The main trout, on Devonshire-street, will be 240 feet, and consist of a central pavilion with wings, flanked at the corners of Water and Milk streets by bold projections, which are terminated against the skyline ornamented with pavilion roofs and clock turrets."

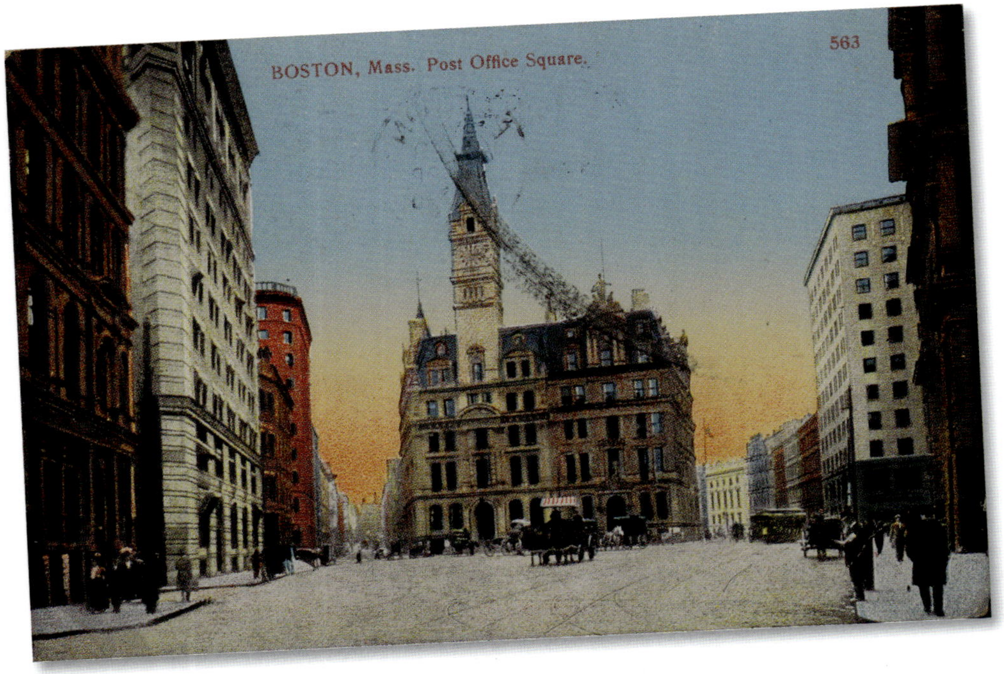

The Norman B. Leventhal Park at Post Office Square, constructed in 1991, has replaced the original Post Office Square. During a spring lunch-break it is difficult to find a place to sit or even stroll through the park because everyone leaves their big office buildings to sit in the sun in this 1.7-acre park on Congress and Pearl. The park sits atop a 1,500-car parking garage, which provides part of the revenue to maintain and operate it.

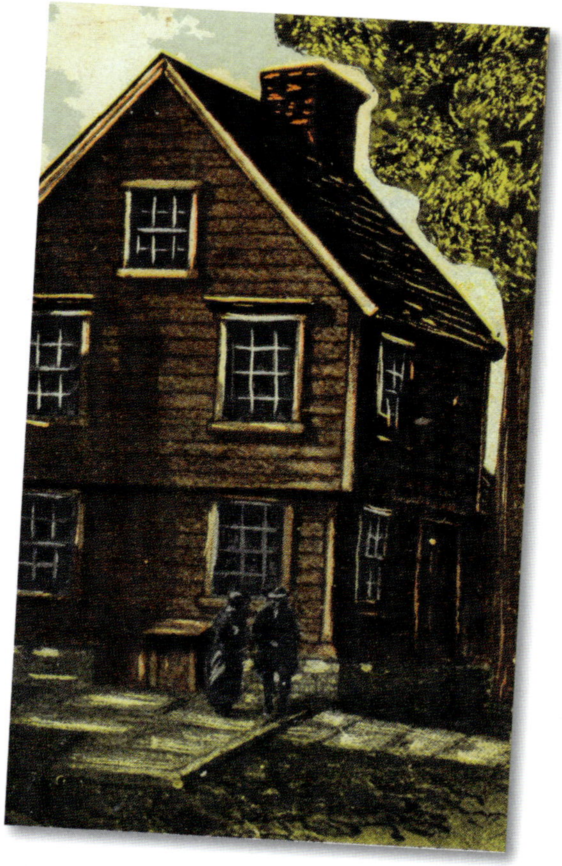

Among these seventeenth century, cobblestone alleys are the remains of one of Boston's oldest neighborhoods and the birthplace of Benjamin Franklin. Benjamin Franklin was born on Milk Street in Boston on January 17, 1706, and baptized at Old South Meeting House. The fifteenth child of a tallow chandler, a maker of candles and soap, Franklin attended Boston Latin School for several years and then became an avid reader. Apprenticed to his brother James, a printer, Ben enjoyed the work and soon became a skilled printer. He also began to write articles under the pseudonym "Mrs. Silence Dogood." Ultimately, Ben decided to run away to Philadelphia.

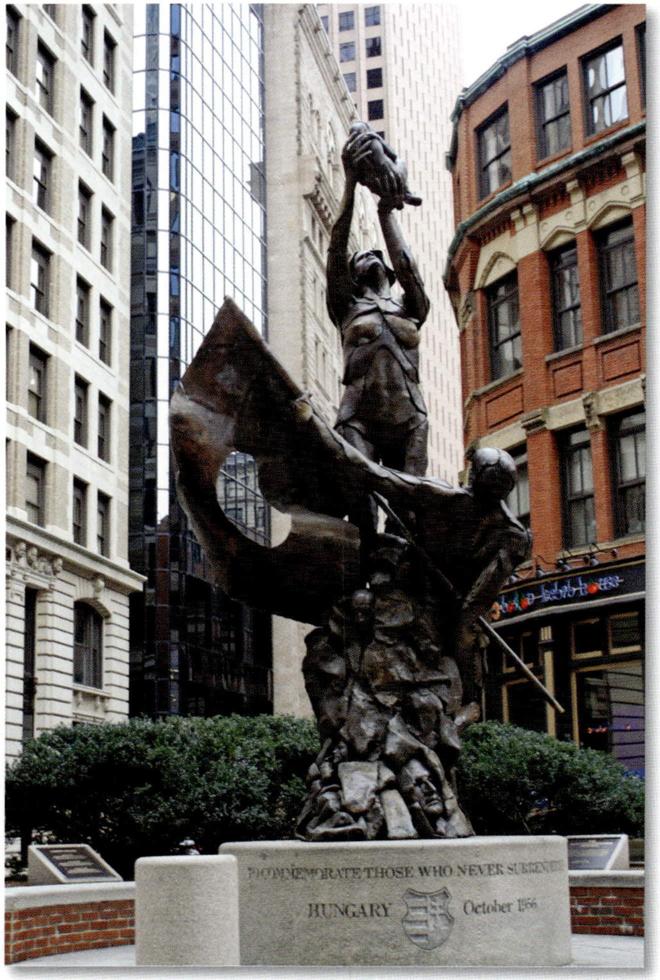

Surrounded by handsome Victorian buildings, this square has been known as Liberty Square long before the Hungarian Revolution. One theory is on August 14, 1765, angry colonials tore down the British Stamp Act office located in this square. A year later, the act was repealed. Another is that the square was named Liberty Square to commemorate the French Revolution. A festive banquet was held here, and a 21-gun salute fired to mark the occasion. The Hungarian Society of Massachusetts commissioned this statue by E. Gyuri Hollos to commemorate the thirtieth anniversary of the Hungarian Revolution. In the fall of 1956, the Hungarian people demanded change, and tens of thousands of students, workers, and other citizens bravely marched through the streets to call for freedom from the Soviet-installed Hungarian communist government. Thousands died fighting, others were tortured and executed, while 200,000 were forced to flee.

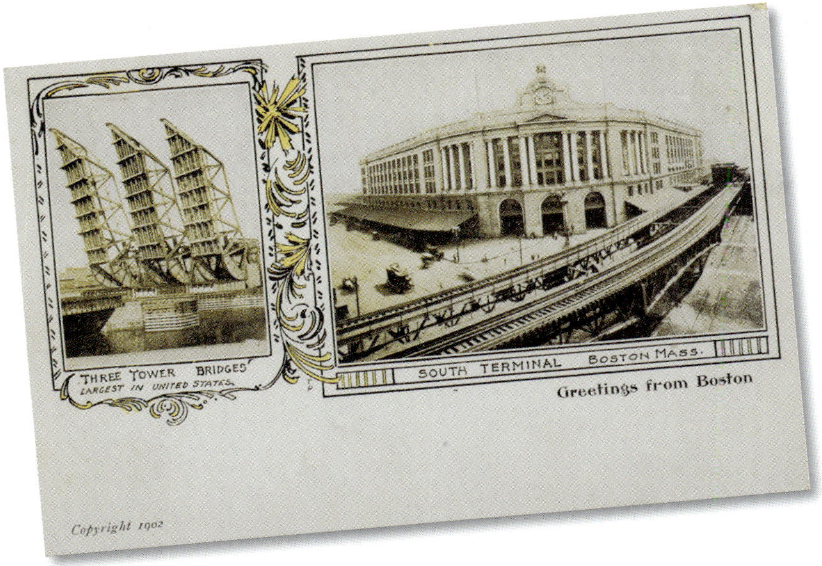

Horse cars gave way to electric trolleys as the nineteenth century progressed. By 1891, the Boston region had 245 miles of trolley track. Increasing congestion inspired the building of the nation's first subway system. Originally, four railroads served Boston. Each had its own terminal.

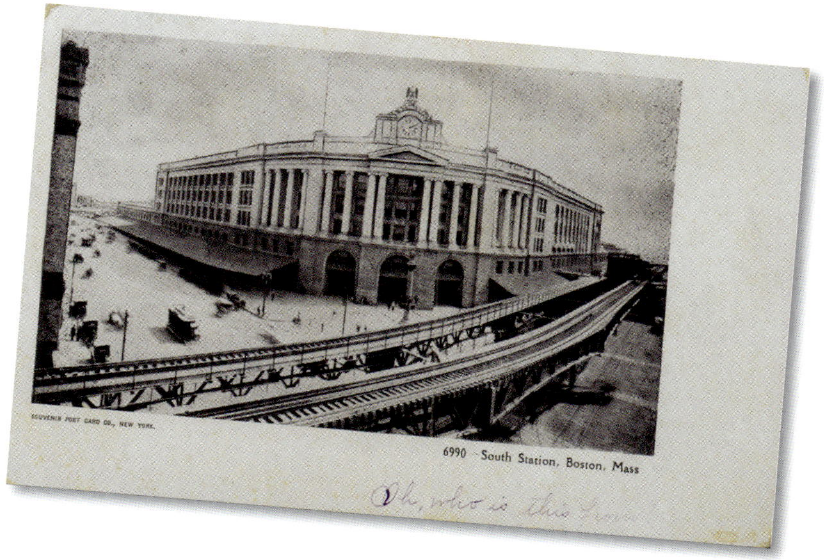

On January 1, 1899, South Station combined many terminals; by 1910, it was the busiest station in the country. After World War II, passenger rail was no longer as popular.

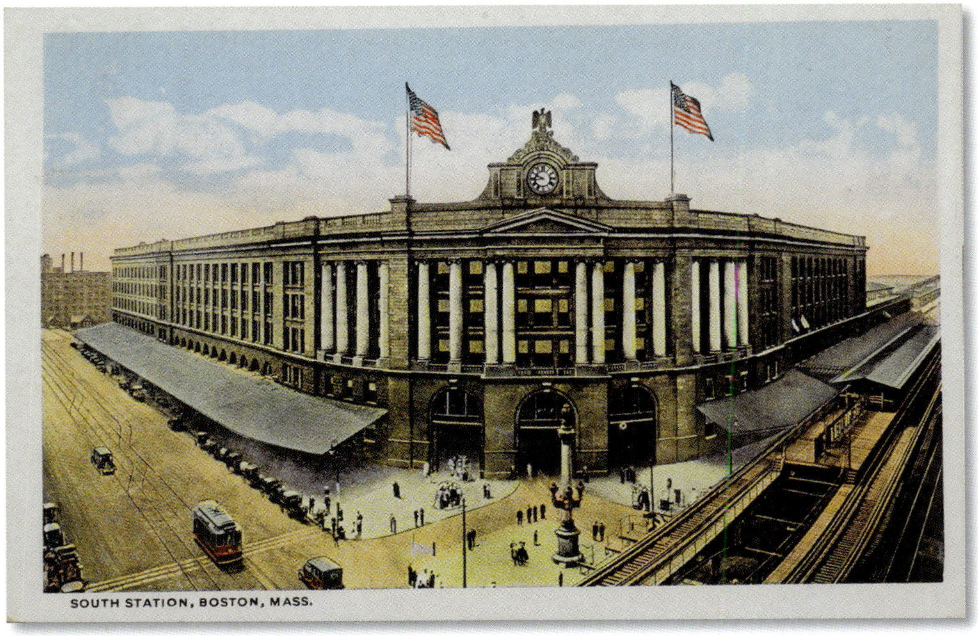

Eventually, the lines stopped running or went bankrupt, and the Boston Redevelopment Authority (BRA) bought South Station. In 1978, the Massachusetts Bay Transportation Authority (MBTA) bought the station, which is now on the National Register of Historic Places. In 1989, the station was renovated.

Chapter 3

The North End and The Waterfront

And this is good old Boston, The home of the bean and the cod, Where the Lowells talk only to the Cabots, And the Cabots talk only to God. –Attributed to Ralph Waldo Emerson

Although most people today associate the North End with great Italian restaurants, a large proportion of the original inhabitants of the North End were shipbuilders and mariners. Since the area was settled in the 1630s, people have lived here. One of the most famous residents was Paul Revere.

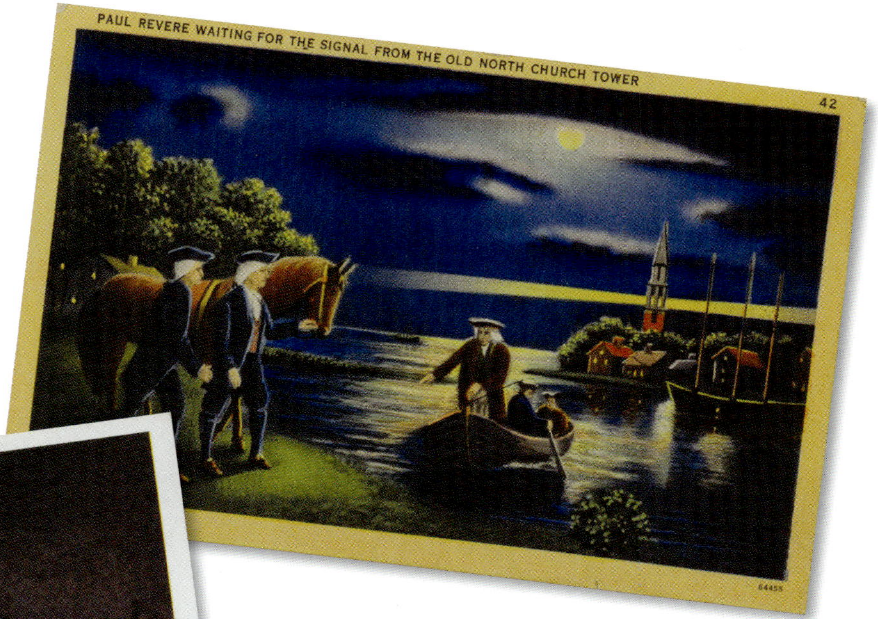

Silversmith and patriot Paul Revere is famous for his midnight ride. Here, he crosses the Charles River as he sets out through the countryside

The North End

Listen my children and you shall hear
Of the midnight ride of Paul Revere,
On the eighteenth of April, in Seventy-five;
Hardly a man is now alive
Who remembers that famous day and year.
He said to his friend, "If the British march
By land or sea from the town to-night,
Hang a lantern aloft in the belfry arch
Of the North Church tower as a signal light,
--One if by land, and two if by sea;
And I on the opposite shore will be,
Ready to ride and spread the alarm
Through every Middlesex village and farm,
For the country folk to be up and to arm.
–Henry Wadsworth Longfellow, from *Paul Revere's Ride*

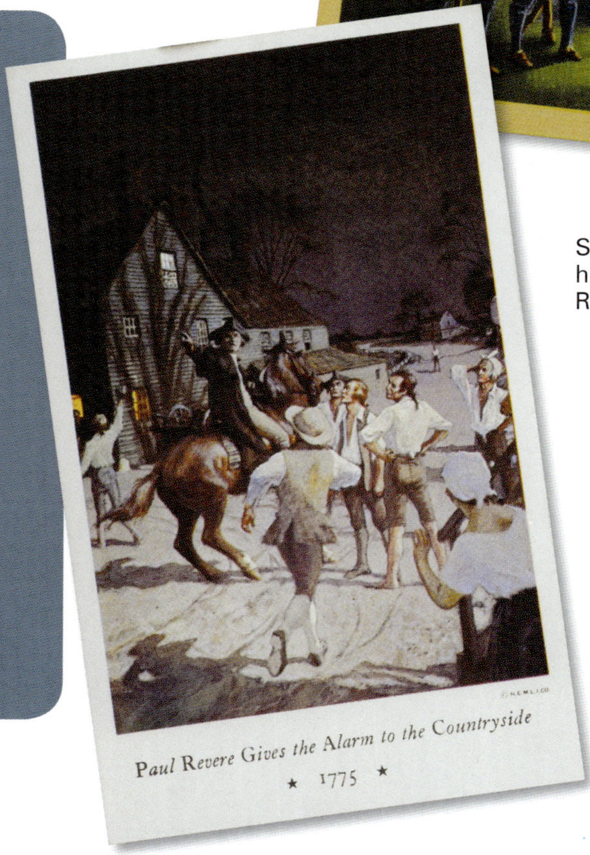

He warned Samuel Adams and John Hancock about the advancing British troops.

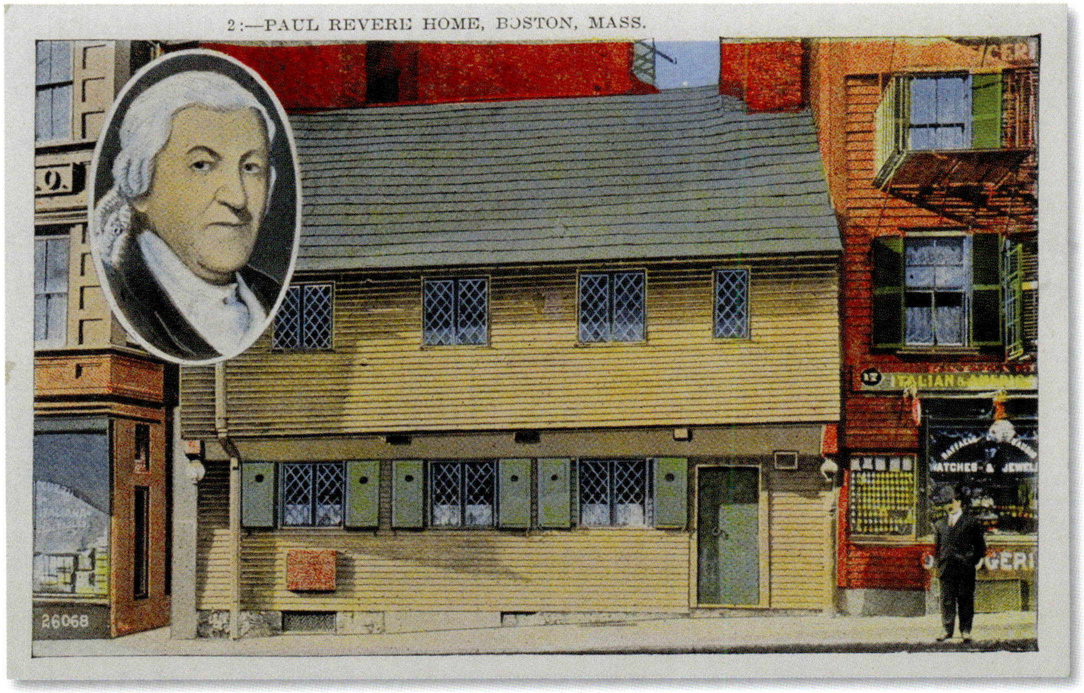

Paul Revere purchased this wood-framed house built around 1680 (19 North Square) in 1770. He left from here for his many missions for the revolutionary cause, including his famous ride to warn the colonists that the "regulars are out." The Revere house has preserved some of the furnishings used by the family and gives a view of everyday life in colonial Boston.

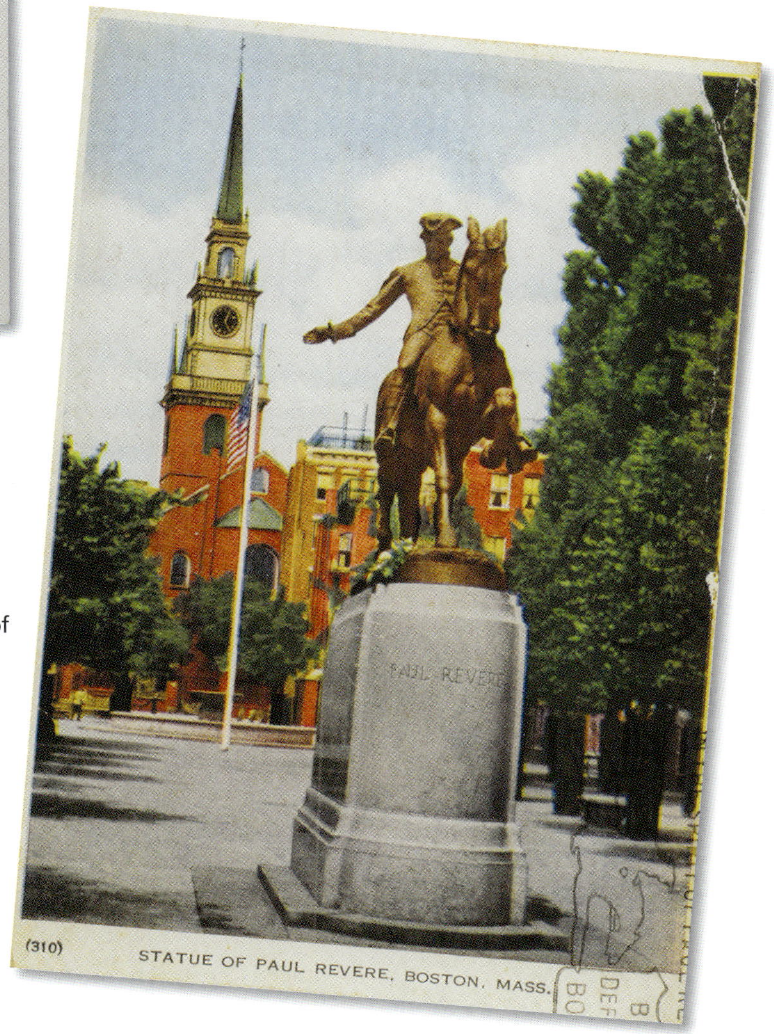

Behind the statue of Paul Revere is Old North Church.

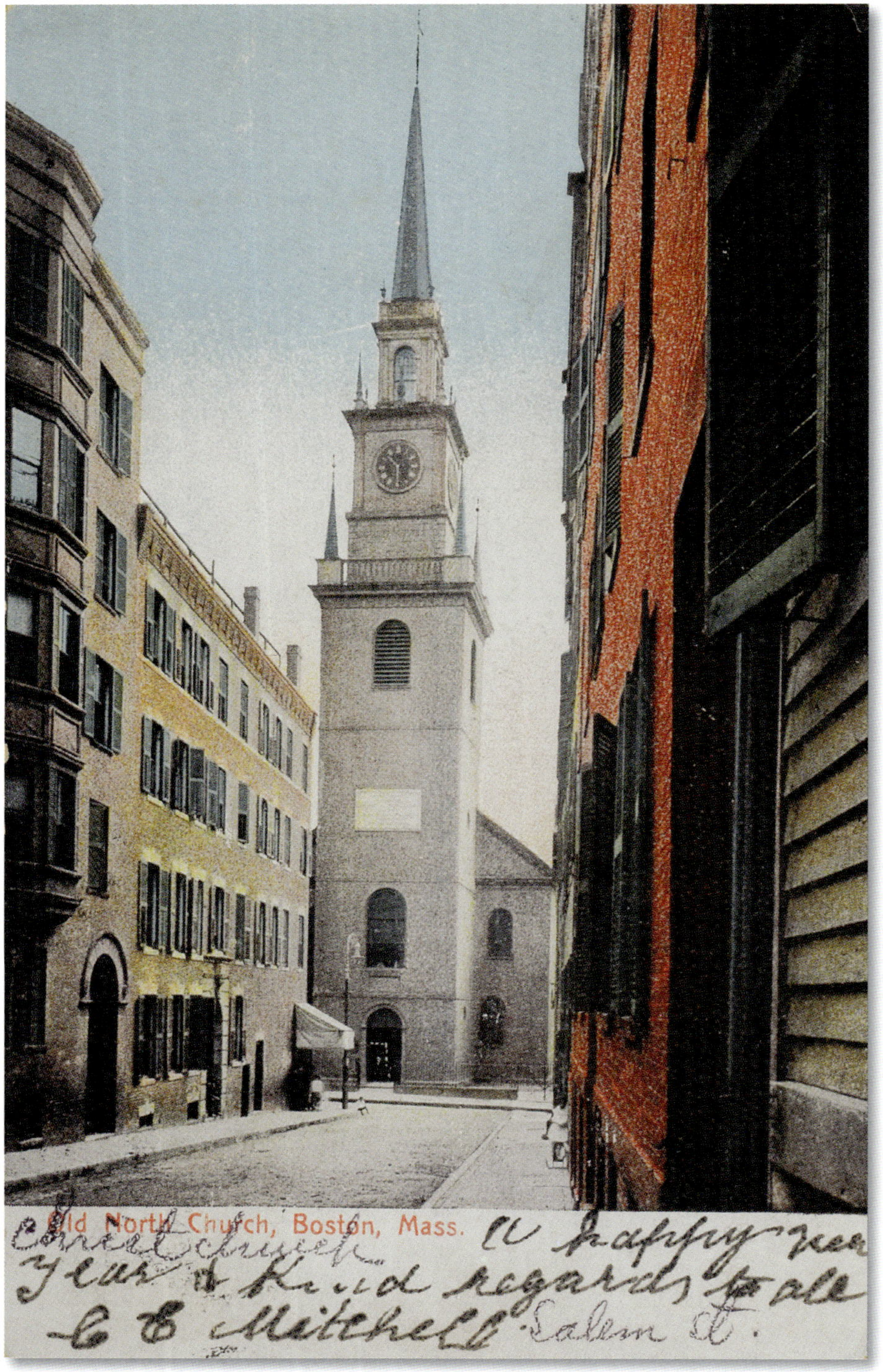

Known as "Christ Church in the City of Boston," the brick Old North Church, an Episcopal church (193 Salem Street) was built in 1723. Not only the most famous church in Boston, it is also the second oldest (the first is King's Chapel). The church found its place into our history books on April 18, 1775, when the sexton Robert Newman hung a pair of signal lanterns in the belfry. These lights warned the patriots of the departure of the British troops to Lexington and Concord.

Its massive brick walls support a 191-foot tall steeple – the tallest steeple in Boston. Visible to ships sailing into port, the steeple has been replaced several times. It also has the first set of bells ever brought to America. Paul Revere was one of the neighborhood bell ringers.

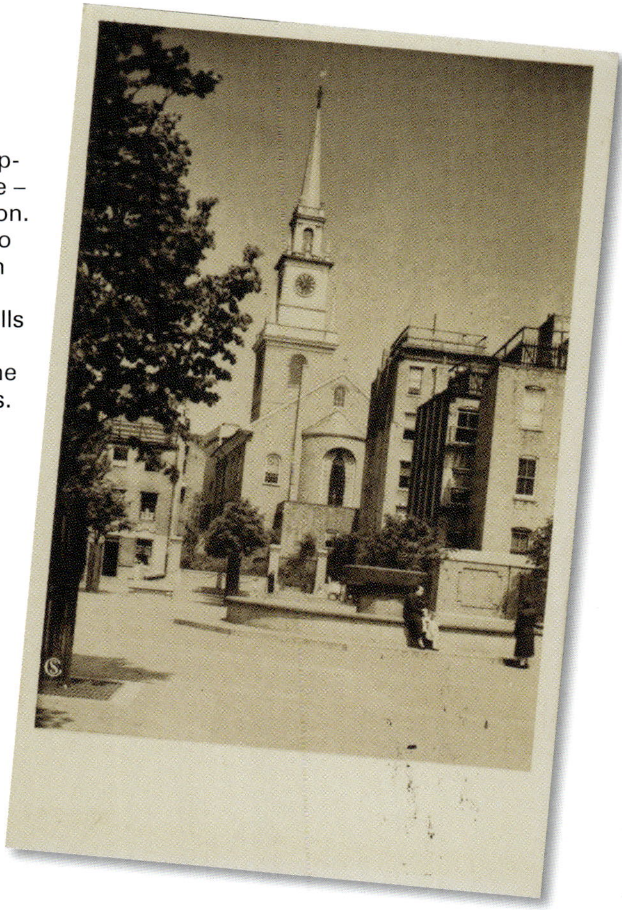

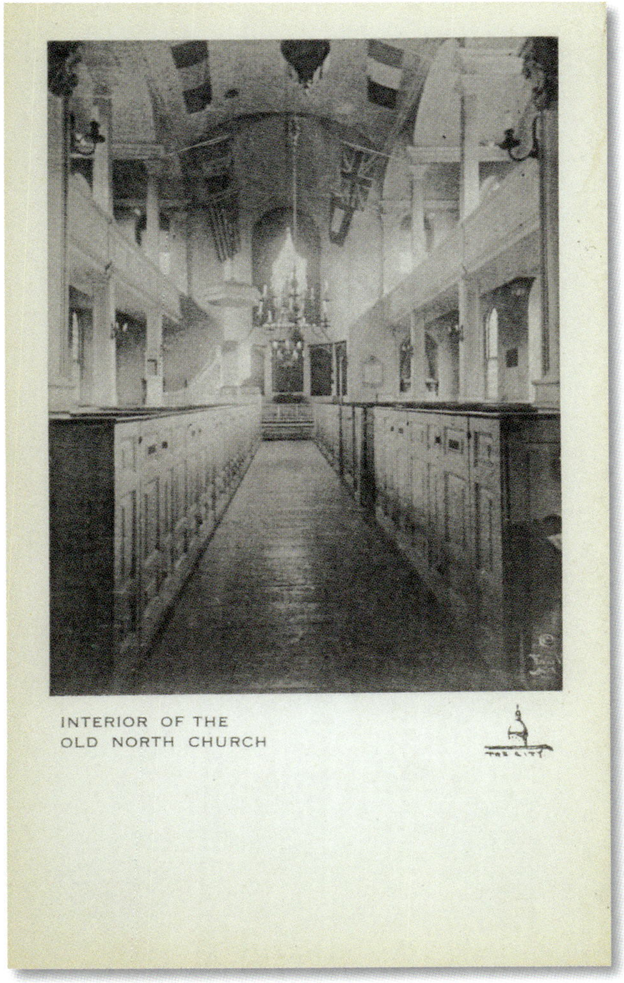

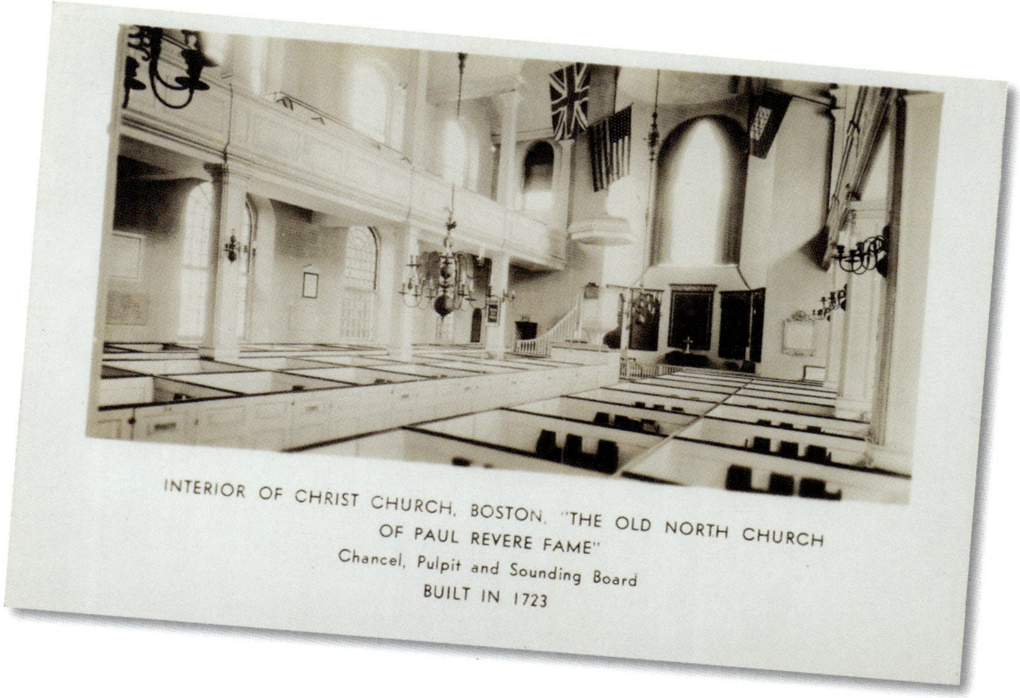

From the steeple of this church, lanterns signaled the approach of the British regulars, "One if by land, and two, if by sea.

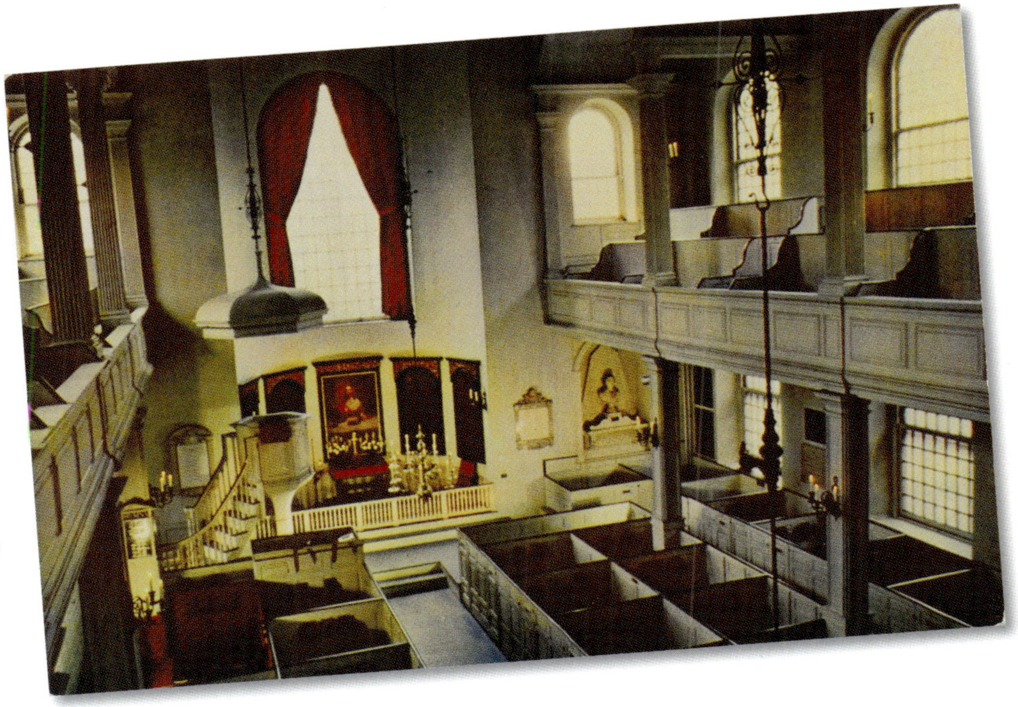

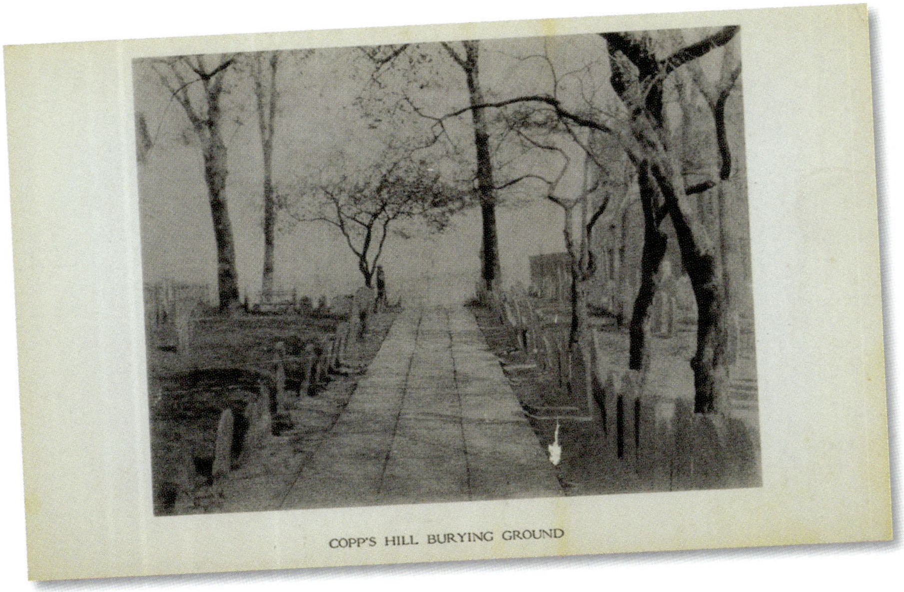

Before it was a burial ground, Copp's Hill was the site of Boston's first windmill. Eventually, Copp's Hill became the largest of the early burial grounds. It contains the remains of many famous people, including three generations of the Mather family, Robert Newman, Prince Hall, a free black man who founded the African Freemasonry Order, and the builder of the *USS Constitution*. On June 17, 1775, British cannon based on the hill fired on American positions across Boston Harbor. The British used the gravestones for target practice, and you can still find the bullet holes.

The Waterfront

Boston, New York, Philadelphia, Charleston, New Orleans, and the rest, are the names of wharves projecting into the sea (surrounded by the shops and dwellings of the merchants), good places to take in and to discharge a cargo (to land the products of other climes and load the exports of our own). I see a great many barrels and fig-drums,—piles of wood for umbrella- sticks,—blocks of granite and ice,—great heaps of goods, and the means of packing and conveying them,—much wrapping-paper and twine,—many crates and hogsheads and trucks,—and that is Boston. The more barrels, the more Boston.
–Henry David Thoreau, *The Writings of Henry David Thoreau*

The Boston waterfront was host to many of the first fortunes made in the New World. During the first half of the nineteenth century, the harbor was filled with sloops, square-riggers, schooners, whalers, and brigs. As shipping interests grew, new wharves were built. The waterfront was a crowded busy place with draft horses pulling wagons filled with goods to and from the brick warehouses; beaver-hatted men sporting blue tailcoats and black stocks walked to and from their counting houses: grimy urchins ran about looking for work or spare coins.

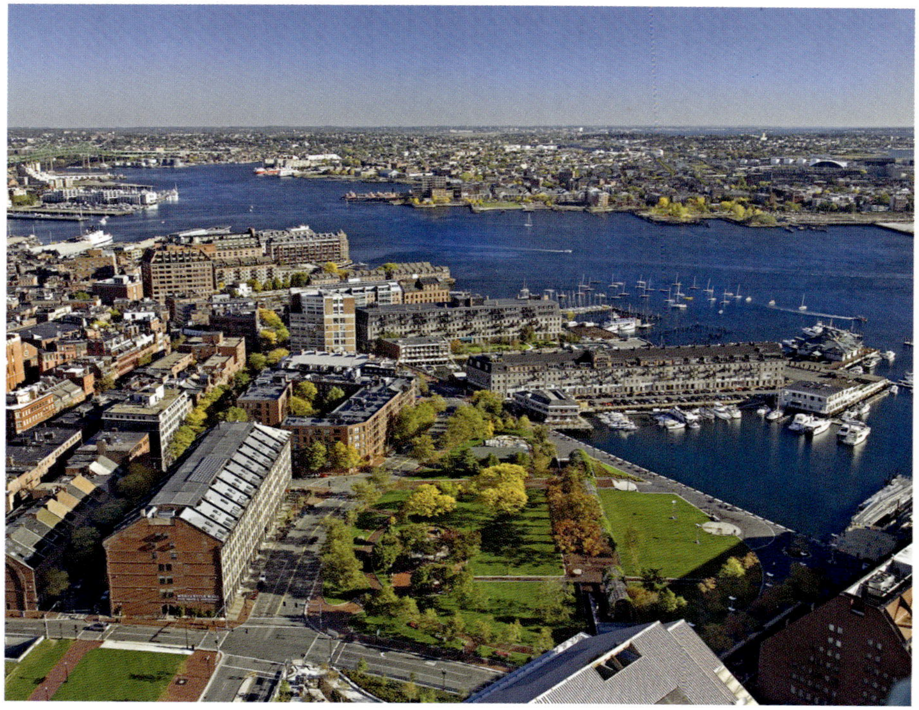

This image looks at Boston's Inner Harbor and on to Christopher Columbus Park, which borders on the North End. Long Wharf is at the lower right, and Commercial Wharf is in the middle. Much of the cargo from America's early shipping passed through Boston's warehouses, which have subsequently been transformed into luxury condominiums and offices. *Courtesy of Paul E. Doherty*

Shipping

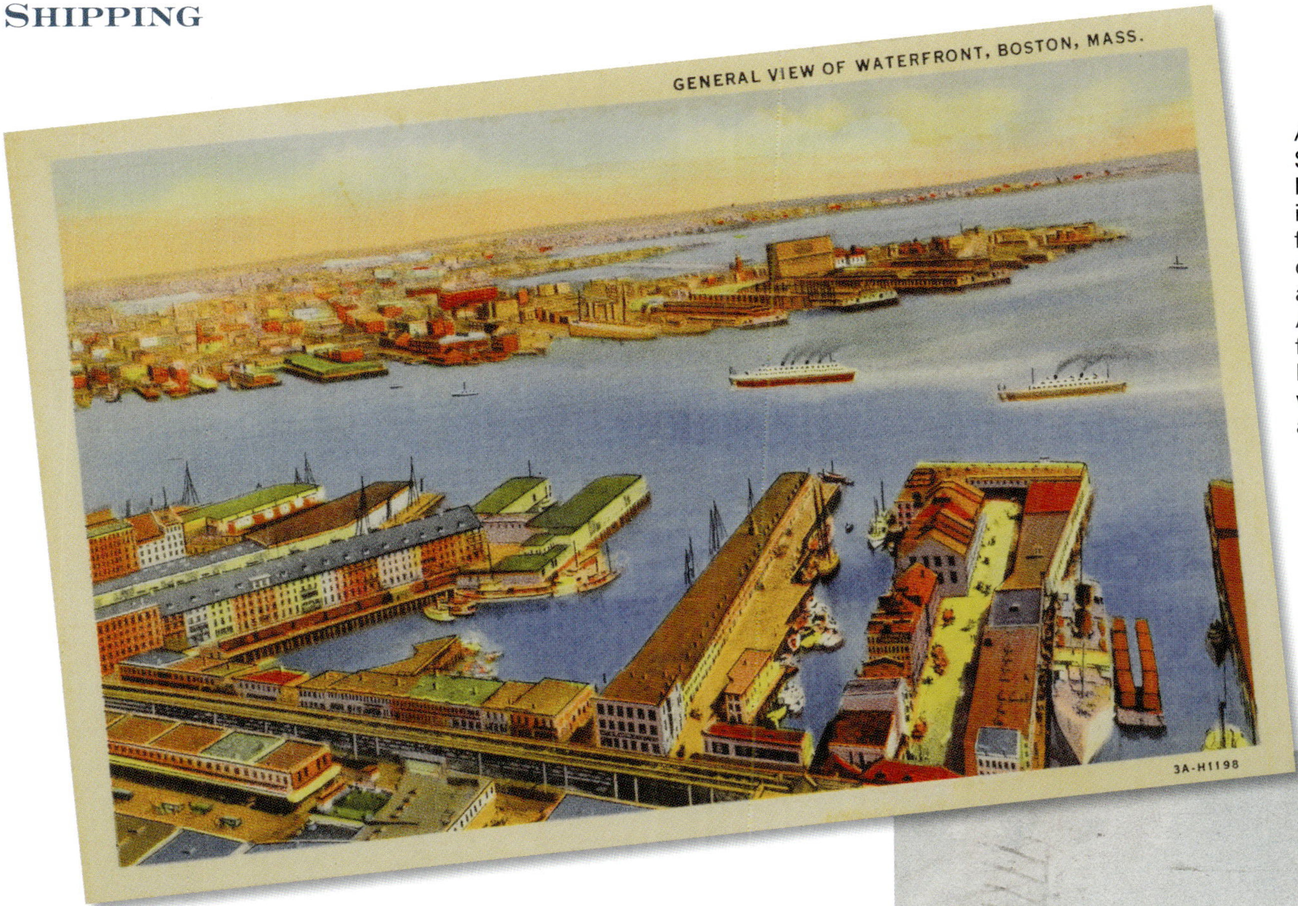

After the Revolutionary War, the new United States sent its own trading ships to China. Most ships sailed west around South America and through to the Pacific. The mariners faced diseases, hurricanes, and other natural disasters to reach Macao, a major port city at the mouth of China's Pearl River. There, American ships received official permission from the Chinese government to sail up the Pearl River to Canton, the only Chinese port where westerners (Americans included) were allowed to trade.

American merchant ships brought back silk, porcelain dinner services and teacups, tealeaves, and spices. With Massachusetts's merchants owning almost one-third of the shipping in the country, the 1807-1815 shipping embargo affected Boston. Once that was over, Boston's maritime industry prospered again

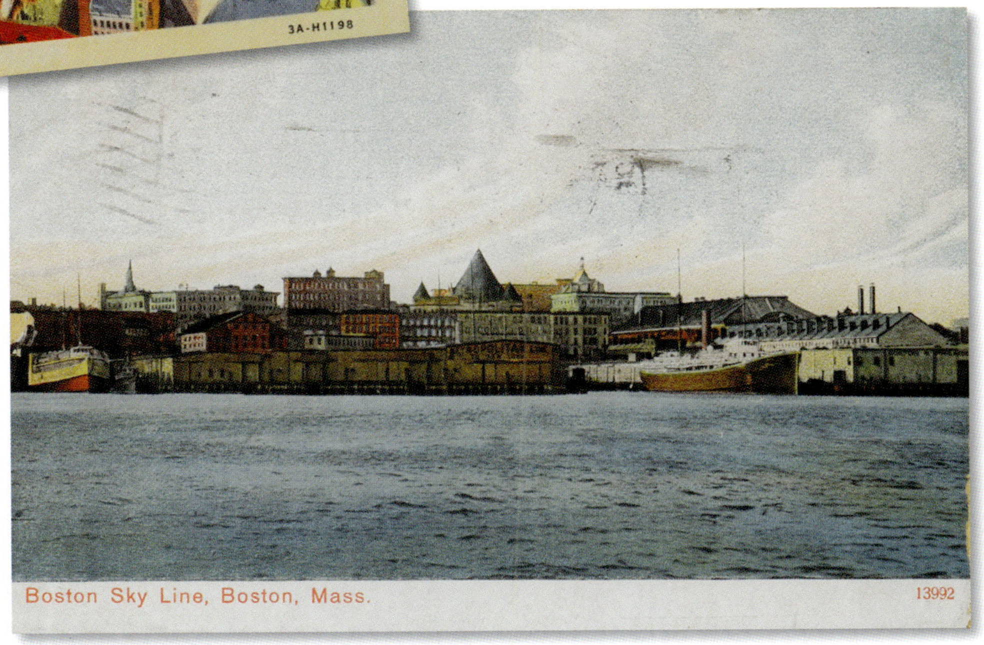

The slave runner had a three-part voyage. The first leg of the voyage from Europe to Africa, the ship carried goods that usually included cloth, brandy, rum and guns. Upon landing on Africa's "slave coast," European and Yankee sailors traded their cargo for African men and women who had been transported from the interior to the west coast of Africa. Once fully loaded with its human cargo, the ship set sail for the Americas, where the slaves were exchanged for sugar, tobacco or some other product. This leg of the journey took approximately eight weeks. The final leg brought the ship back to Europe. Through this system, called the Triangle Trade Route, perhaps 10–12 million people were sold into slavery. It lasted for three hundred years until many countries abolished slavery.

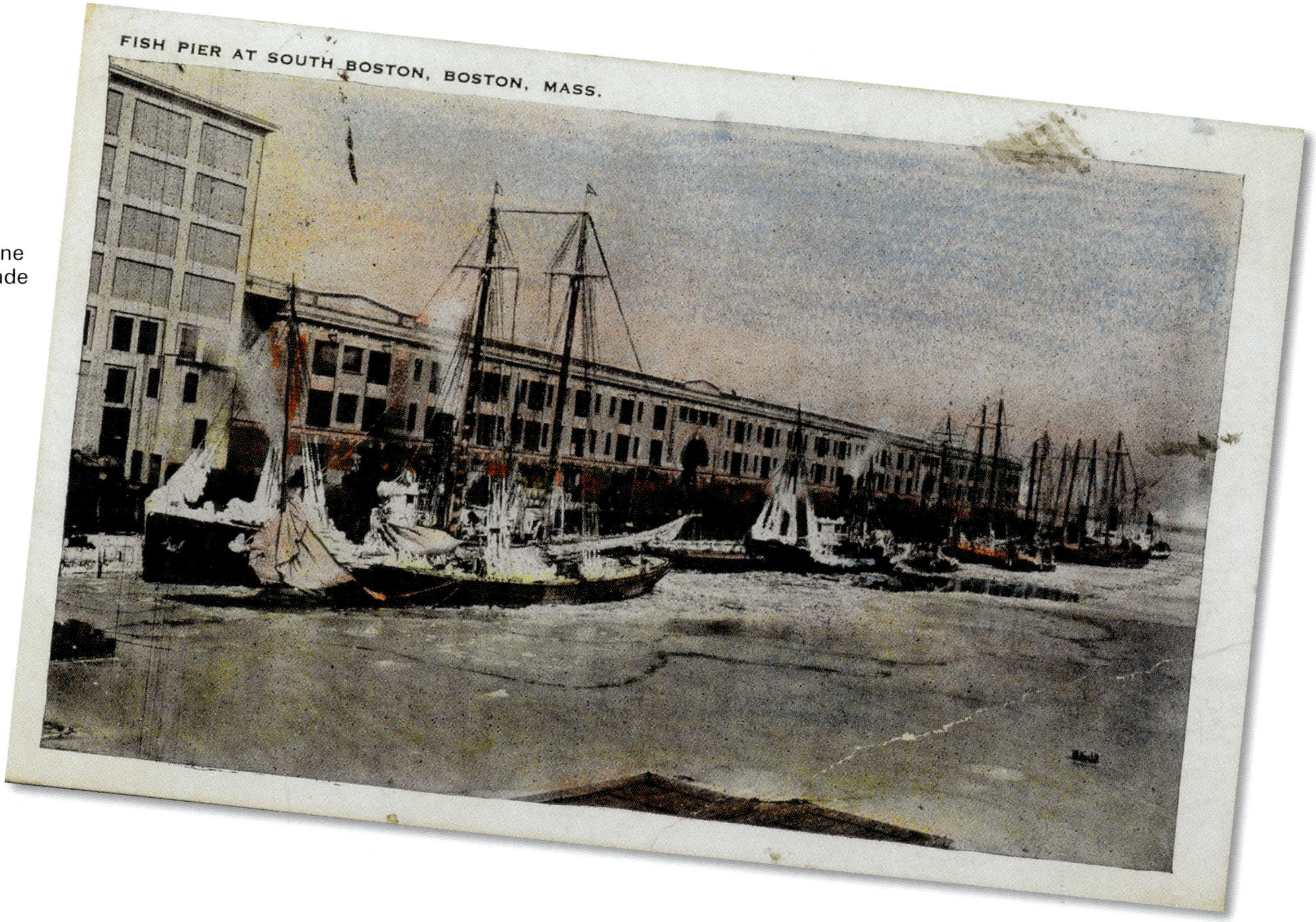

Some made their fortune through the triangle trade route.

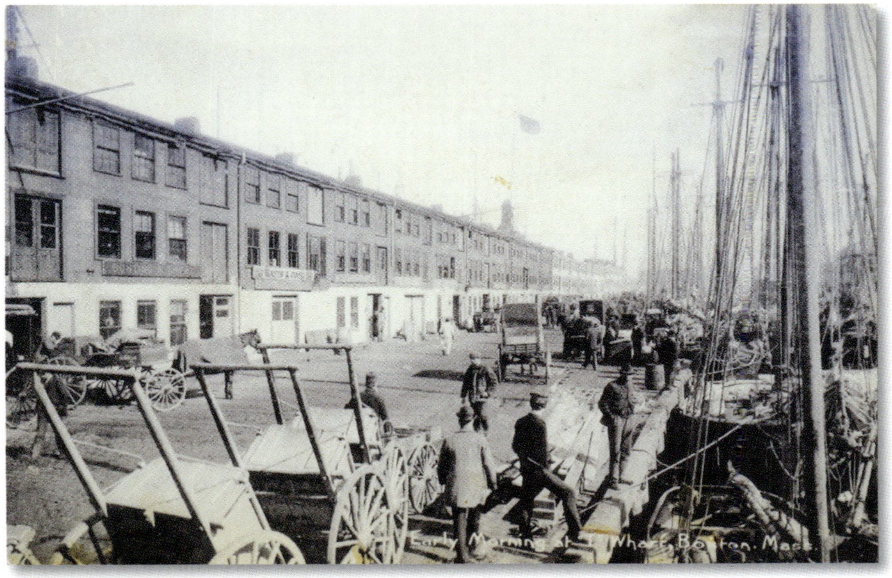

Others smuggled while some became whalers or cod fishermen.

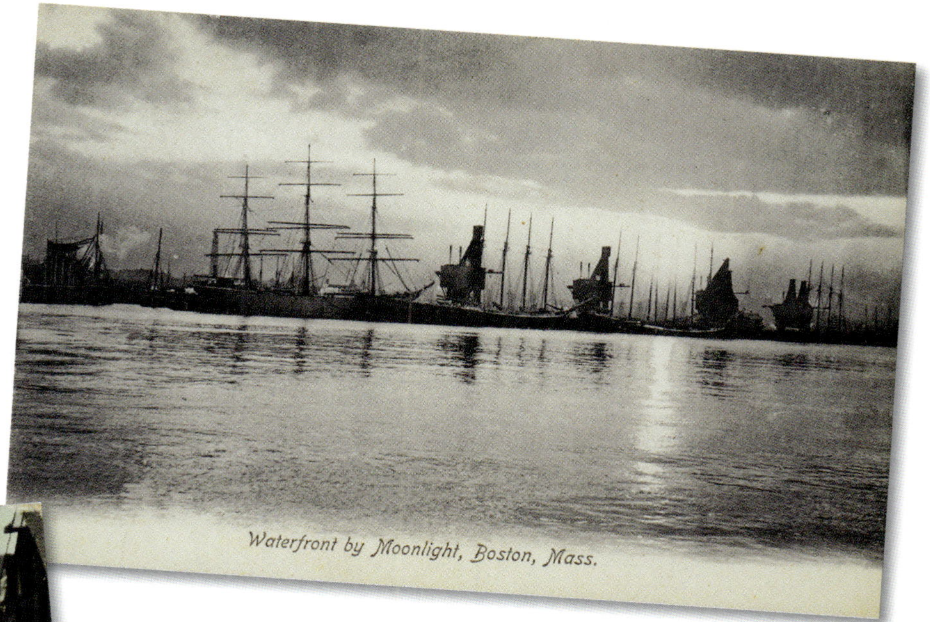

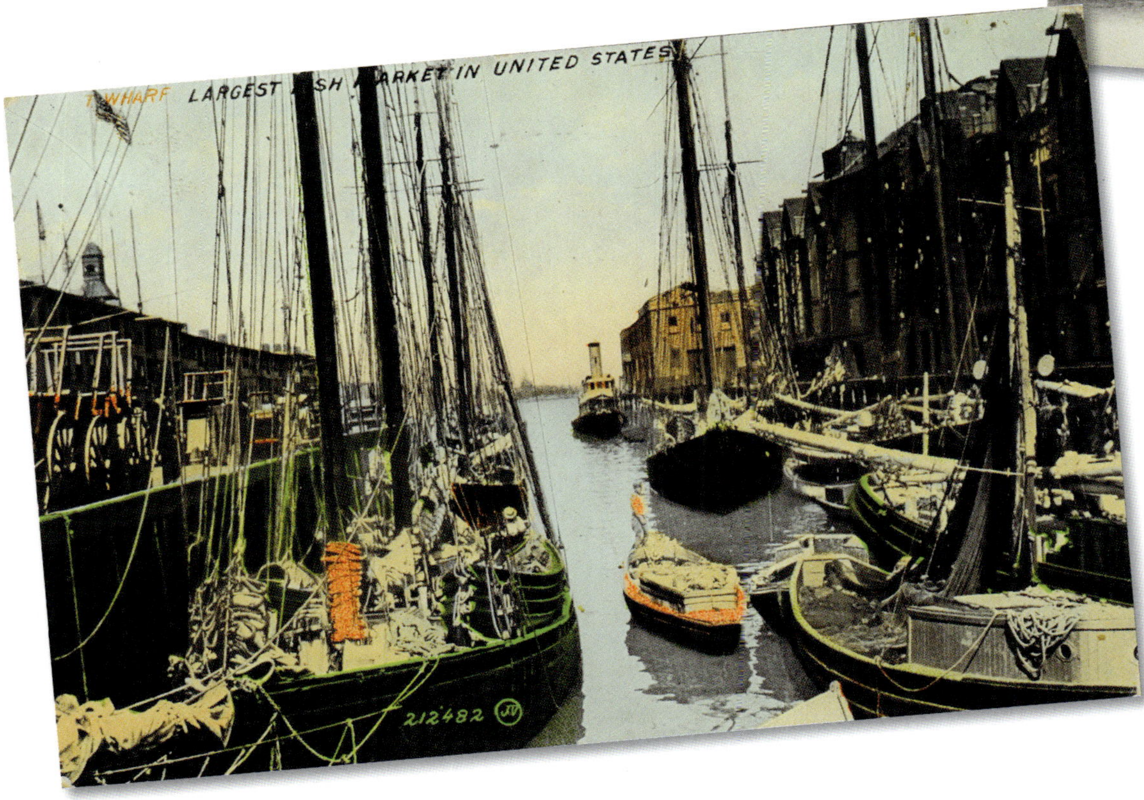

The busy port was a jungle of sails, masts, and spars reflecting the flourishing sea trade. Its excellent harbor and nearby shallow ocean banks to the east added fishing to its commercial base.

In those early years, Boston workers were mast makers, riggers, rope makers, sail makers, shipwrights, chandlers, and seamen. The call of the sea remains part of Boston folklore.

With its available supply of timber, New England became an important shipbuilding center. Its shipyards built warships for the British and the fledgling American navy and merchant ships for trade. The discovery of gold in California kindled a rebirth of the Massachusetts shipbuilding industry and the advent of the beautiful clipper ships.

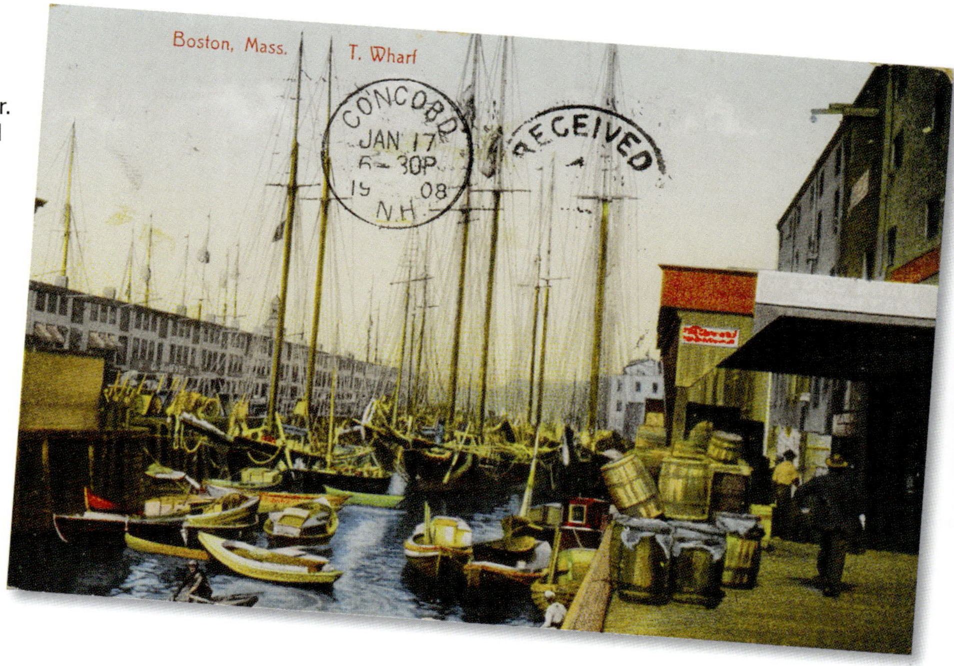

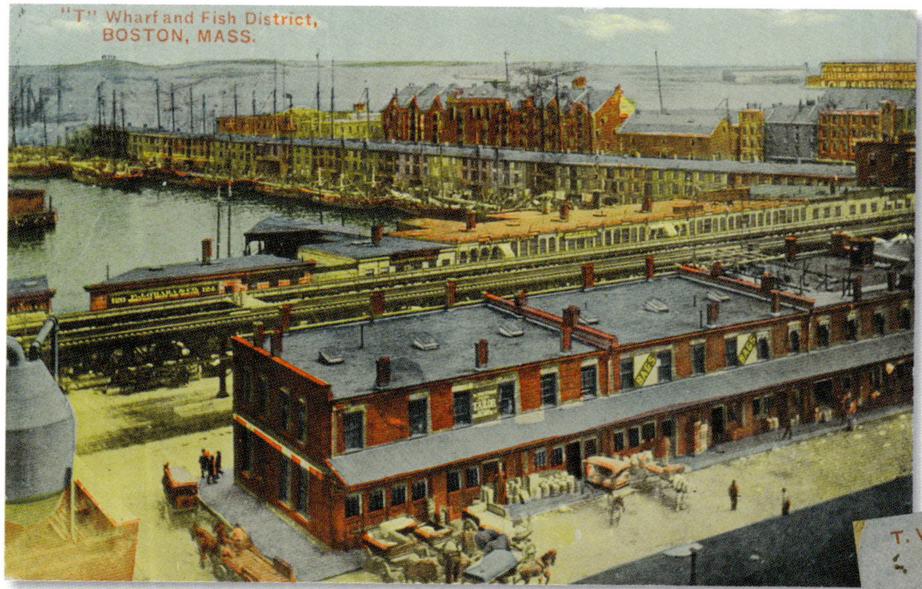

Demolished in 1967, the long wooden T-Wharf building was built in 1882-1883.

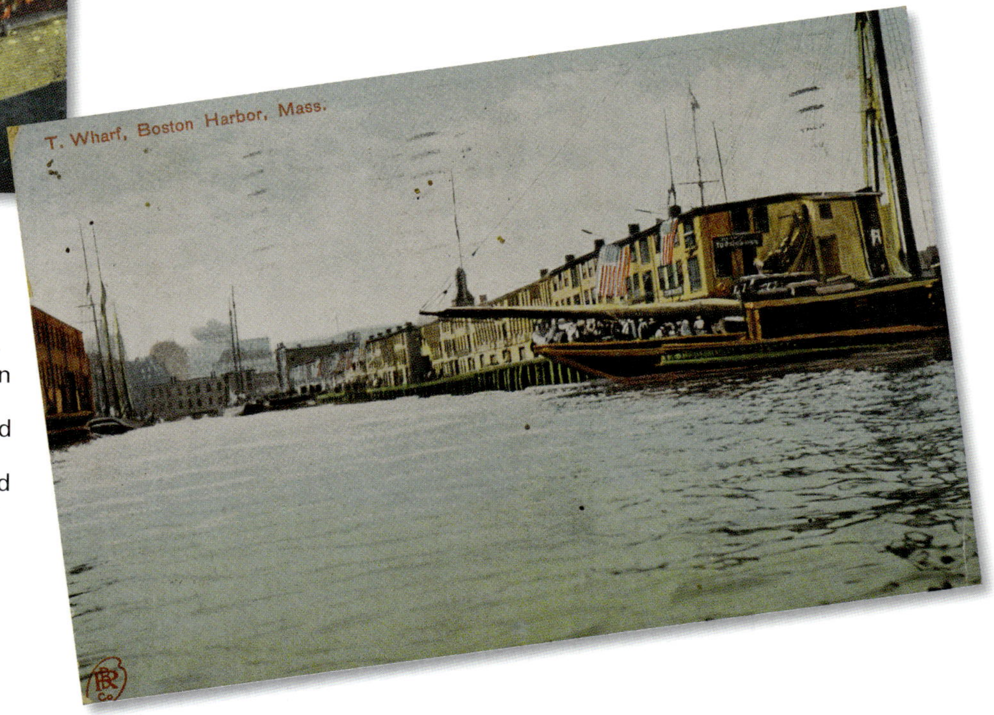

Dozens of wharves lined the waterfront early in the nineteenth century. Over the decades, the wharves have been silted in, and new, longer wharves built. The rigging for these ships was produced in narrow ropewalks, or roofed sheds with open sides. A foreign visitor described Long Wharf as a "noble pier eighteen hundred to two thousand feet long with a row of warehouses on the north side for the use of merchants" (State Street Trust Company, p. 20). He also said that it extended so far into the bay that it could unload large ships. The landfill projects over the last two centuries have shortened its land end.

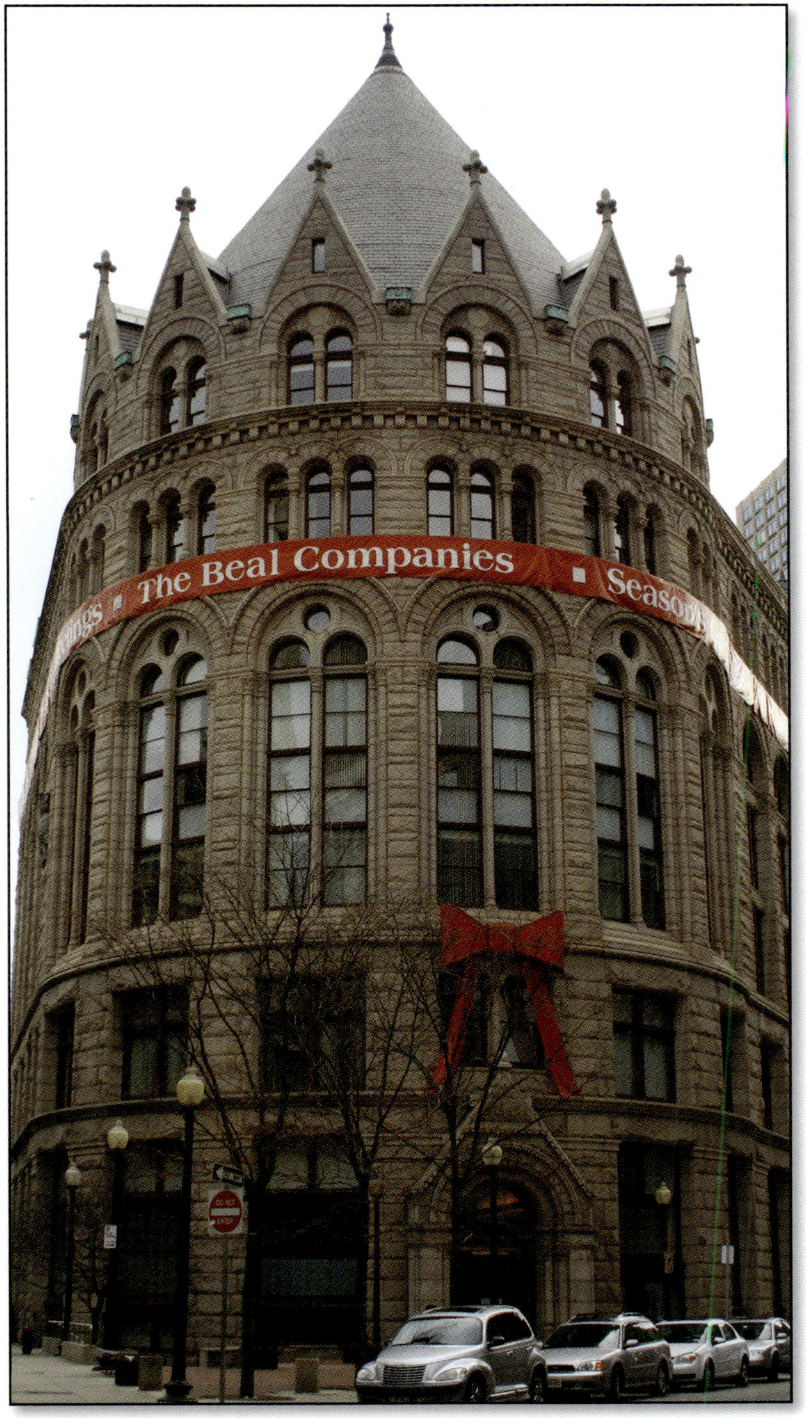

Shepley, Rutan and Coolidge designed the Richardsonian Romanesque Grain Exchange building. Boston was one of the largest grain exporters by the end of the nineteenth century. *Courtesy of D. Peter Lund*

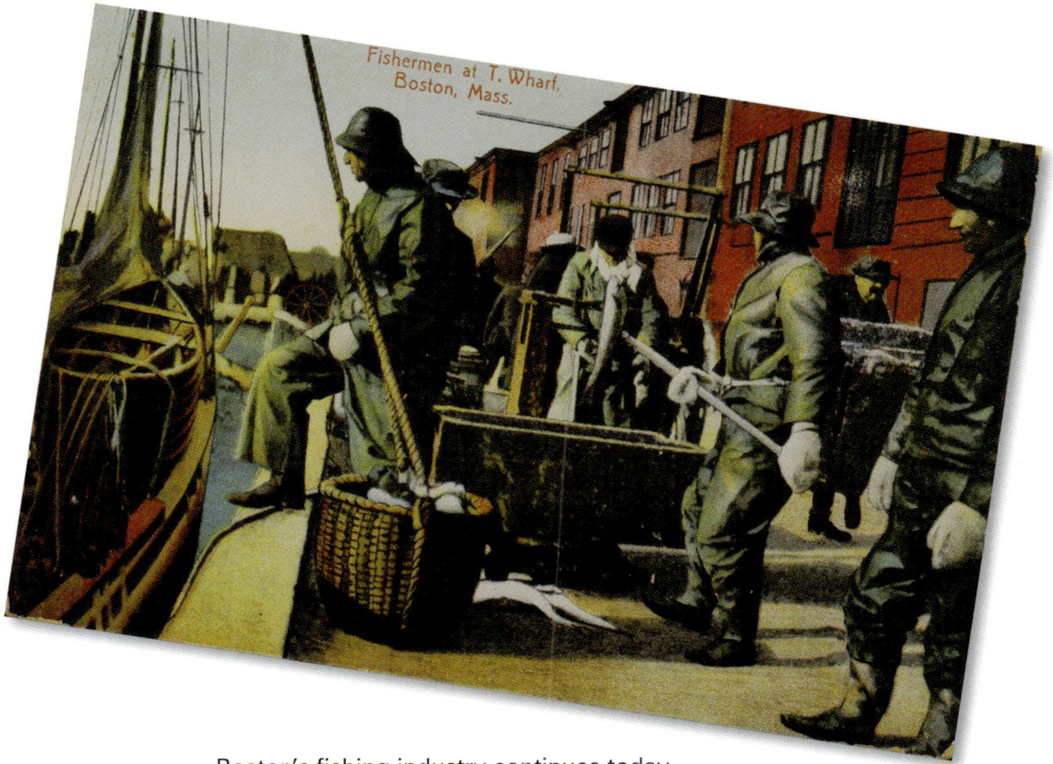

Boston's fishing industry continues today.

Cruiseport Boston is now considered one of the fastest growing high-end cruise markets in the country. Thousands of passengers come to Boston each year.

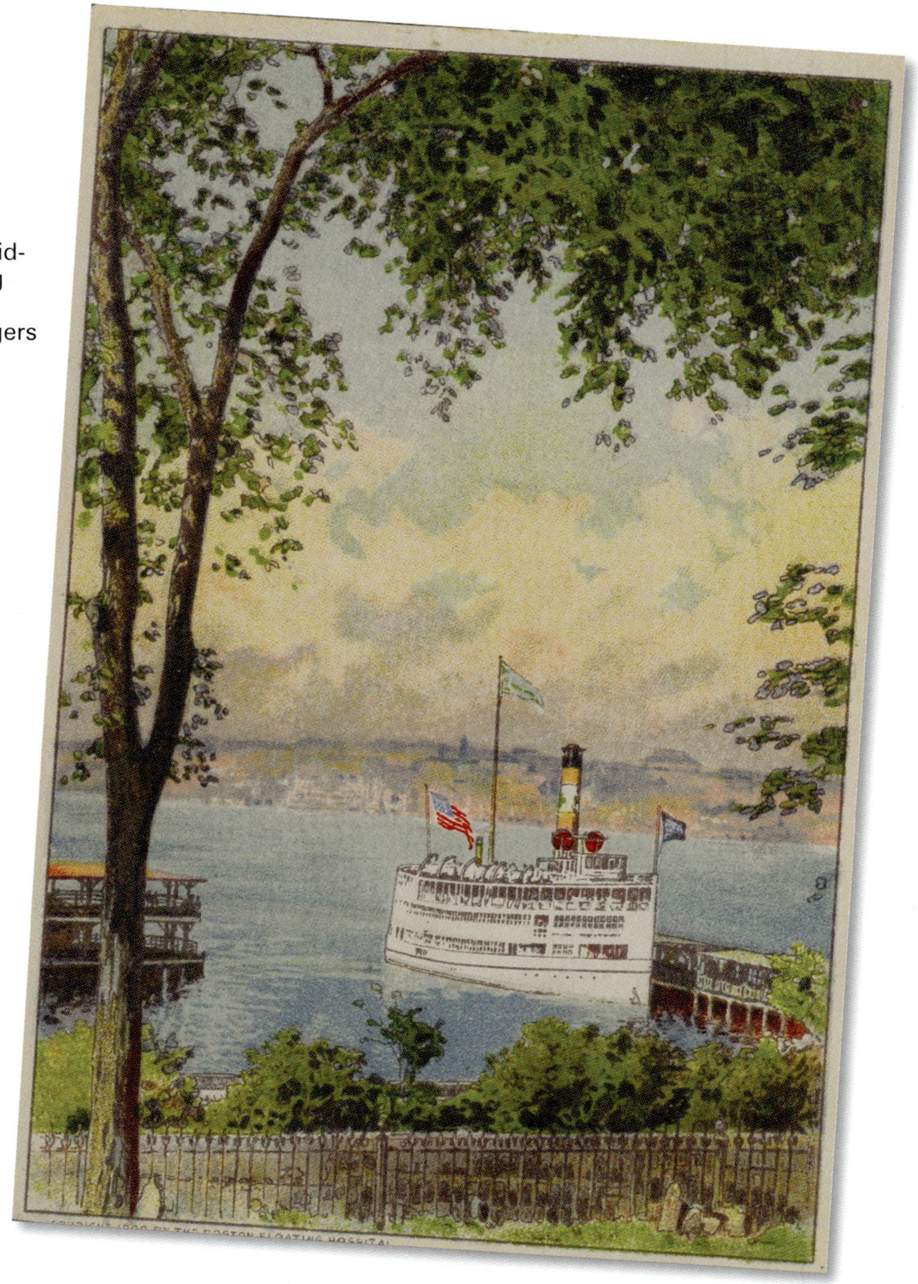

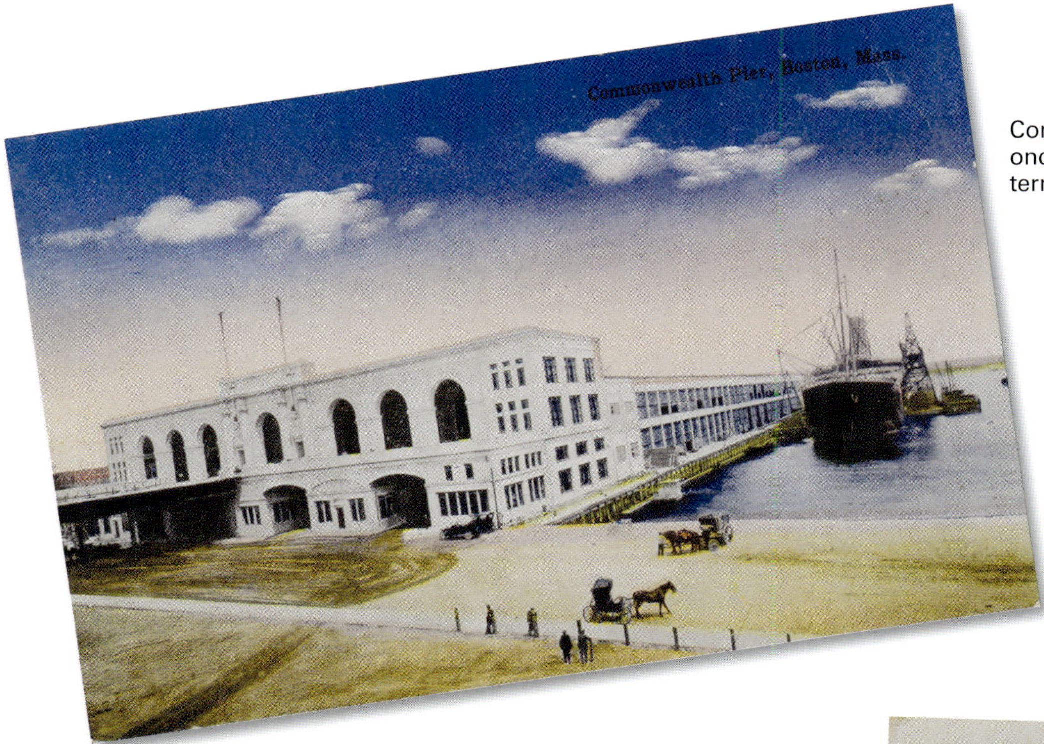

Commonwealth Pier was once the largest steamship terminal in the nation.

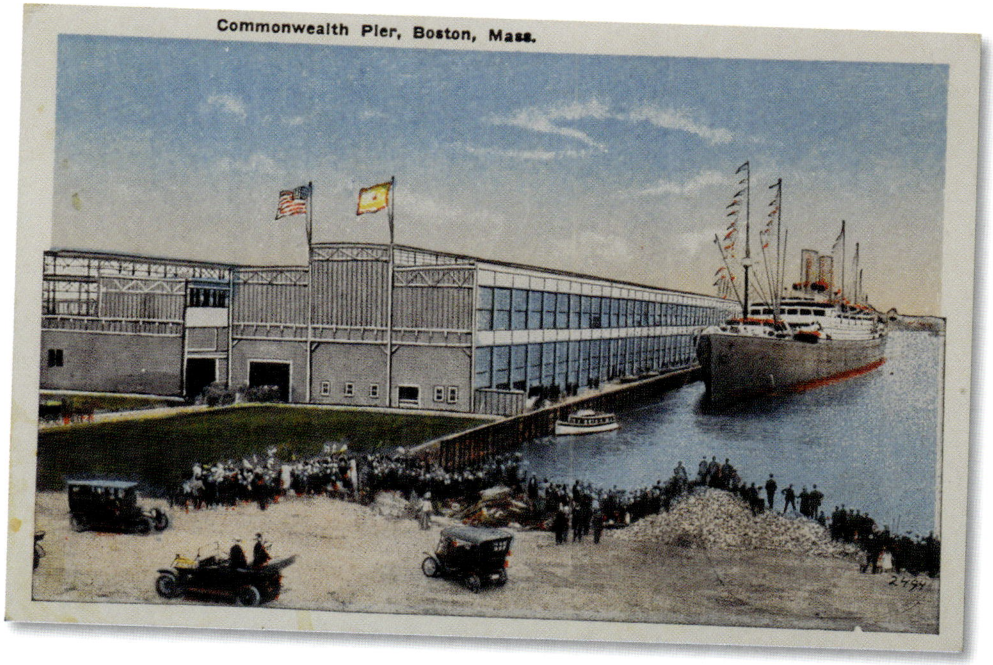

Notice the differences in transportation.

The Custom House

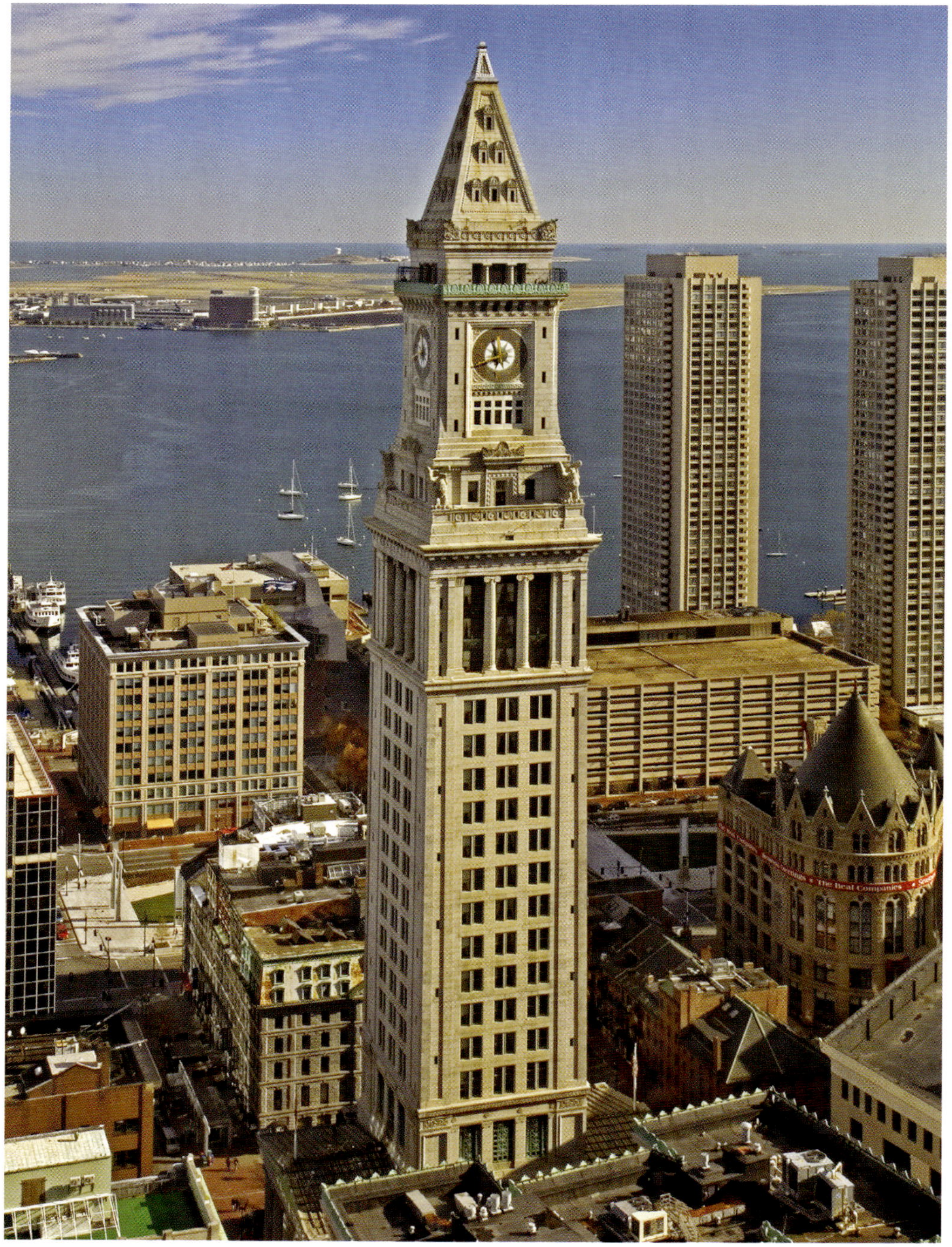

The Custom House today with its 495-tower overlooking Boston Harbor. To the right can be seen the Grain Exchange building and Harbor Towers. *Courtesy of Paul E. Doherty*

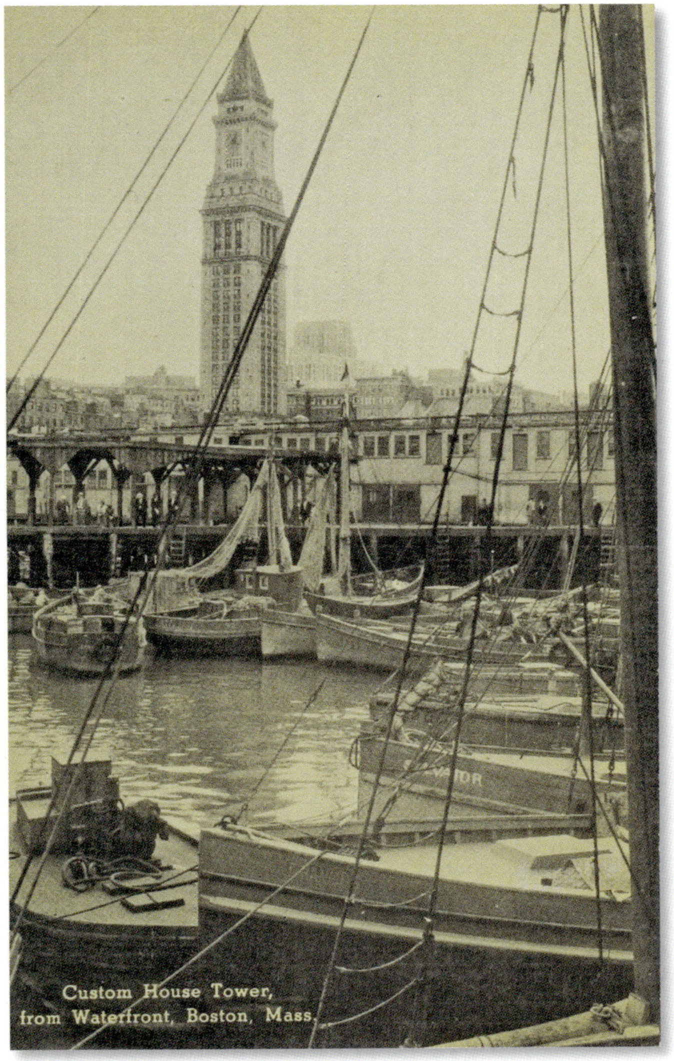

By the nineteenth century, Boston ships were trading worldwide, bringing goods from Europe, Asia, Africa, West Indies, and South America to the United States. To oversee this maritime commerce, President Andrew Jackson authorized the building of a Custom House (India Street at State Street) in 1835. The subsequent landfill has caused it to be about a quarter-mile from the water. Today, this splendid Quincy granite, Greek Revival skyscraper is in McKinley Square, in the Financial District. The present tower, designed by Peabody & Stearns, was completed in 1915.

Designed by Ammi Burnham Young, Custom House opened August 1, 1847. At that time – before the waterfront was filled in – Boston's waterfront extended right to the building, which was built at the end of the city docks, to facilitate inspection and registration of cargo. Here, side-whiskered merchants and government officials dressed in long coats and sporting canes watched and waited for their ships to come in. For many years, the building housed the port's immigration detention station. The 1850 *Boston Almanac* describes the original Custom House building as: "Situated at the head of the dock between Long and Central Wharves, fronts east on the dock, west on India Street, and is in the form of a Greek Cross, [with] the opposite sides and ends being alike. It is 140 feet long north and south, 75 feet wide at the ends, and 95 feet through the centre.... It is built on about 3,000 piles, fully secured against decay; the construction throughout is fire proof and has the very best kind." The monolithic columns weighed forty-two tons each.

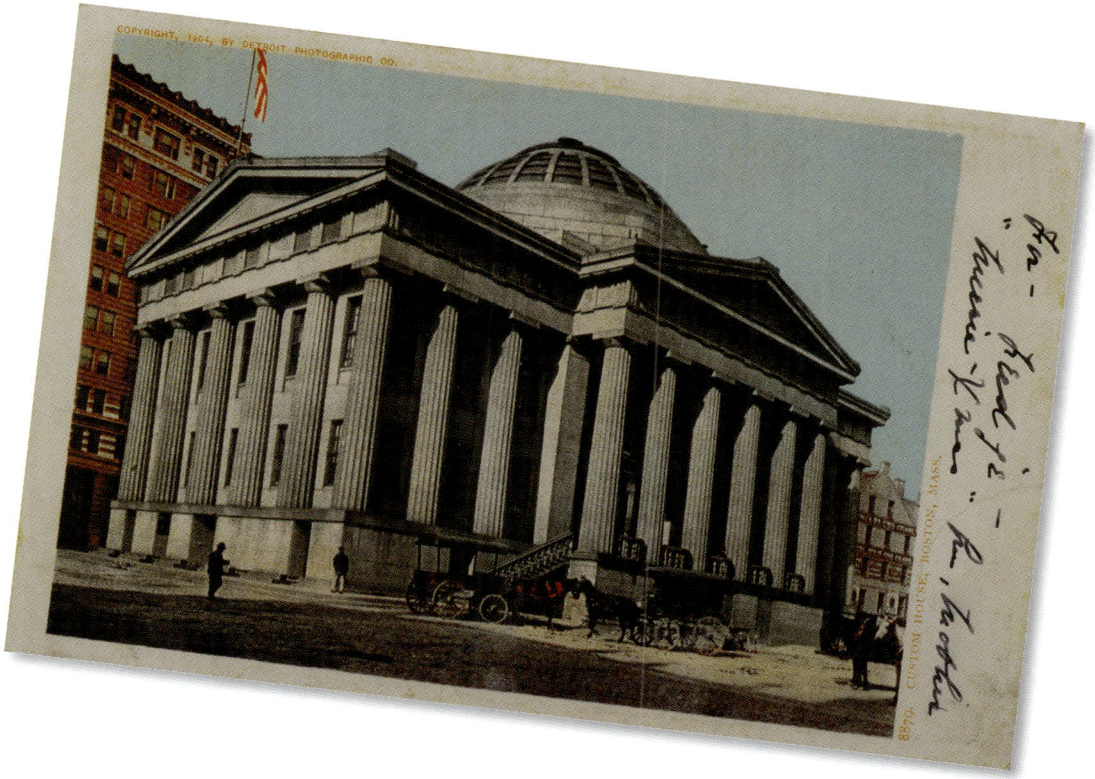

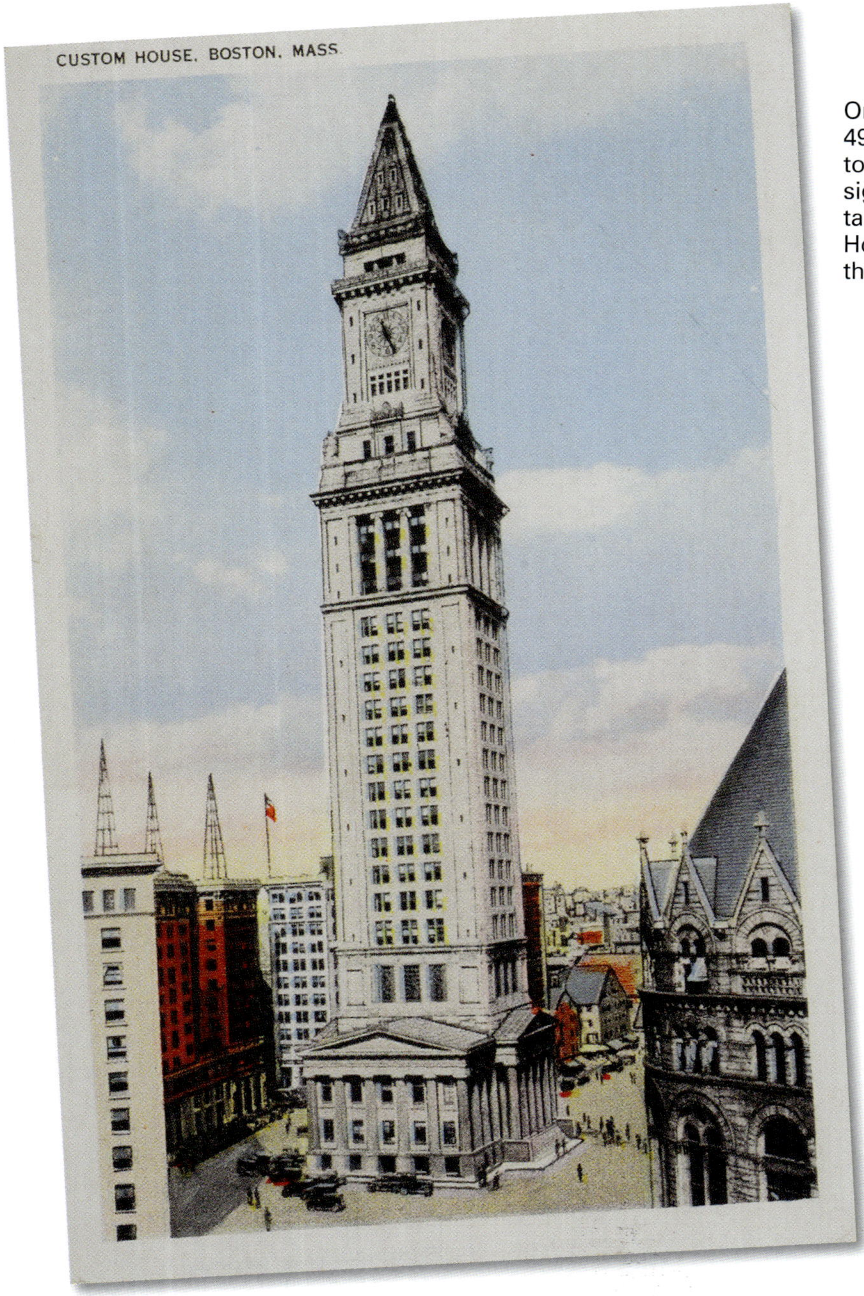

Originally, the building had a glass dome. Today, a 495-foot, classic revival style tower, built from 1913 to 1915 according to Peabody and Stearns's design, soars skyward. For more than thirty years the tallest building on the Boston skyline, the Custom House is a tangible reminder of the importance of the sea in Boston's history.

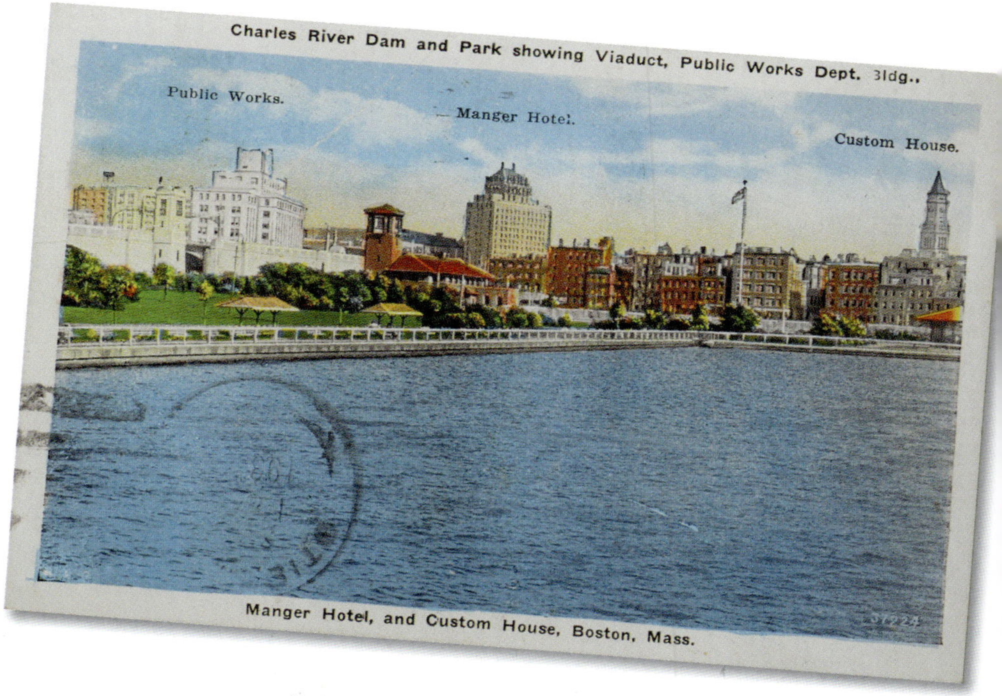

The tower was completely renovated in the 1990s, and now is a timeshare owned by Marriott Vacations. The building has luxurious rooms, harbor and city views, a full-service concierge, and an open observation deck on the 25th floor.

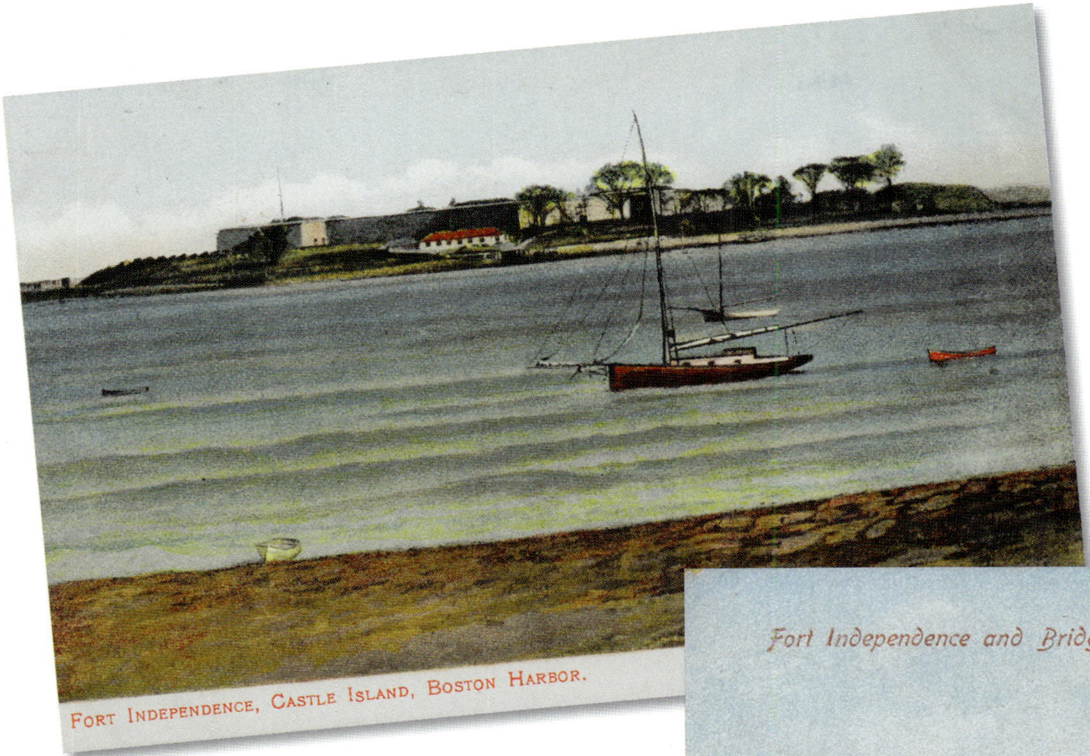

The first fort on Castle Island was built in 1643, making it the oldest fortified military site in North America. A National Historic Landmark, the present fort is the eighth generation of forts built on the island. When the British evacuated Boston in 1776, they destroyed their fort on Castle Island. General George Washington appointed Colonel Richard Gridley, his chief engineer, to refortify the island, and Colonel Paul Revere commanded the forces stationed there. After the Revolution, Massachusetts state forces garrisoned Castle Island. Later it was used as a prison.

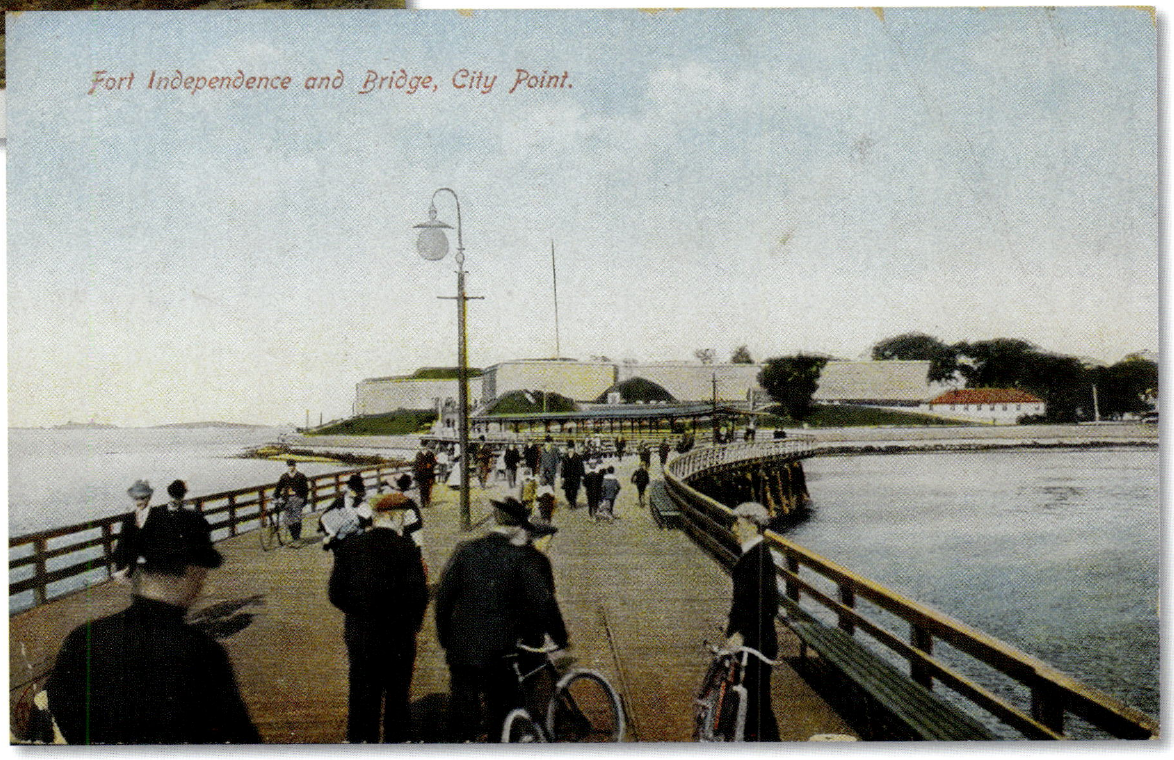

Today, the island and fort are a lovely excursion.

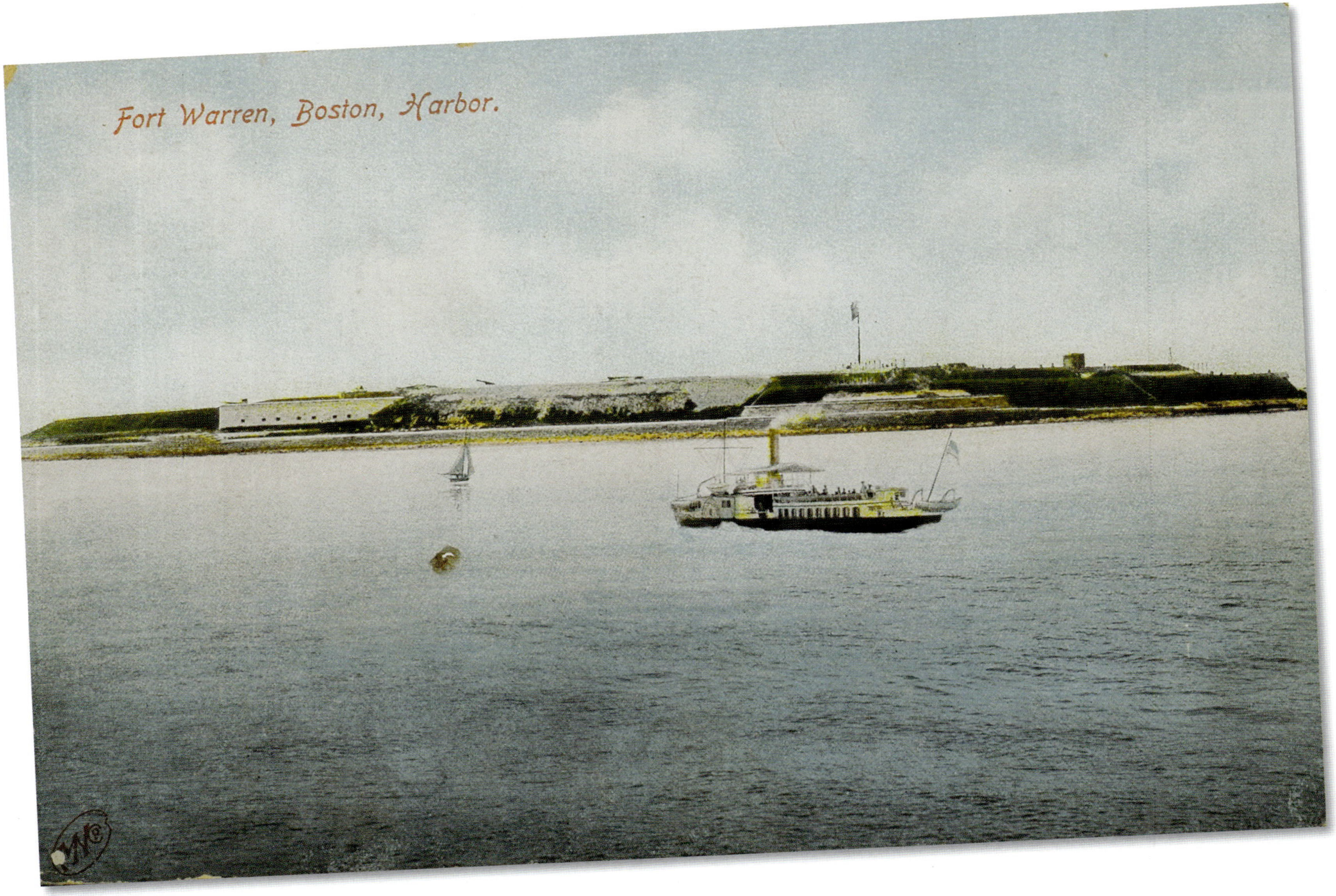

Named for Revolutionary war hero Dr. Joseph Warren who sent Paul Revere on his famous ride, Fort Warren is a historic fort on the 28-acre Georges Island at the entrance to Boston Harbor. The stone fort was completed shortly after the beginning of the American Civil War. Fort Warren defended the harbor in Boston, Massachusetts, from 1861 through the end of World War II. During the Civil War, it served as a prisoner-of-war camp and a jail for political prisoners. It was permanently decommissioned in 1947 and is now a National Historic Landmark.

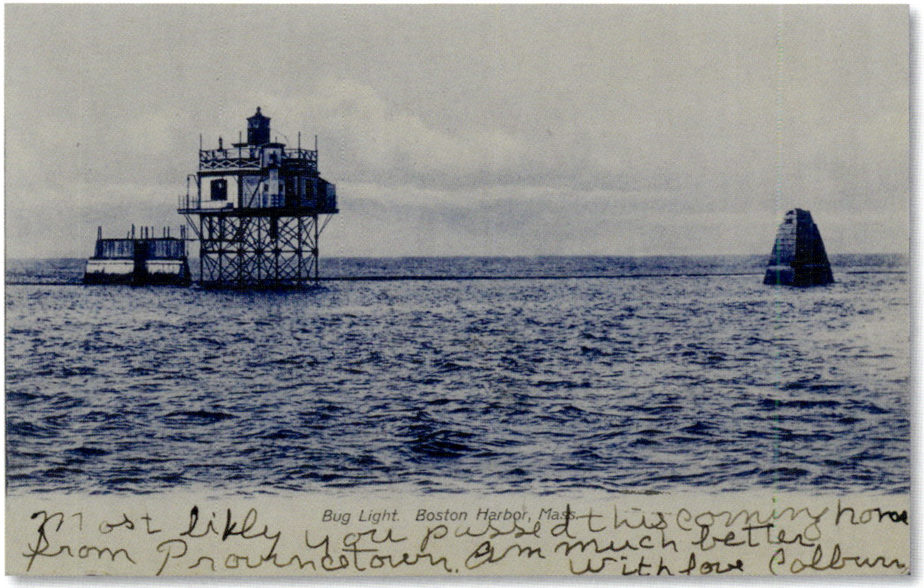

Boston Harbor navigational aids guide the many boats and ships that sail it today.

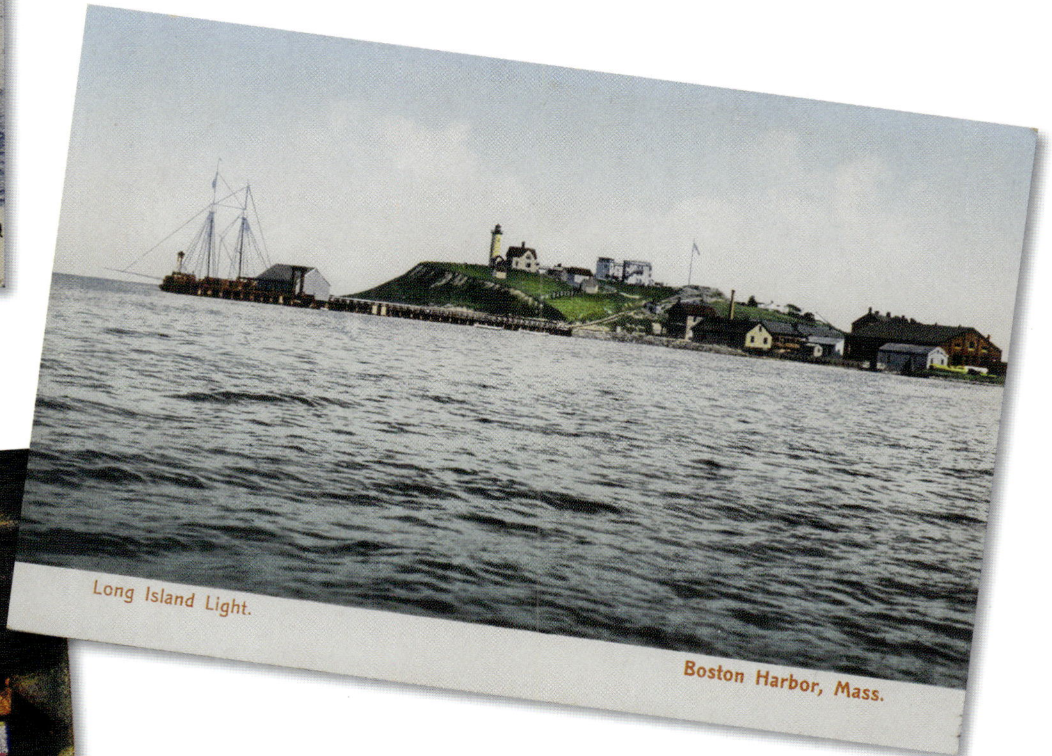

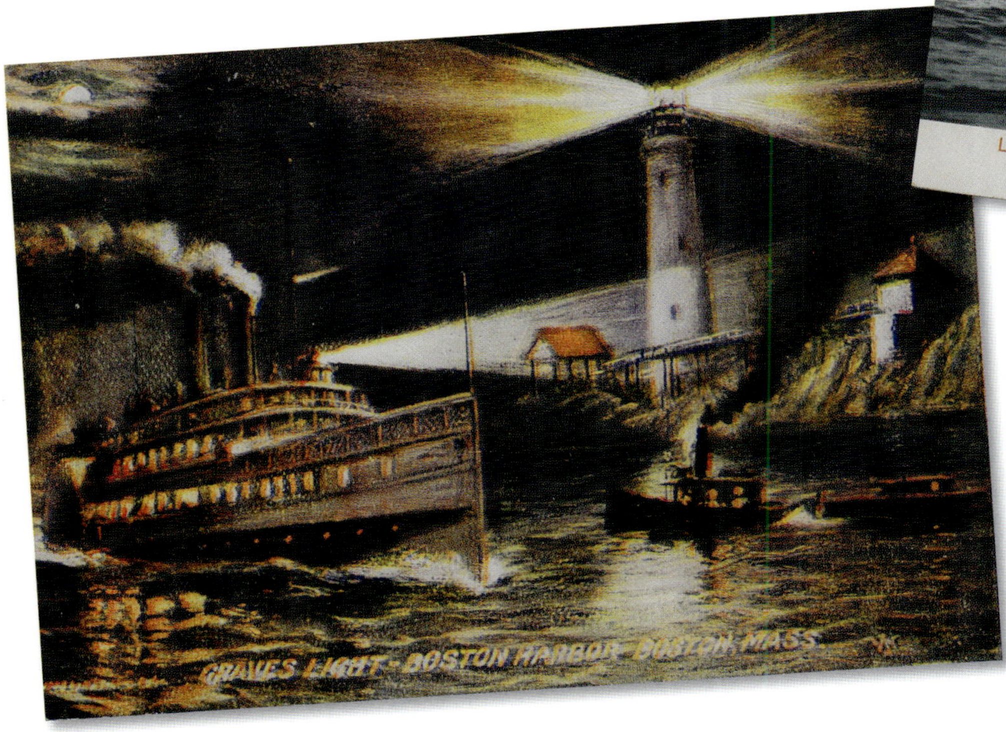

Despite all the waterfront reclamation, the Boston coastline is famous for its innate beauty. By the 1920s, seaside pleasure became popular.

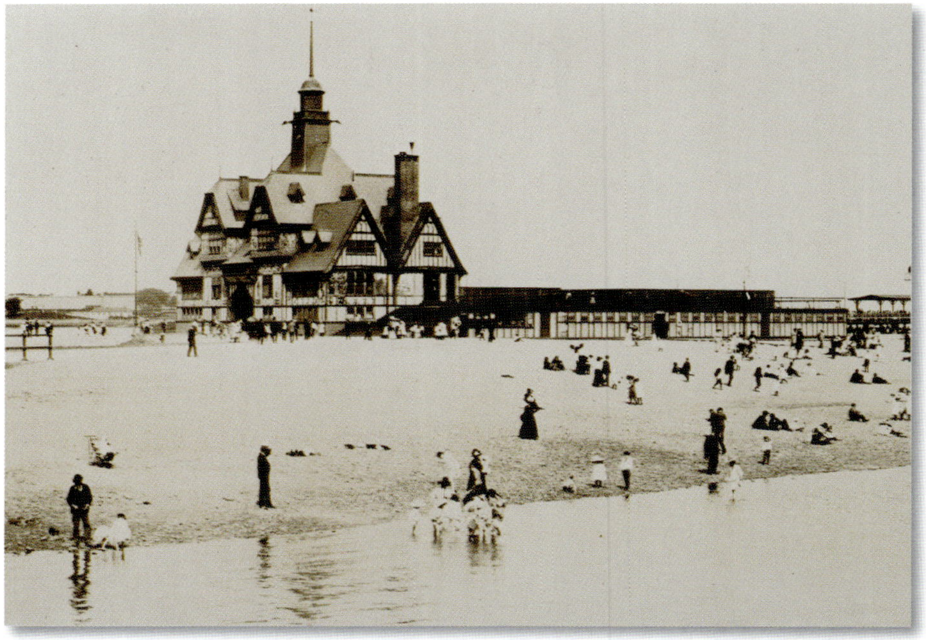

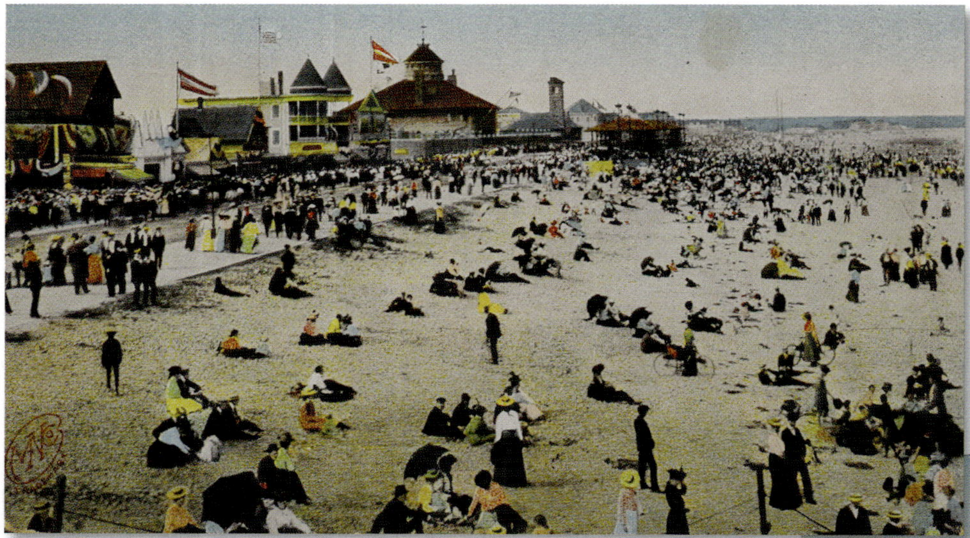

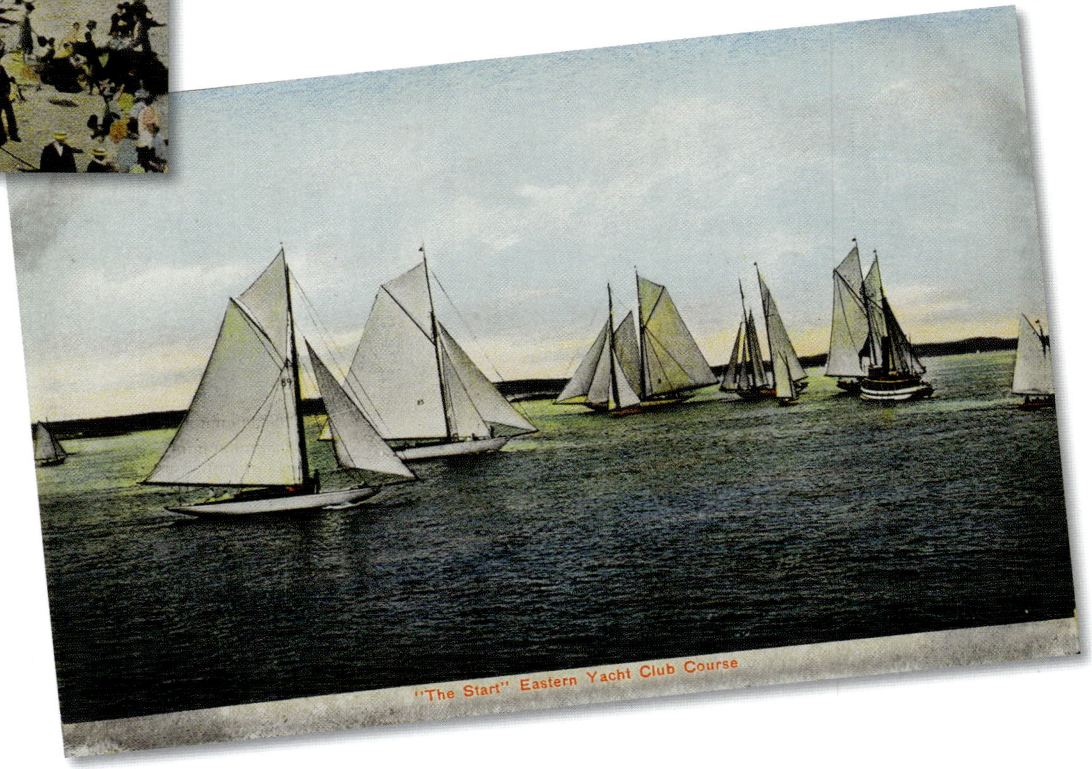

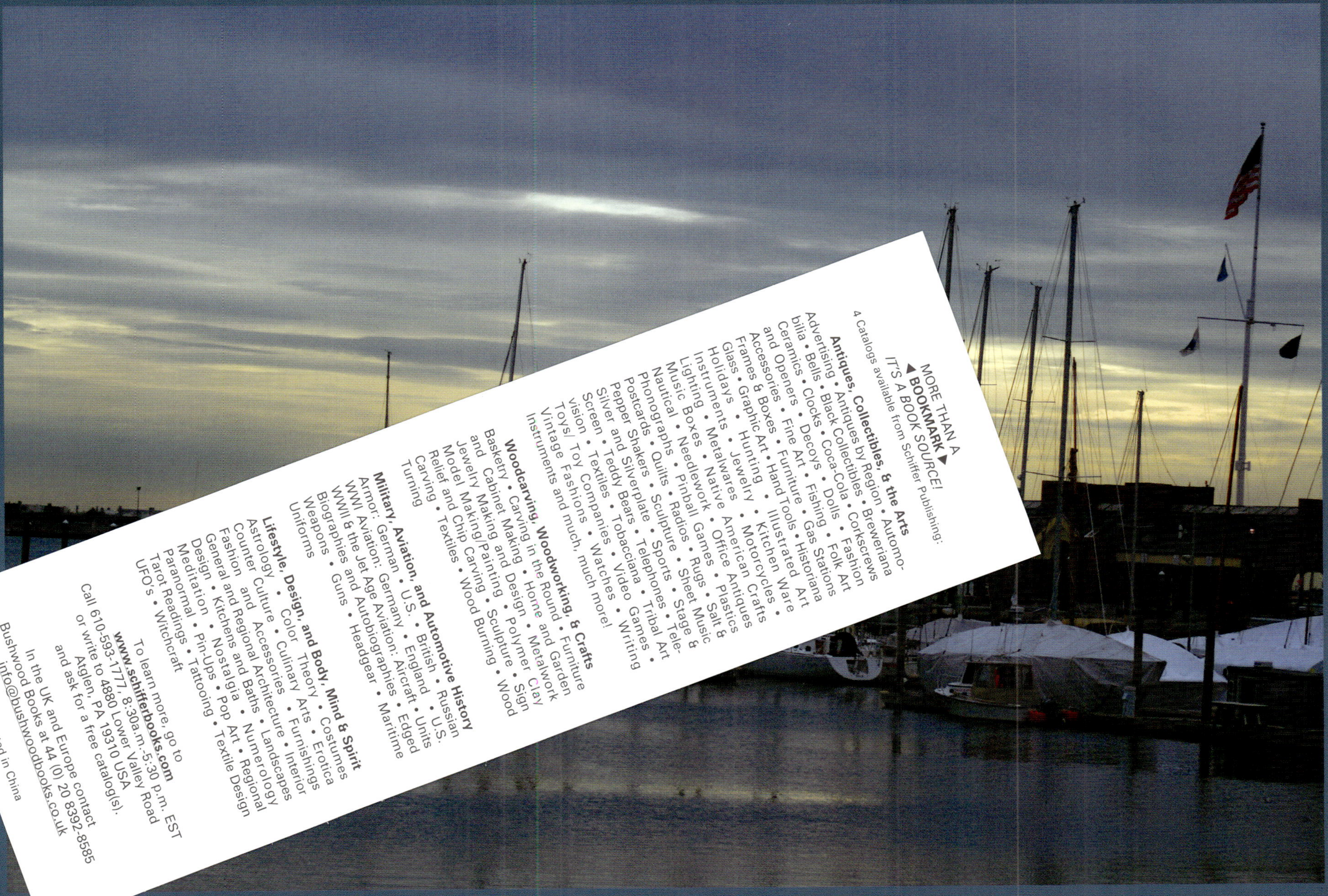

Chapter 4

The Massachusetts State House and Beacon Hill

Boston State-house is the hub of the solar system. You could not pry that out of a Boston man if you had the tire of all creation straightened out for a crowbar. –Oliver Wendell Holmes, *The Autocrat of the Breakfast Table*, vi.

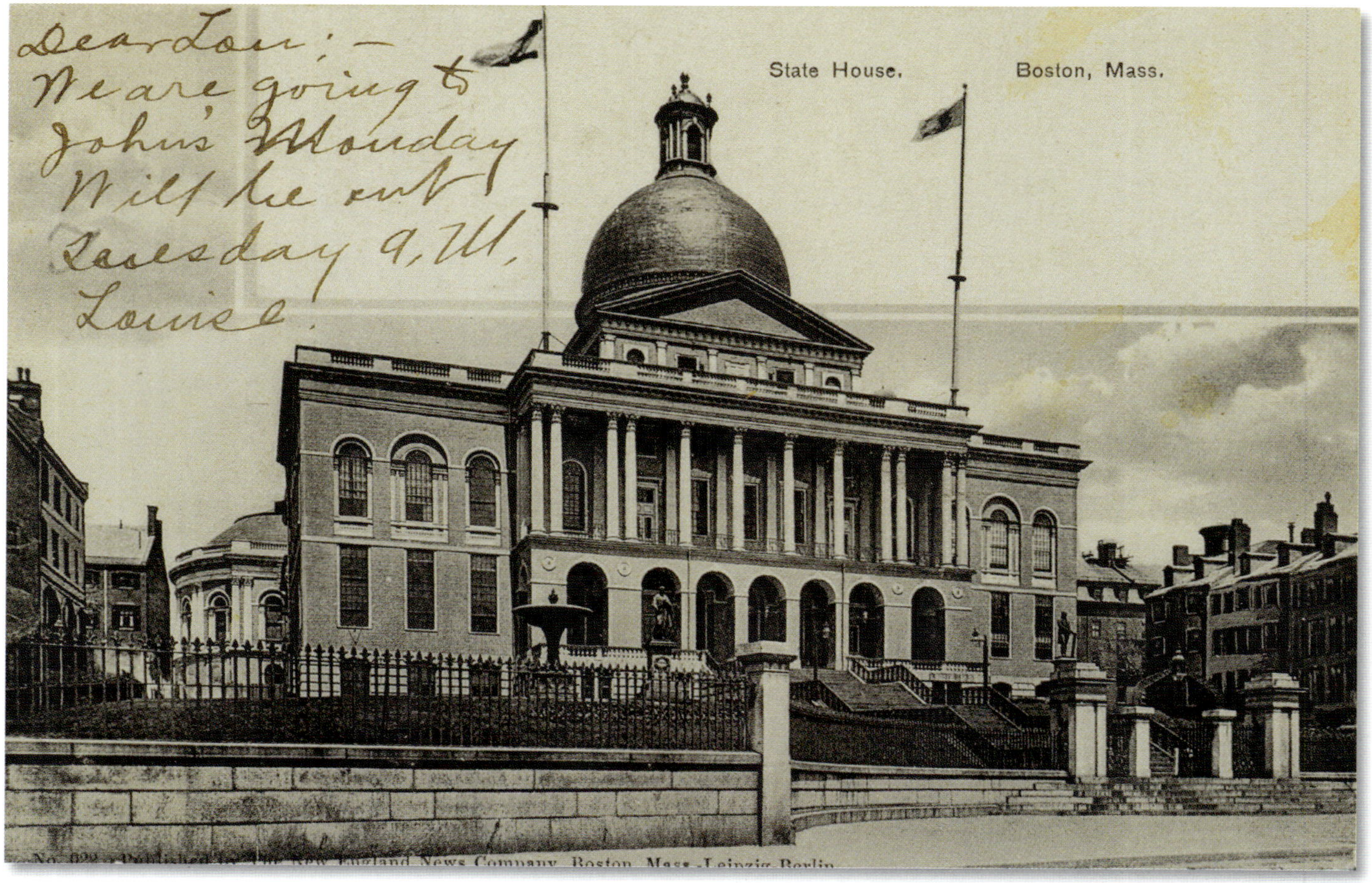

In 1713 the seat of the Massachusetts government was the old State House at the corner of King (now Washington) and State Streets. After the Revolution, state leaders wanted a larger and more elegant home to better reflect the prosperous new republic and spacious enough to accommodate an expanding government. In 1795, they paid the heirs of John Hancock for a cow pasture, close to the summit of the south side of Beacon Hill, overlooking Boston Common and the Back Bay. A young native-born architect, Charles Bulfinch, was chosen to design the building.

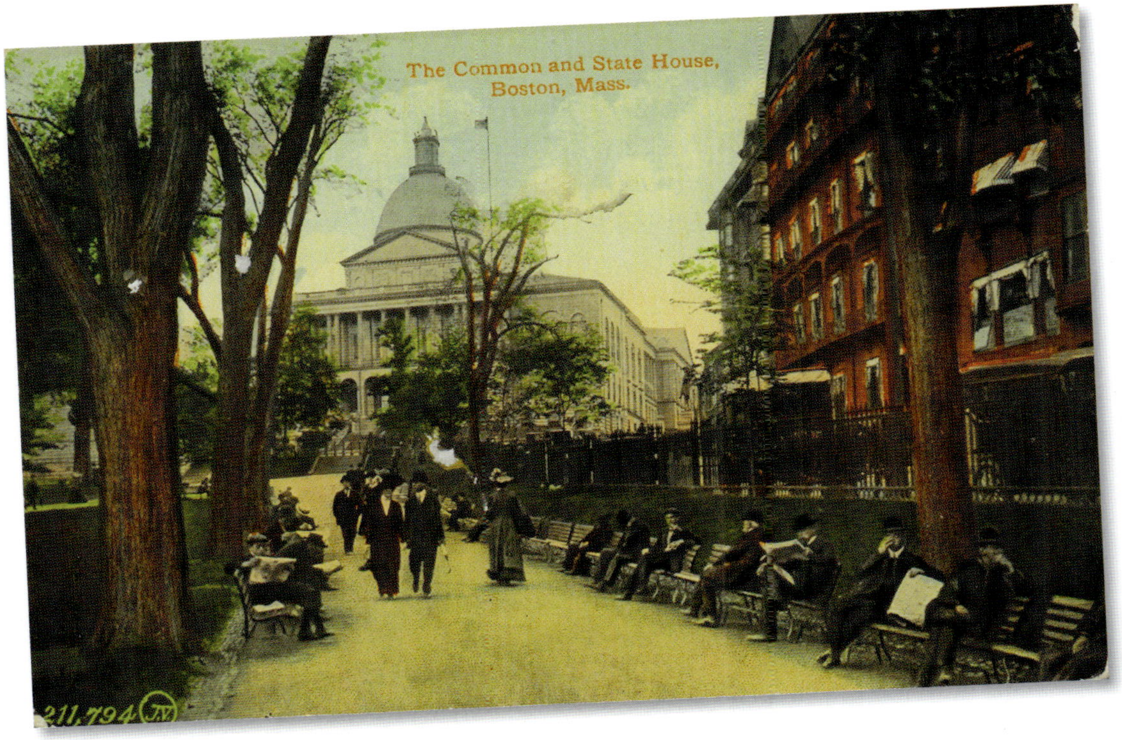

Samuel Adams and Paul Revere laid the cornerstone of the Massachusetts State House on July 4, 1795, making it the oldest existing building on Beacon Hill. Revere also provided nails and copper for the construction of the dome.

Completed by January 1798, the building and grounds cover two city blocks. Paul Revere covered the dome in copper in 1802. At its peak, Bulfinch placed a gilt pinecone to symbolize the forests that made it possible for the early settlers to survive. The dome was gilded in 23-karat gold leaf in 1874.

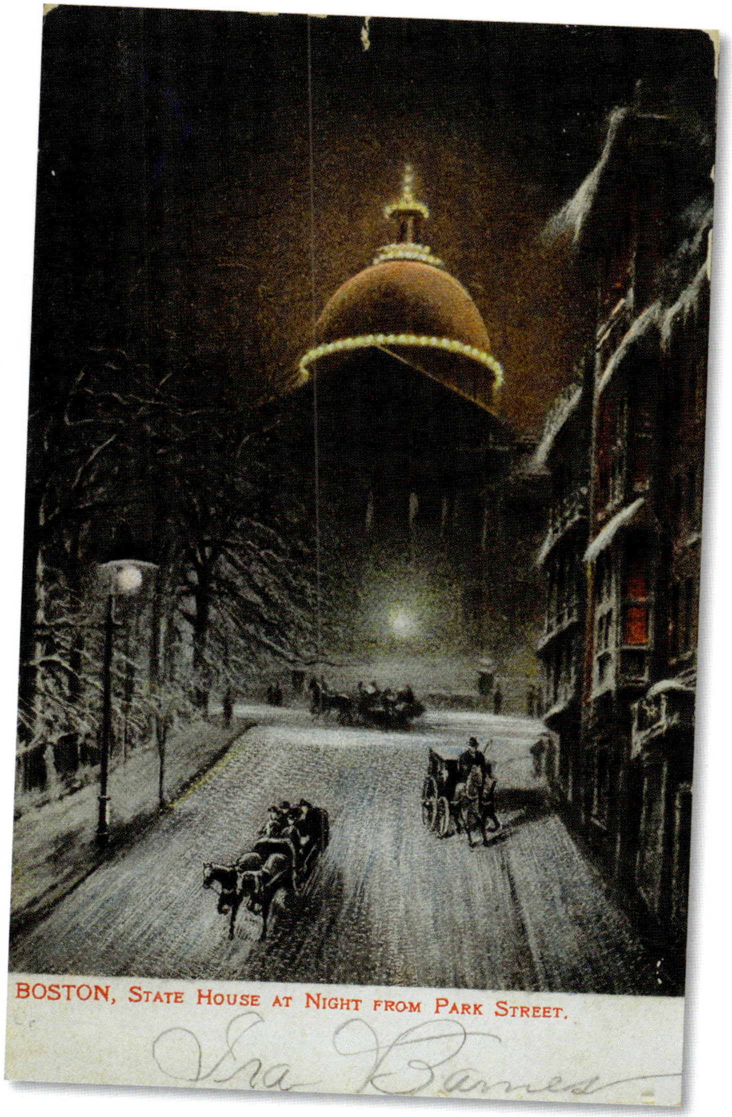

Widely acclaimed as one of the more magnificent and well-situated buildings in the country, the State House dome dominated the Boston skyline until the advent of the skyscraper. It has served as a model for the U. S. Capitol Building and other state capitals.

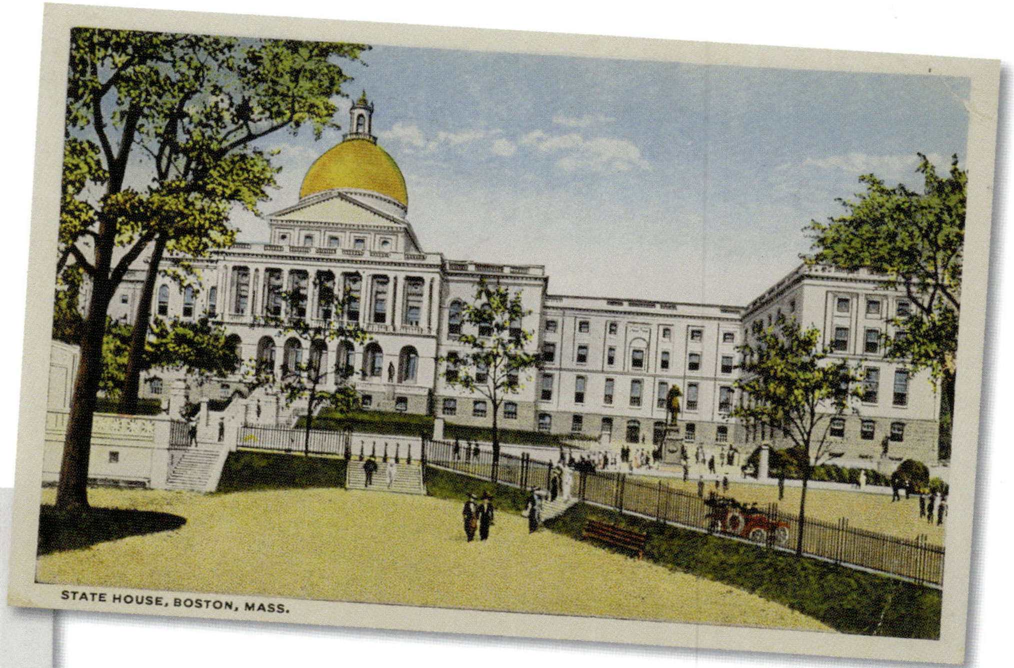

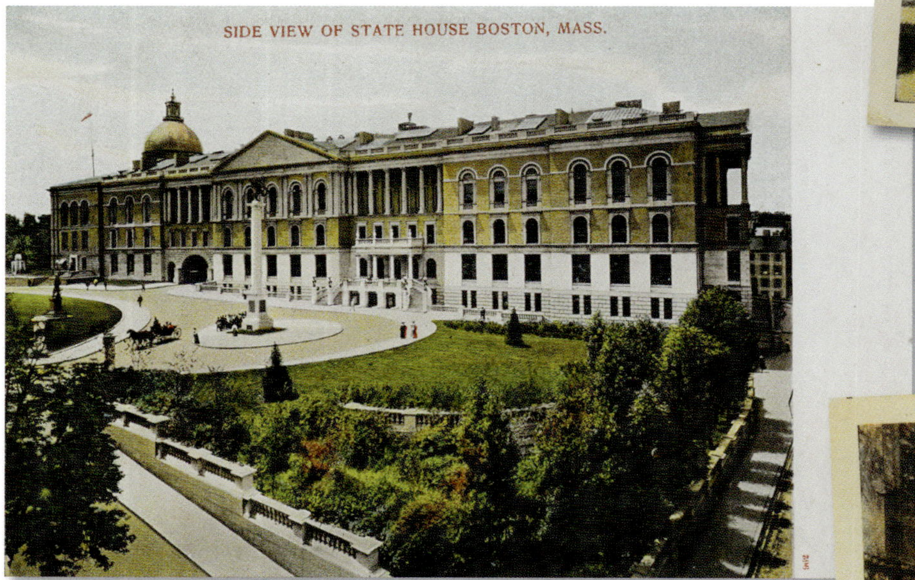

A side view of the State House.

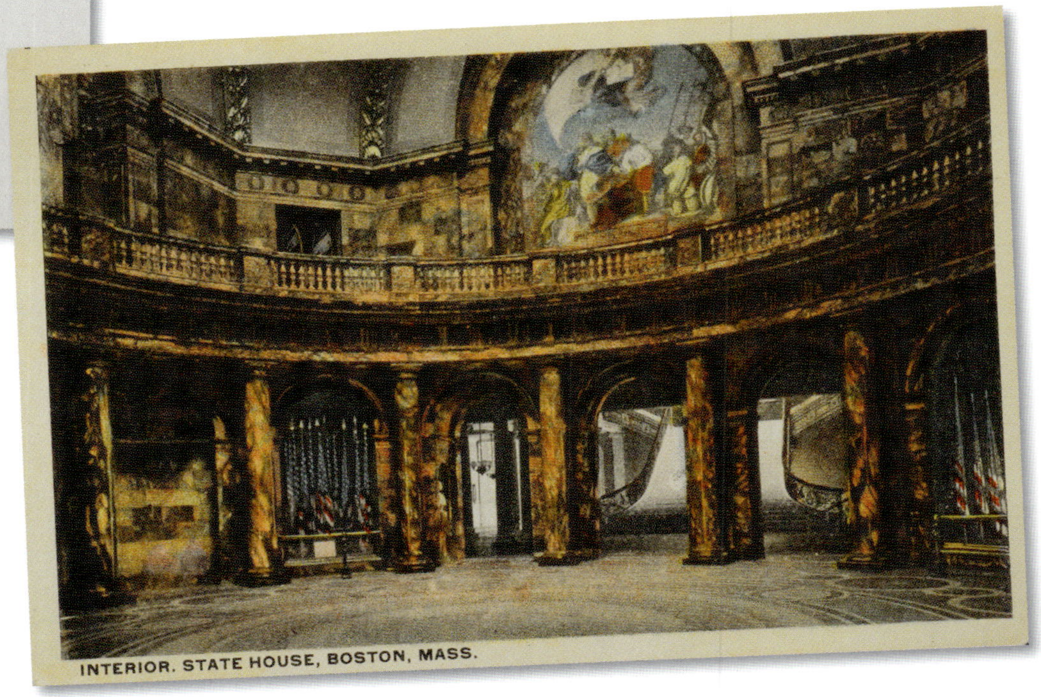

Sited directly beneath the dome, the Senate Chamber features a Bulfinch-designed sunburst ceiling.

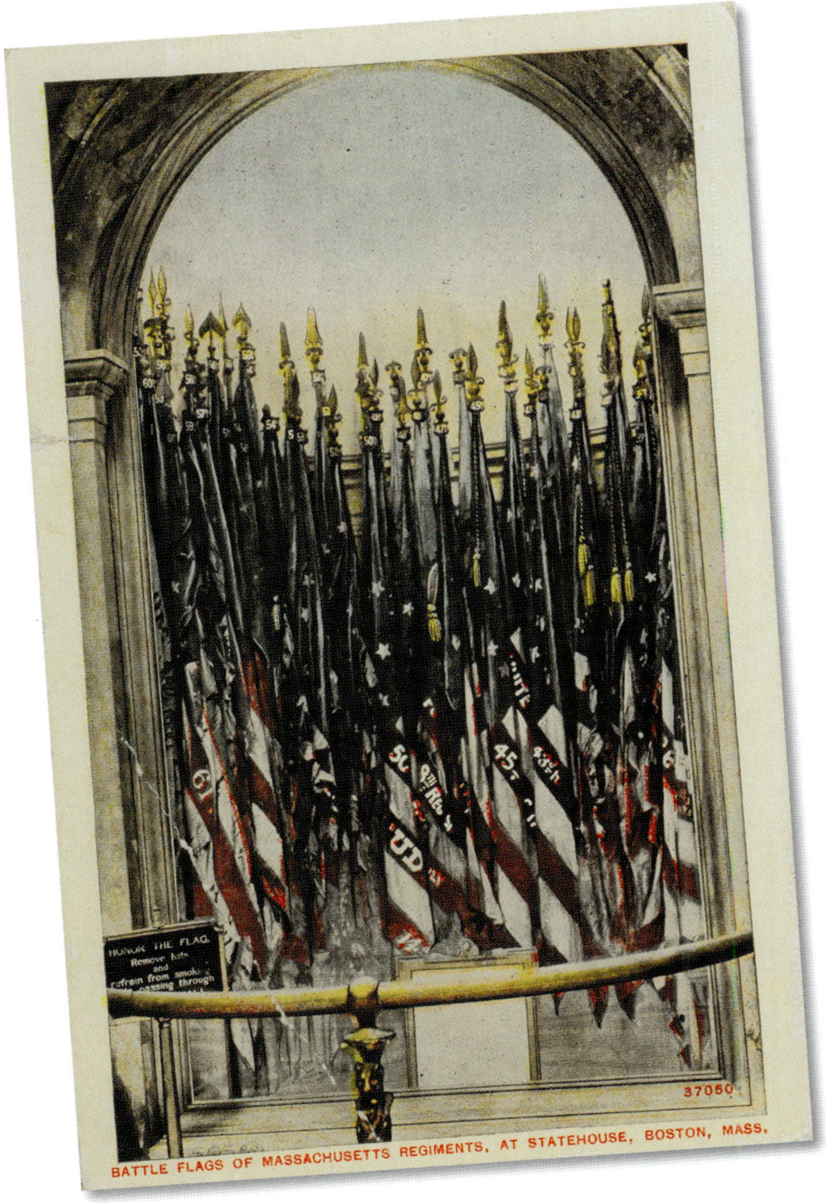

Completed in 1990, the flags of all 351 cities and towns in the Commonwealth decorate the Hall of Flags. The purpose of the room is to hold state functions, as Massachusetts does not have a Governor's Mansion.

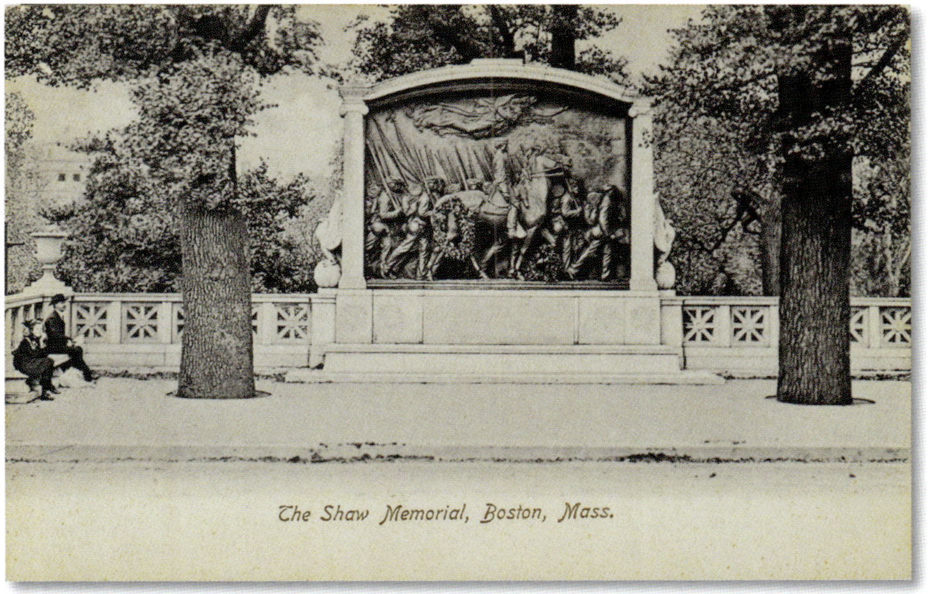

Sculpted by Augustus Saint-Gaudens, the Robert Gould Shaw Memorial is opposite the State House. This poignant bas-relief commemorates the first regiment of emancipated African-Americans formed in Boston during the Civil War. Robert Gould Shaw, son of an old Boston family, led them. He and many of his men died during the assault on Fort Wagner in South Carolina in 1863.

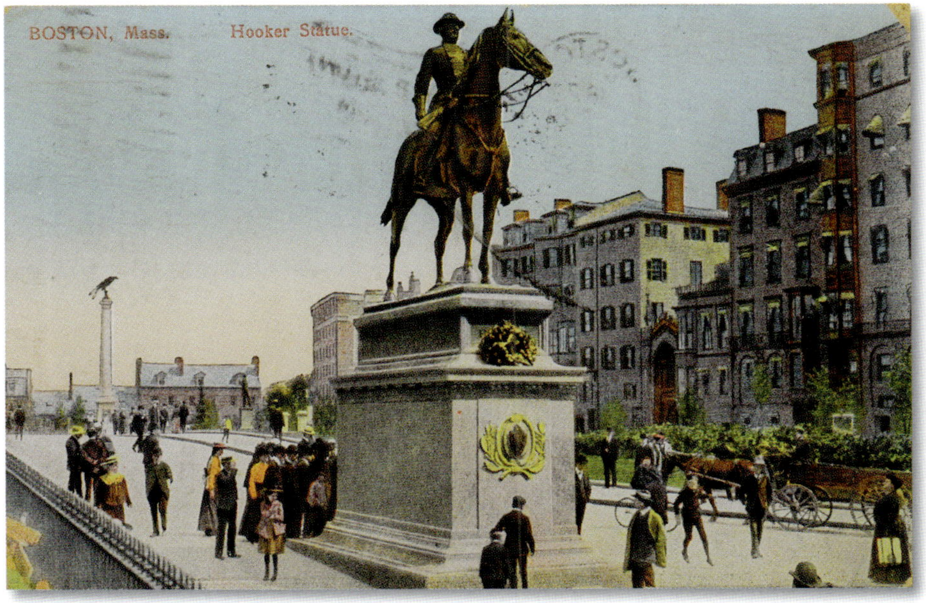

Adjacent to the state house is a bronze statute of General Joseph Hooker. Known as "Fighting Joe," he was a career U.S. Army officer and a major general in the Union Army during the American Civil War.

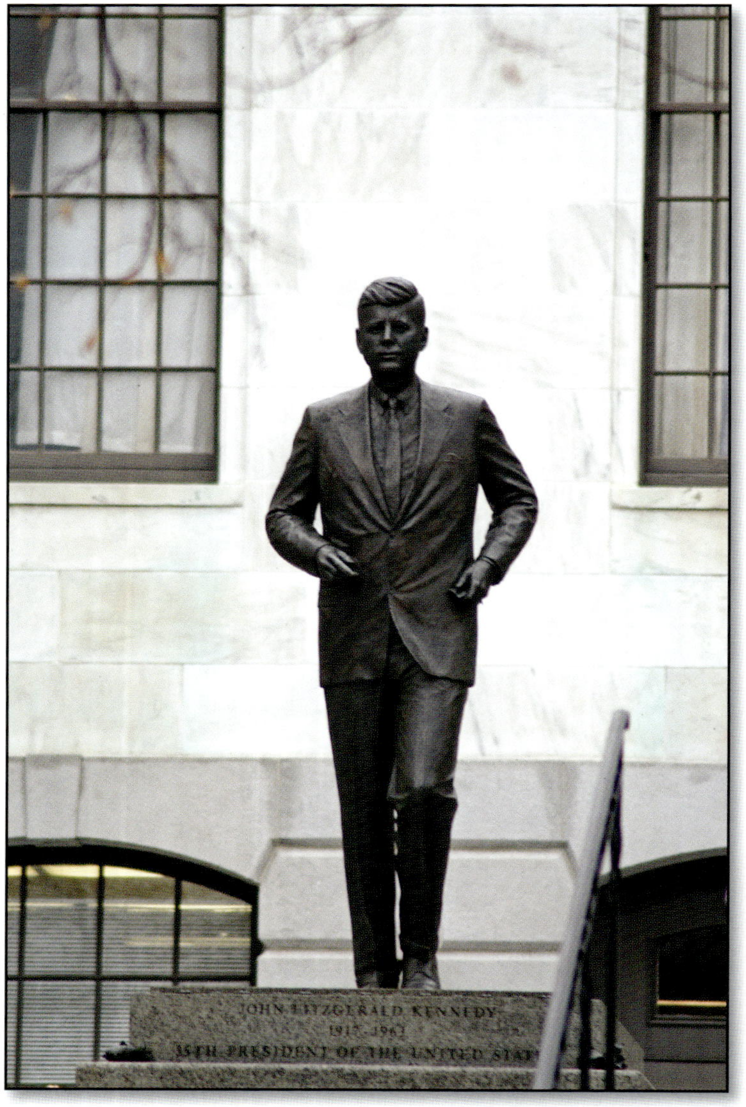

The statue of John F. Kennedy, the 35th President of the United States, is located in the west wing plaza. A gift from the people of the Commonwealth of Massachusetts, it was dedicated on May 29, 1990. Sculptor Isabel McIlvain depicts Kennedy confidently striding forward, hand in pocket. *Courtesy of D. Peter Lund*

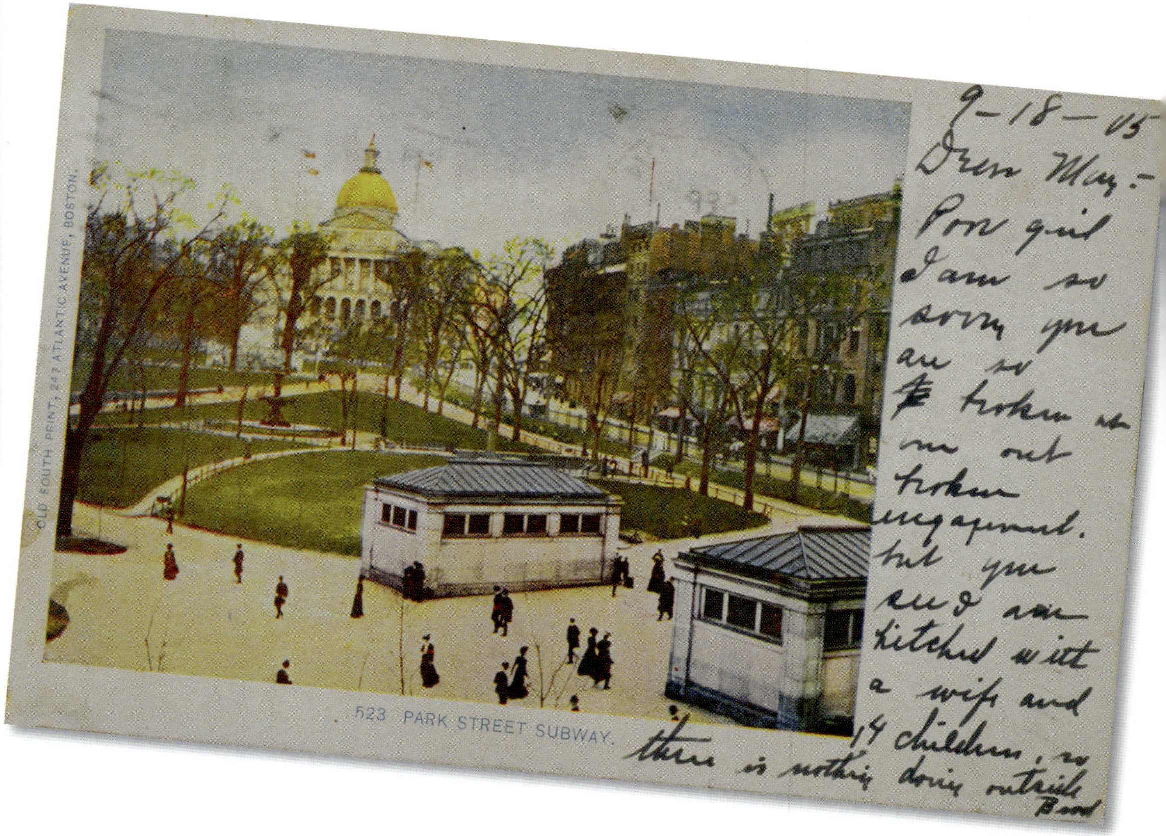

The train station and the State House.

The only respectable street in America. – Henry James about Mount Vernon Street

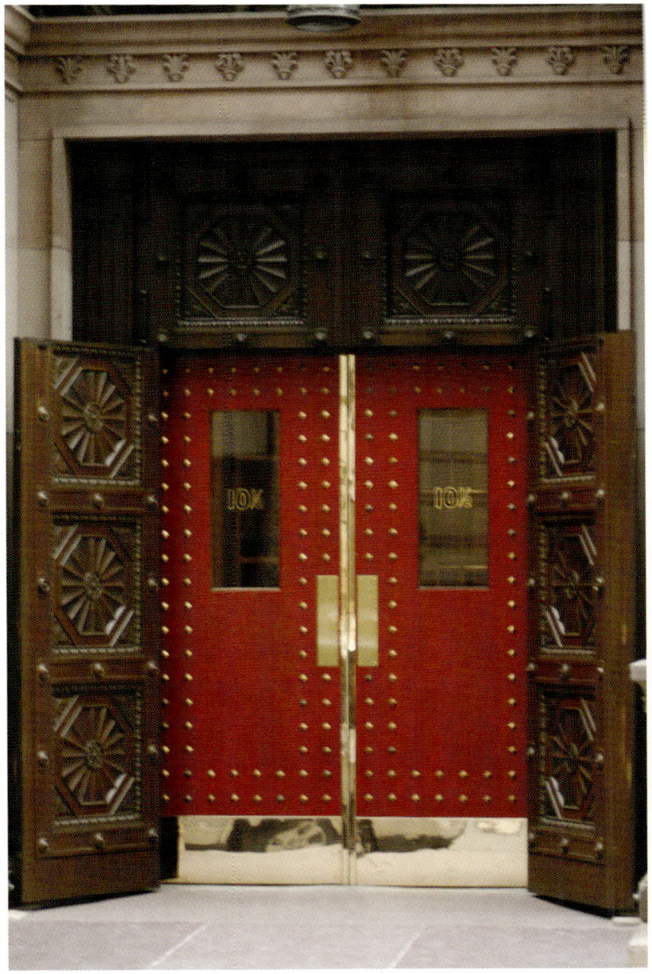

The Boston Athenaeum designed by Edward Clark Cabot is sited at 10 ½ Beacon Street. First organized in 1805 by the Anthology Society, a literary club, the Athenaeum had several homes before this one was opened in 1849. The society wanted "a reading room, library, museum and laboratory" in the central part of the city. Although the laboratory was soon dropped, the library and art gallery were immediately successful. Today, the library contains over 600,000 volumes. Its former art gallery was removed to the Museum of Fine Arts when that was established. *Courtesy of D. Peter Lund*

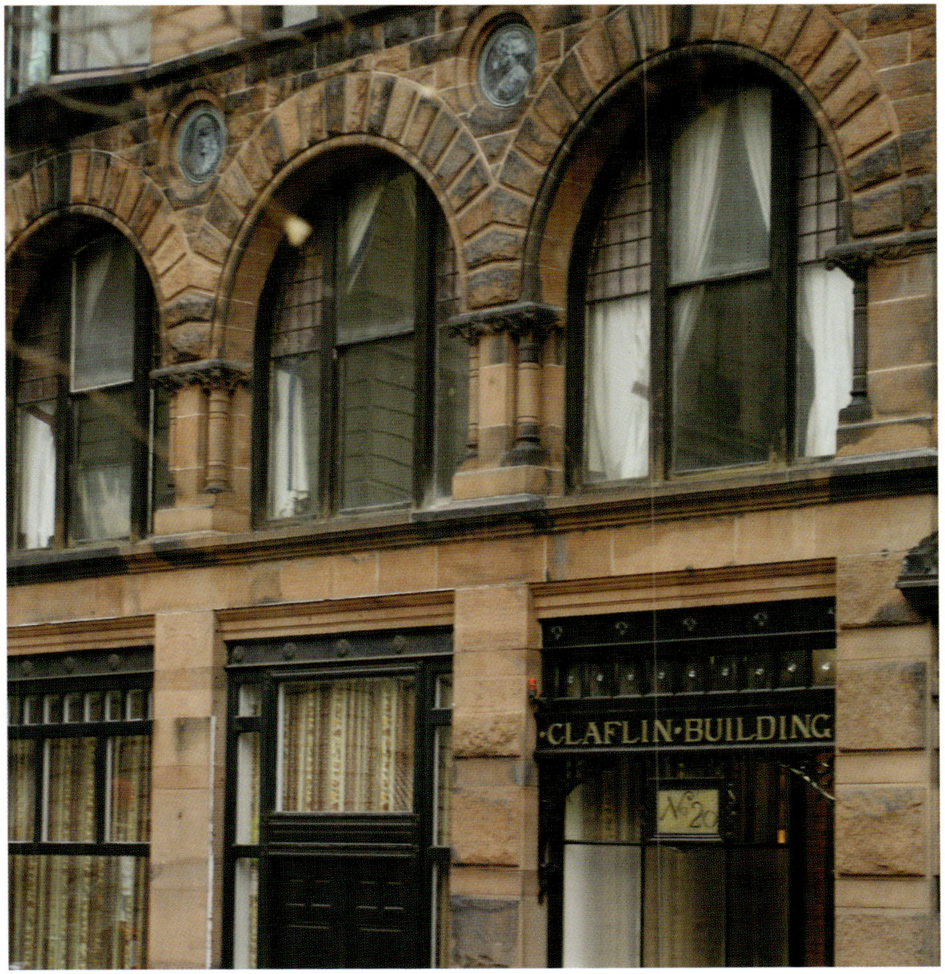

Designed by William Preston, the Claflin Building (18-20 Beacon Street), dating from 1882-1884, has a rugged Richardsonian dark stone facade. On the second floor, terra-cotta portrait plaques of the artists Albrecht Durer and Anthony van Dyke separate the three window arches, which terminate in paired columns. The building was the first home of the Boston University College of Liberal Arts. *Courtesy of D. Peter Lund*

Beacon Hill

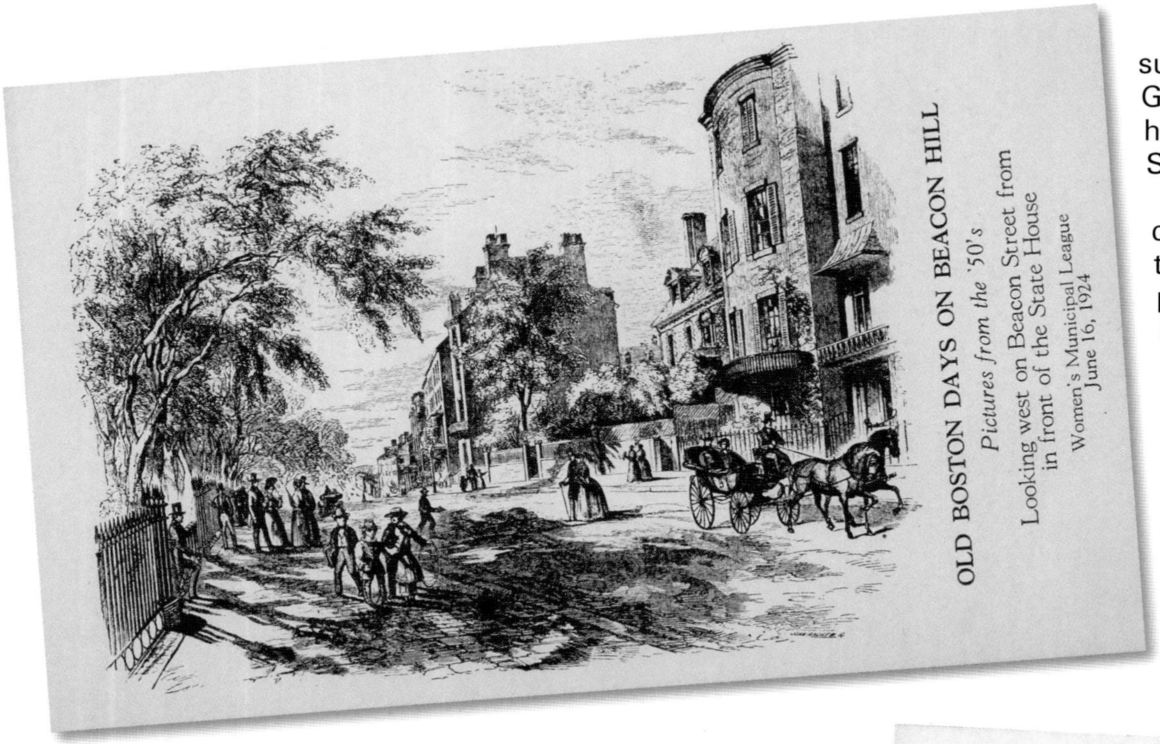

Initially, the Puritans called the Shawmut peninsula Trimountain because it had three hills. In 1634, Governor Winthrop erected a beacon on the central hill, "to give notice to the country of any danger." Subsequently, that hill was known as Beacon Hill.

Until the State House was built, Bostonians considered Beacon Street to be fairly remote. In the 1790s, the Mount Vernon proprietors acquired property from John Singleton Copley's estate. They leveled the peak of Beacon Hill, slowly carting down the gravel, which was subsequently used to create Charles Street. They intended to build an upscale residential neighborhood of handsome mansions with generous gardens. Today, Beacon Hill is an elegant neighborhood of Federal-style row houses lining the narrow, gas-lit streets. Most of the buildings are made of brick and date back to the nineteenth century

Beacon Hill was developed from pastureland owned by the portrait artist John Singleton Copley in the 1790s.

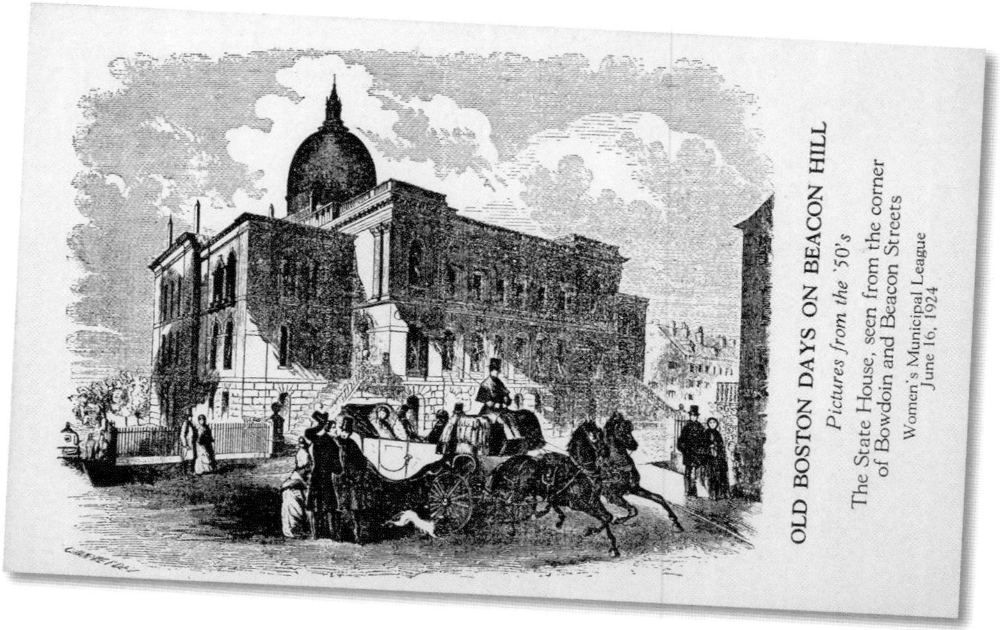

Although it took several decades, most of the Mount Vernon proprietors chose to build their private homes on the hill. To this day, one can still see the Federal-style windows, balustrades and iron railings in this area.

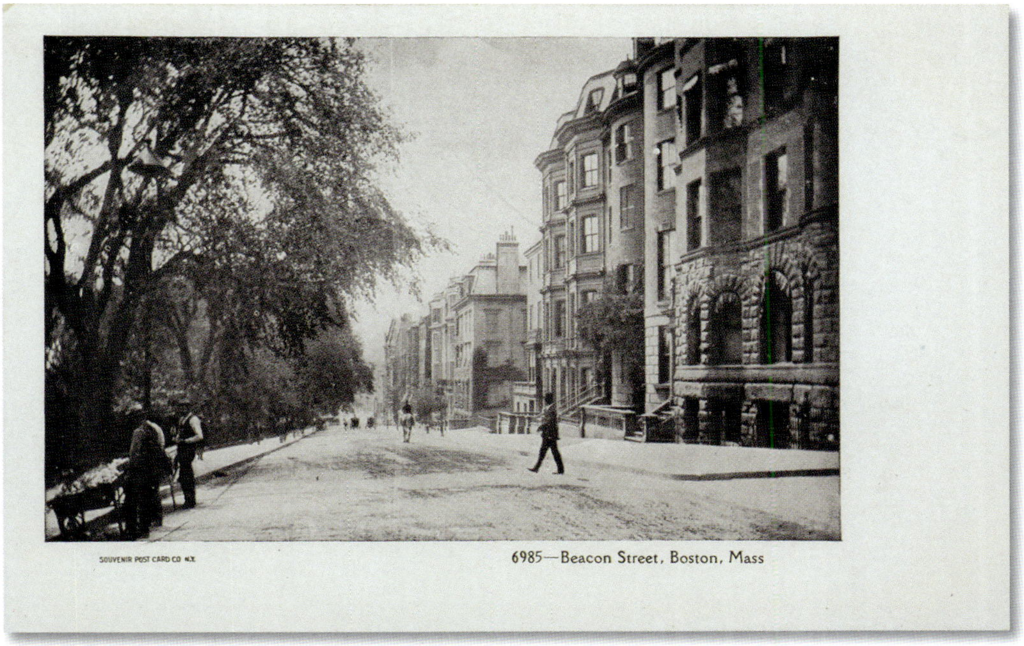

The south slope, facing the Boston Common (to the left), is where the wealthy and powerful lived. Charles Bullfinch designed many of the well-proportioned red brick houses in Federal style, some with ornate reliefs.

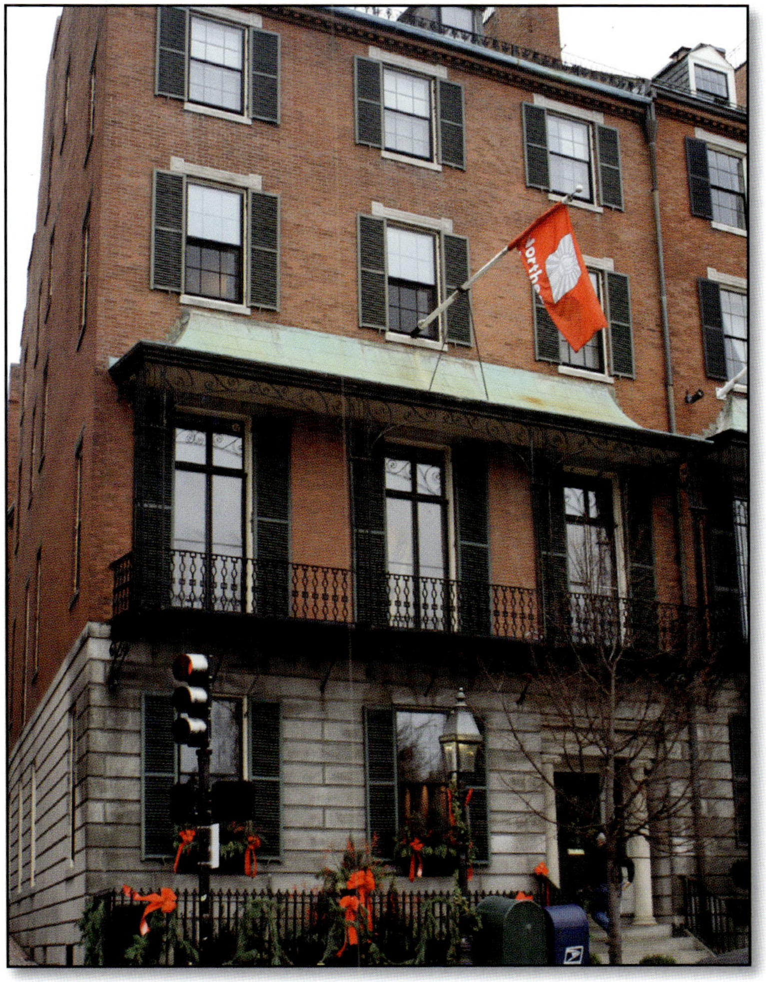

In 2006, Northeastern University (Boston) bought this five-story townhouse, which sits on the west pasture of the estate once owned by John Hancock. Built in 1825 for Nathaniel Pope Russell, a leading China trade merchant, the house has had a series of owners. In 1909, it became the headquarters of the publishing house Little, Brown and Co. Today, it is the official residence for Northeastern University's president. *Courtesy of D. Peter Lund*

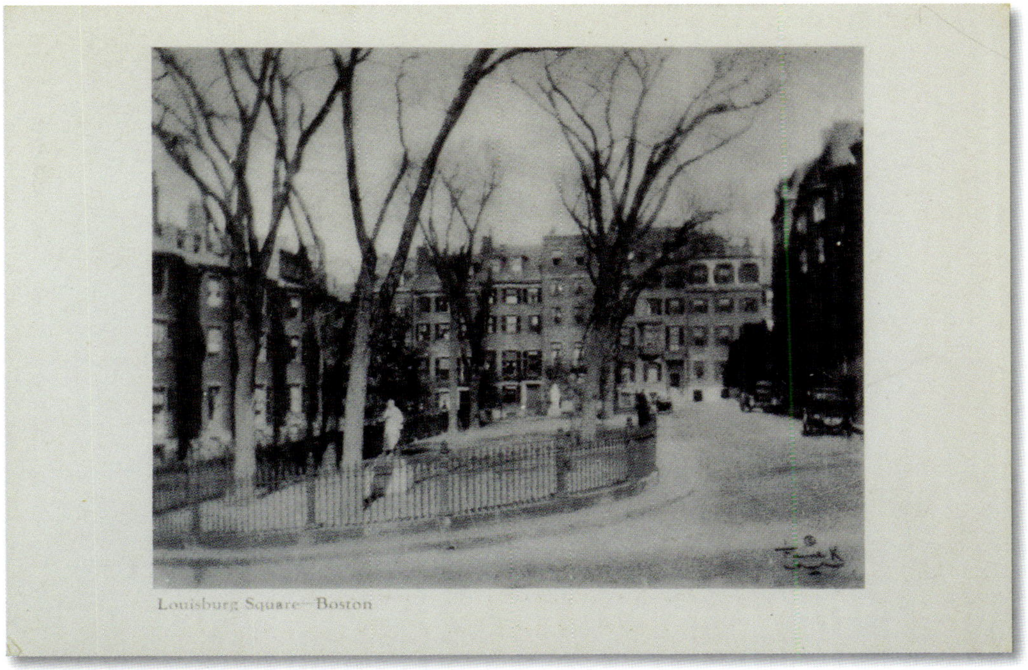

Developed in the 1830s as a shared private preserve, Louisburg Square is still a highly desirable address. Supposedly, Christmas Eve carol singing and candlelit windows began at Louisburg Square. The red brick houses surrounding the square are joined together to protect the tree-shaded fenced park. A statue of Christopher Columbus presented by a wealthy Greek merchant in 1850 stands at its center.

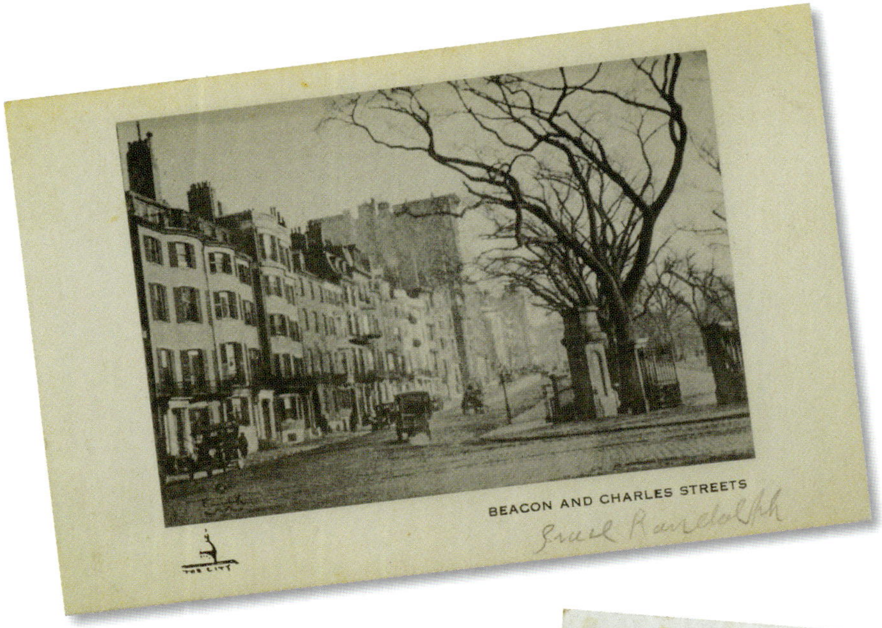

Charles Street is an elegant shopping area lined with upscale grocers, restaurants, specialty and antique stores. Originally, the city street paralleled the Charles River banks, but a later landfill moved it back several hundred feet.

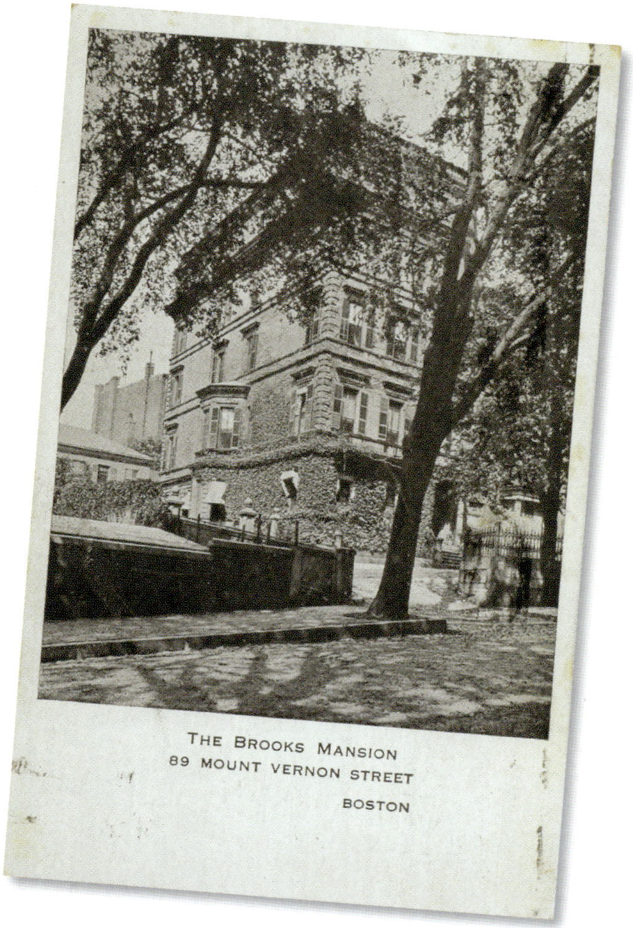

H.H. Richardson designed the Trinity Church rectory in 1879-1881. Known as the Brooks Mansion, it housed the Reverend Phillips Brooks. Later, a fourth story was added. Under Brooks' direction, H.H. Richardson designed one of his most famous works: Trinity Church in 1872 after The Great Boston Fire had destroyed the first church.

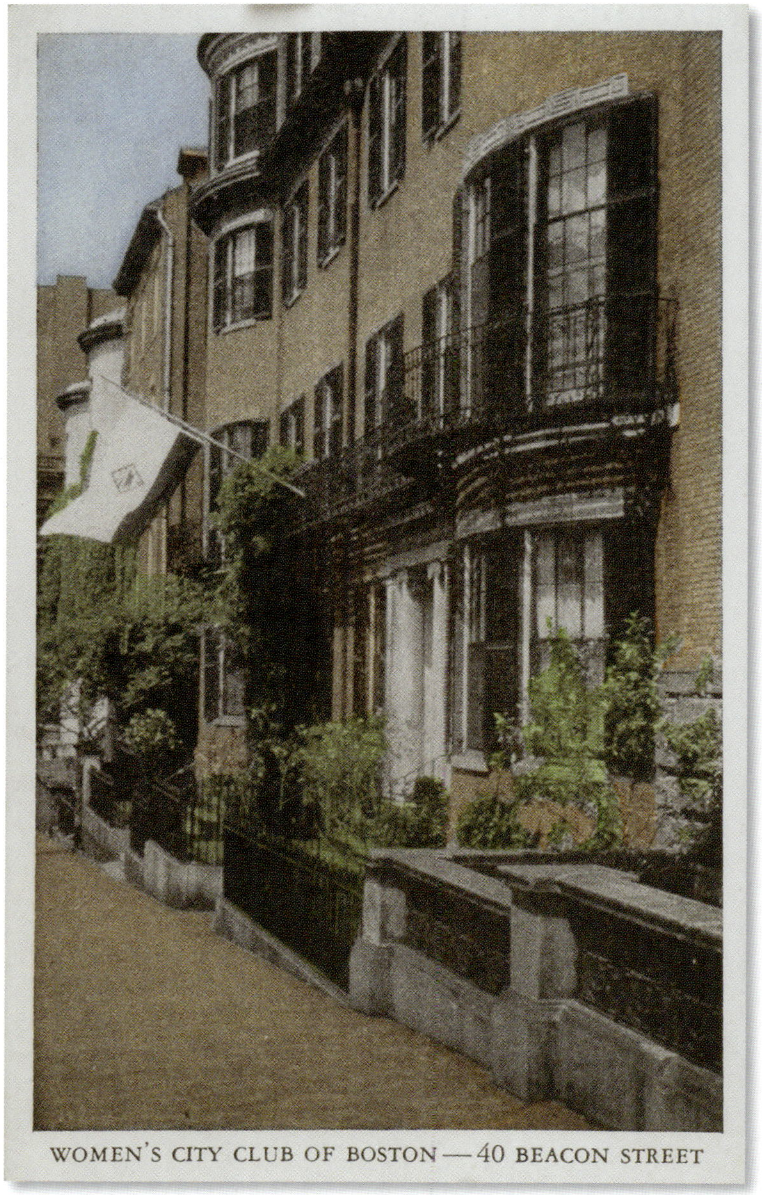

This stately mansion once housed the Women's City Club of Boston.

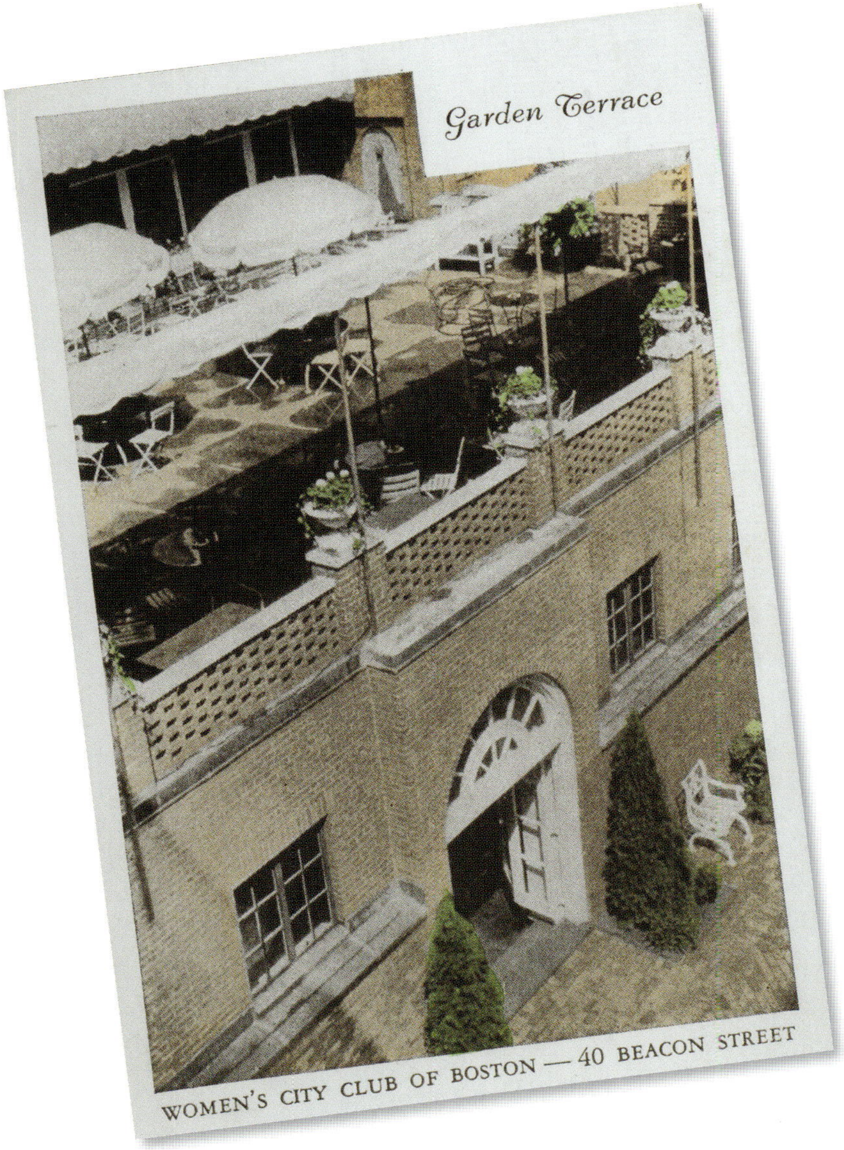

Founded in 1914 as a service club for women, the Women's City Club membership rose to 5,000 by the mid-1920s.

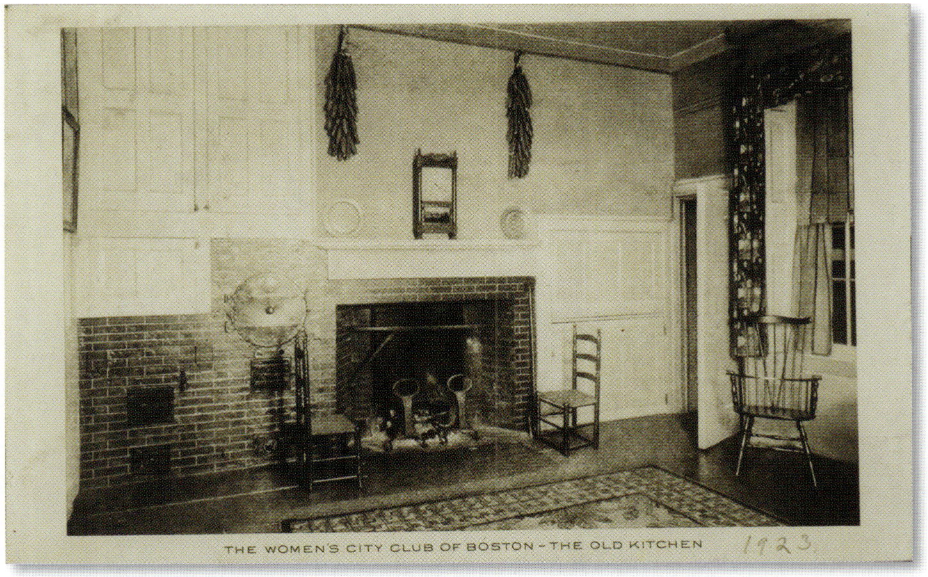

The Women's City Club sold its building in 1992 and now shares space with the Union Club.

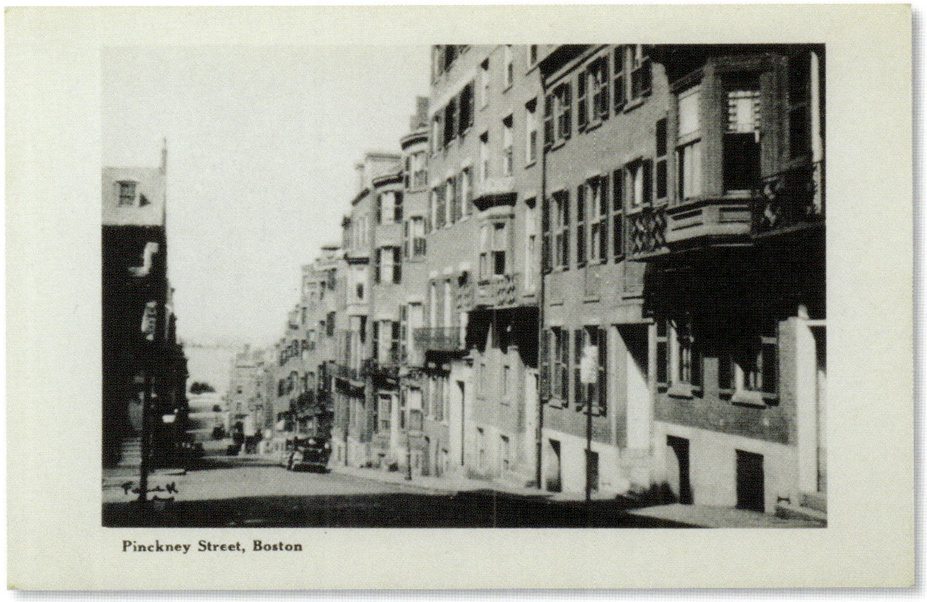

Pinckney Street was originally used for stables for the Mount Vernon Street mansions. Many famous people have lived on Pinckney Street including John J. Smith, Louisa May Alcott, John P. Marquand, and Elizabeth Peabody.

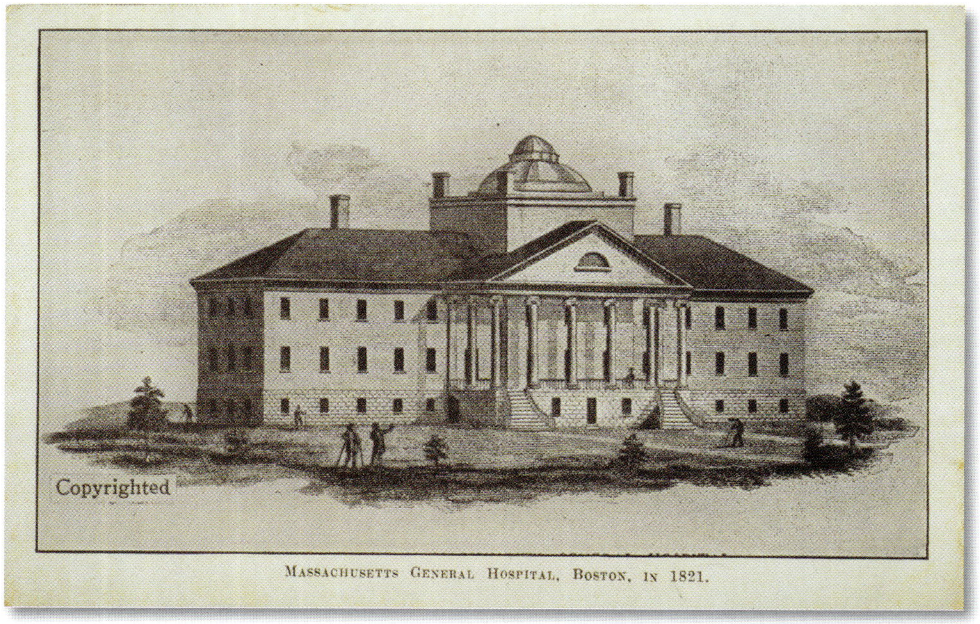

Founded in 1811, the world-renown Massachusetts General Hospital (Fruit Street) is built of local Chelmsford granite and is the third oldest general hospital in the United States. Charles Bulfinch designed the handsome Greek revival main building in 1817. The hospital is now a large complex of buildings surrounding the original Bulfinch building. Known as MGH or Mass General, it is one of the world's leading teaching and research hospitals. On October 16, 1846, one of the first demonstrations of the efficacy of ether took place here.

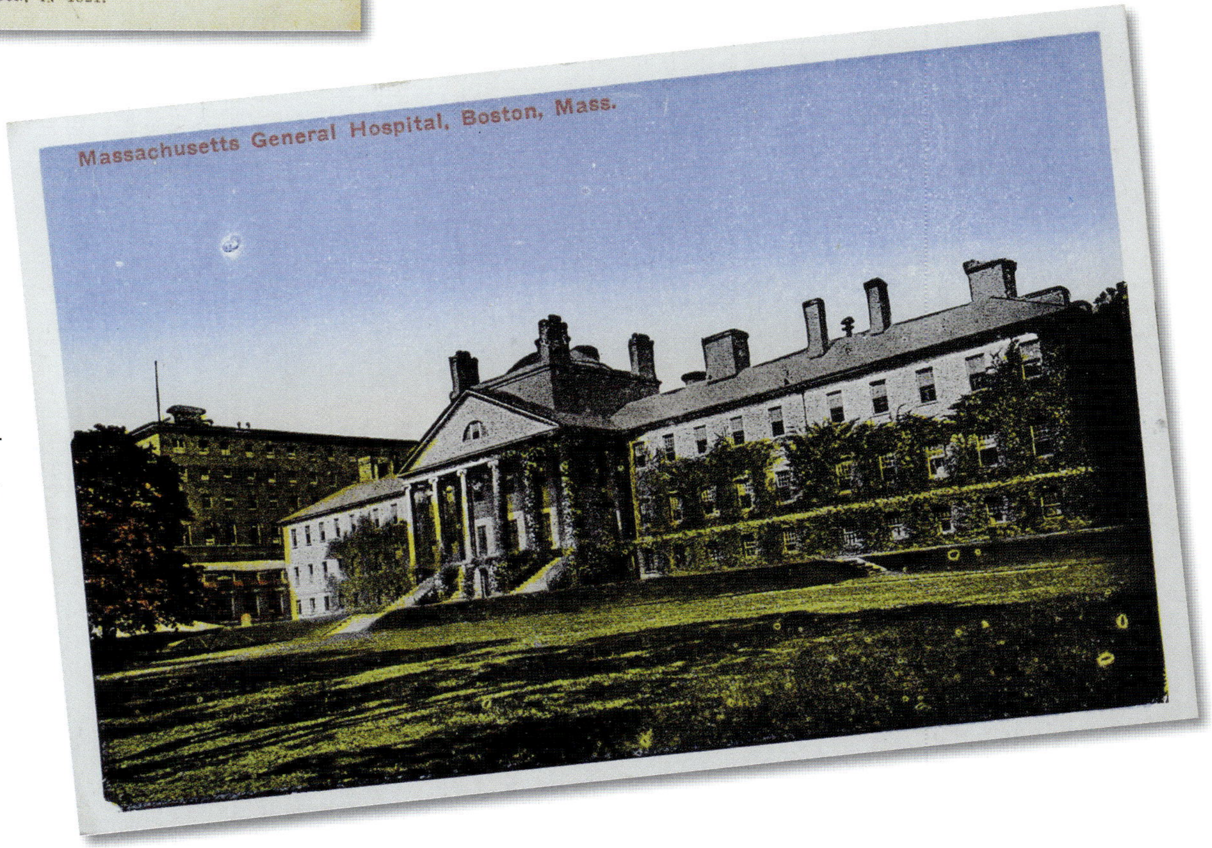

With more than 10,000 employees, the hospital is the largest non-governmental employer in Boston. It is sometimes jokingly described as "The Medical-Industrial Complex." It consistently ranks as one of the country's top hospitals in *U.S. News and World Report*.

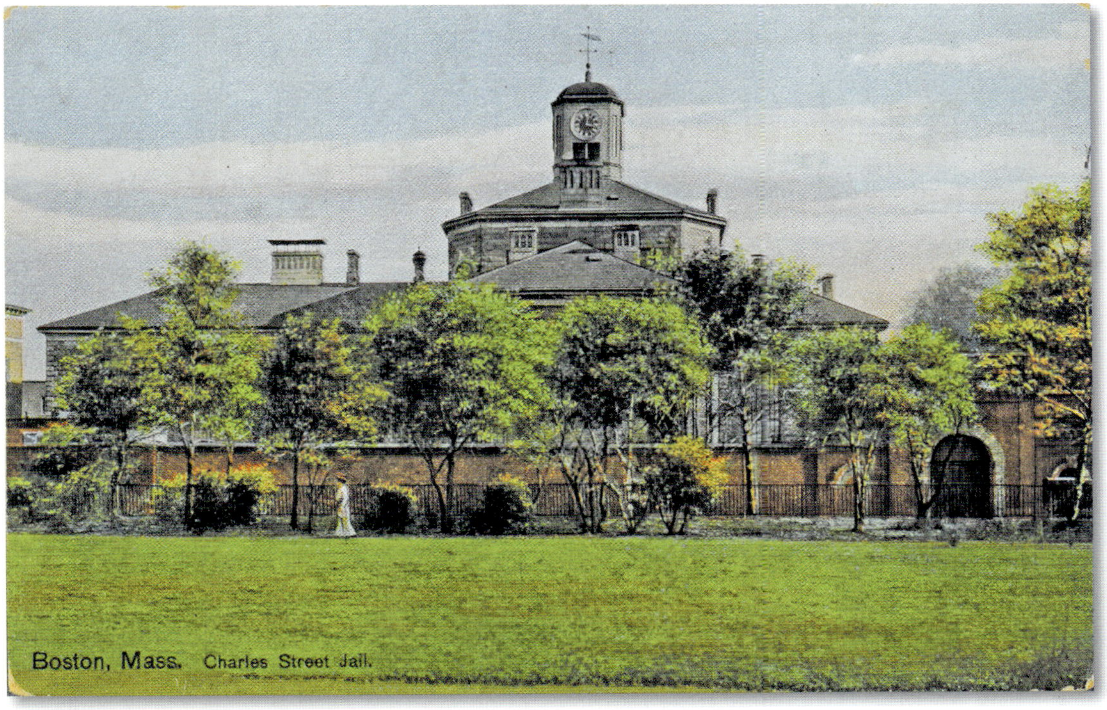

The Charles Street Jail (215 Charles Street) is listed in the state and National Registers of Historic Places. Architect Gridley and James Fox Bryant with prison reformer Rev. Louis Dwight designed it in a cross with four wings of Quincy granite extending from a central, octagonal rotunda with a 90-foot atrium. Thirty arched windows, each 33 feet high, provided ventilation and natural light. Over the years, the jail has housed a number of famous inmates including James Michael Curley, Sacco and Vanzetti, suffragists imprisoned for protests when President Woodrow Wilson visited Boston in 1919, and World War II prisoners from the German submarine *U-234*. After the jail was closed in 1990, Cambridge Seven Associates redesigned it as a 300-room luxury hotel. The design incorporated the cupola that was cut out of the original building plan because of insufficient funds. The new hotel is named "Liberty"; its bar is named "Alibi"!

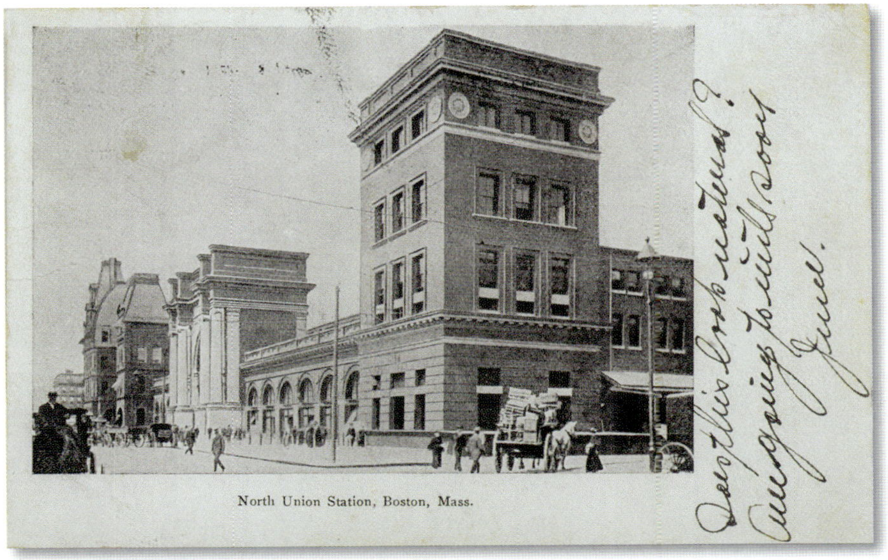

North Station (at Causeway and Nashua Streets) is a major transportation hub, physically attached to the former Fleet Center, now called TD Banknorth Garden. It was the main station for the old Boston & Maine Railroad.

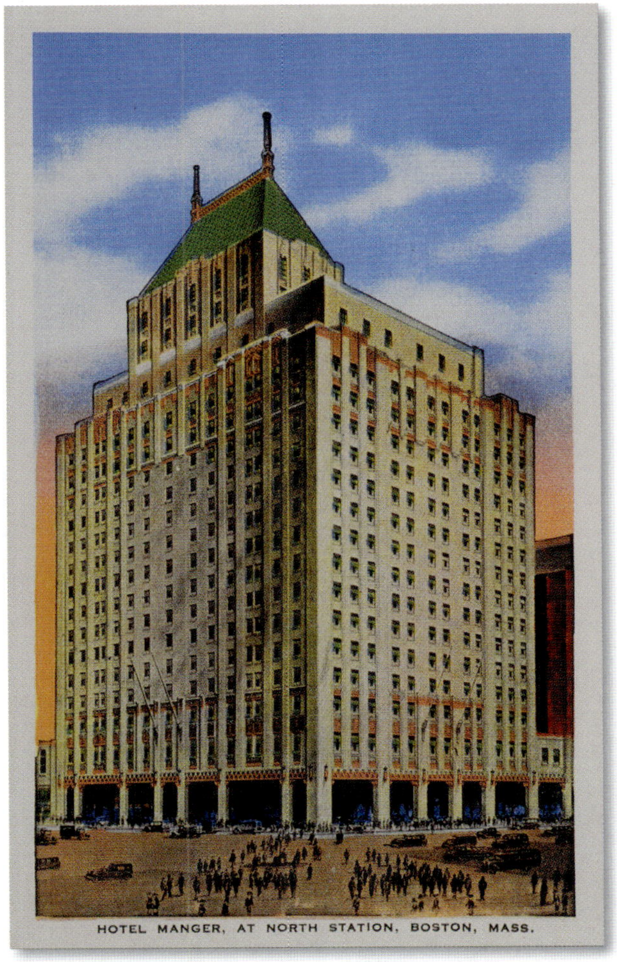

The former Hotel Manger was built in 1928 at North Station.

Chapter 5

The Common and The Boston Public Garden

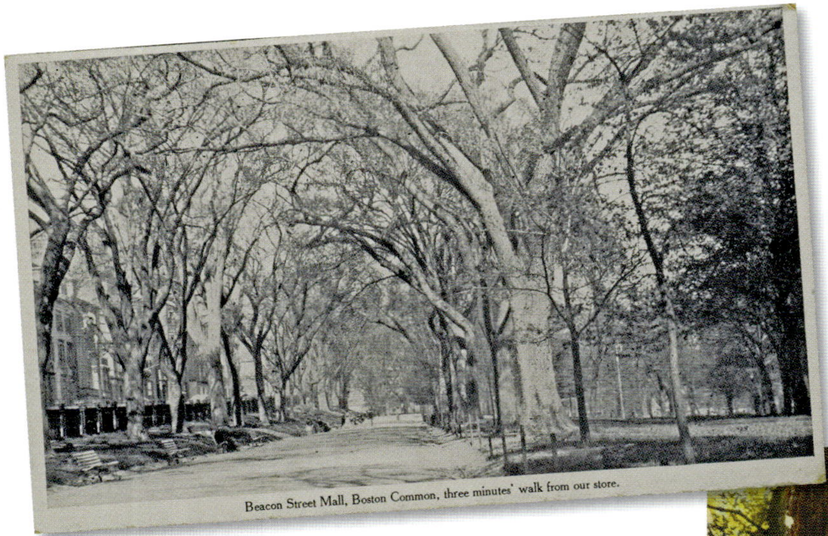

...could but just keep my feet upon the sidewalk, so bubble-like, balloony were my sensations – the full rich foliage, the hills, the water, inflated me. Oh that Common – that Eden in miniature." –Sophia Hawthorne, *Harris*, p. 21.

In English counties, common land or a common is a piece of land owned by a community, which residents can use for grazing their livestock. The approximately 50-acre Boston Common dates back to 1634, making it one of the oldest city parks in the country. The original owner was William Blackstone, who sold the plot of land to the Puritans. By 1646, grazing was restricted to seventy milk cows, but four sheep could be substituted for one cow!

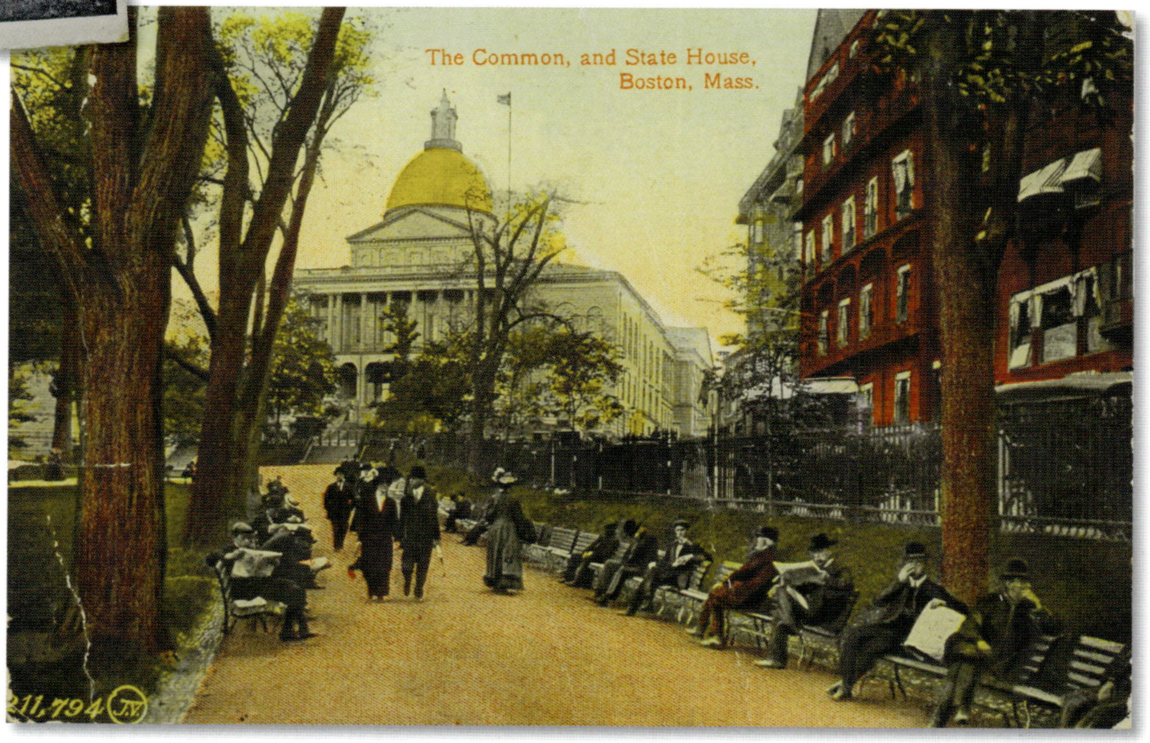

Boston Common is the anchor for the Emerald Necklace, a system of connected parks that winds through many of Boston's neighborhoods. With its grand sweep down from the majestic State House, the Common provides an uninterrupted view of green expanse, historic city buildings, and people. It contains walking paths, promenades, a Frog Pond for skating, play areas, and a war monument. The park hosts concerts, church services, protests, and other sorts of gatherings. Both Martin Luther King Jr. and Pope John Paul II have made speeches from there,

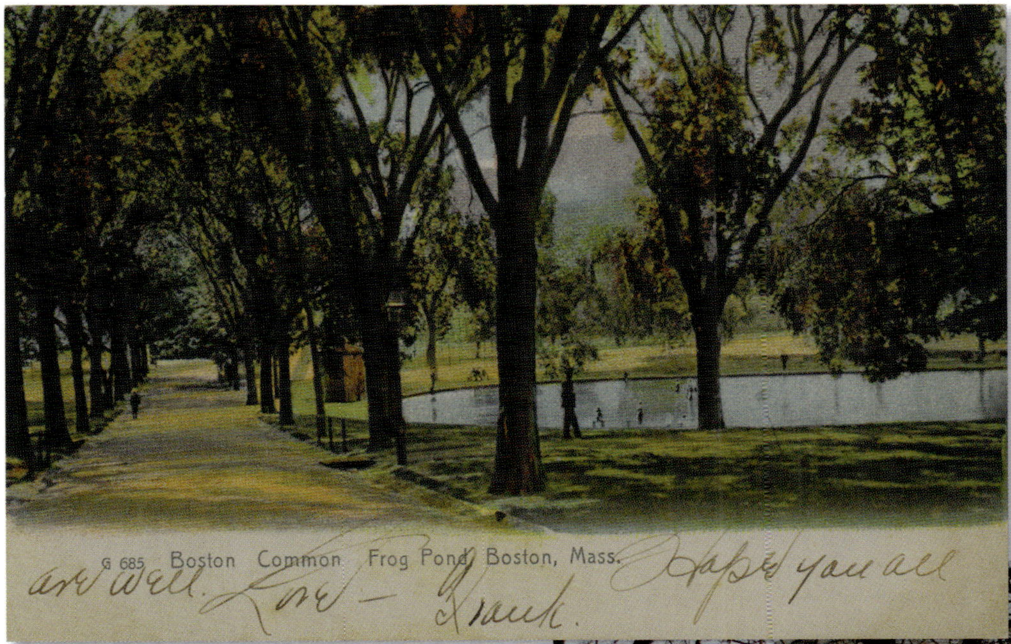

Boston Common played a role in our War for Independence. It became a campground for British troops when an armed fleet of eight British ships arrived in October 1768. In April 1775, British troops left from the Common to face colonial resistance at Lexington and Concord. Until 1817, the Common was a site for public hangings, such as Mary Dyer's. By 1830, an ordinance banned cows from the Common, and seven years later a Public Garden was established on the reclaimed land west of the Common.

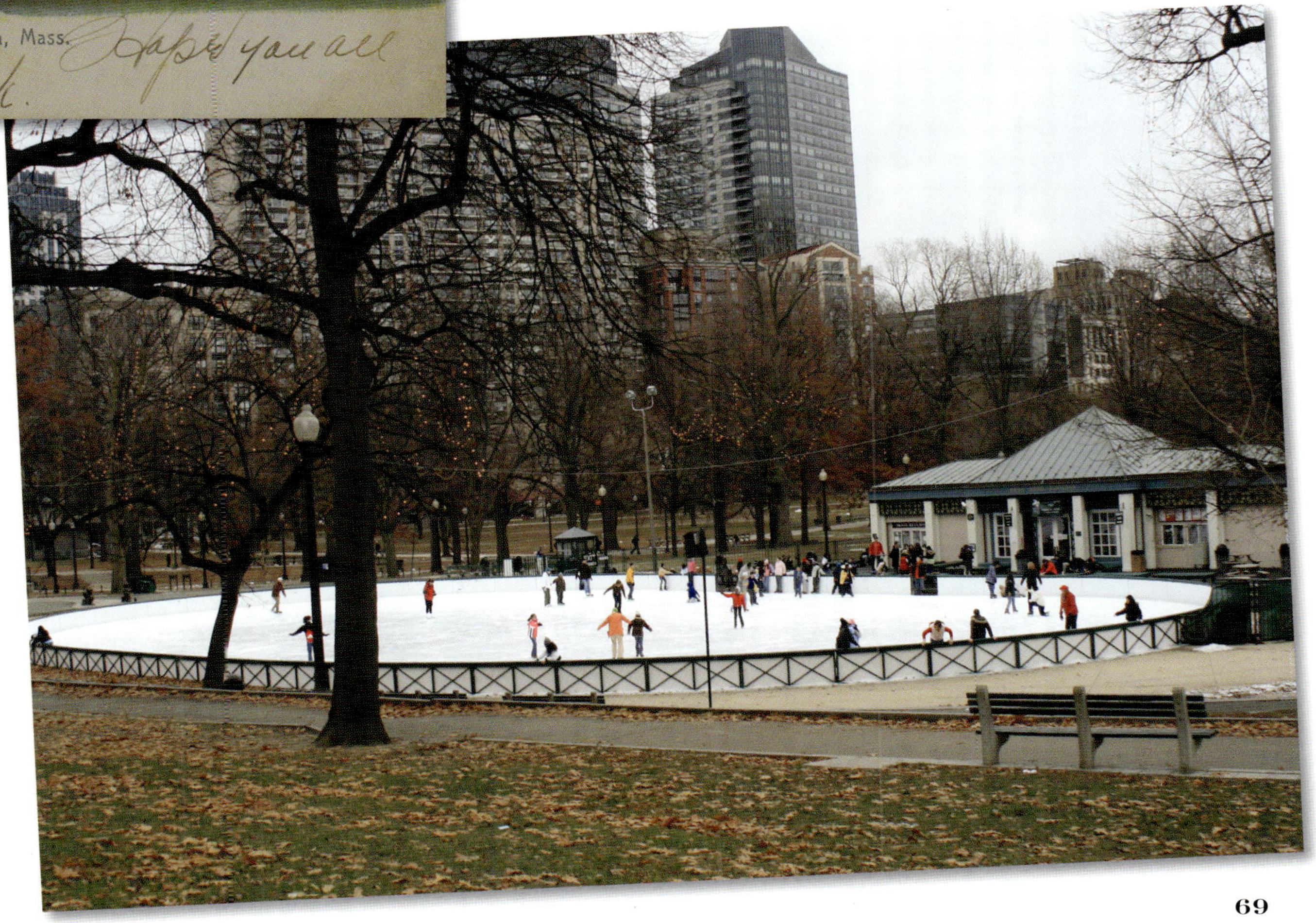

During the winter, the Boston Common Frog Pond is a wonderful place to go ice skating! *Courtesy of D. Peter Lund*

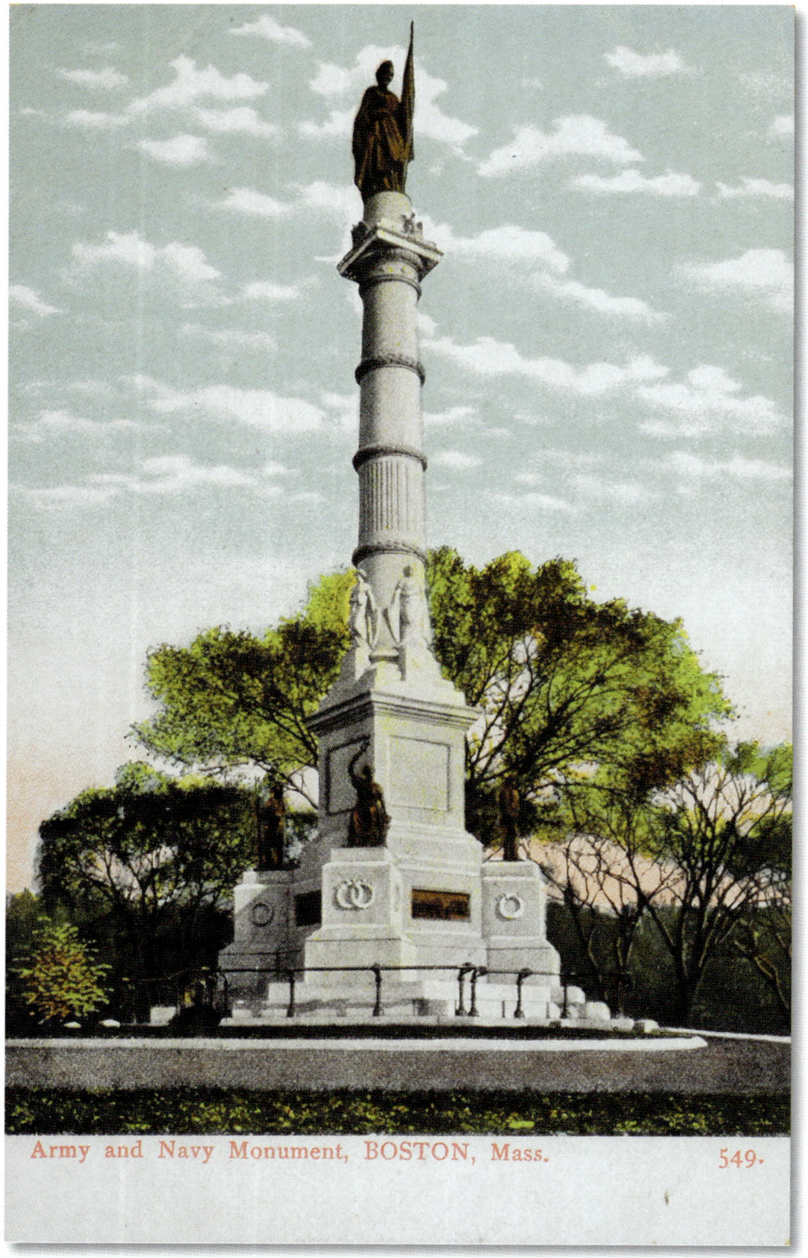

The Soldiers' and Sailors' Monument was dedicated on September 17, 1877, when the President of the United States reviewed the state's entire militia force. Designed by Martin Millmore, four projecting pedestals sustain four, eight-foot bronze statues representing Peace, the Sailor, History, and the Soldier.

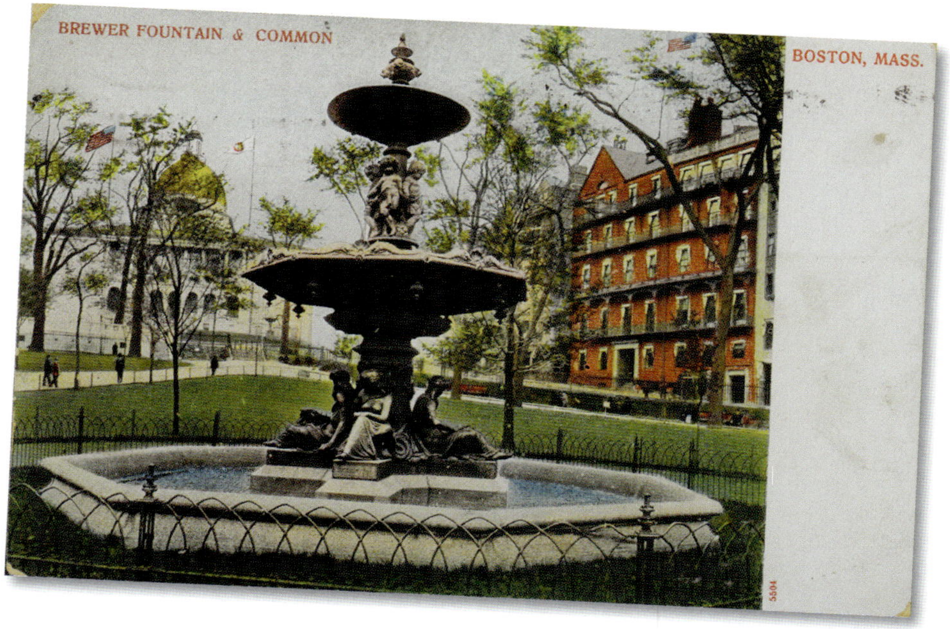

Donated by Gardner Brewer in 1868, the Brewer Fountain, which rarely has any water flowing, is a bronze replica of a French original that won a gold medal at the 1855 Paris World's Fair. The figures represent mythological figures (e.g., Neptune) associated with water. At some point, the fountain was relocated to its current location within view of the State House.

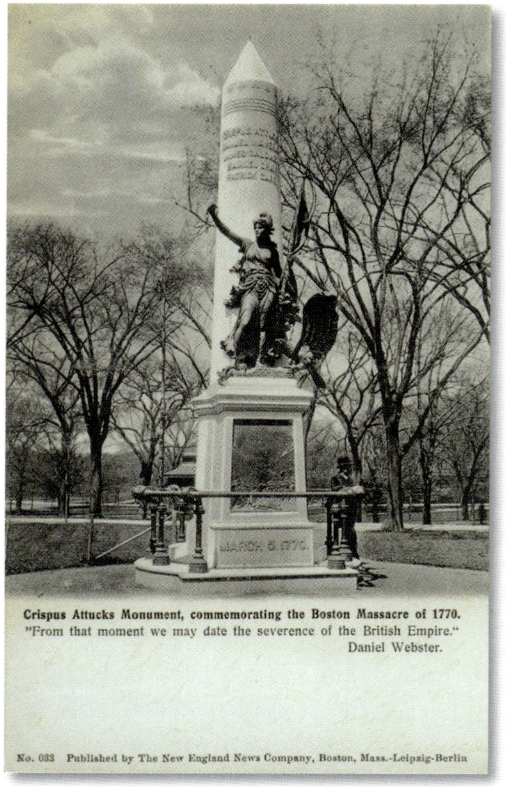

This bronze Boston Massacre Memorial "represents the Revolution breaking the chains of tyranny by depicting the events before the Old State House on March 5, 1770."

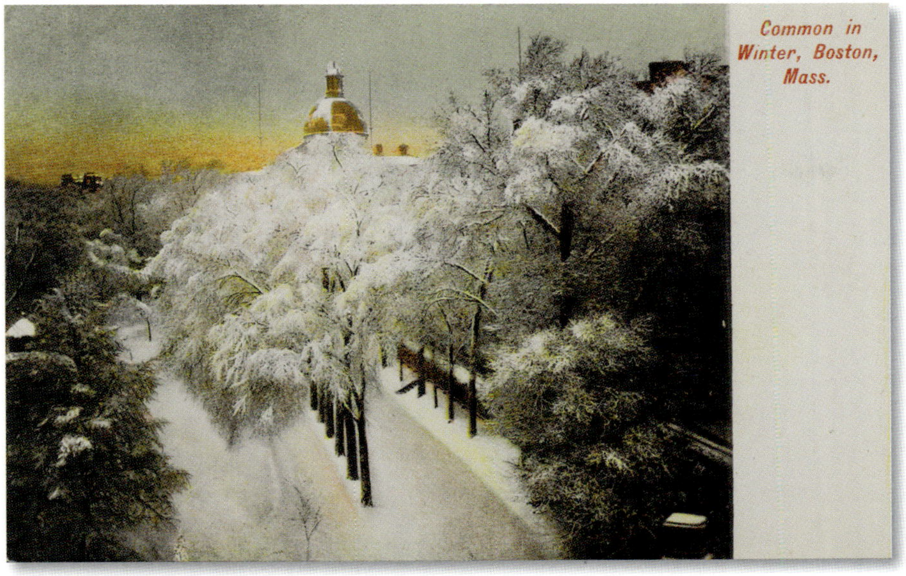

Once used for livestock grazing, the Common is the city's largest park. In 1910-1913, Olmstead Brothers oversaw a massive landscape renovation.

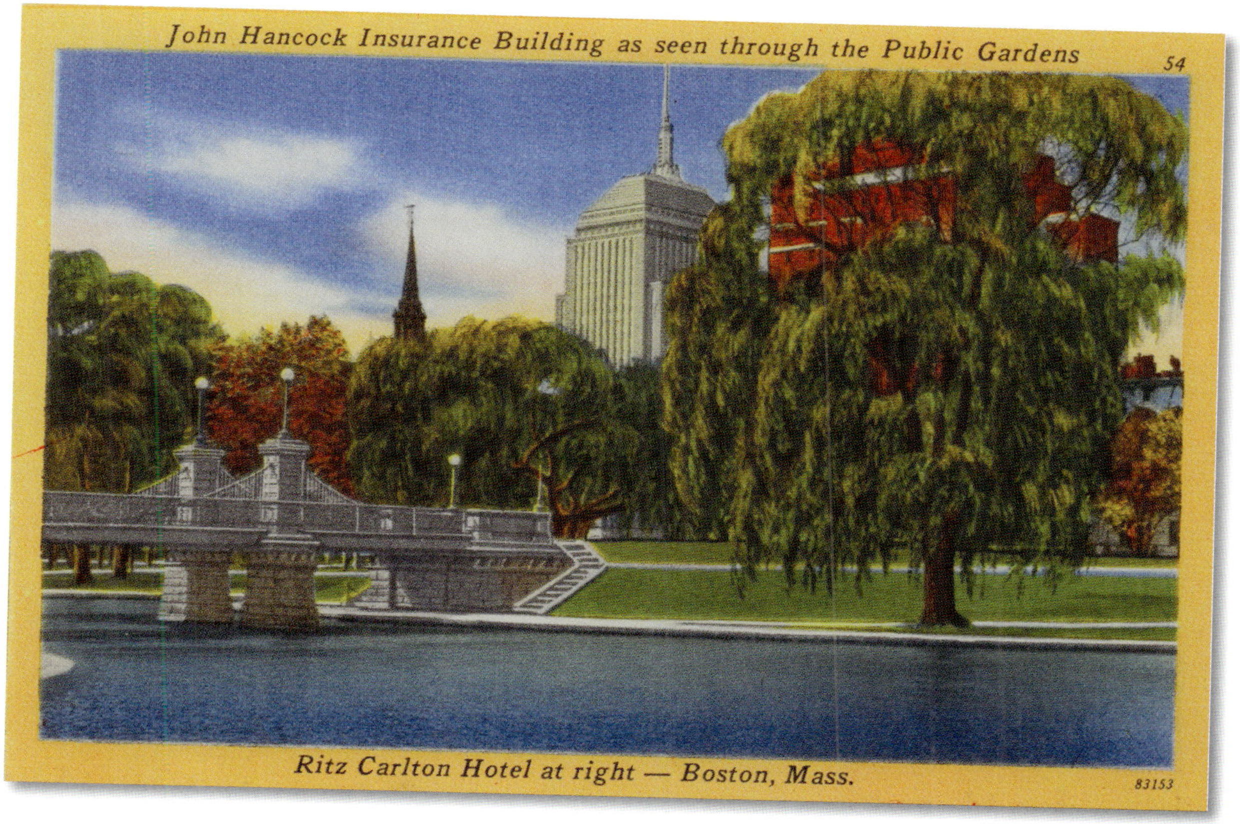

Although the Common and the Garden are adjacent (bisected by Charles Street) and serve a unified purpose, the two parks differ significantly.

The Common is more pastoral, while the Public Garden is the first American botanical garden. Under Mayor Quincy, the city secured the land now known as the Public Garden. Previously, it had been a great mud flat, which became the site of the ropewalks. Then it was marsh-land, which was covered by Back Bay water at high tide. In 1850, these marshes were filled to become a 24-acre Public Garden.

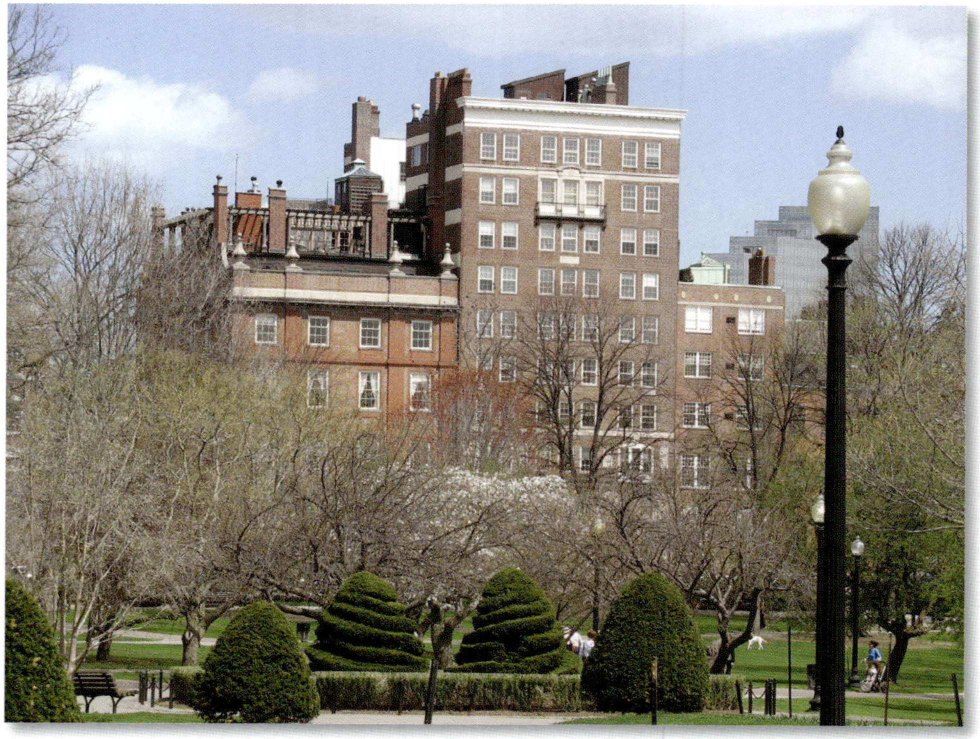

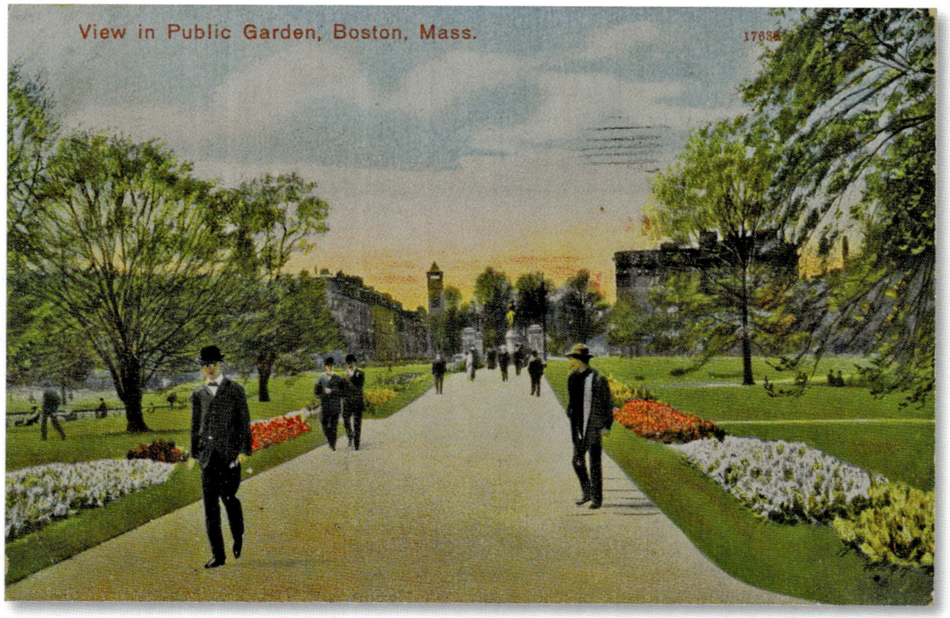

The city considered several landscape plans before returning to its English roots and selecting the English-style garden scheme of George Meacham in 1869.

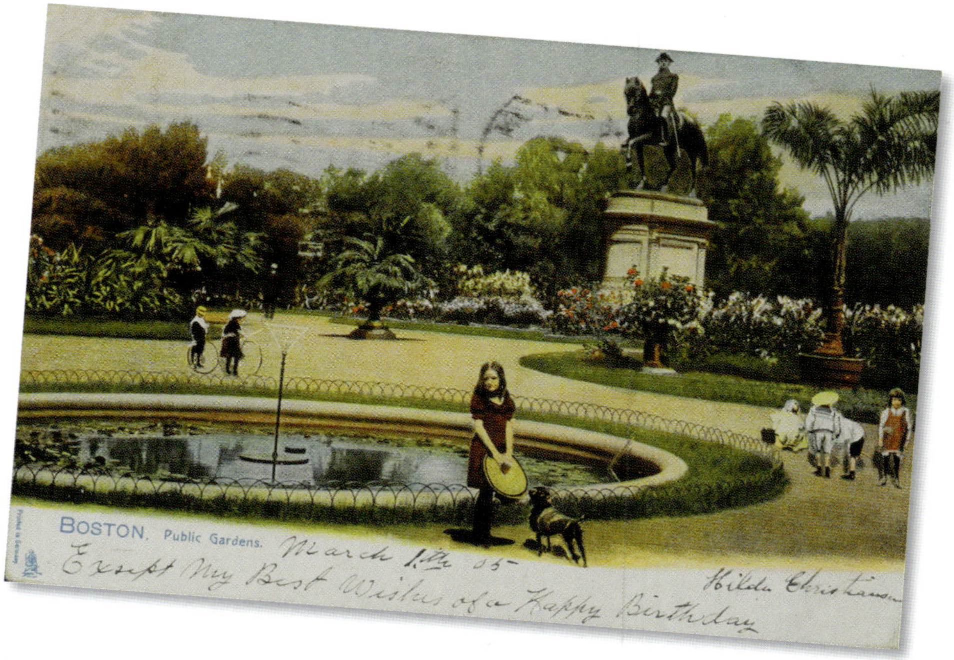

Established in 1837, the Public Garden is known for its series of formal plantings. Boston Brahmin and philanthropist Horace Gray paid for the first bed of tulips in the nation to be planted here. Dahlias, pansies, and cannas bloom in the summer. Ornamental trees offer shade, and young Bostonians play happily.

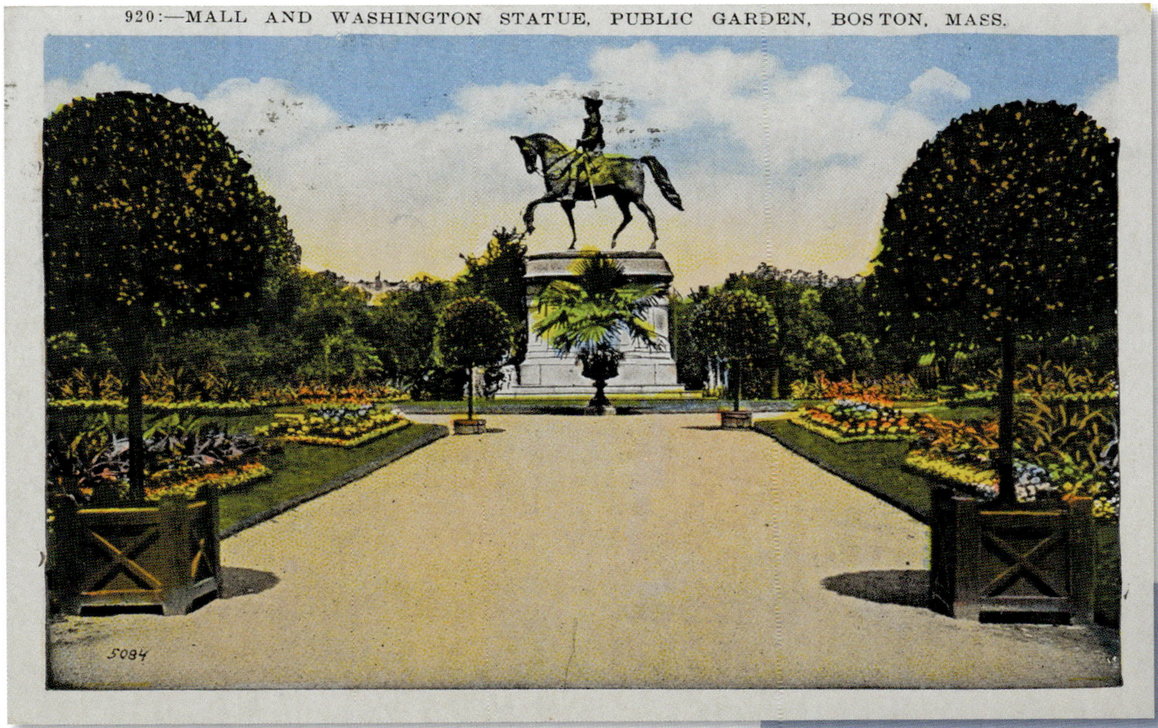

A favorite scene is The Mall and the statute of George Washington. The first equestrian statue in Boston, it was the fourth in the United States.

Designed by the American-born sculptor, Thomas Ball, and cast in bronze in Chicopee, Massachusetts, the George Washington statue was dedicated in 1869. George is shown surveying the field. Since then, Washington's "field" has been covered with buildings.

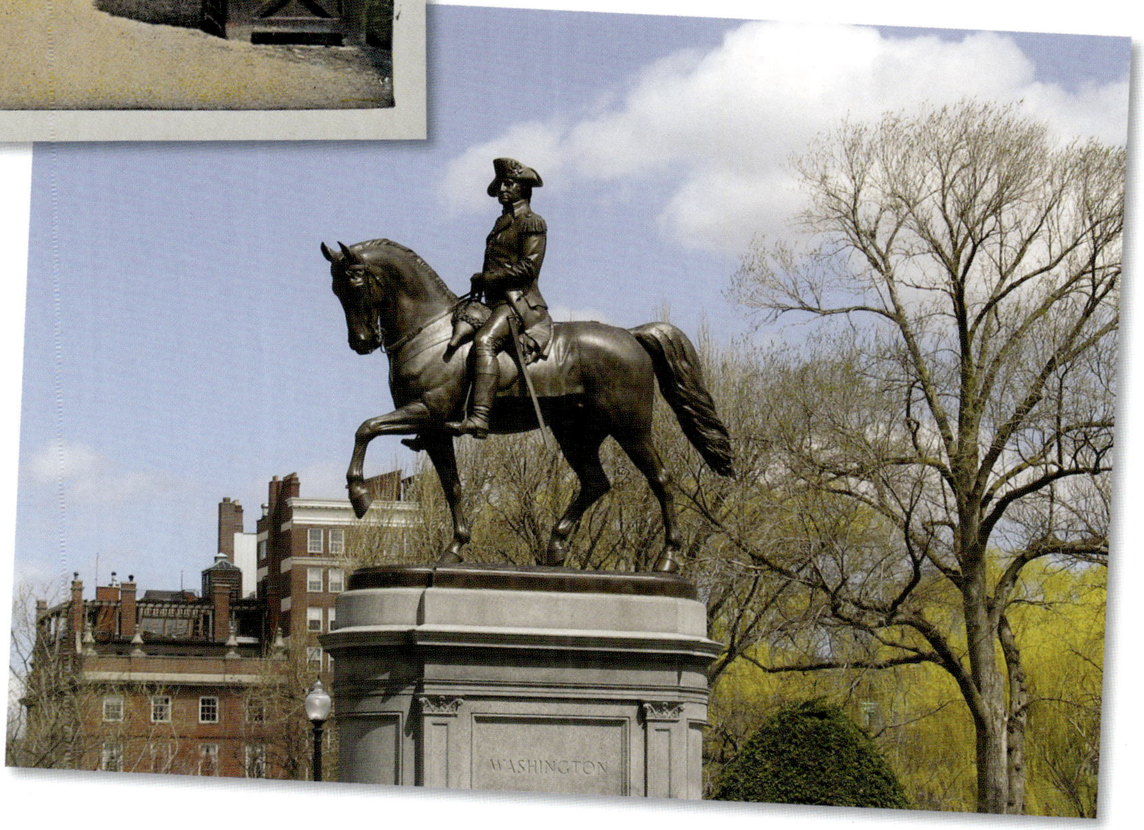

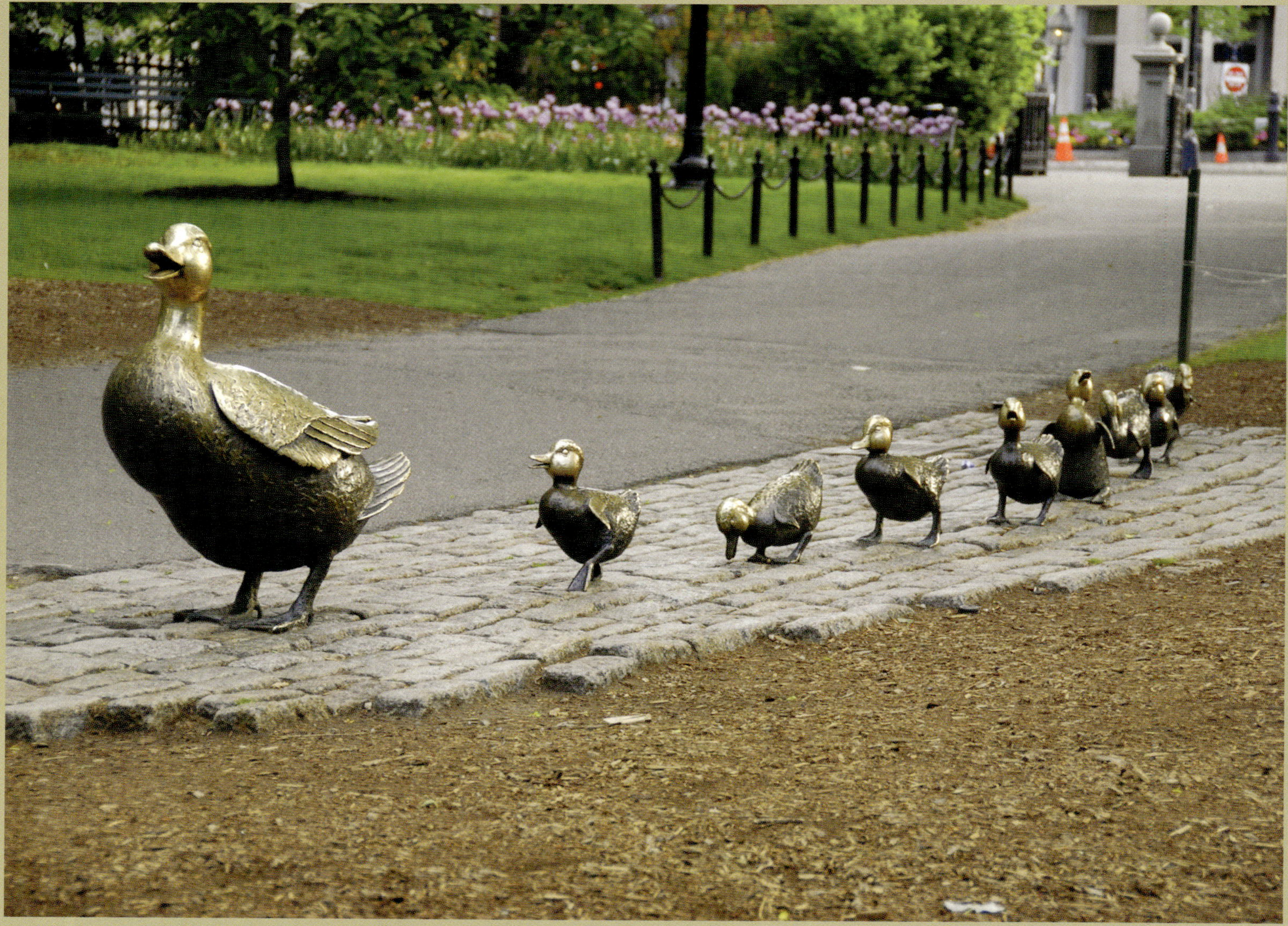

One of the most popular statues is the set of bronze ducklings from the children's story *Make Way for Ducklings* located between the pond and the entrance at Charles and Beacon Streets. *Courtesy of Linda Williamson*

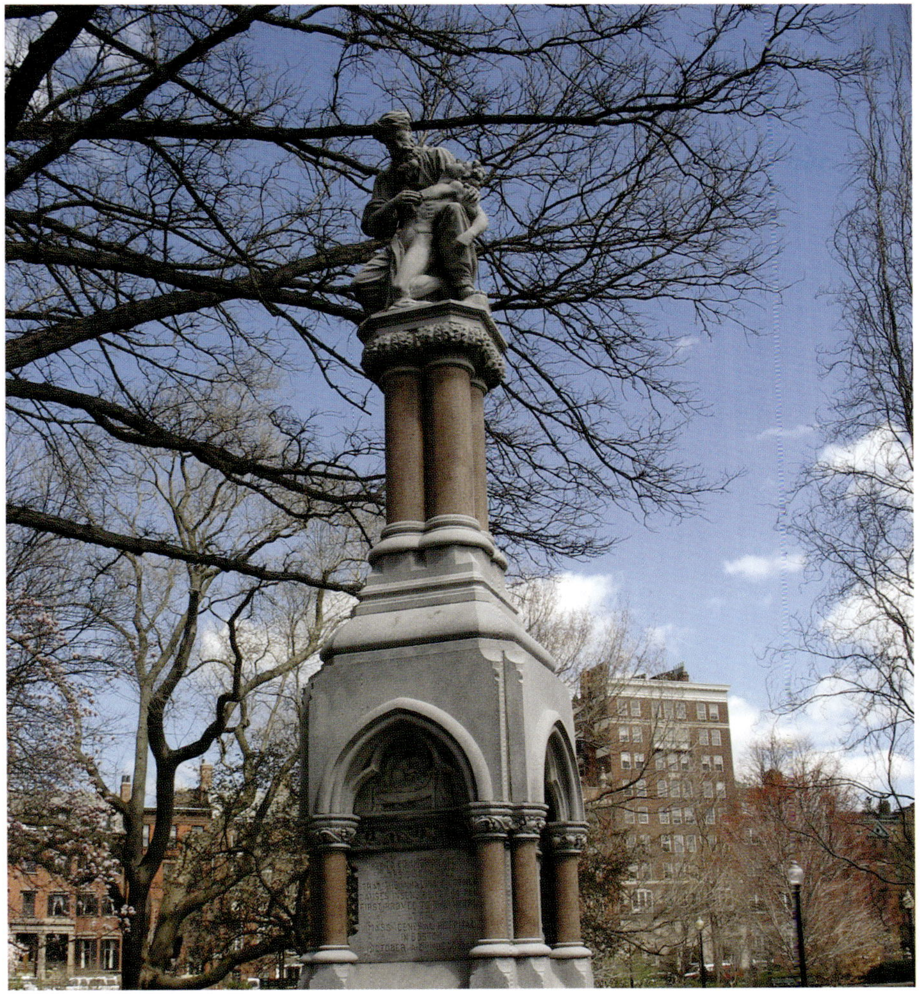

This 140-year-old monument commemorates the first use of ether as an anesthetic under the Etherdome at Massachusetts General Hospital on October 16, 1846. Sited in a prominent spot in the Boston Public Garden, it is supposedly the world's only monument to a drug.

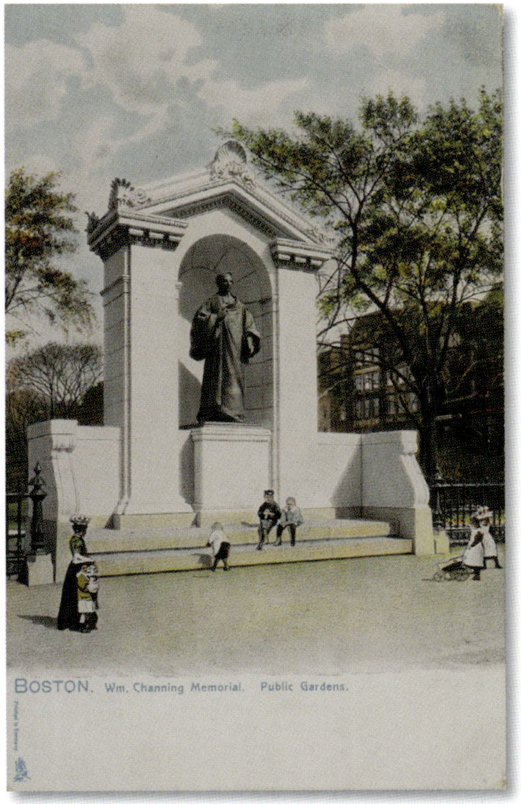

Sculpted by Herbert Adams, the William Channing Memorial commemorates William Ellery Channing, the pastor of the Arlington Street Church. Admired for his articulate and liberal sermons, he had a major influence on the New England Transcendentalists.

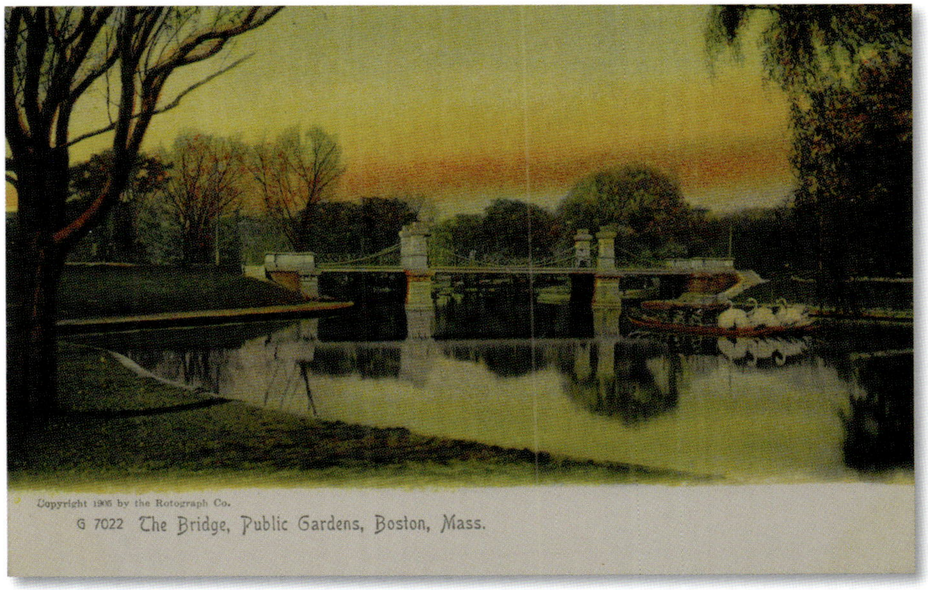

The Public Garden has a lovely lagoon. During the warmer seasons, one or more swans dwell in the vicinity of the pond complimenting the Swan Boats.

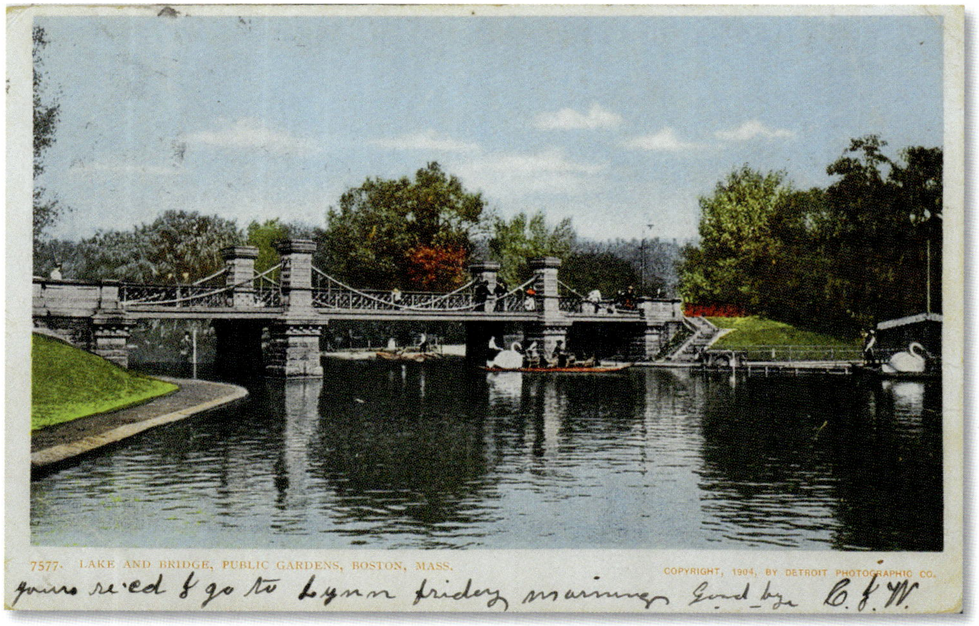

A small iron suspension bridge, designed by William Gibbons Preston, spans the four-acre pond.

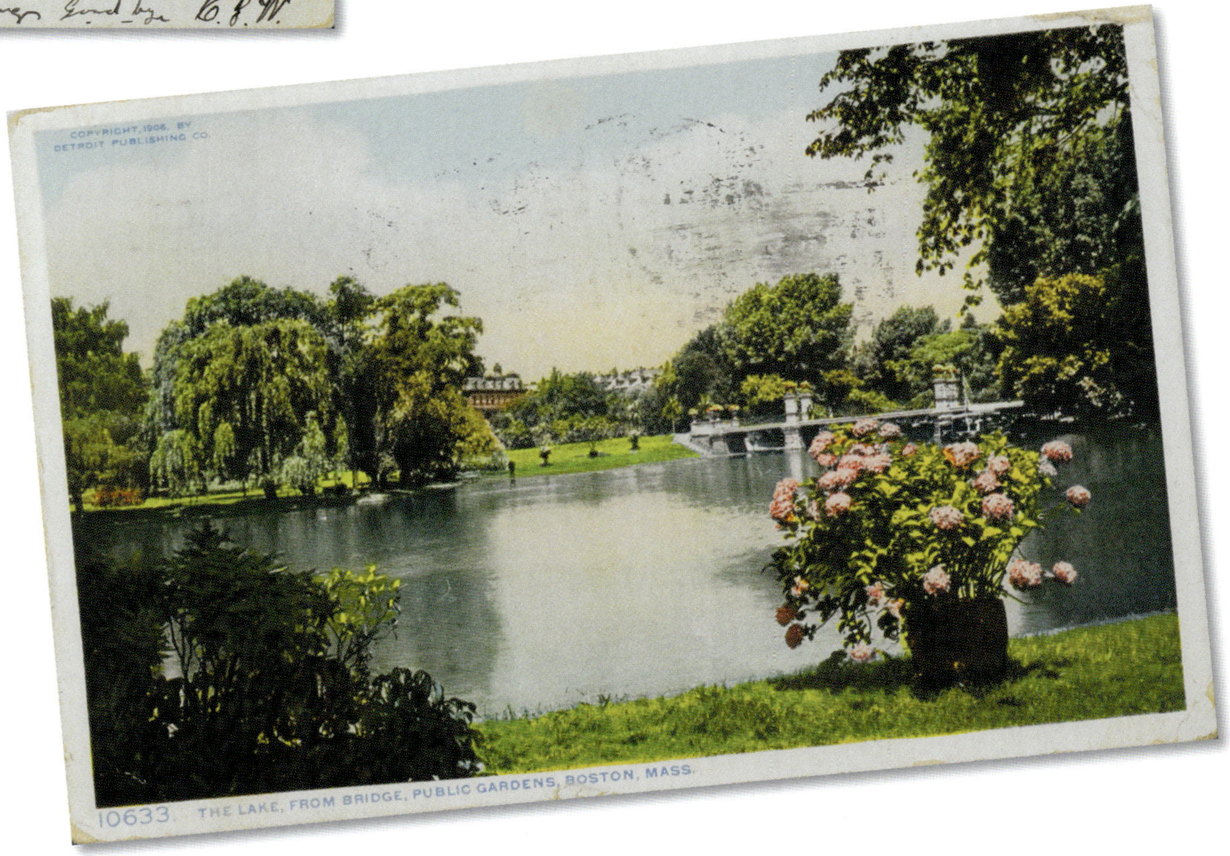

Everyone visits the Public Garden. New England winters can be long; a beautiful garden makes it all worthwhile.

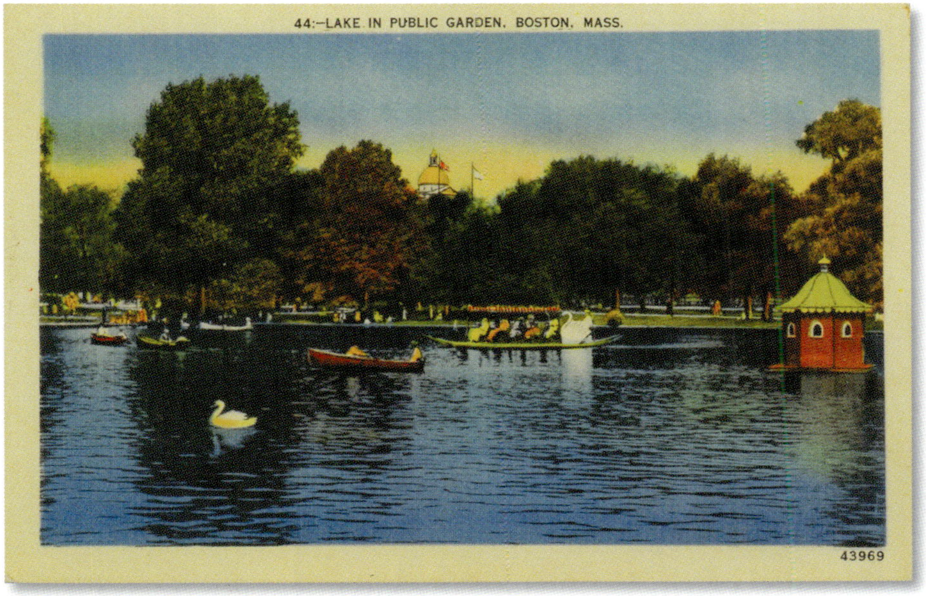

The legendary pedal-powered Swan Boats, which arrive each April, are one of its greatest attractions. They are rarely empty.

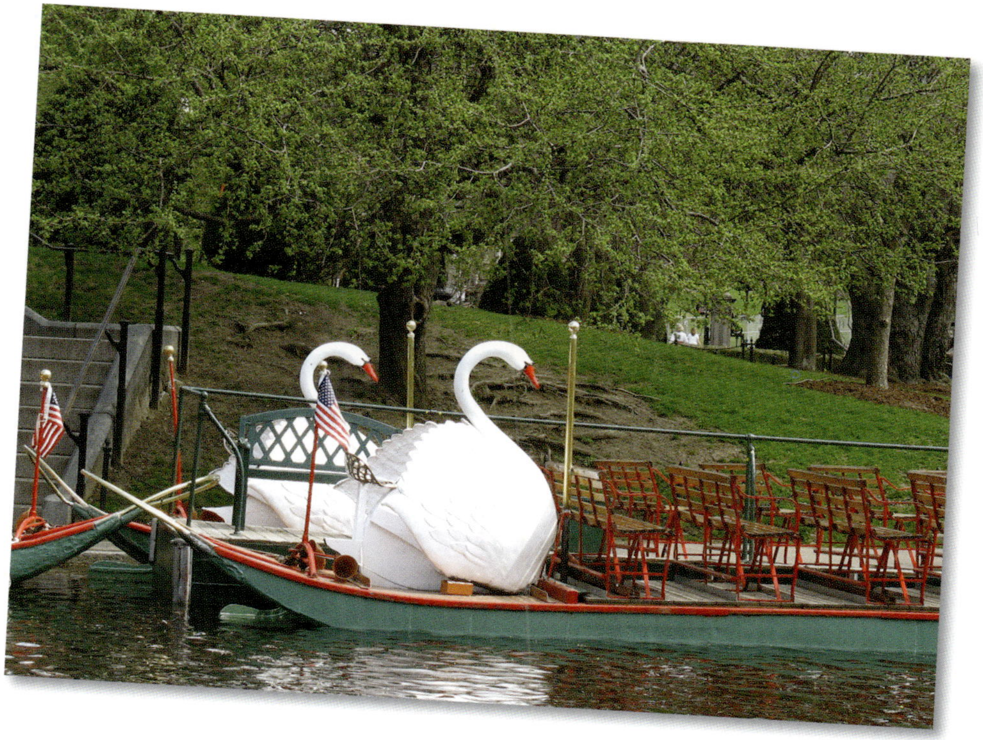

Inspired supposedly by Wagner's "Lohengrin," the Swan Boats have been there since 1877.

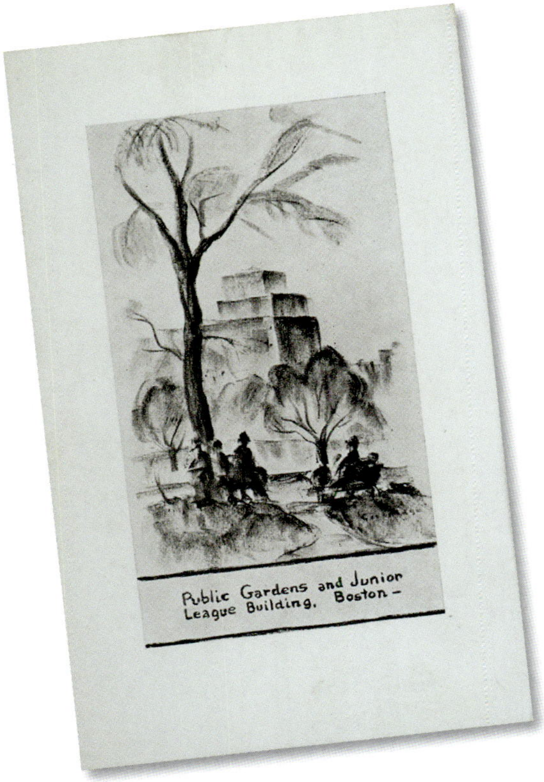

Established in 1906, the Junior League of Boston is a group of young women interested in educating other young women in the social needs and problems of the greater Boston Metro community. At the turn of the century, debutantes of the season were invited to join a sewing circle each year. Originally created to sew clothing and bandages for Union soldiers during the Civil War, these sewing circles had become purely social groups. In 1906, one of the young debutantes felt it was time for Boston's sewing circles to be more useful. Following several months of discussion, the sewing circles of old joined together to form a new group to interest young women in the local social problems and needs.

CHAPTER 6

BACK BAY

I know no place at which an Englishman may drop down suddenly among a pleasanter circle of acquaintance, or find himself with a more clever set of men, than he can do at Boston. –Anthony Trollope, *North America*

Back Bay, with its impressive nineteenth century mansions and tree-lined streets, attracted many visitors, wonderful residences, magnificent churches, and cultural entities. It certainly wasn't like this originally.

In the early eighteen hundreds, Back Bay was characterized as "an open cesspool" (State Street Trust Company, p. 29). Until Boston decided to fill Back Bay, the city's growth was restricted. When Back Bay was filled in, Boston suddenly recognized approximately 570 acres of build-able land from this audacious urban project, which replaced the tidal marsh just south and west of downtown Boston with tons of sand and gravel. New residences and public buildings were erected on pile-driven foundations. Today, the Back Bay area is a place of long straight streets, something which is quite novel in Boston — an area that is known for its crooked and narrow streets.

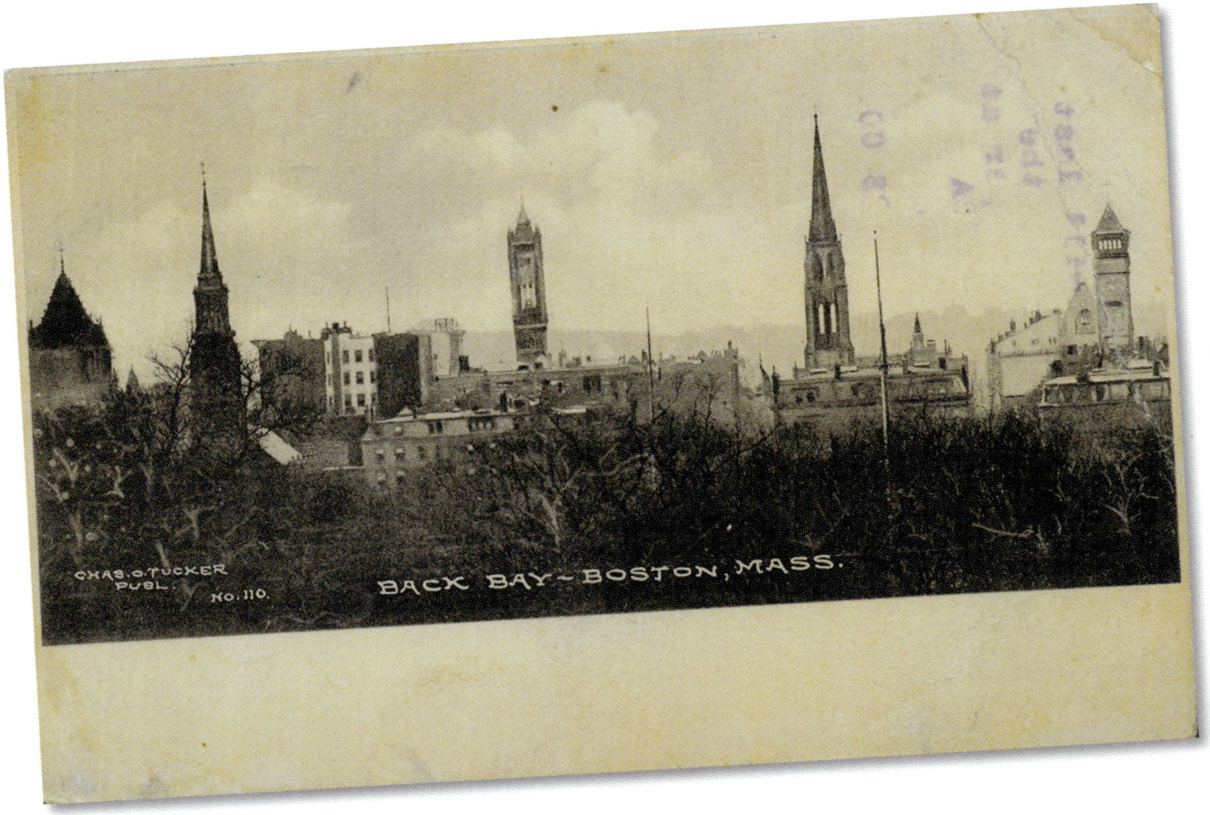

Adjacent to the Common was a brackish swamp known as the Back Bay. With the aid of the newly invented steam shovel, Boston began filling in this odiferous marsh. The reclaimed mudflat became a center for cultural institutions as well as fashionable residences.

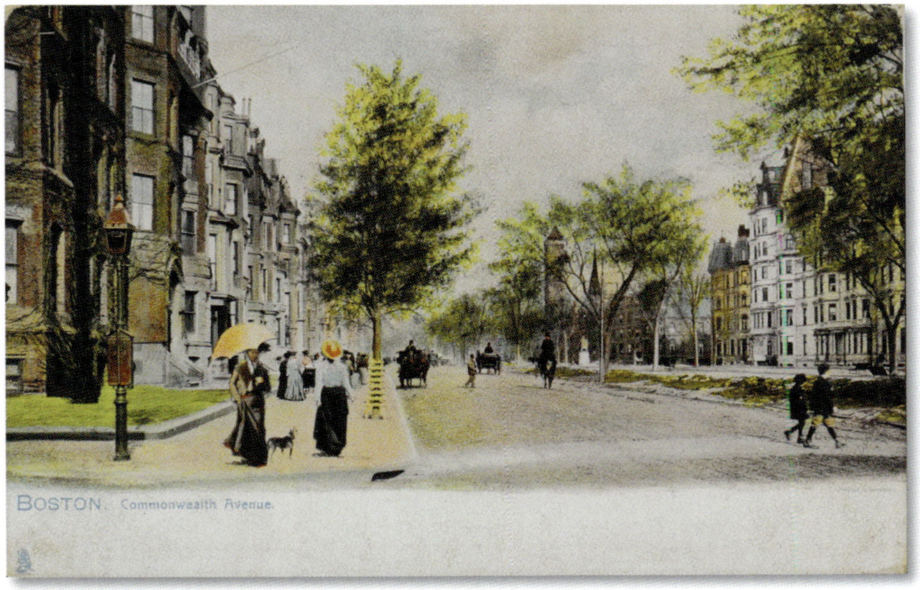

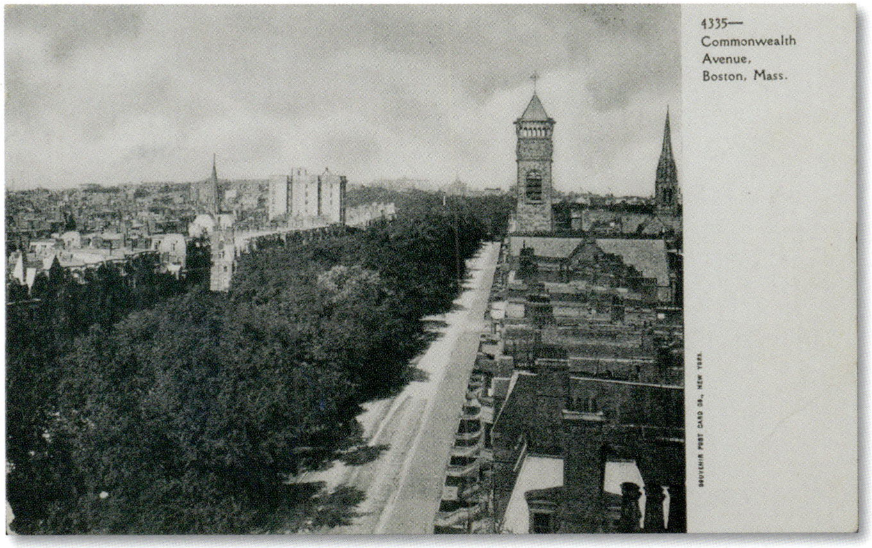

Commonwealth Avenue is the spine of Back Bay. At its end, between the new infill and Boston Common, is Boston Public Garden.

As this ambitious urban design project was completed, turreted brick and stone houses were built along Commonwealth Avenue. This upscale residential district sports sculptural detail, towers, and well-planted small gardens in front of each handsome house.

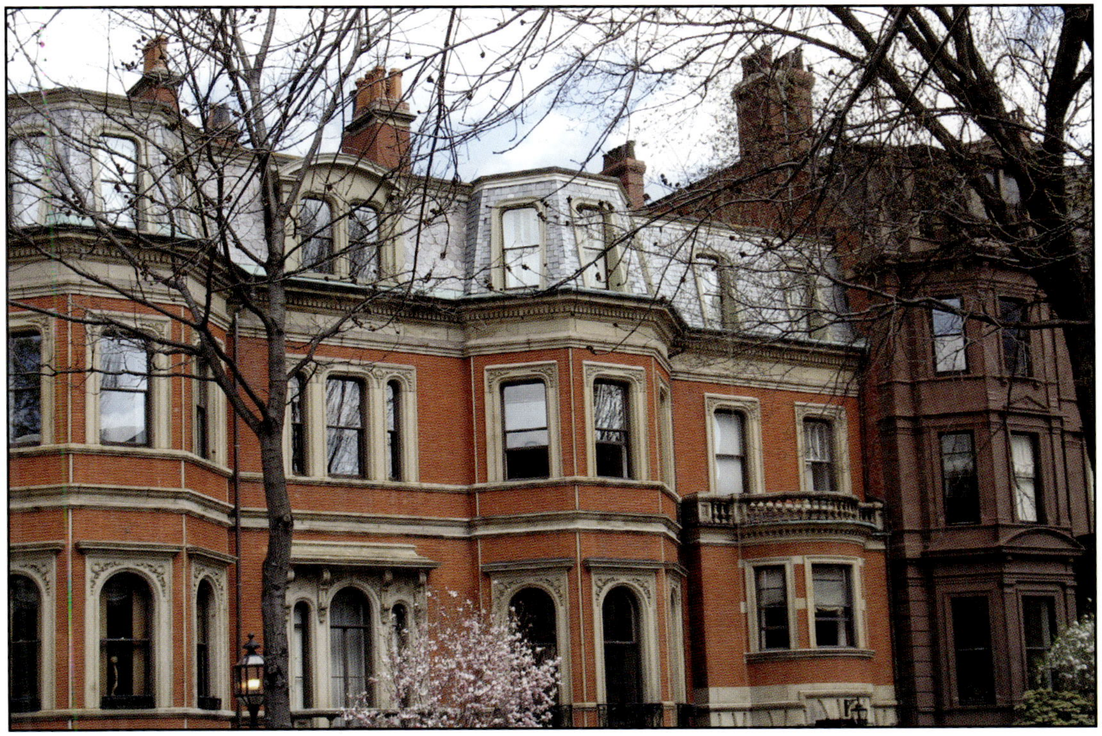

Many Back Bay buildings are red brick and brownstone Queen Anne Revival.

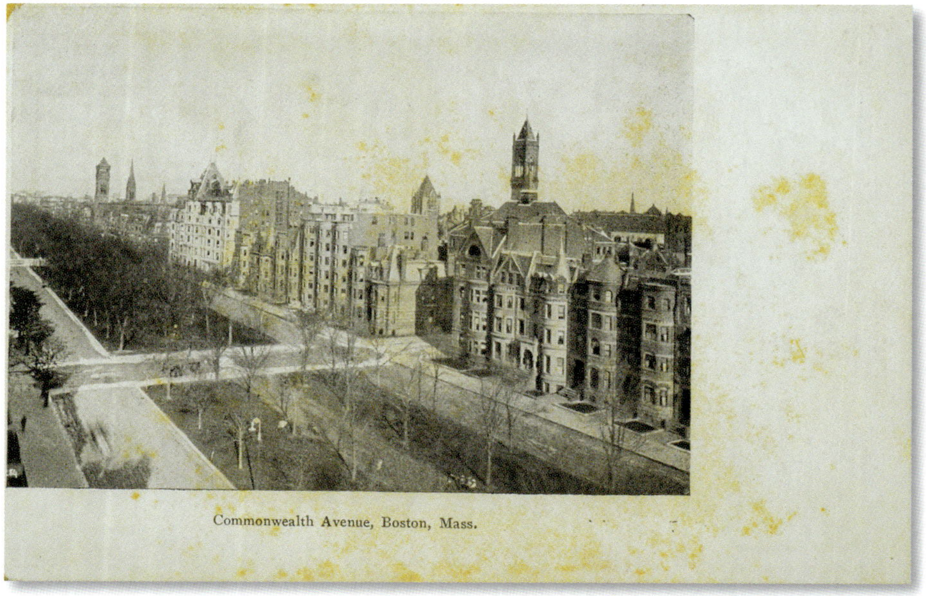

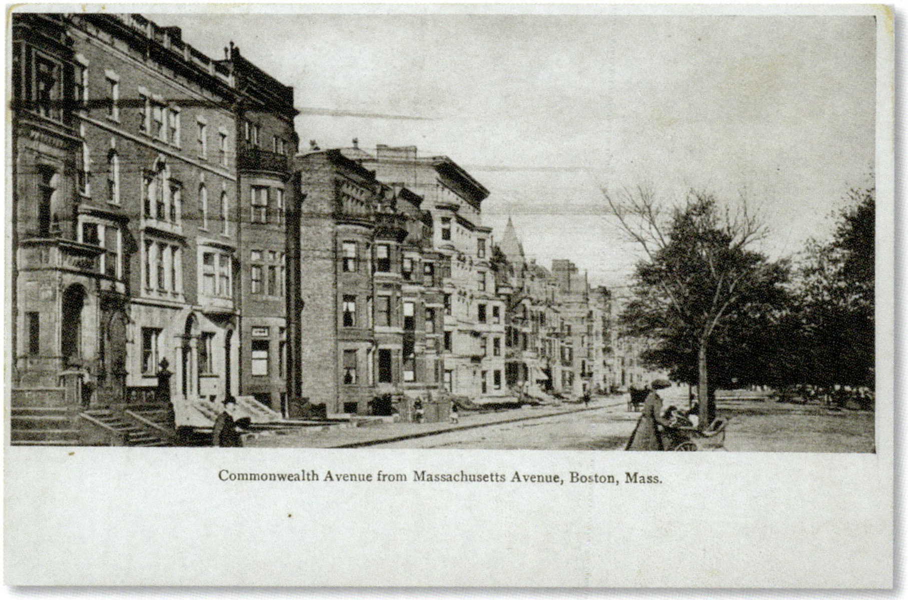

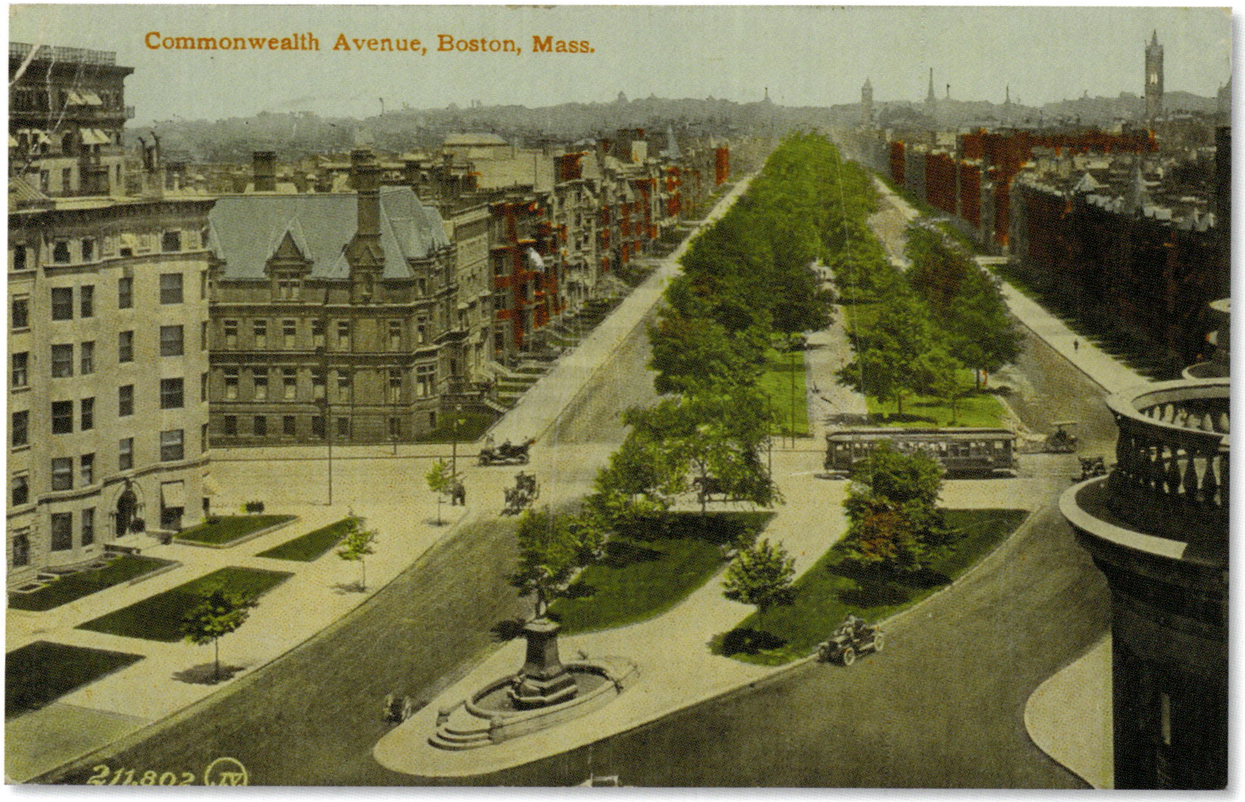

Architect Arthur Gilman modeled the 200-foot wide Commonwealth Avenue on the Champs Elysees of Paris, France, arranging statues and landscaping down the avenue's center mall from the Public Garden to the Fens.

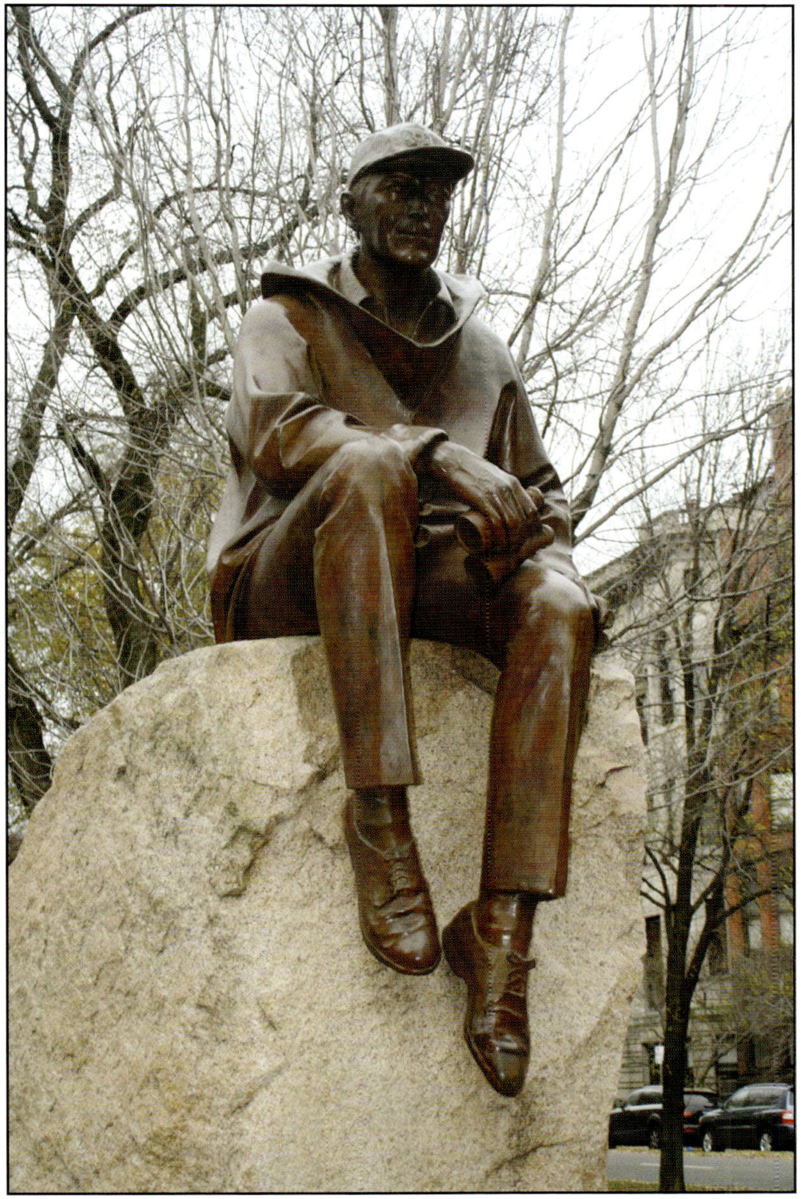

One statue is that of Rear Admiral Samuel Eliot Morison, United States Naval Reserve, a Boston-born historian, who is noted for producing authoritative works of readable maritime history. He was awarded two Pulitzer Prizes, two Bancroft Prizes, and the Presidential Medal of Freedom. This bronze statue of Morison can be found on the Commonwealth Mall between Exeter and Fairfield Streets. *Courtesy of D. Peter Lund*

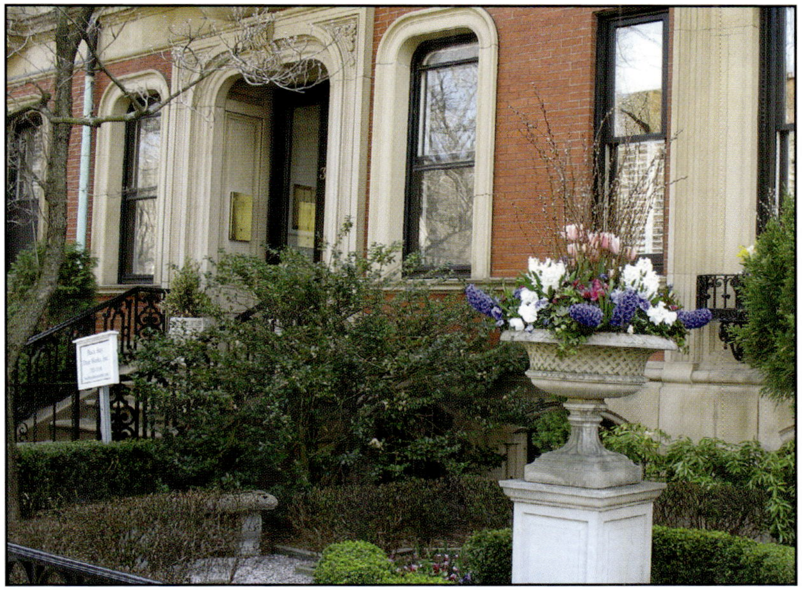

Gilman restricted all lots so that the houses were set back 20 feet from the property line. That step permits each house to have a small garden.

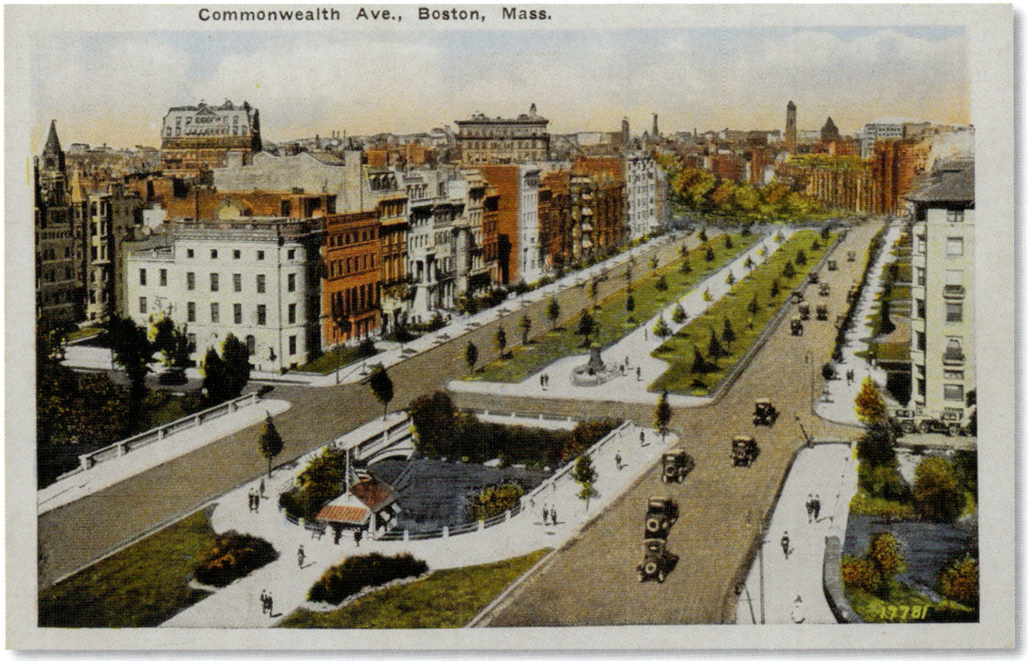

Instead of imitating the earlier Colonial style of narrow winding streets, he laid out the streets surrounding Commonwealth Avenue in a logical grid-like pattern – and named them in alphabetical order. This is one area in Boston where you can easily find your way.

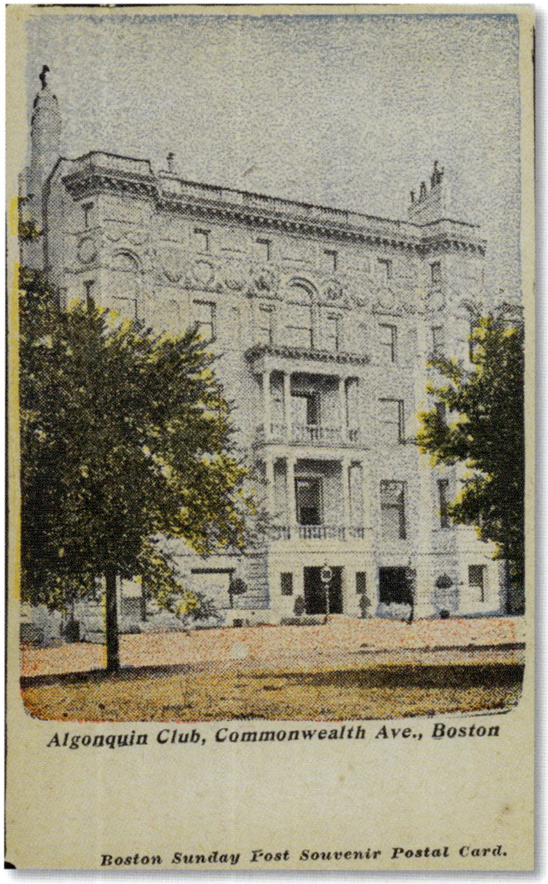

Thirty prominent Bostonians organized the Algonquin Club of Boston (217 Commonwealth Avenue) in 1885 for "good fellowship." Stanford White's design resulted in this stately Renaissance structure in 1887. One architectural note of interest is the porch superimposed on the double Ionic columns.

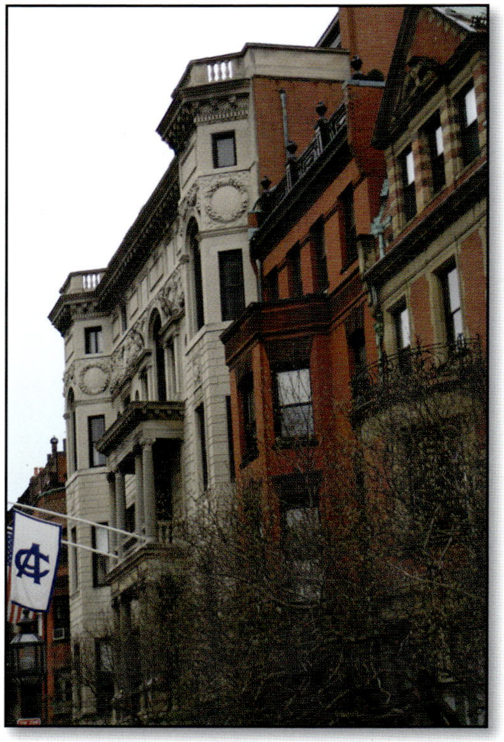

Over the years, presidents, heads of state, foreign dignitaries, and preeminent local and national leaders have enjoyed visiting the Algonquin Club.

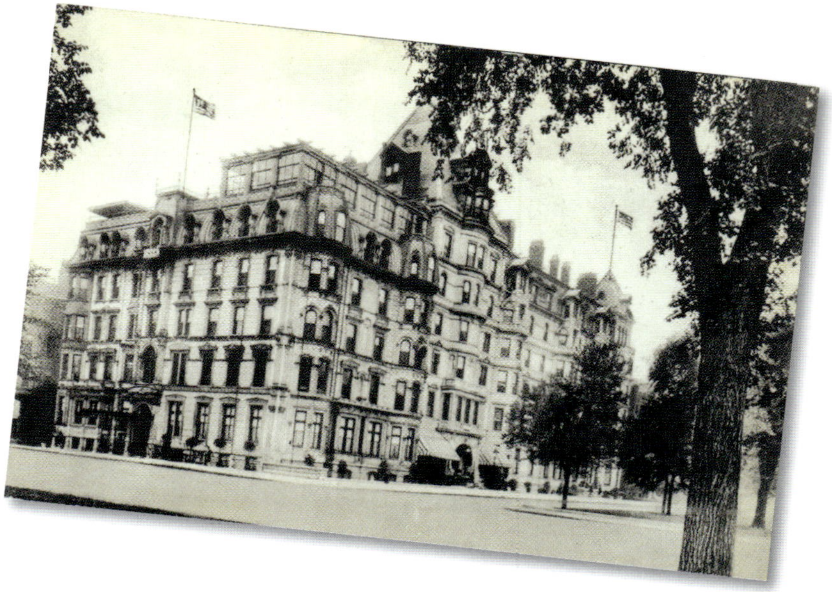

Built in 1871, the Vendome Hotel located at Dartmouth Street and Commonwealth Avenue was known for its lavish style. Presidents Harrison and Cleveland stayed there as did industrial tycoons Andrew Carnegie and John D. Rockefeller. An addition to the hotel was the site of a fatal fire, which killed nine firemen. The building still stands.

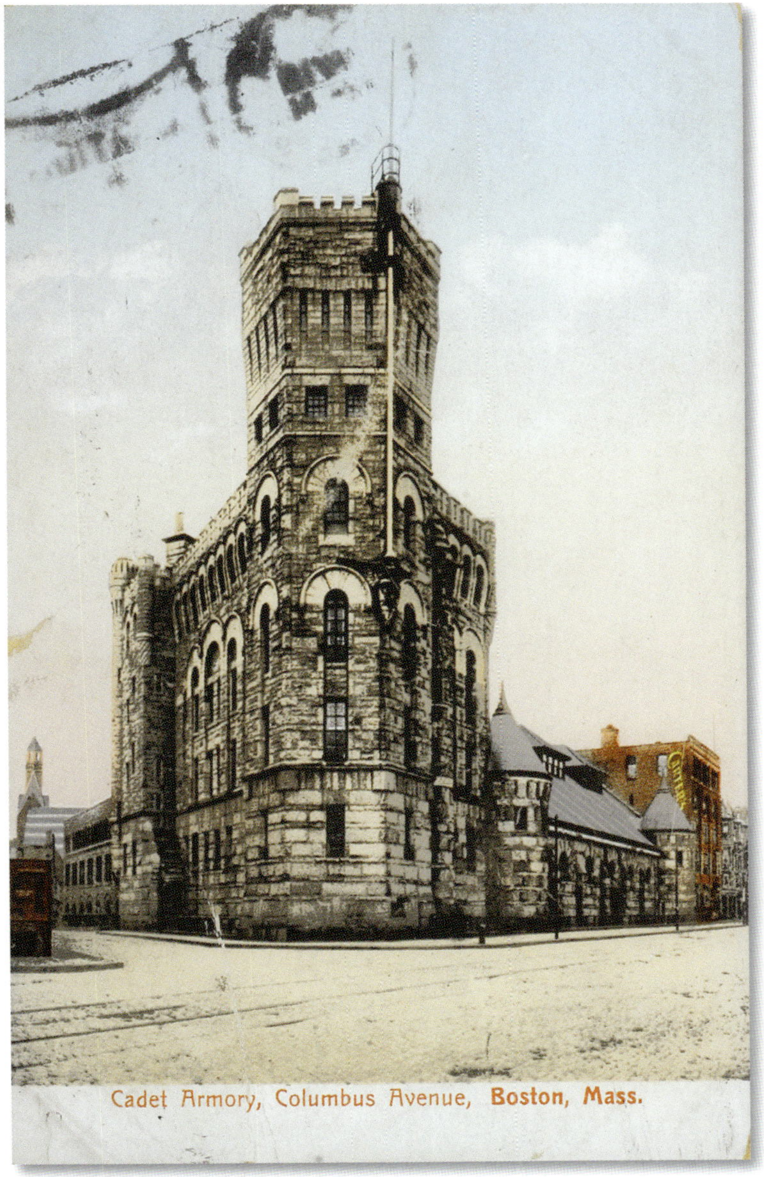

The First Corps Cadet Armory (Arlington and Columbus) was built in 1891. The First Corps of Cadets was chartered in 1741 to serve as a bodyguard to the governor. Subsequently, the cadets have helped to suppress civil disturbances. This famous Boston landmark is known for its fort-like appearance. It has battlements, turrets and a drawbridge. Today, it is an office building and exhibition hall.

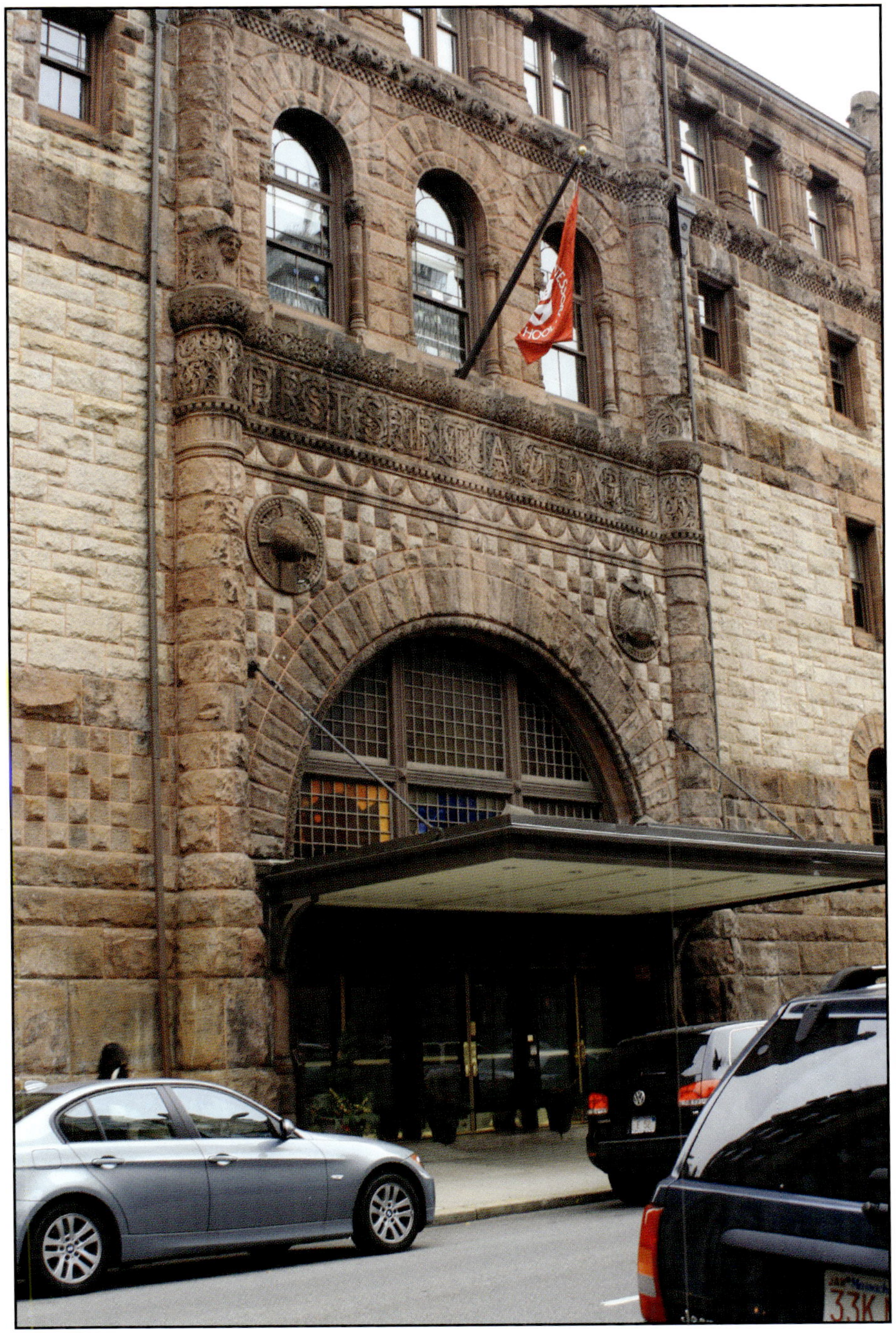

H. W. Hartwell and W. C. Richardson designed The Exeter Street Theater (26 Exeter Street) in the Romanesque Revival style. Built in 1884-1885, it was designed as the Church of the Working Union of Progressive Spiritualists, who originated in the spiritualist movement of the 1840s, but whose members also believed that spirits could materialize and speak with the aid of a human medium. It became a movie theater in 1914. Its elaborate granite and brownstone facade resembles that of Trinity Church. *Courtesy of D. Peter Lund*

Copley Square

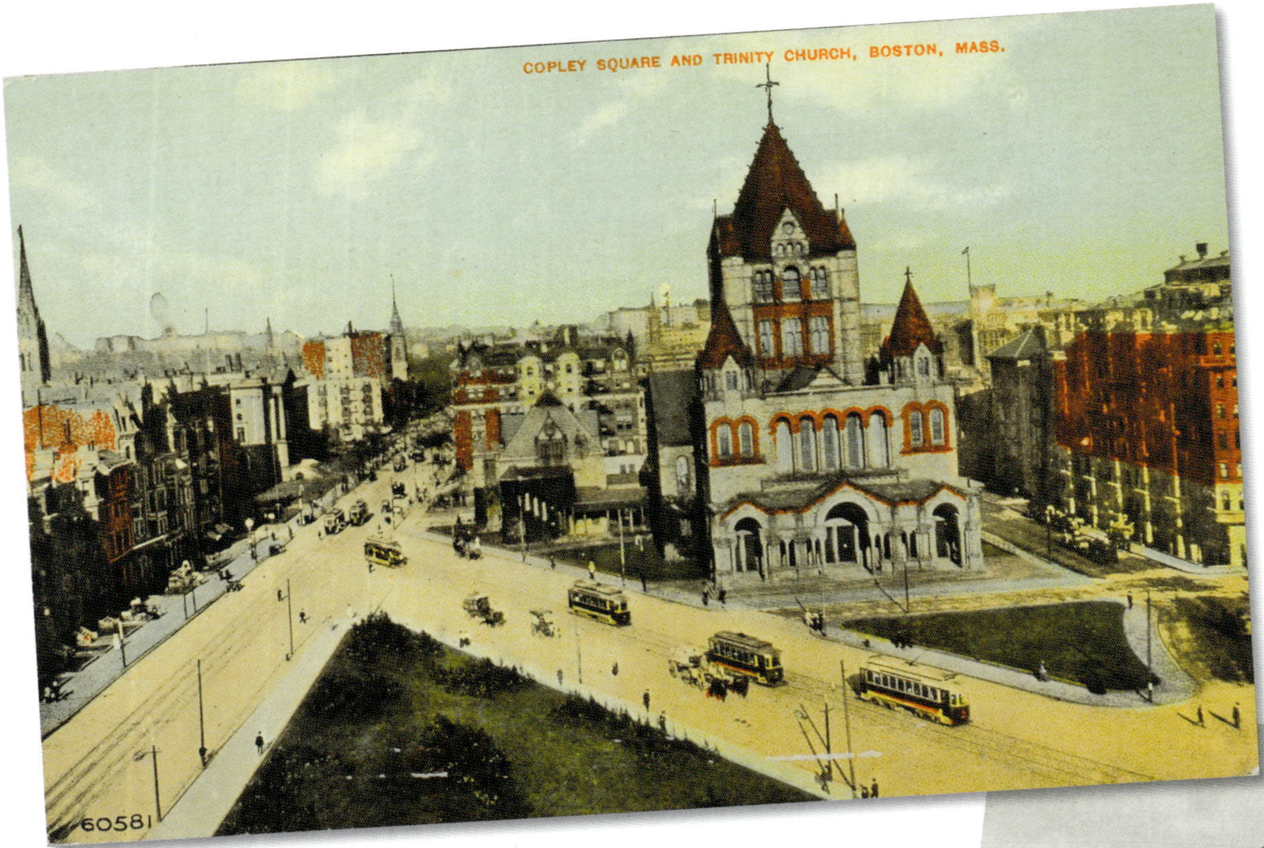

In 1870, Copley Square was developed. It was named after John Singleton Copley, a Boston painter who was born in 1737. In this image, the Public Garden is in the background, and Trinity Church is in the foreground.

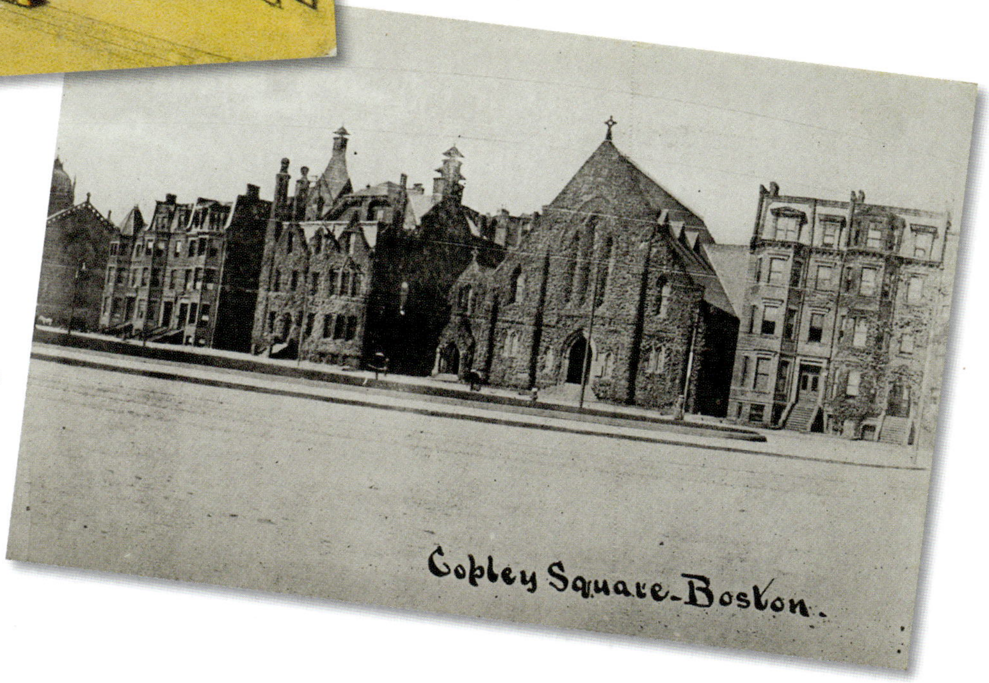

Today, Copley Square, with its brick walkways, seating, and fountain, is a wide green space in the middle of the city.

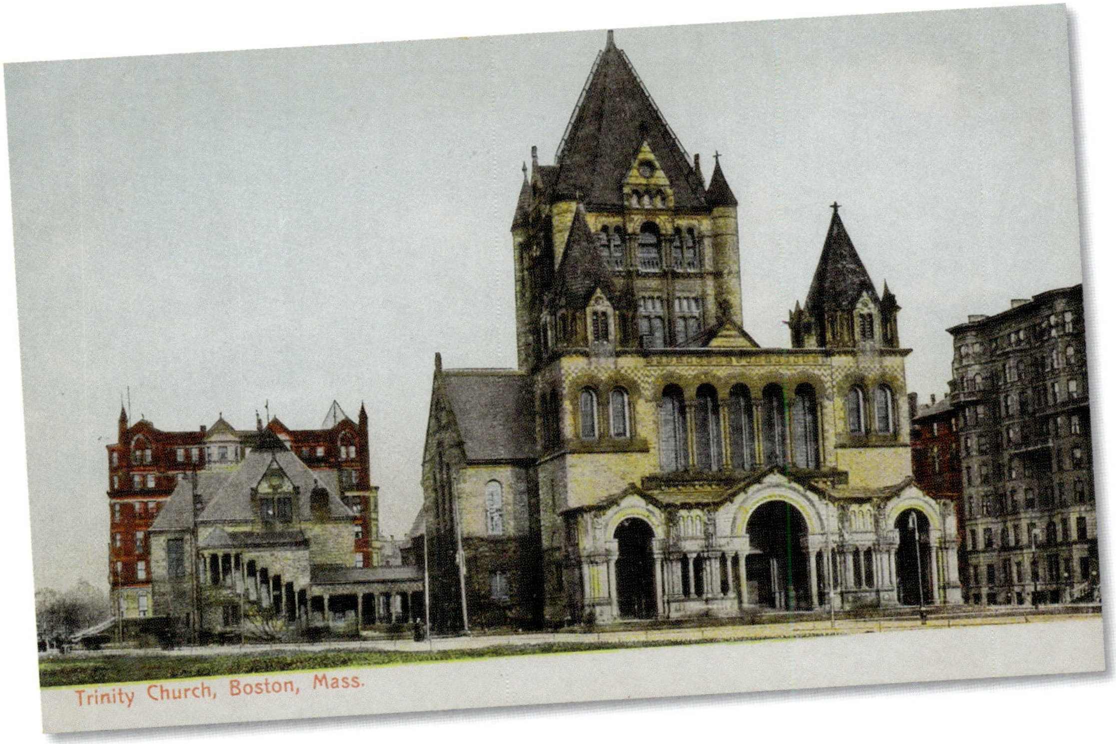

After a fire destroyed the first church structure, H.H. Richardson designed Trinity Church, which still stands today. Completed in 1877, Trinity Church was one of the most ambitious church building projects in the nation. Built of Dedham granite and brownstone, the building is in the form of a Latin cross with a large central tower rising 211 feet on four huge piers. Shepley, Rutan and Coolidge designed the west porch and its towers added in 1897. Some have nicknamed the church "The Church of the Holy Bean-blowers" because of the giant angels with gilded trumpets at each corner of the roof.

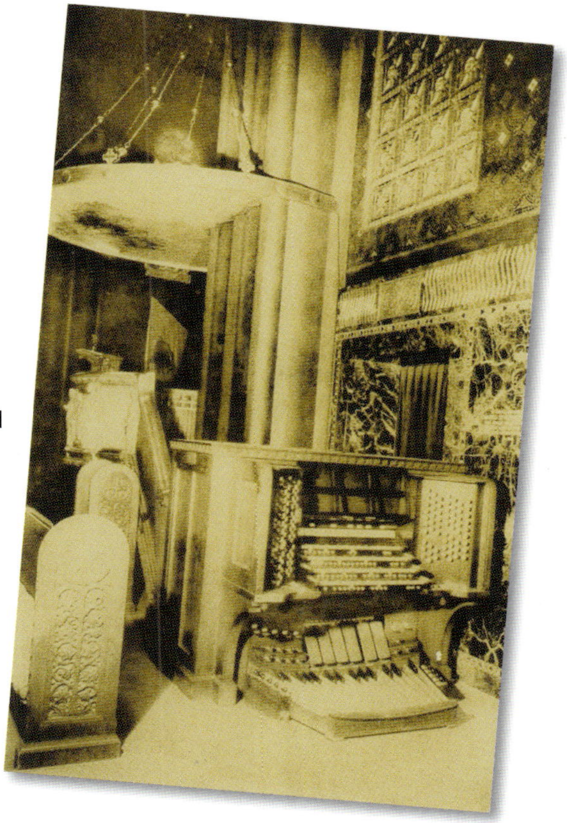

Richardson plastered and painted the interior granite walls in gold, blue-green, and sienna.

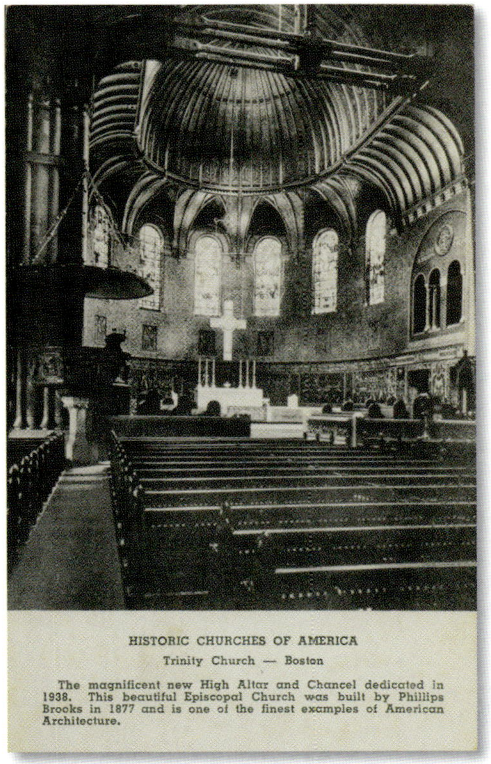

Four thousand and five hundred piles were driven into the Back Bay gravel landfill to support the weighty tower, which could not rest easily on Back Bay's swampy reclaimed land. In 2005, a massive renovation and restoration project involving repairing stones in the facade, restoring stained glass and murals, repairing some of the wood pilings due to a fluctuating water table, and lowering the basement to create additional space was undertaken. A National Historic Landmark, the church has been named one of the "Ten Most Significant Buildings in the United States" by the American Institute of Architects.

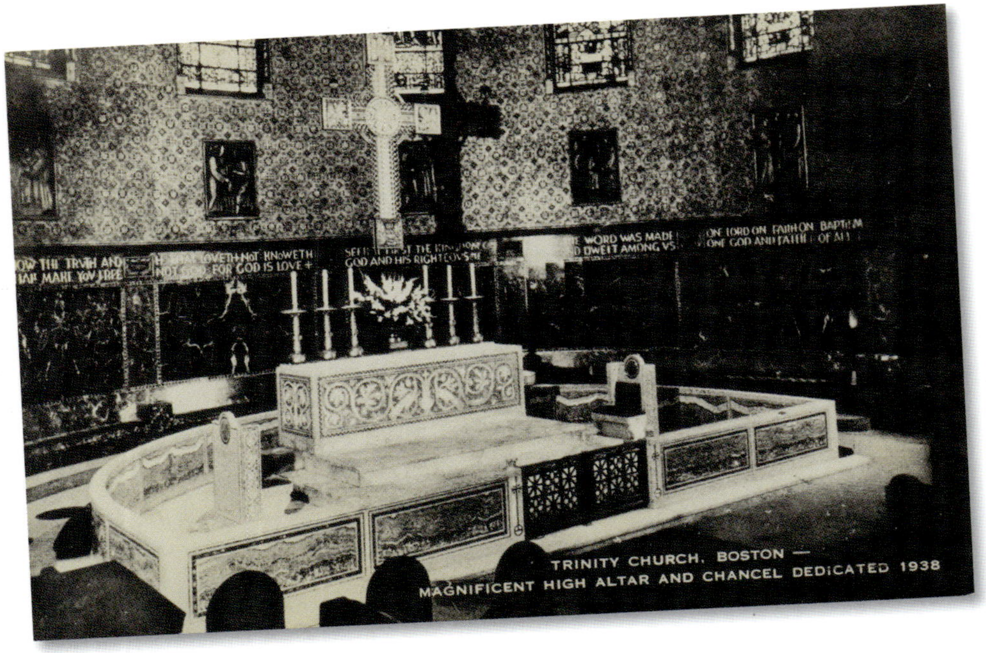

John La Farge and Augustus Saint Gaudens produced frescoes, sculpture, and stained glass for the church.

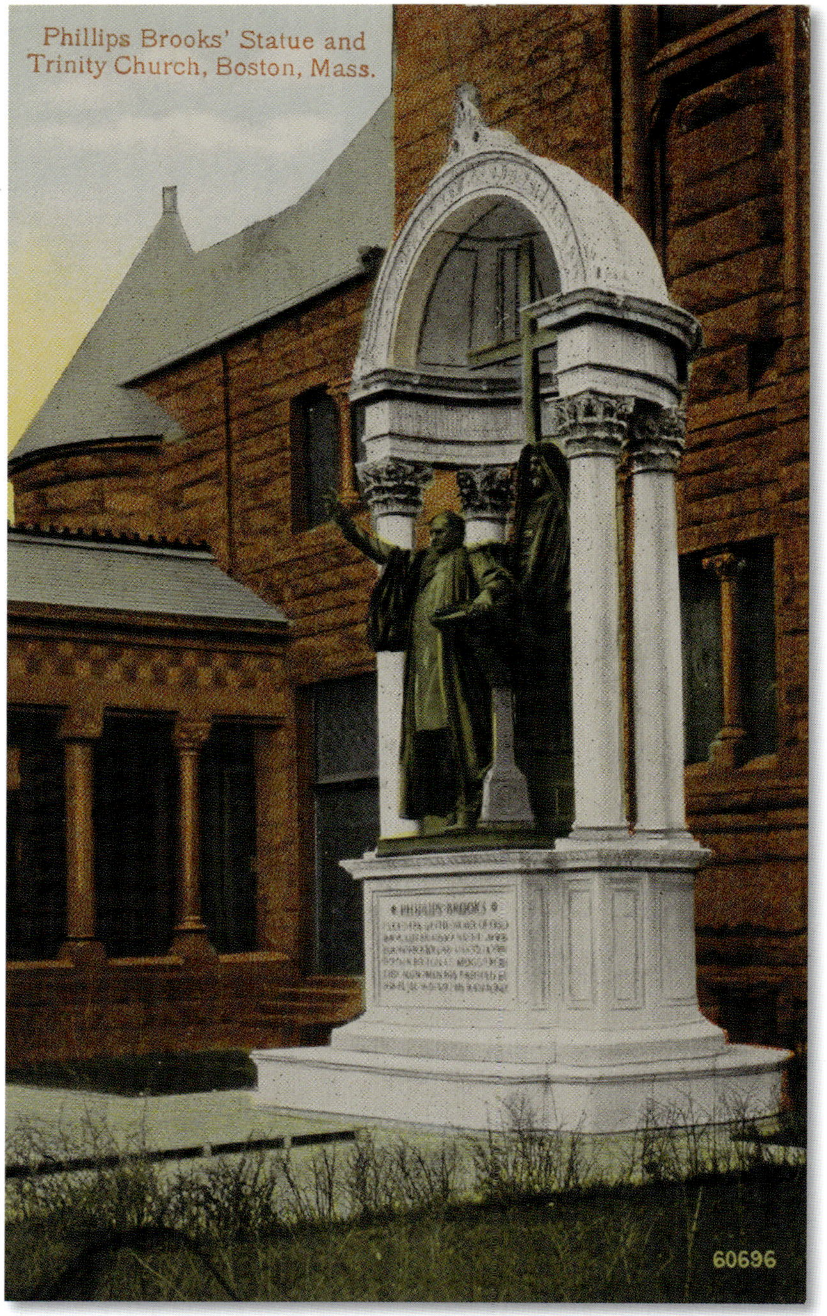

Phillips Brooks, a Harvard graduate, became American Protestantism's most respected figure in the last half of the nineteenth century. As the rector of Trinity Church in Boston, he was famous for his powerful sermons. The first American to preach in the Royal Chapel at Windsor, he was elected bishop of Massachusetts in 1891. Brooks was not known for his theological works but rather his charismatic preaching. He wrote the Christmas hymn "O Little Town of Bethlehem." In this Augustus Saint-Gaudens statue, he is shown here with Christ touching his shoulder in approval.

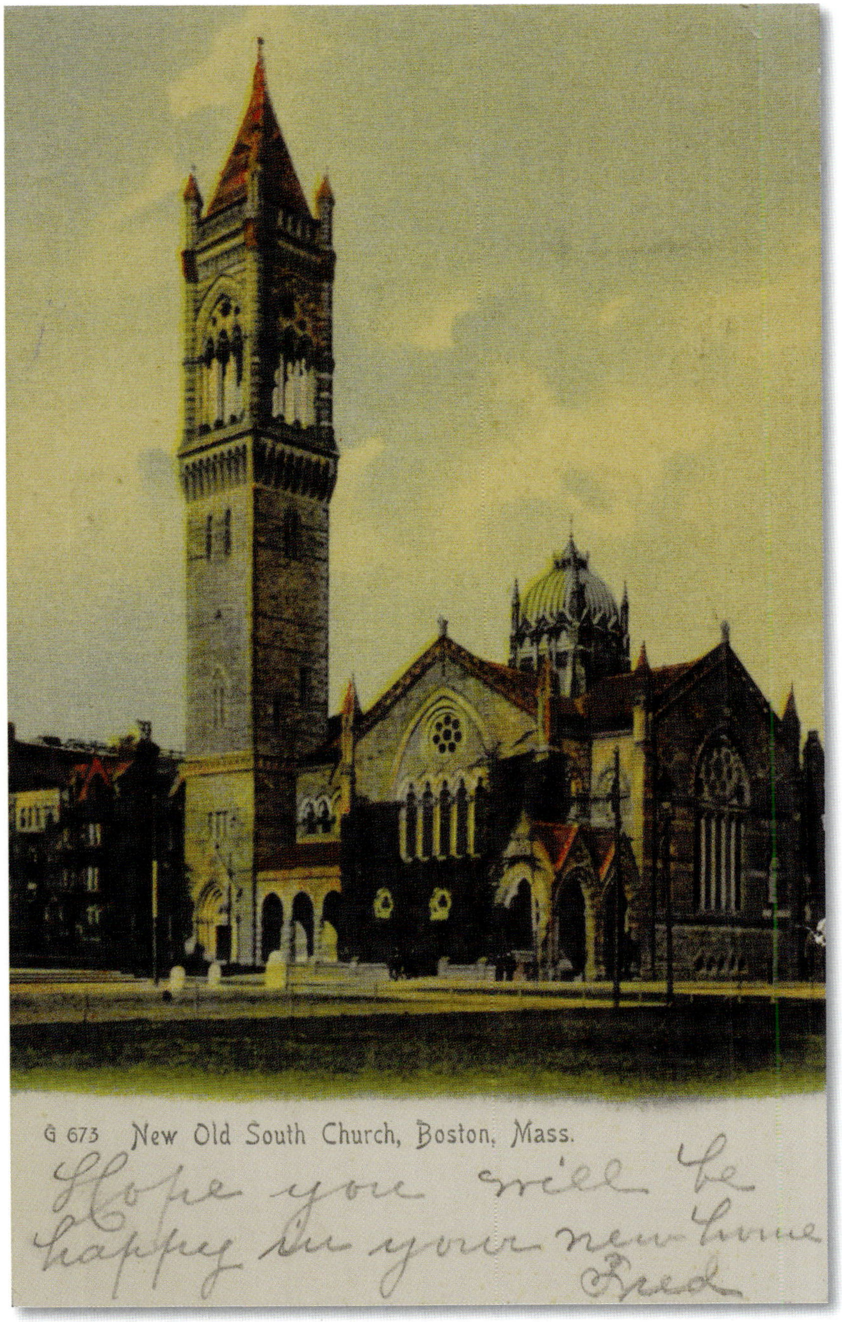

Built in 1875, the New Old South Church (645 Boylston Street) houses the former Third Congregational Church that moved from Old South Meeting House. Cummings and Sears designed the church building in a North Italian Gothic style with a 220-foot bell tower. This United Church of Christ (historically related to the Congregationalists) is home to one of the older religious communities in the United States, organized by dissenters from Boston's First Church in 1669, and from that time known as the Third Church in Boston.

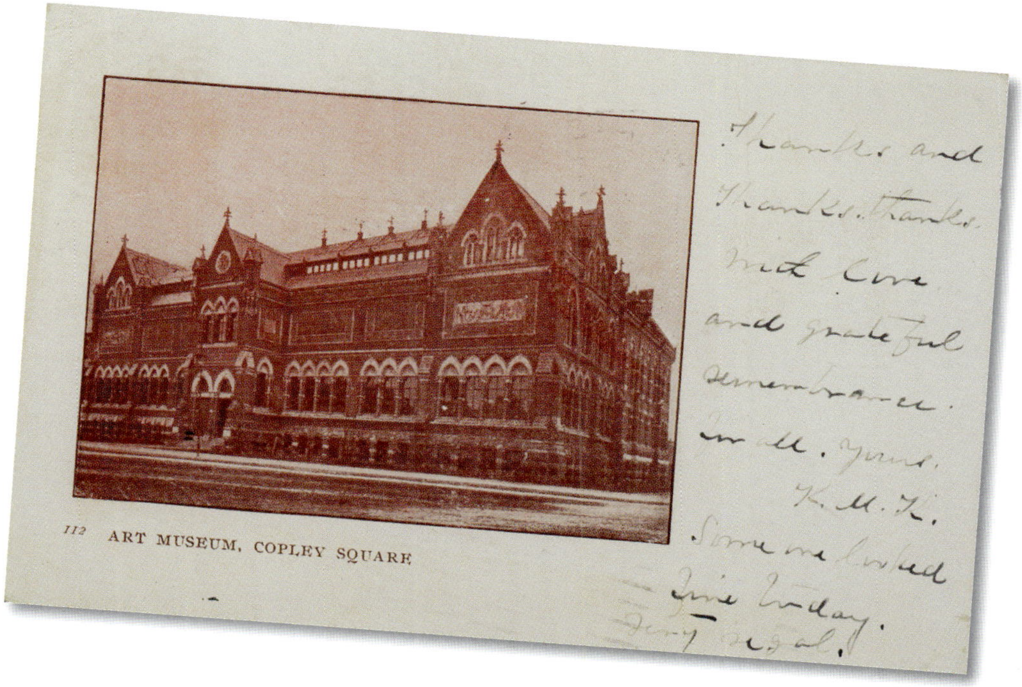

Designed by Sturgis and Brigham, the original building for the Museum of Fine Arts was erected in 1877. It was one of the first American buildings to use terra cotta for decoration on the exterior.

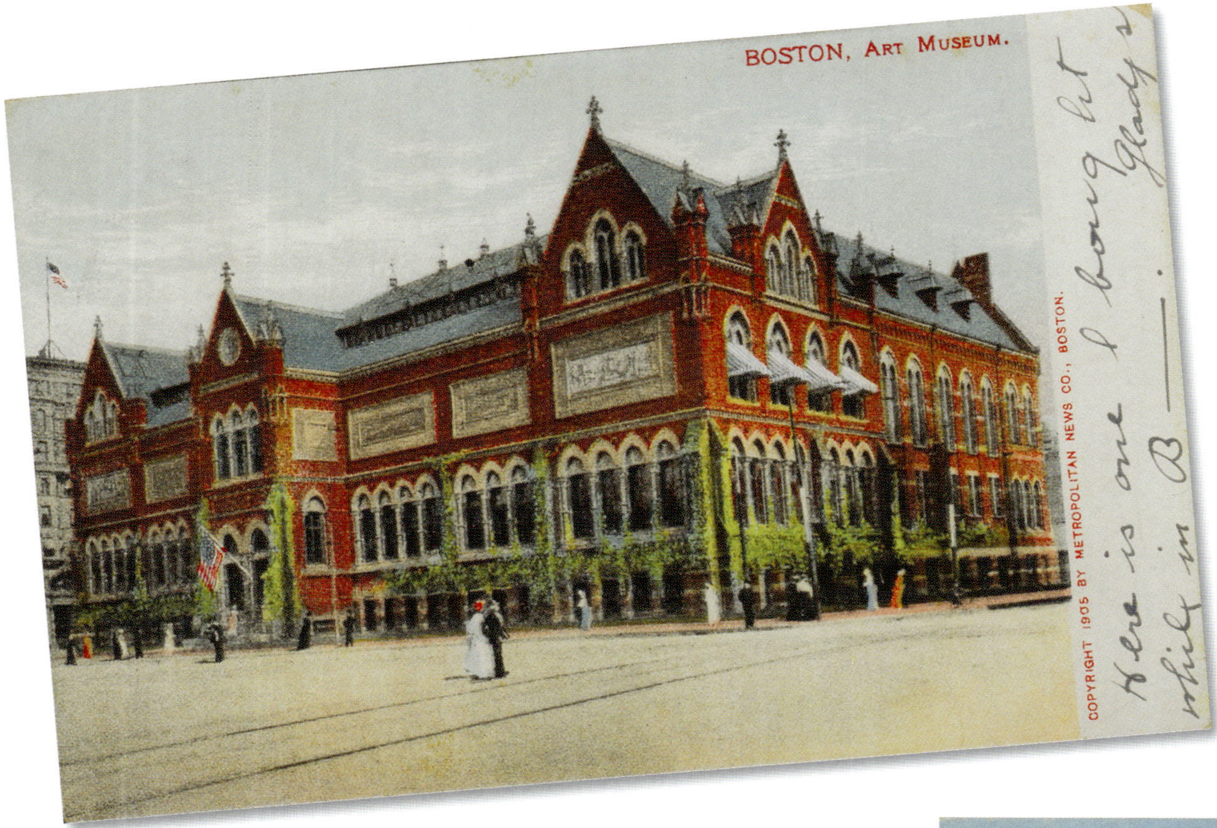

Constructed in a vibrant brick Victorian Gothic style with polished columns topped with terra cotta capitals, the building proved to be too small within thirty years. The trustees voted to move to Boston's Fenway in the beginning of the twentieth century.

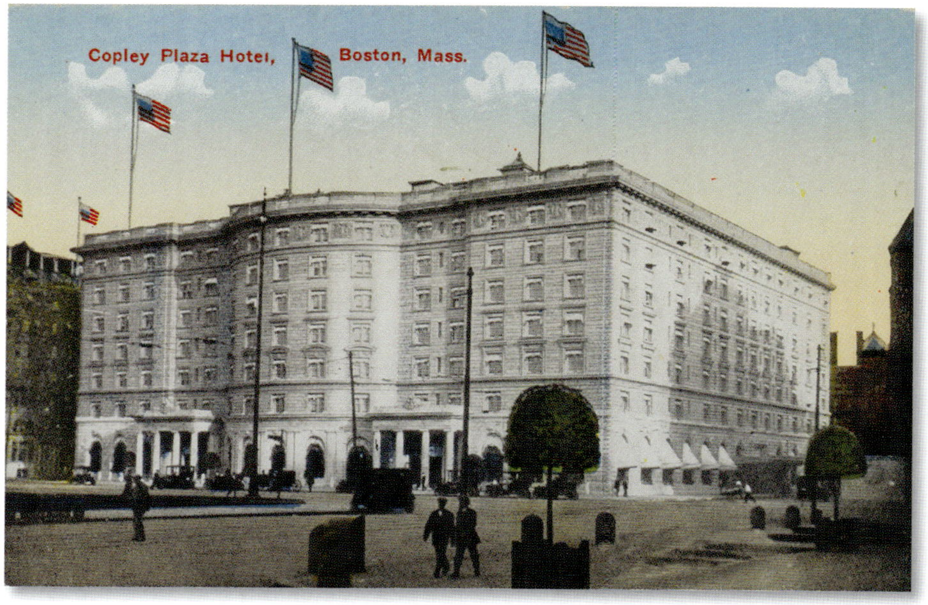

The Fairmont Copley Plaza Hotel (138 St. James Avenue), which was built on the original site of the Museum of Fine Arts in 1912, faces the square. Its architect was Henry Janeway Hardenbergh. At its opening, Mayor of Boston John F. Fitzgerald, President Kennedy's grandfather, presided over a reception of over 1,000 national dignitaries, civic leaders, captains of industry, and stage and movie stars. Rooms had been booked as early as 16 months in advance.

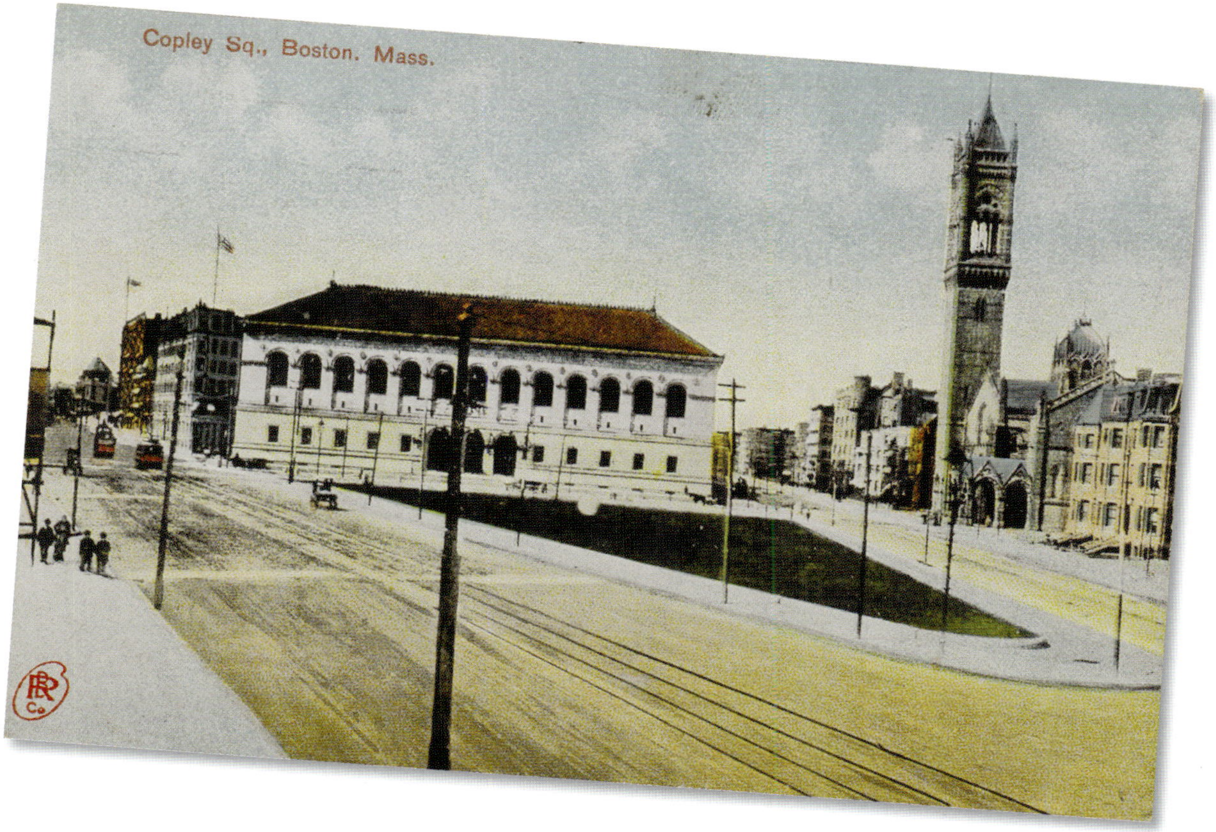

The Boston Public Library (700 Boylston Street) is one of the largest municipal public library systems in the United States. "Free to All" is inscribed above its entrance. It is the first publicly supported municipal library in the United States, the first large library open to the public in the United States, and the first public library to allow people to borrow books and other materials and take them home to read and use. All adult residents of the Commonwealth are entitled to borrowing and research privileges, and the library receives state funding. Its collections have expanded through generous gifts of books and funds.

Founded in 1848, the library quickly outgrew its space and needed a new building. Designed by McKim, Mead and White and built from 1888 to 1895, the library's design was based on Rome's Renaissance palaces. Once the library was built, Boston builders began to favor its Renaissance Revival style.

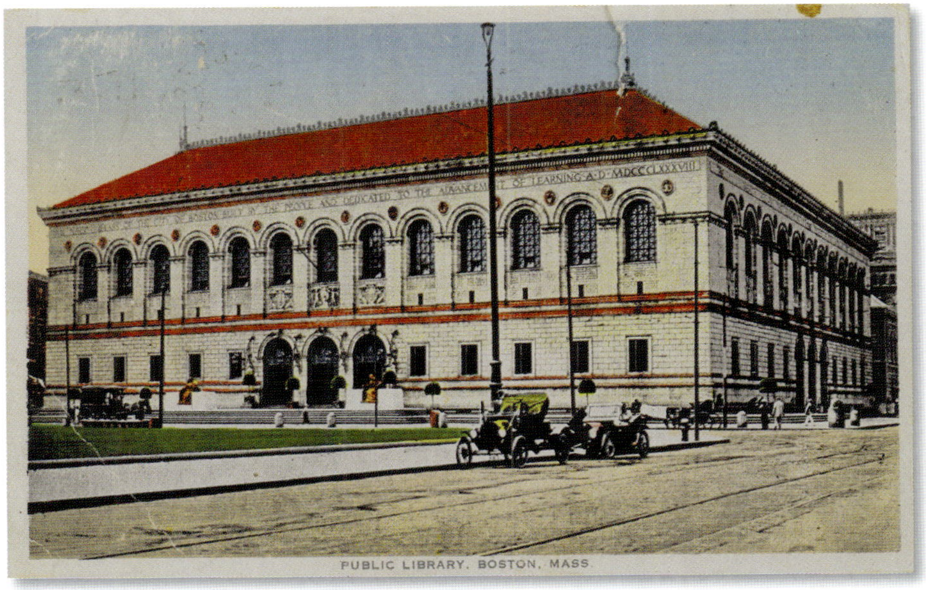

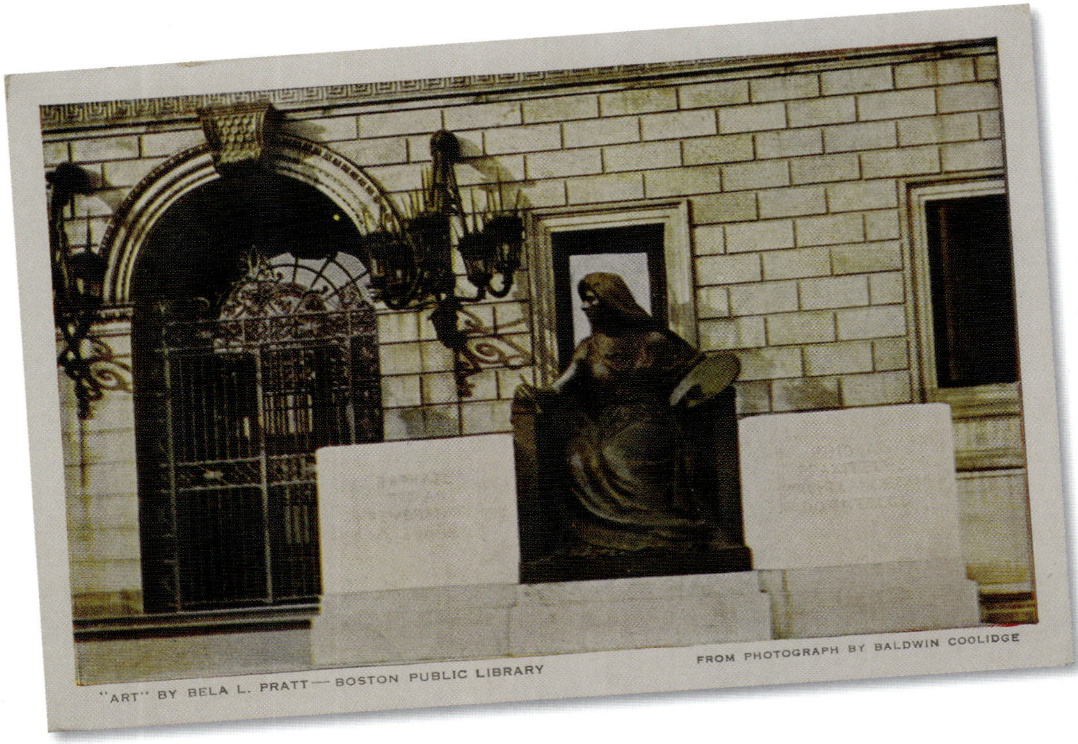

In addition to its many millions of books, the library boasts over a million rare books and manuscripts, a wealth of maps, musical scores, and prints. Because of the extent of the collections, many items are displayed on a rotating basis. The building boasts work by many famous artists. Sculptor Daniel Chester French fashioned the huge bronze doors that represent music and poetry, knowledge and wisdom, and truth and romance. French painter Puvis de Chavannes executed the murals that adorn the staircase and the second floor gallery. John Singer Sargent's murals of Judaism and Christianity decorate a third floor gallery.

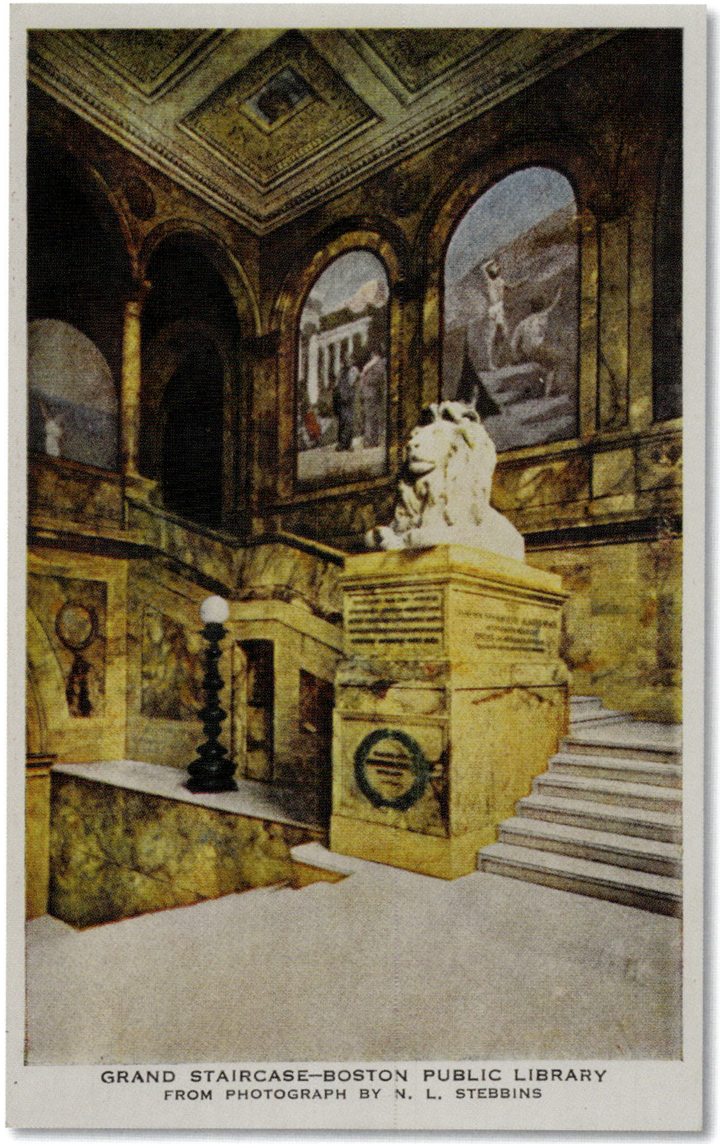

Stairway murals painted by de Chavannes adorn the grand staircase.

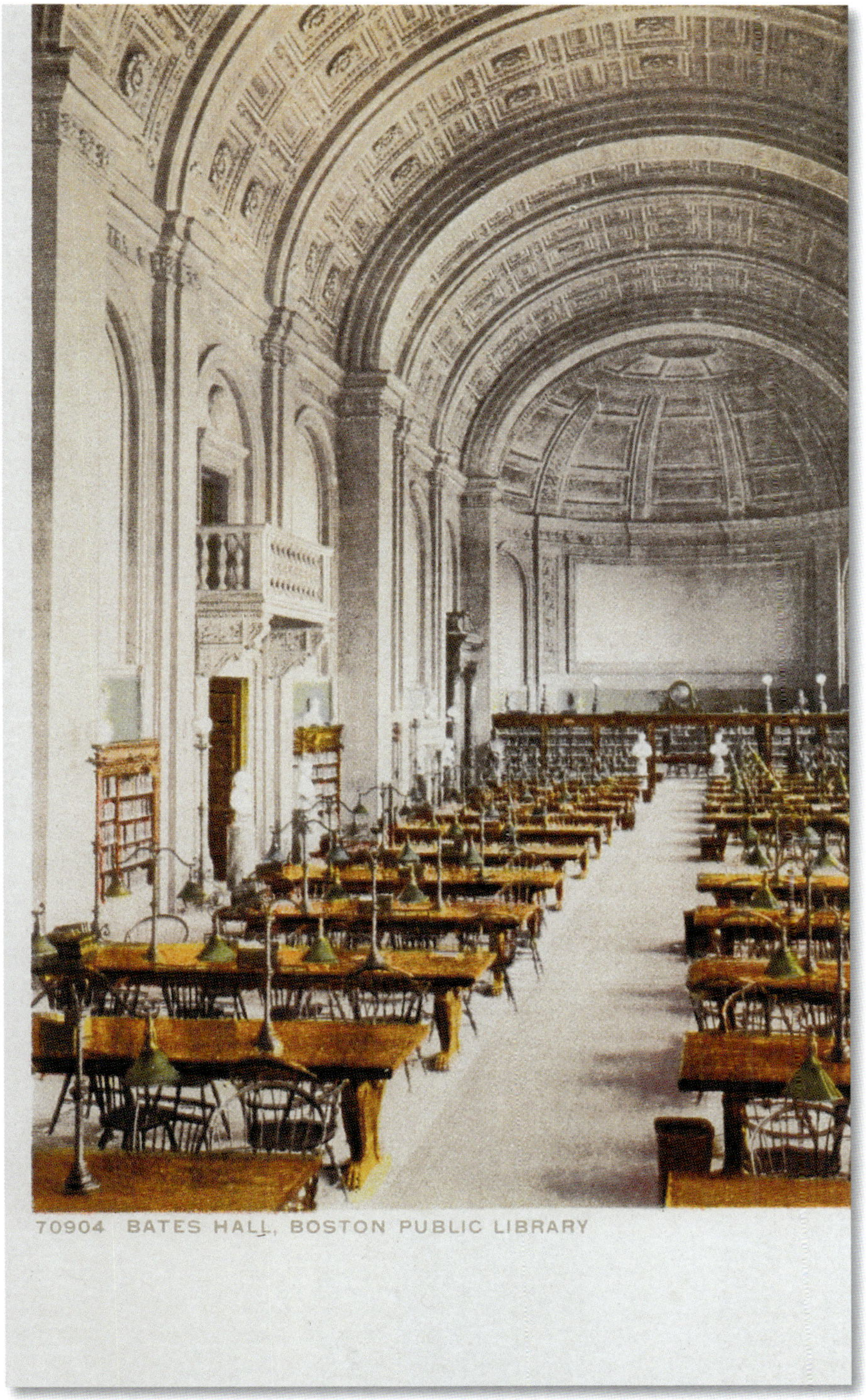

In 1852, after reading the first Annual Report published by the Trustees of the Boston Public Library, Joshua Bates donated $50,000 for the purpose of purchasing books for the new library. His one condition was that "the building shall be such as to be an ornament to the City, that there shall be a room for one hundred to one hundred and fifty persons to sit at reading tables, and that it be perfectly free to all." The Boston City Council enthusiastically accepted the offer, and the Reading Room remains one of the most historically significant spaces of this National Historic Landmark. Lit by high arched windows, it is 218 long, 42 feet wide, and 50 feet high. Its barrel-vaulted ceiling is particularly noteworthy.

The New England Mutual Life Insurance Company building was erected in 1940-1941. It is the first chartered mutual life insurance company in the United States. Its rapid expansion in the late 1980s, led to changing its name to The New England and a large office tower building being constructed in 1988.

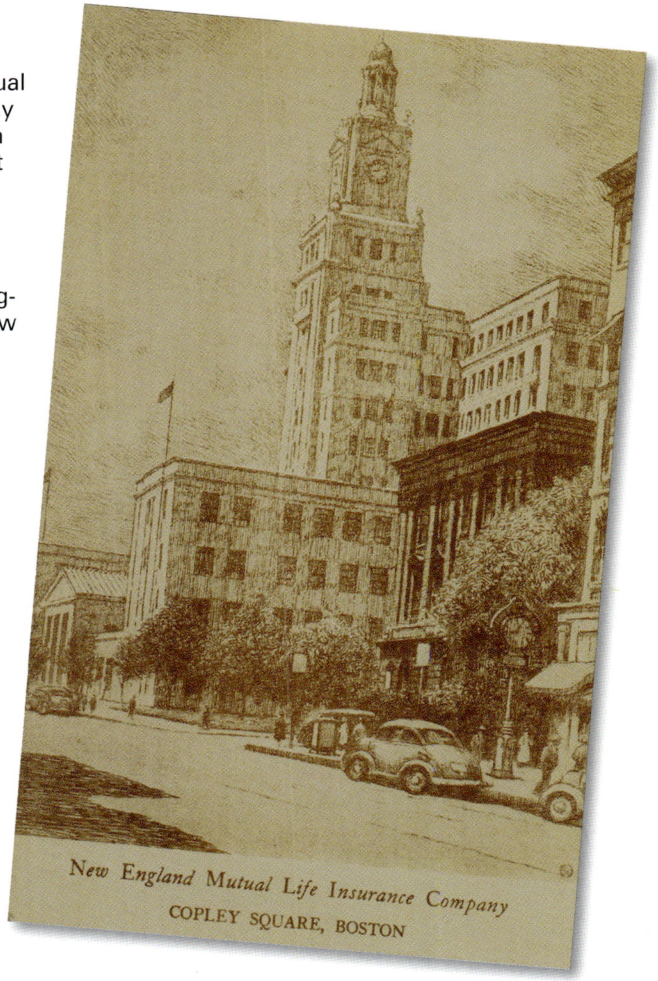

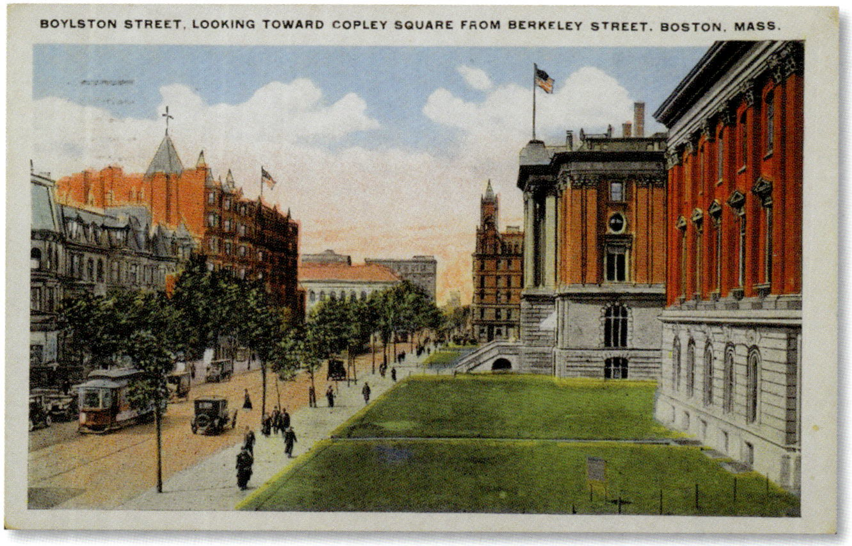

Boylston Street looking towards Copley Square. The library is in the distance on the left.

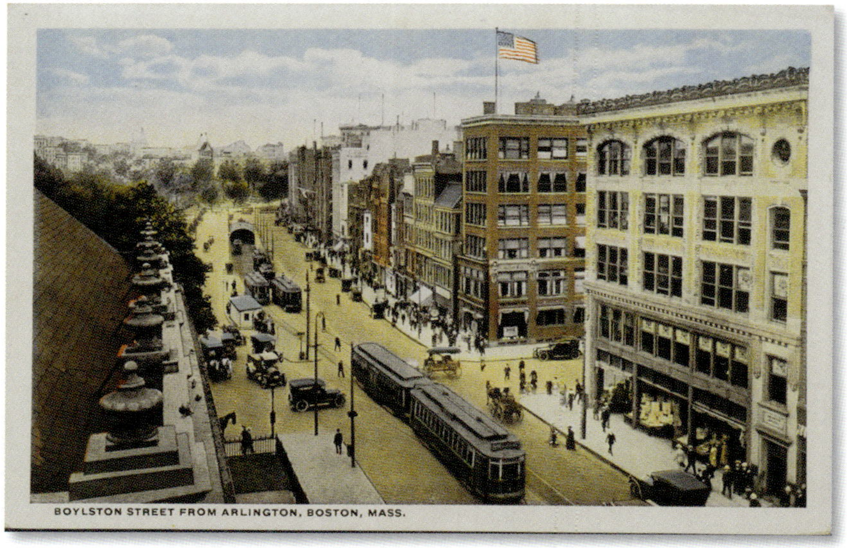

Boylston Street from Arlington Street.

Built in a French Academy style, The Museum of Natural History (234 Berkeley Street) was designed by William Gibbons Preston and built in 1863. The large freestanding building has elaborate Corinthian pilasters and carved animal heads on the keystones. Later, the building housed upscale clothiers. When the Natural History Museum moved to its new building, its name changed to The Museum of Science.

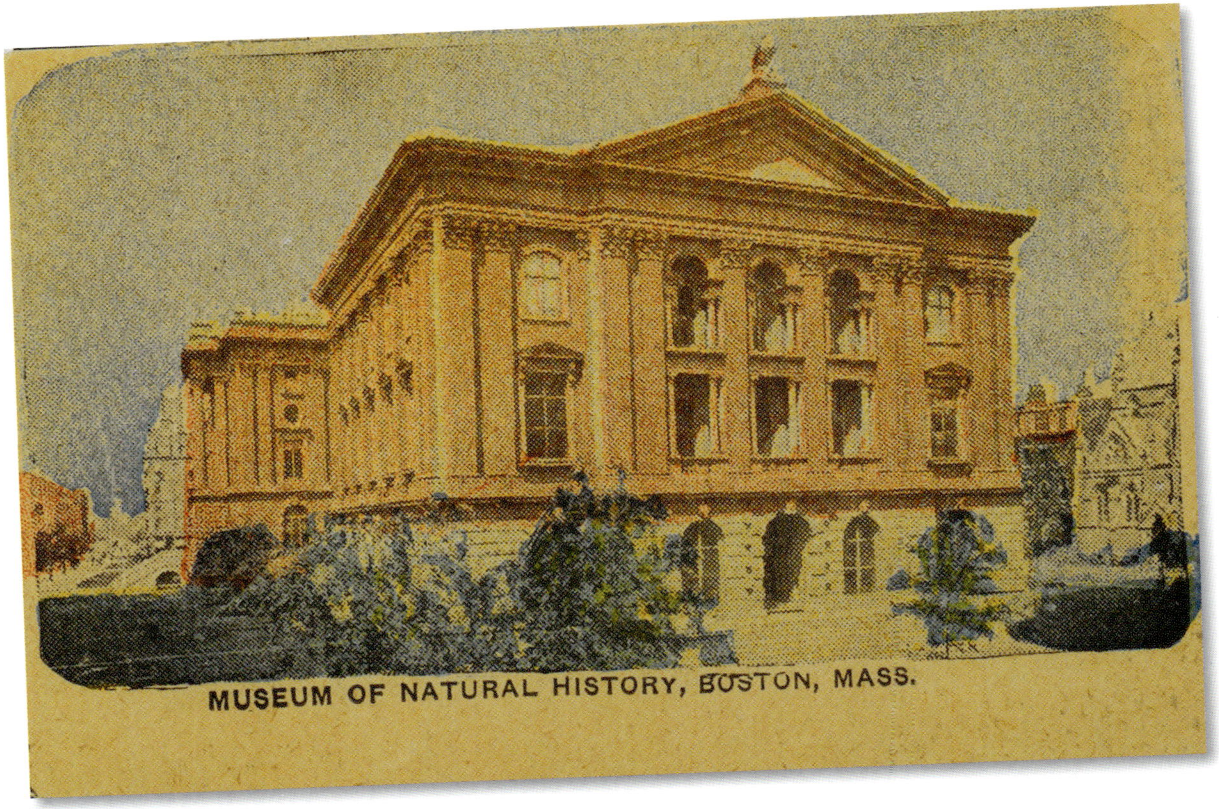

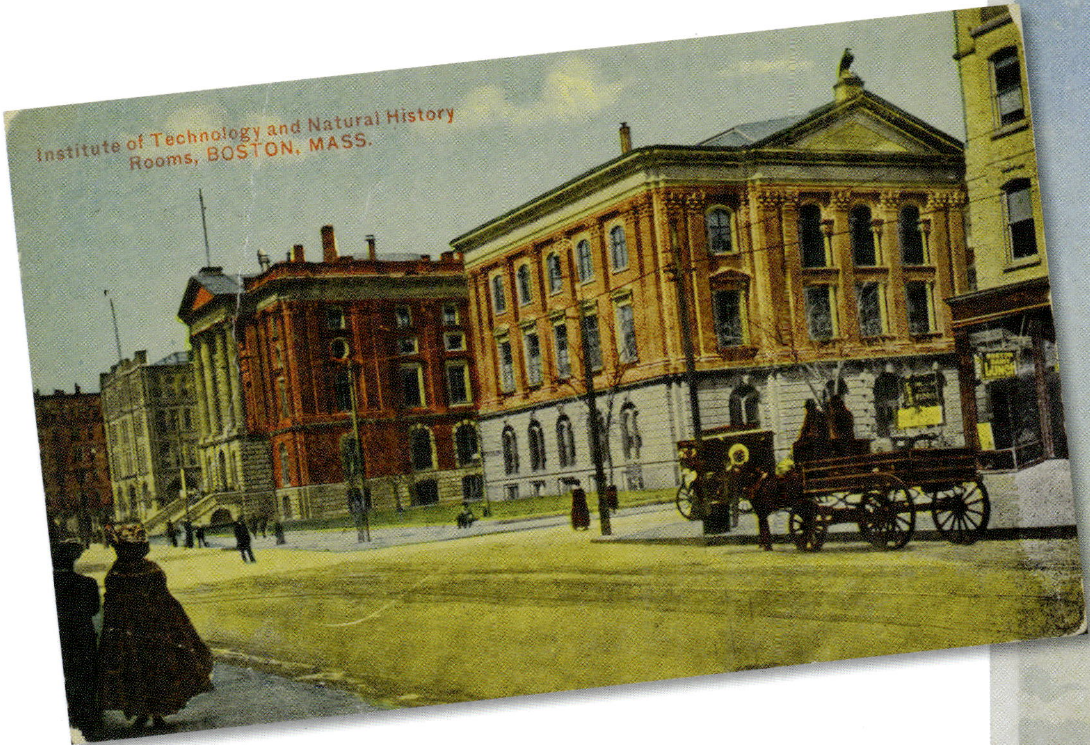

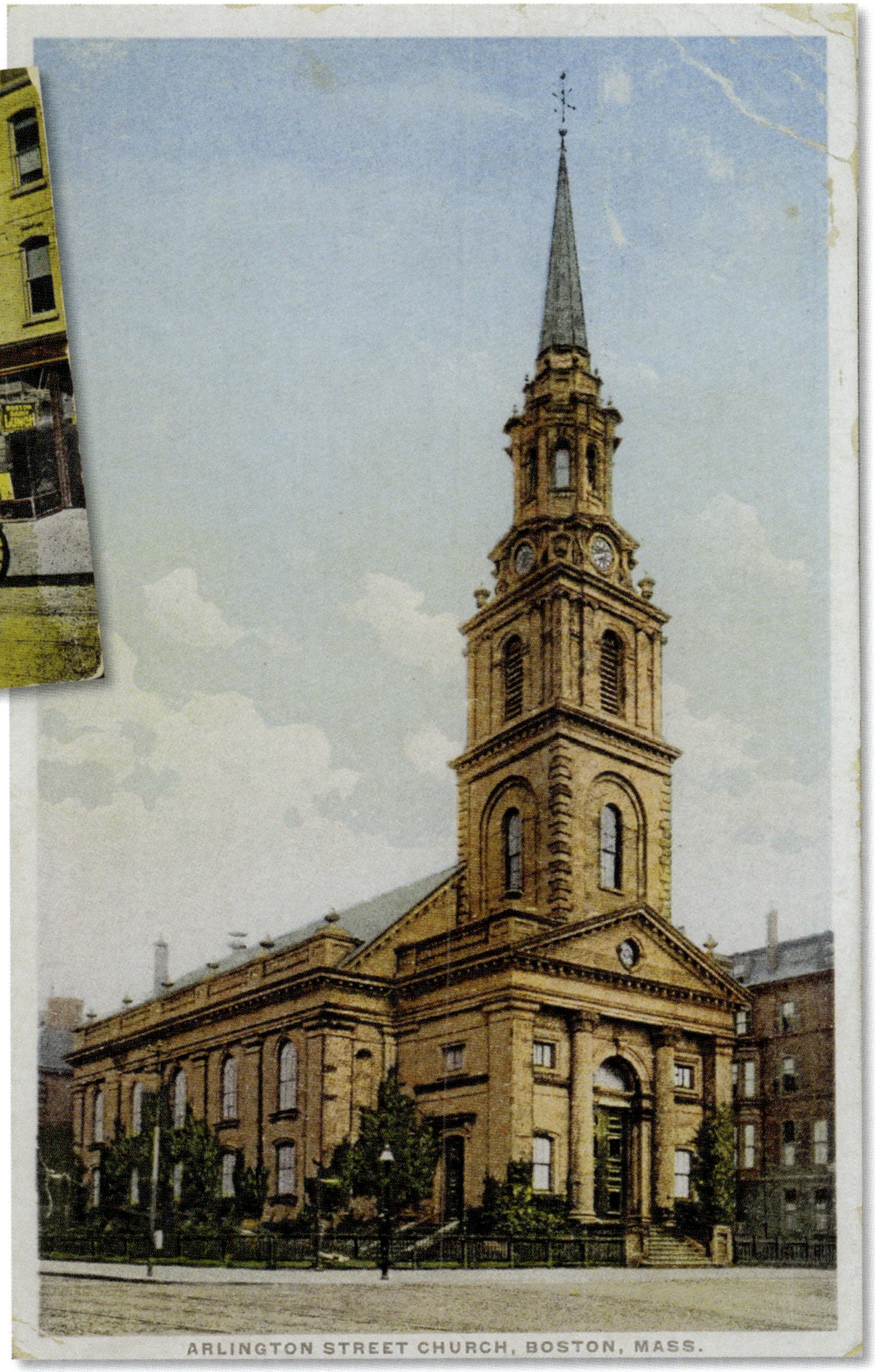

Its companion is the 1866 Rogers Building on Boylston Street. William Barton Rogers, a natural scientist and first president, founded MIT, a precedent-setting educational institution intended to meet the technical challenges of the United States as it became increasingly industrialized. Two days before the bombardment of Ft. Sumter in 1861, the Commonwealth of Massachusetts approved a charter for the incorporation of the "Massachusetts Institute of Technology and Boston Society of Natural History." The institute's first students were admitted in 1865.

The Arlington Street Church (351 Boylston Street) integrates Georgian and Italian styles. Designed by Arthur Gilman, its balanced rows of high Corinthian pillars rising to a barrel-vaulted ceiling in the sanctuary are noteworthy; the Tiffany stained glass memorial windows were given from 1895-1930. The church is famous for its pastor, William Ellery Channing, who founded the American Unitarian Association and its offering of sanctuary to oppressed individuals and groups.

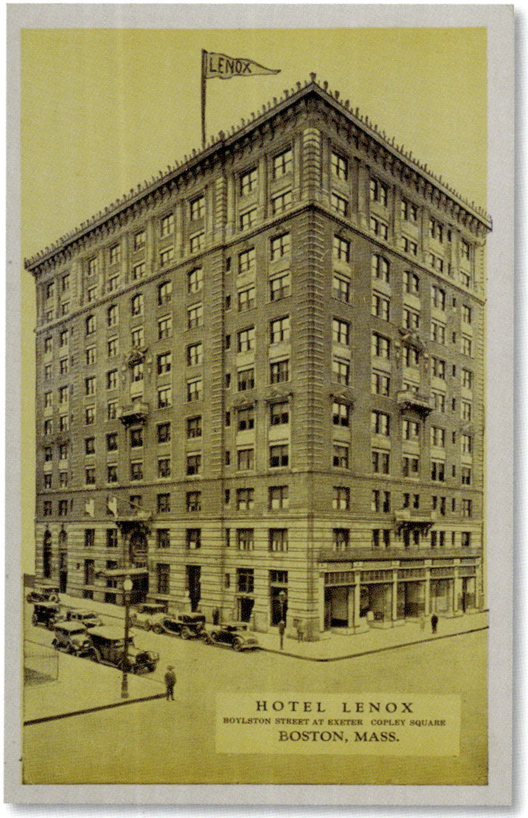

Hotel Lenox (710 Boylston Street) is a small hotel with working fireplaces in its corner rooms.

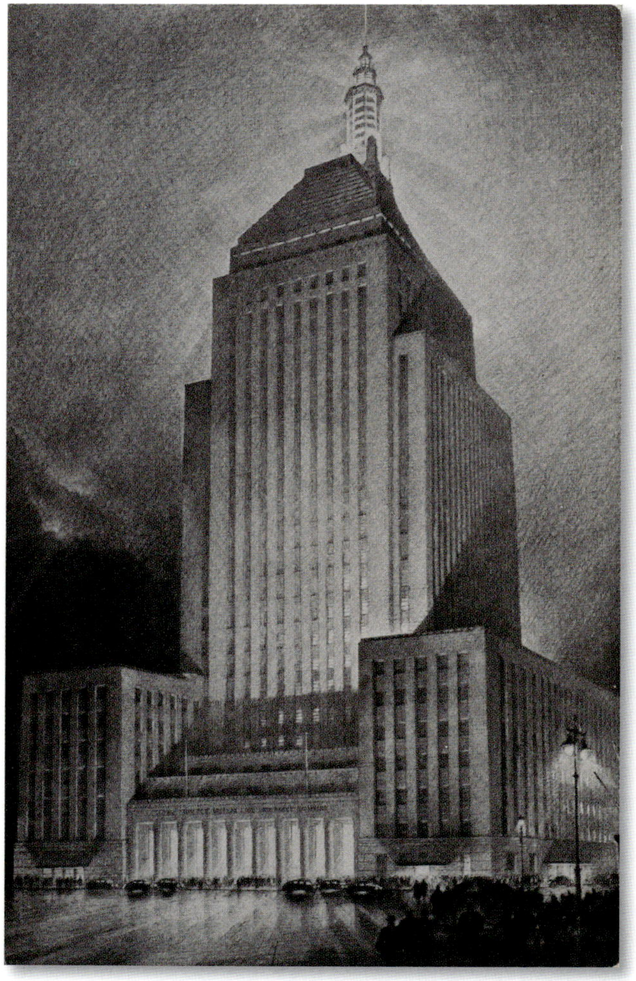

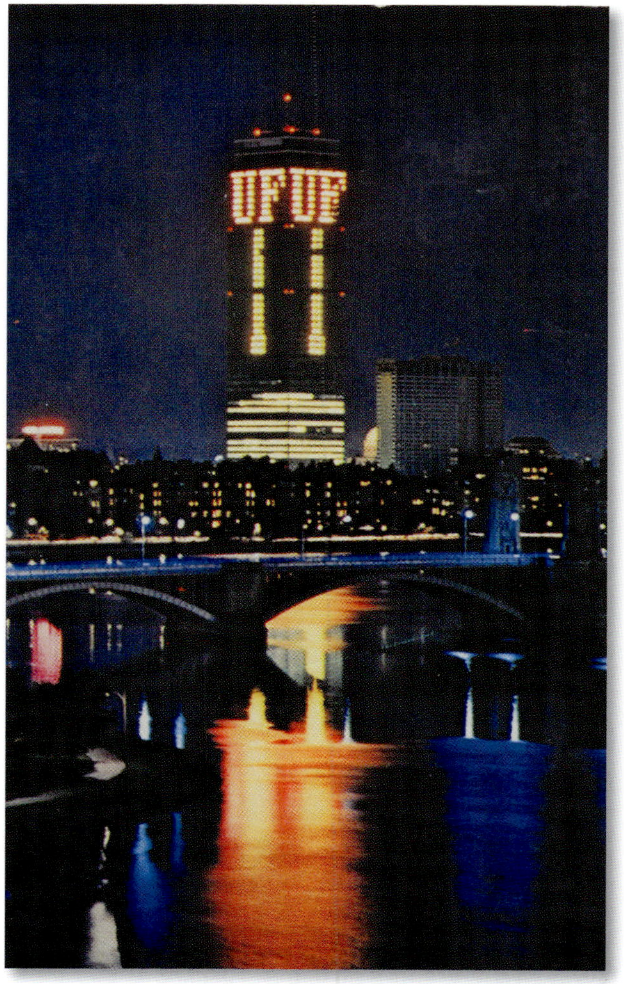

When it was erected in 1965, the Prudential Tower (800 Boylston Street) was the tallest skyscraper in Boston, rising 52 floors. Now, John Hancock Tower is higher. Today, interior walkways link the building with the Hynes Convention Center and the Sheraton Back Bay Hotel, and the upscale Copley Place shopping mall. At its base are offices and a shopping center. Known as The Pru, its lights are often used to spell out slogans such as "go Sox" or UF for United Fund.

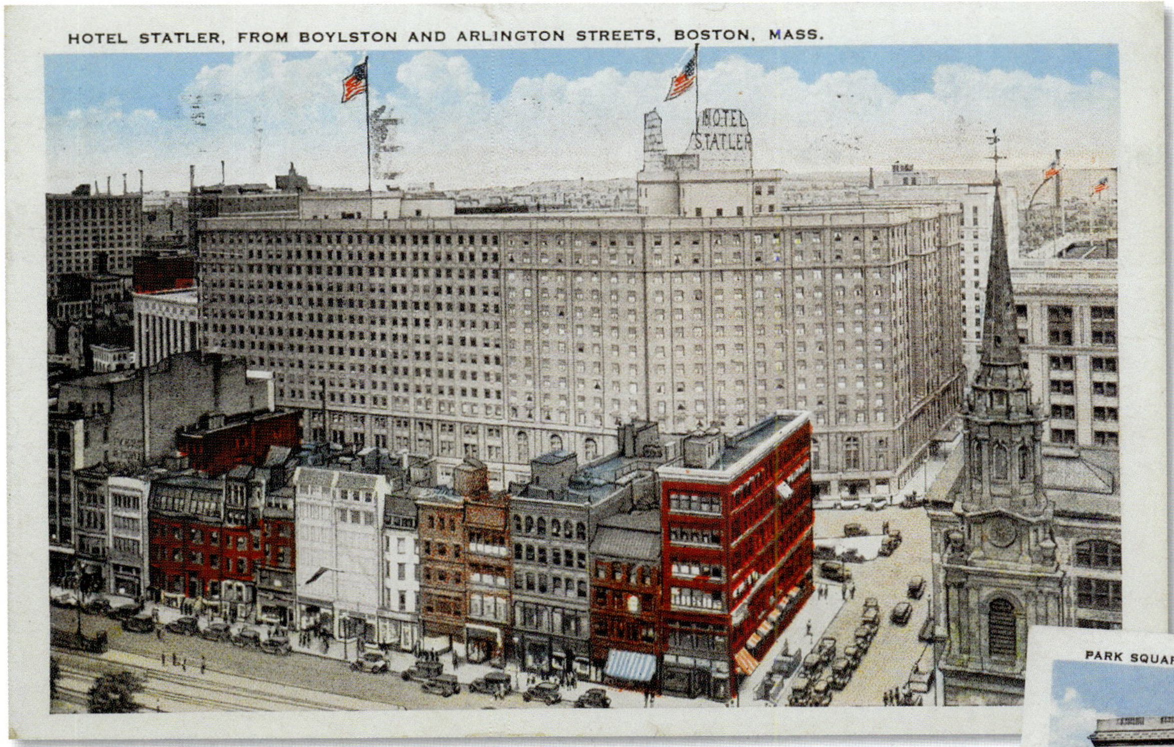

Park Square is sited approximately on the spot where the thin strip of land called the Neck by the colonials joined the pear-shaped peninsula. In the colonial period, the Neck was often awash at high tide. When the South Bay flats and marshes were made into land, it became the Victorian South End. Founded by Ellsworth Milton Statler, the Statler Hotel chain was one of the United States' early chains of hotels catering to traveling businessmen and tourists. This Boston hotel was built in 1927.

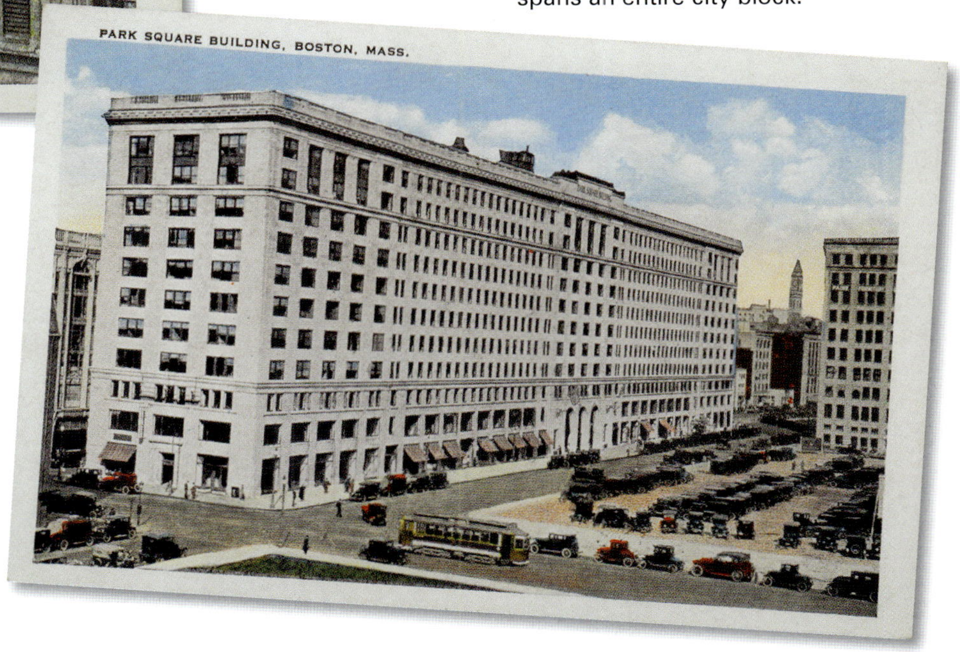

Built in the early 1920s, the landmark Park Square Building spans an entire city block.

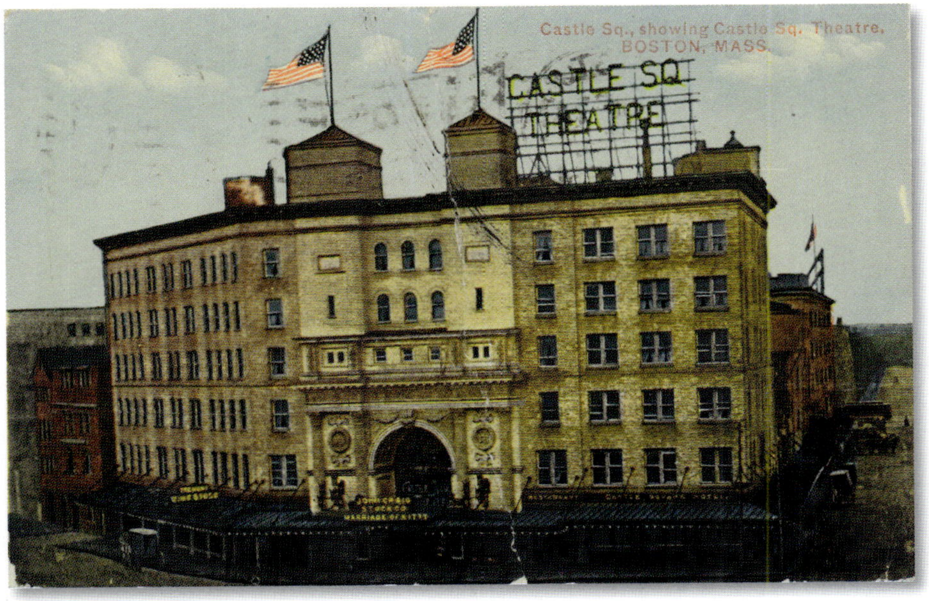

The now demolished Castle Square Theater in Boston's South End was the relatively small but grand home of opera and touring plays.

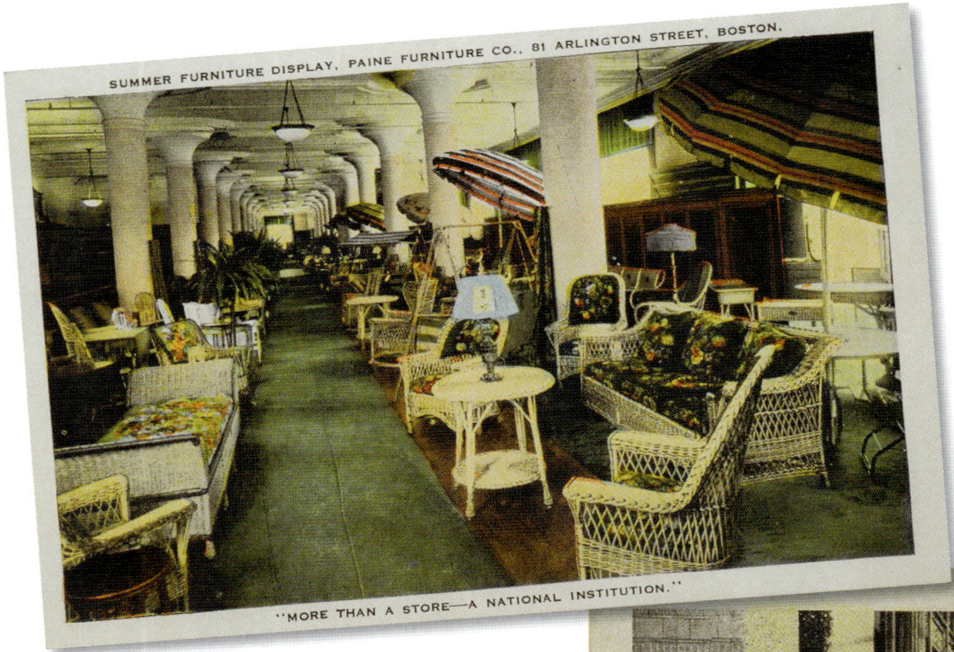

Paine Furniture Company in Park Square. In 1835, Leonard Shearer, a young cabinetmaker, founded the company. Later, he found an apprentice John S. Paine; their siblings joined them; and by 1872, they built the first block-size Paine store on Canal Street. In 1914, the store moved to a stunning new ten-story showroom and manufactory in Park Square.

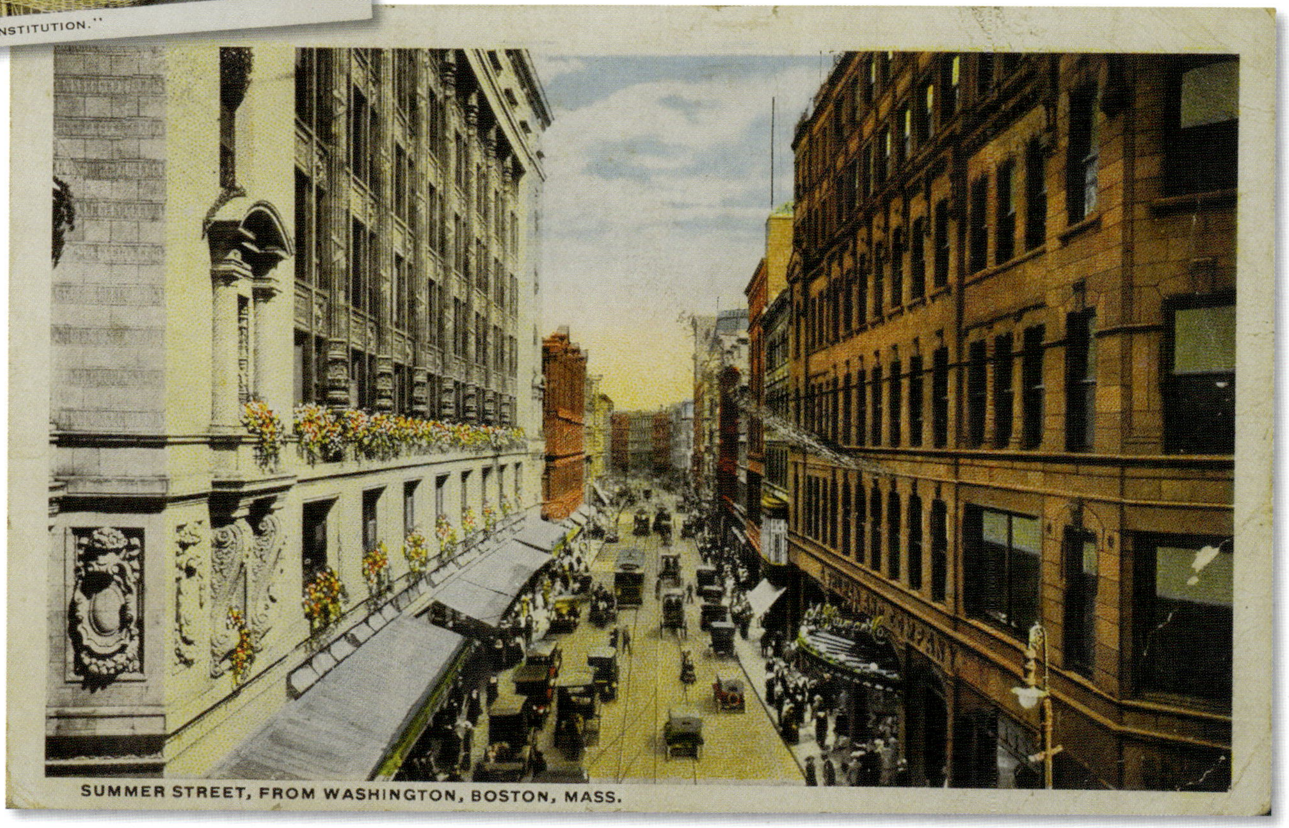

Boston may not be the biggest city in the nation, but it is a busy one with a good deal of history.

CHAPTER 7

DOWNTOWN

Within a few years after the first settlement, Boston grew to be the metropolis of the whole English America. –Cotton Mather

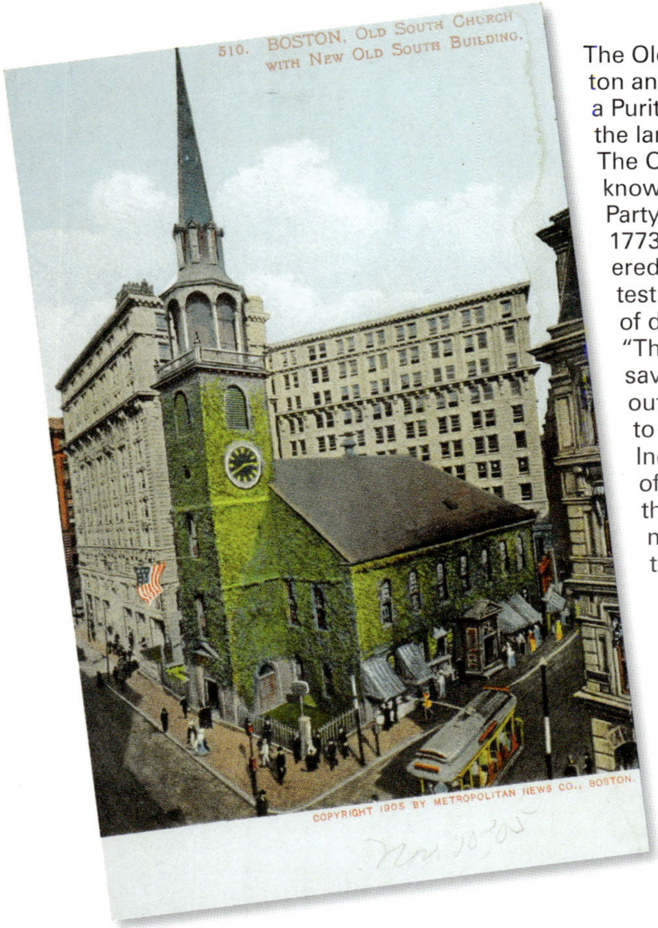

The Old South Meeting House (Washington and Milk Streets) was built in 1729 as a Puritan house of worship. It was also the largest building in colonial Boston. The Old South Meeting House is best known as the site where the Boston Tea Party was organized. In the winter of 1773, more than 5,000 colonists gathered at Old South in a meeting to protest the tax on tea. After many hours of debate, Samuel Adams announced, "This meeting can do nothing more to save the country!" Protestors stormed out of the Old South Meeting House to the waterfront where, disguised as Indians, they dumped three shiploads of tea into the Boston harbor. Today, the Old South Meeting House is a museum where they recreate the tea party debates.

On the 150th anniversary of the Irish Famine, Boston's Irish community unveiled a bronze sculpture to commemorate the fortitude of the Irish families and a memorial park (Washington and School Streets) on June 28,1998. Because of the Queenstown-Boston sailing schedule of the Cunard Steamship Company, many escaped the potato blight by coming to Boston, where they settled in the city.

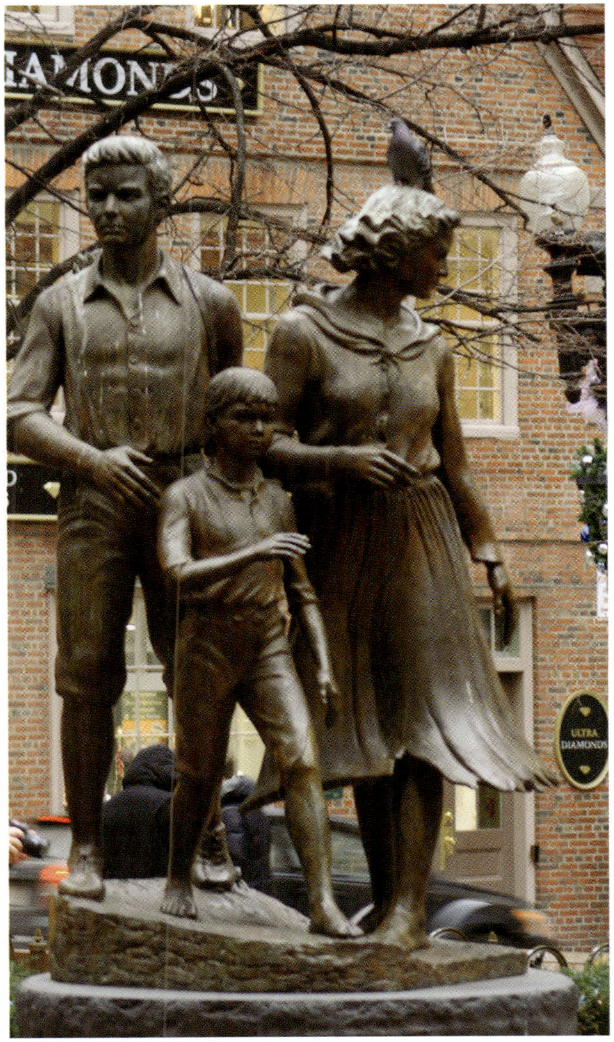

When Sir Edmund Andros arrived to govern the colony in 1686, he wanted to hold Anglican services. Eventually, he built an Anglican chapel on the public burying ground since no resident would sell land for a non-Puritan church. The present-day, King's Chapel (58 Tremont Street) with its four -foot thick walls was constructed from dark Quincy granite in 1749-1754. Its architect was Peter Harrison.

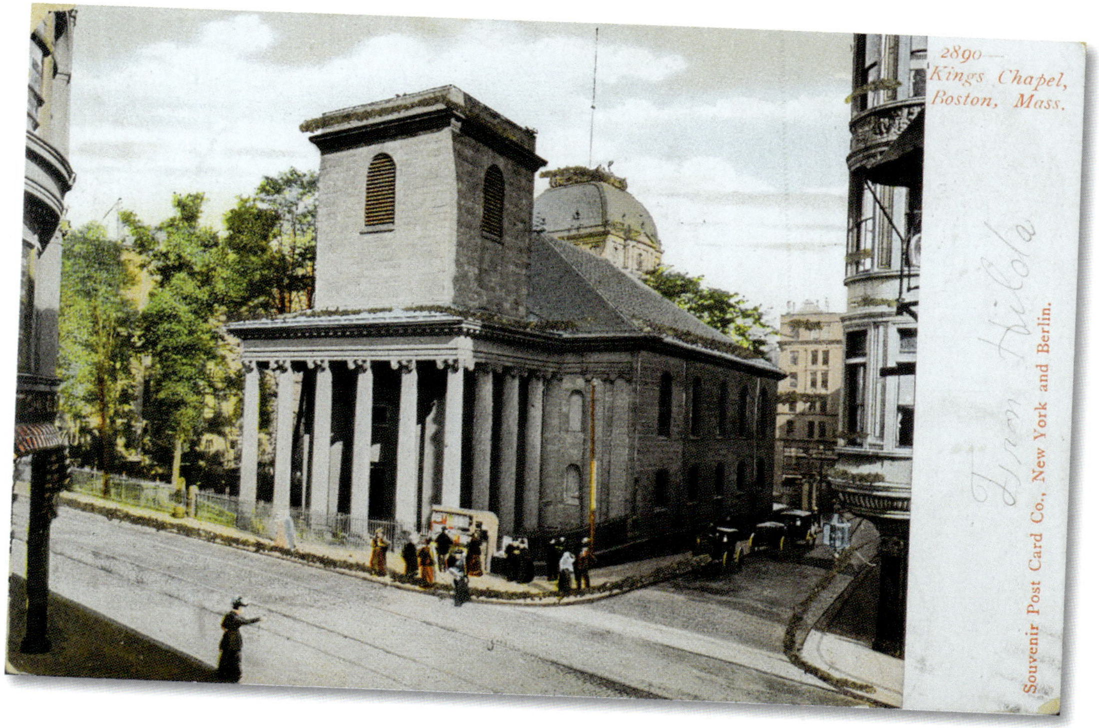

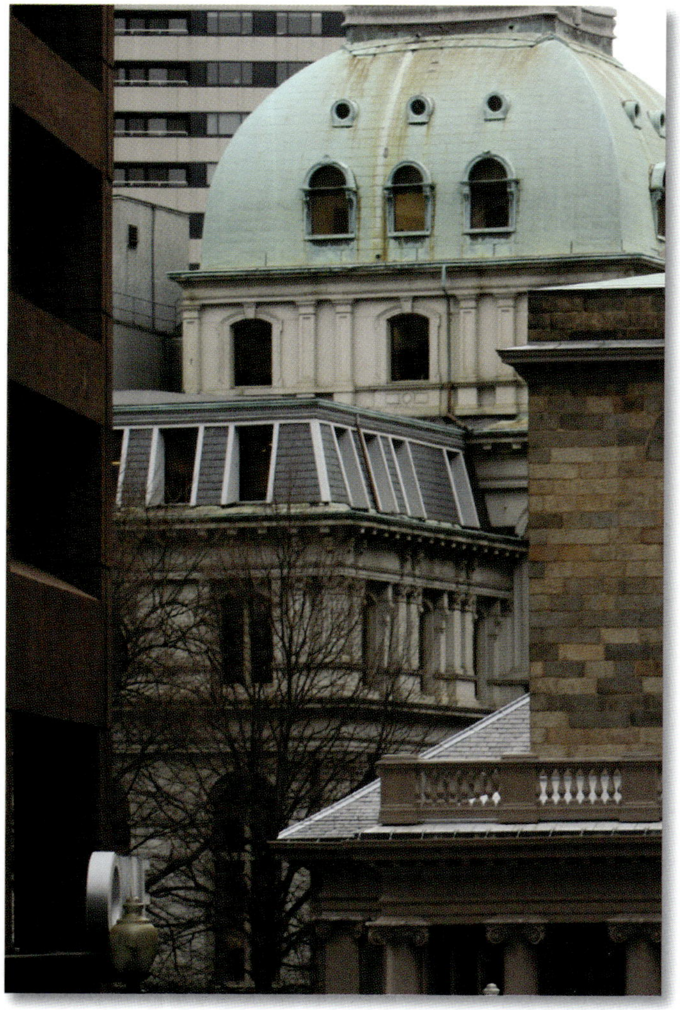

During the American Revolution, the chapel sat vacant and was referred to as the "Stone Chapel." It was reopened in 1782 and became Unitarian under James Freeman, who revised the Book of Common Prayer along Unitarian lines.

The sanctuary's raised pulpit shaped like a wine glass dates from 1717, making it one of the oldest in the nation. The high ceilings, open arches, and clear glass windows give this church the feeling of spaciousness and light. The current bell, cast in England, was hung in 1772. In 1814, it cracked, and Paul Revere recast it. It has been rung at services ever since.

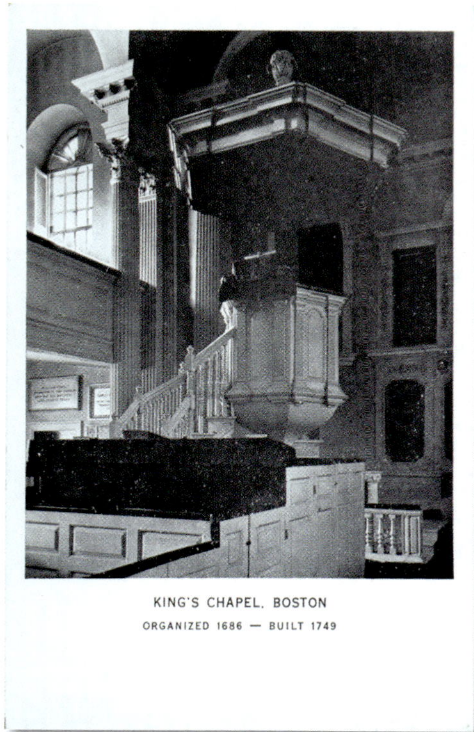

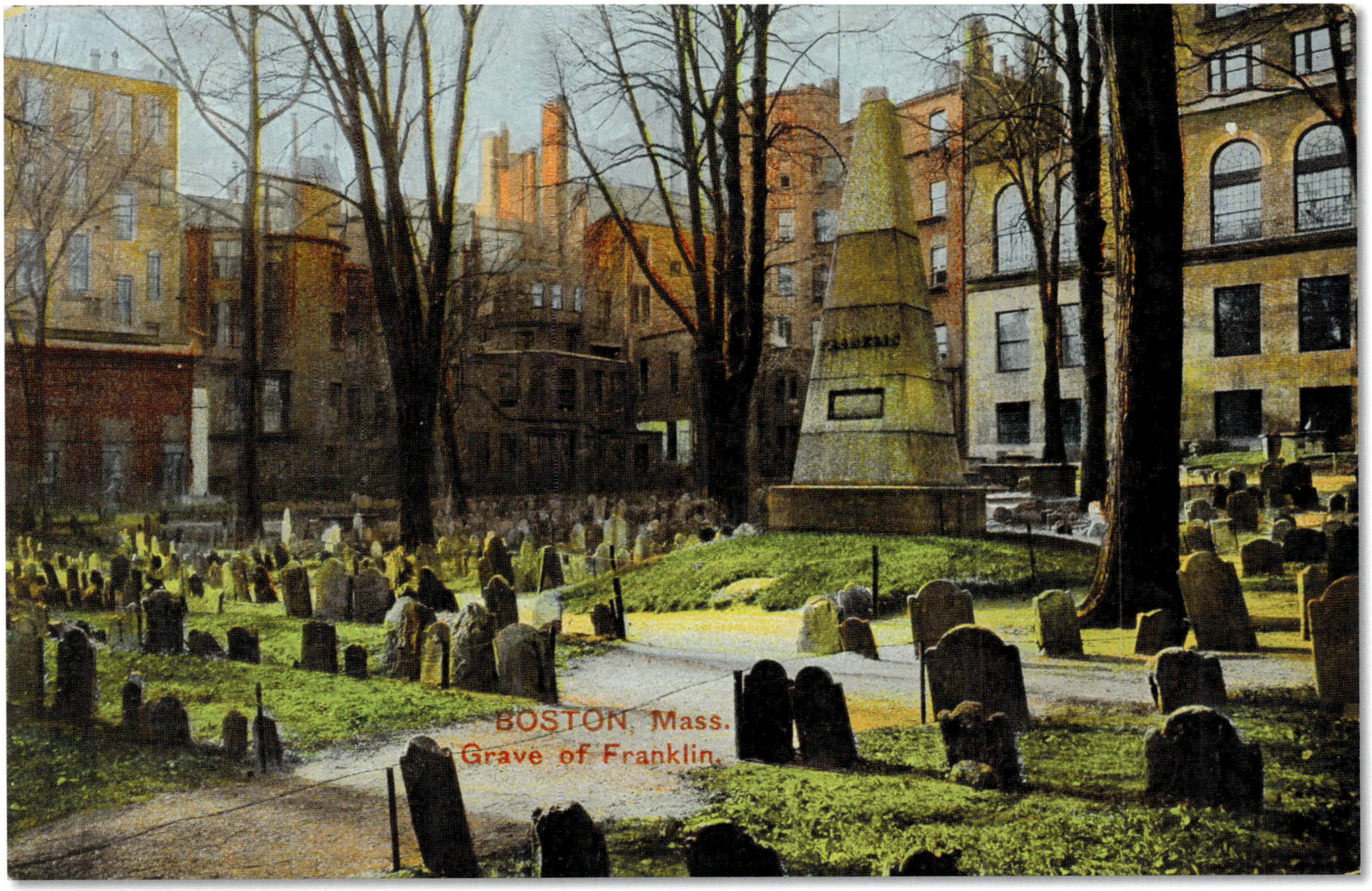

Dating back to the seventeenth century, the Granary Burying Ground (Tremont Street) was named after the early colonial grain storage facility that stood on the adjacent site of the Park Street Church.

Dating back to the seventeenth century, the Granary Burying Ground (Tremont Street) was named after the early colonial grain storage facility that stood on the site adjacent to the Park Street Church.

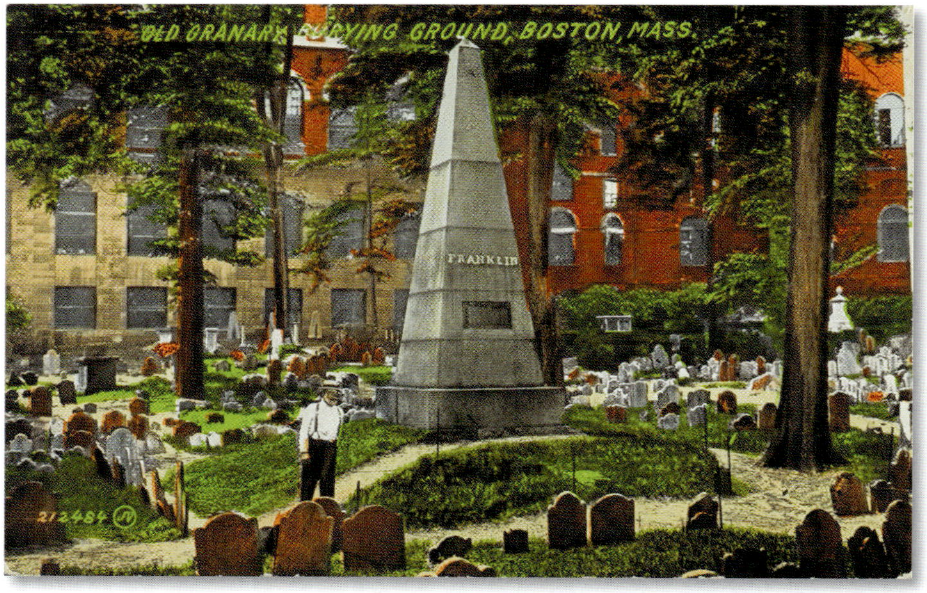

Many early Bostonians are buried there. It serves as the final resting place for many notable Revolutionary War-era patriots, including three signers of the Declaration of Independence, nine governors, and the five victims of the Boston Massacre. Paul Revere's grave can be found here as well as that of John Hancock and Samuel Adams. The obelisk in the center marks the tomb of Benjamin Franklin's parents.

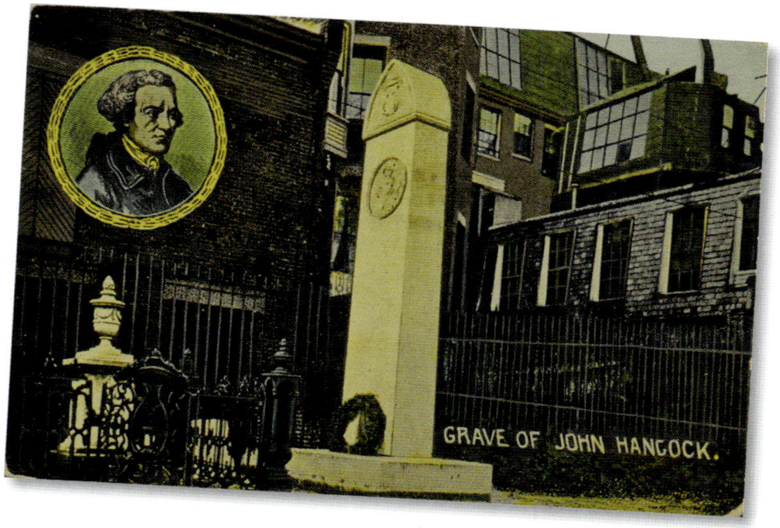

John Hancock, the American patriot leader, governor of Massachusetts for nine times, and signer of the Declaration of Independence from Massachusetts is buried here.

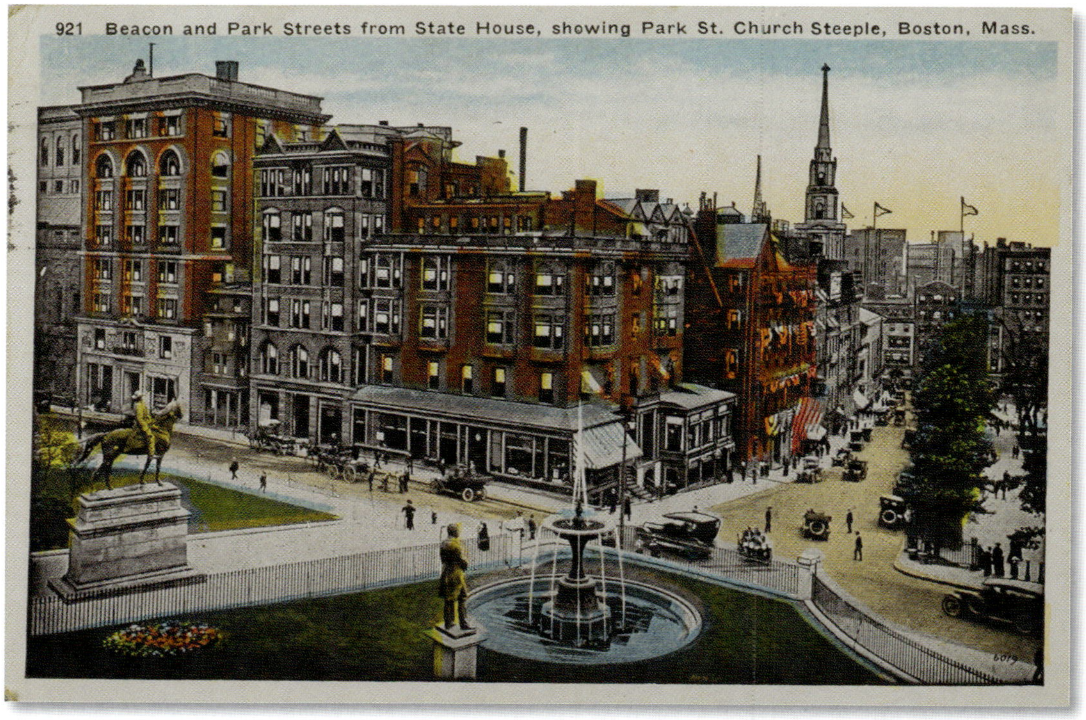

Eager citizens wanting to live near the new Bulfinch-designed State House developed Park Street, which had been a narrow lane with dilapidated houses. At one point, Boston's poorhouse was located near this area. Today, the statue of Civil War General Joseph Hooker (see lower left) dominates it. The Common is to the right.

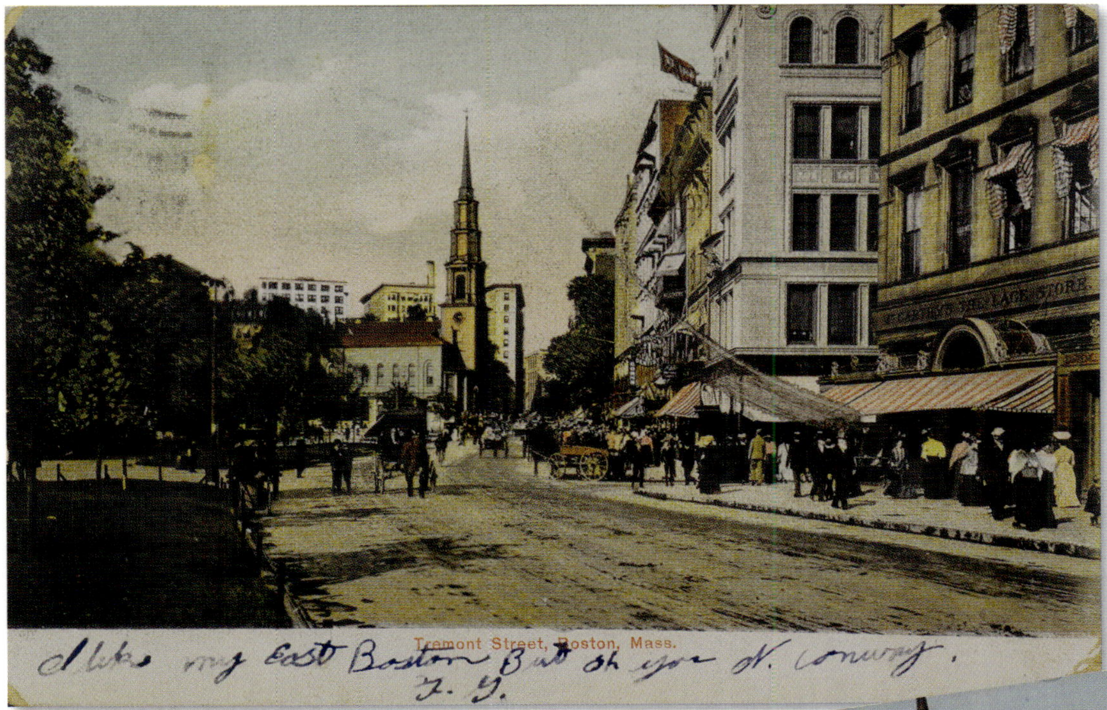

Tremont Street faces Boston Common (left). Park Street Church is in the background.

Since its founding in 1809 by parishioners wanting to establish a Congregational church in the heart of Boston, the 217-foot spire of Park Street Church has dominated the intersection of Park and Tremont Streets. Peter Banner was the architect. Henry James, who described the 270-foot steeple as "perfectly felicitous," commented that the building was "the most interesting mass of brick and mortar in America" (Harris, p. 138).

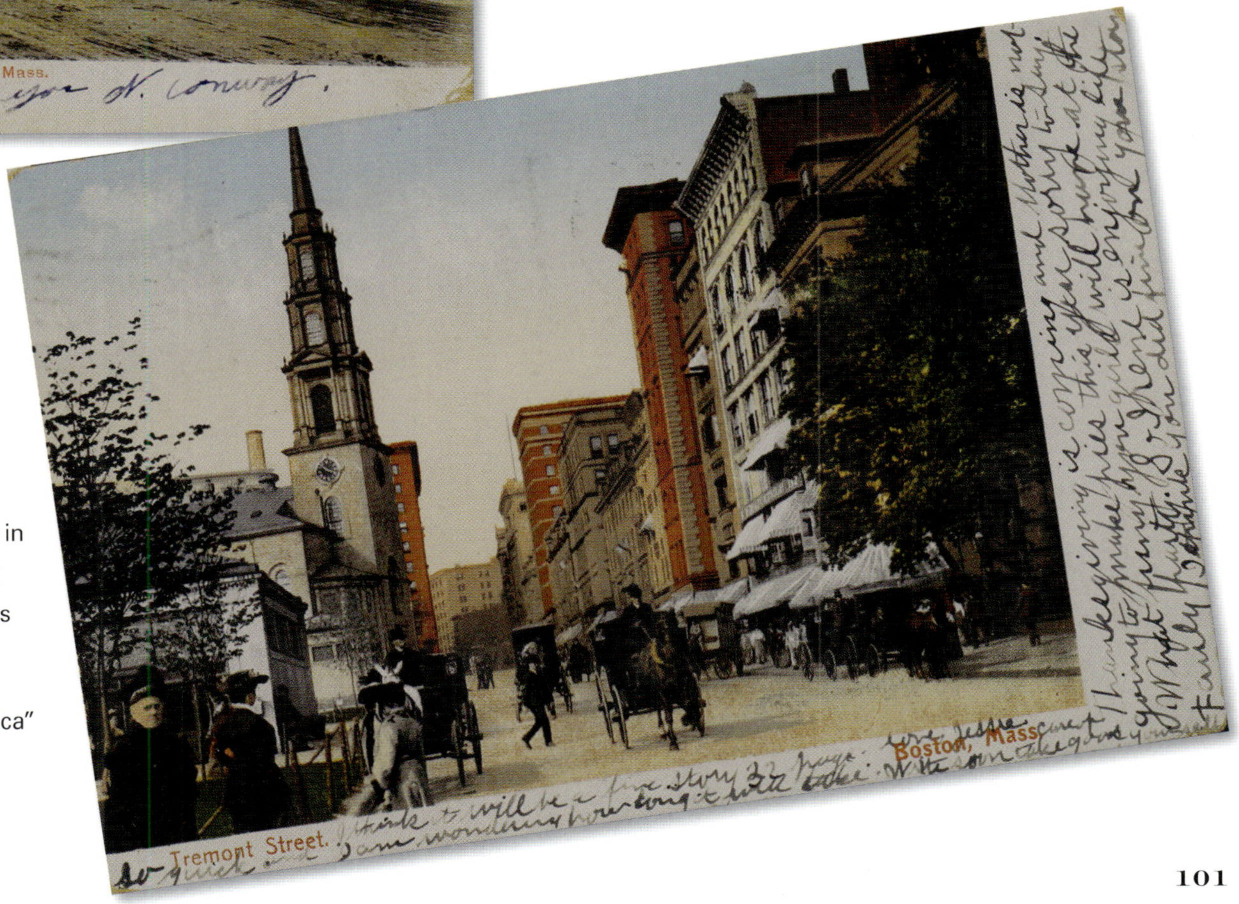

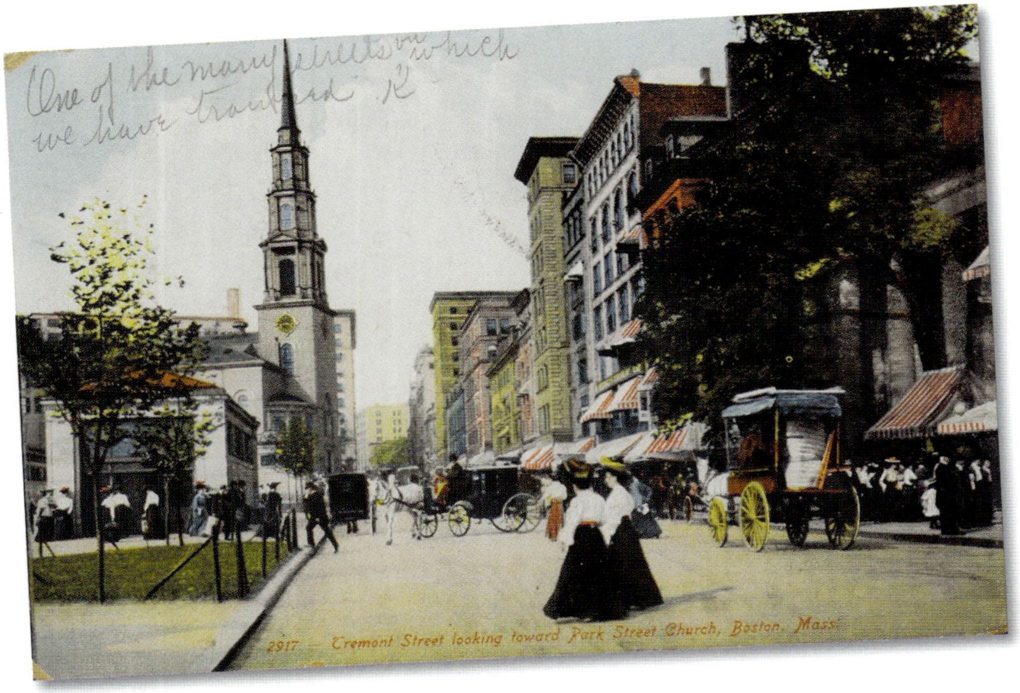

Sunday services were a serious business. Sermons were two to three hours long, and sticks were kept available to rap the heads of dozing adults and misbehaving children. In addition, two men were employed on Sundays to patrol the church grounds and chastise any children found playing or climbing trees in Boston Common. Over the years, Park Street Church pioneered a number of ministries, including the longest running radio broadcast program in the country and the first prison ministry program in America. Its site is nicknamed "Brimstone Corner" because gunpowder was stored in the church's basement during the War of 1812 and because of the fiery sermons that have resounded from its pulpits over the centuries.

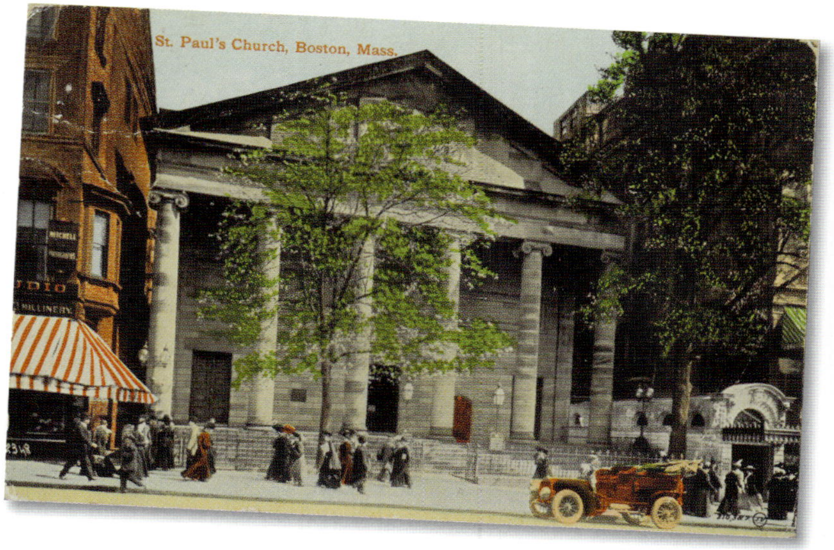

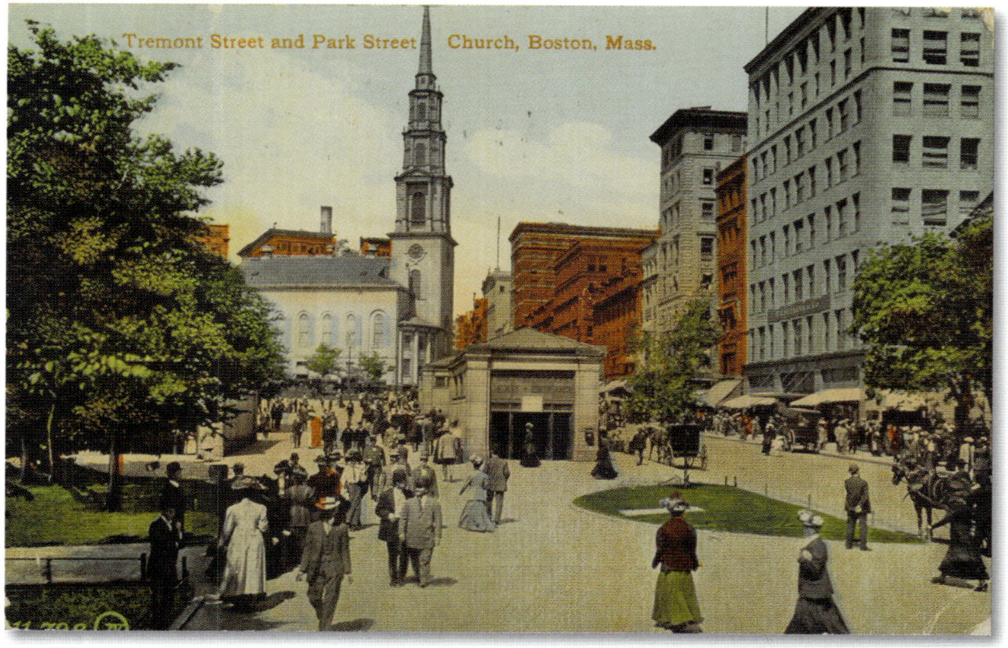

In 1818, a group of wealthy and influential Boston patriots, who wanted to establish a distinctly American Episcopal parish, commissioned Alexander Parris and Solomon Willard to construct a Greek Revival temple. The classical Greek portico of six, brown sandstone Ionic columns on the granite building of the Cathedral Church of St. Paul (138 Tremont Street) contrasts with the other Colonial and Gothic religious buildings. This cathedral is the see of the Episcopal Diocese of Massachusetts.

In 1829, William Lloyd Garrison preached his first abolitionist sermon from the pulpit of Park Street Church. Some members of the congregation thought he should be lynched. Two years later, the church children's choir premiered "America." In this image, the "T" entrance is visible

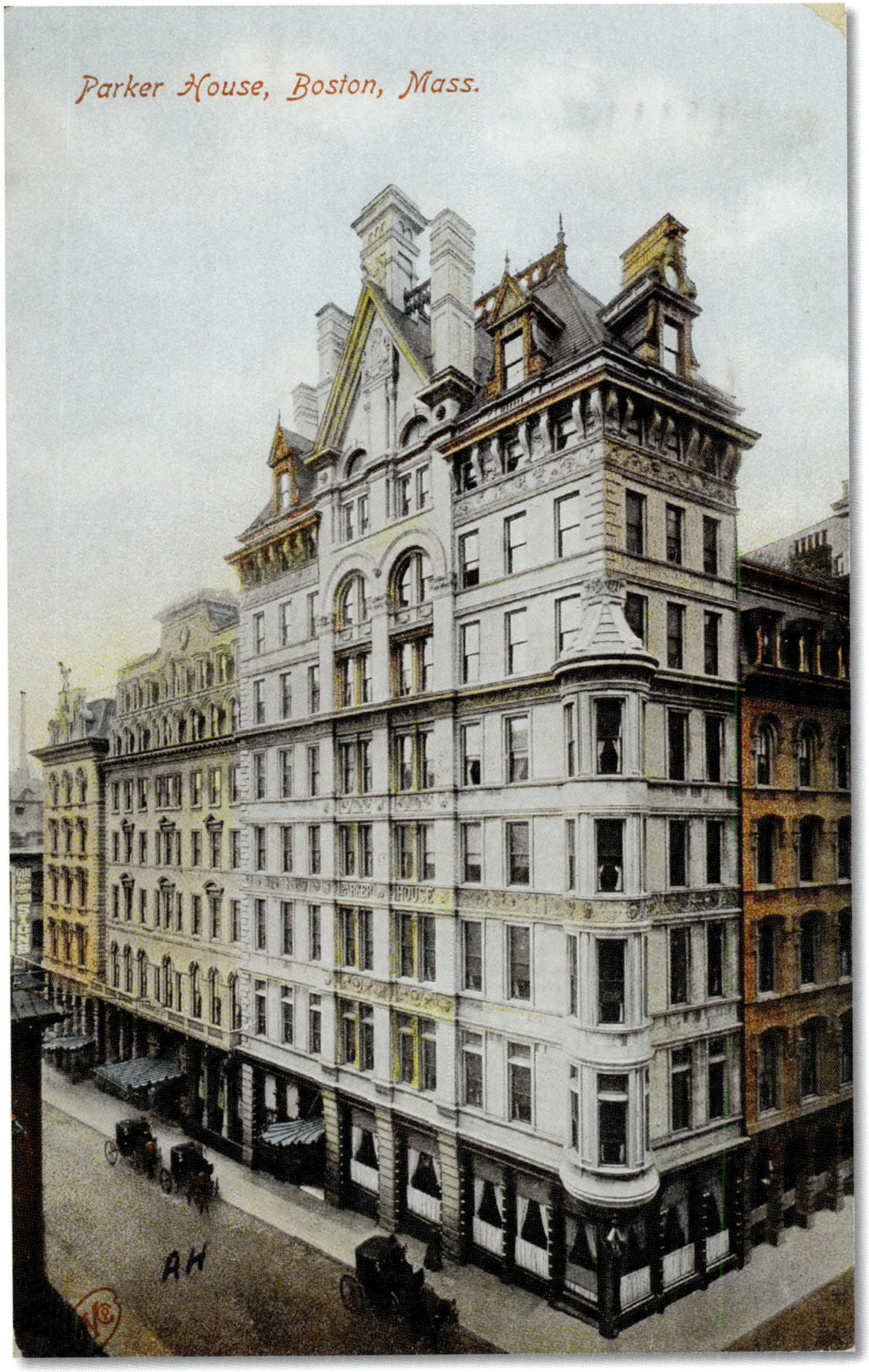

Parker House, birthplace of Parker House Rolls and Boston Cream Pie, opened its doors in 1855, which leads to its claim that it is the longest continuously operating hotel in the United States. In 1825, with less than one dollar in his satchel, a young Maine boy, named Parker, arrived in Boston. By 1832, the ambitious young Parker bought a cafe for $432, and renamed it Parker's Restaurant. In 1854, he built an ornate, five-story, Italianate-style stone and brick hotel at 60 School Street, faced in gleaming white marble. The first and second floors featured gracefully arched windows, while marble steps led from the sidewalk to the marble foyer within.

Sarah Bernhardt, John Wilkes Booth, and Judy Garland; Emerson, Thoreau, Hawthorne, and Longfellow; Babe Ruth and Ted Williams; Ulysses S. Grant, James Michael Curley, Franklin Roosevelt, Jack Kennedy, and Bill Clinton are among the many famous people who have wined and dined here.

A century ago, New England was the world's shoemaker. Early New England shoemaking had involved one craftsman making a pair of shoes a day in one-room cottages. Once shoe stitching and lasting operations became mechanized, the New England shoe industry was born. Massachusetts's factories churned out millions of pairs and shipped them throughout the country.

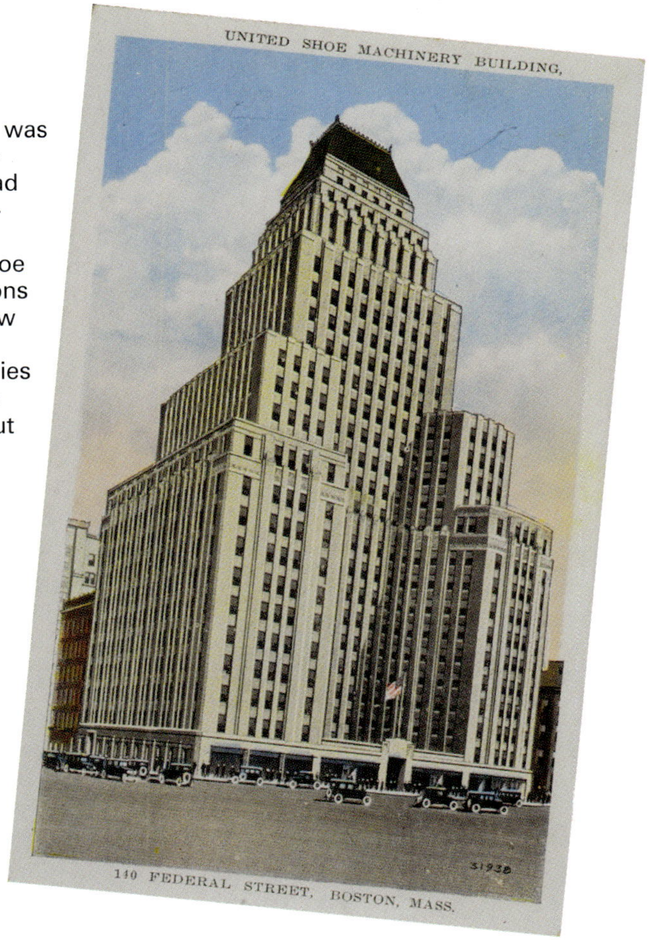

Looking north at the intersection of Boylston and Tremont Streets. The State House is in the far left.

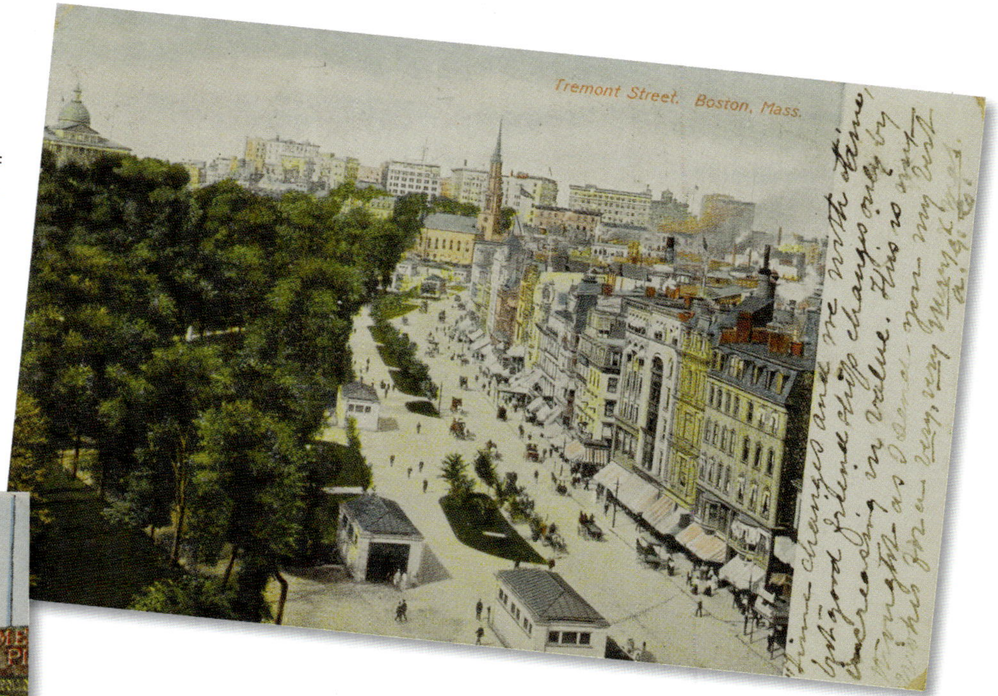

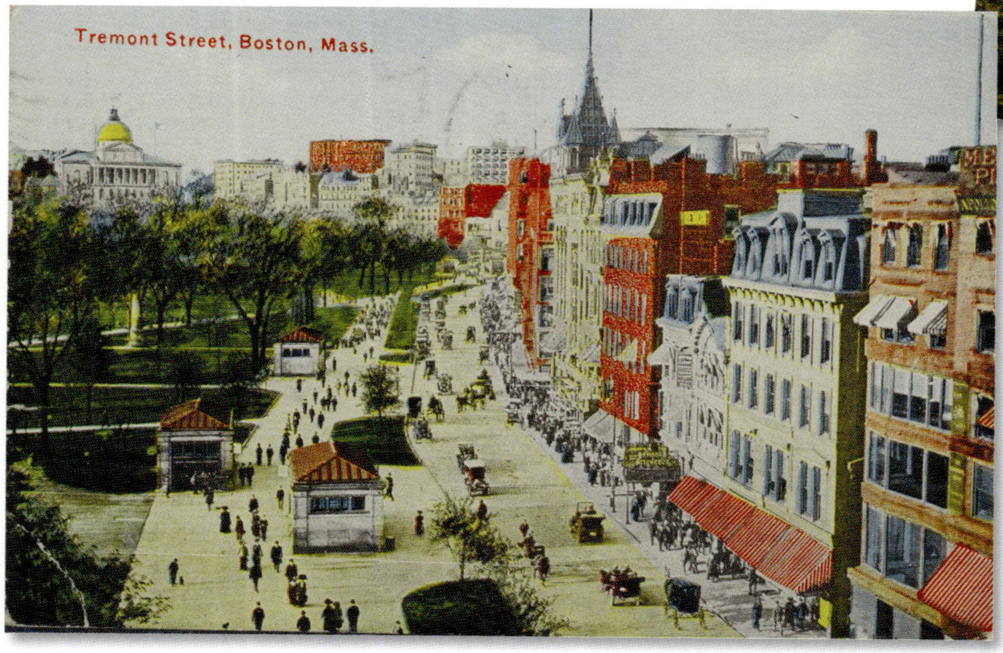

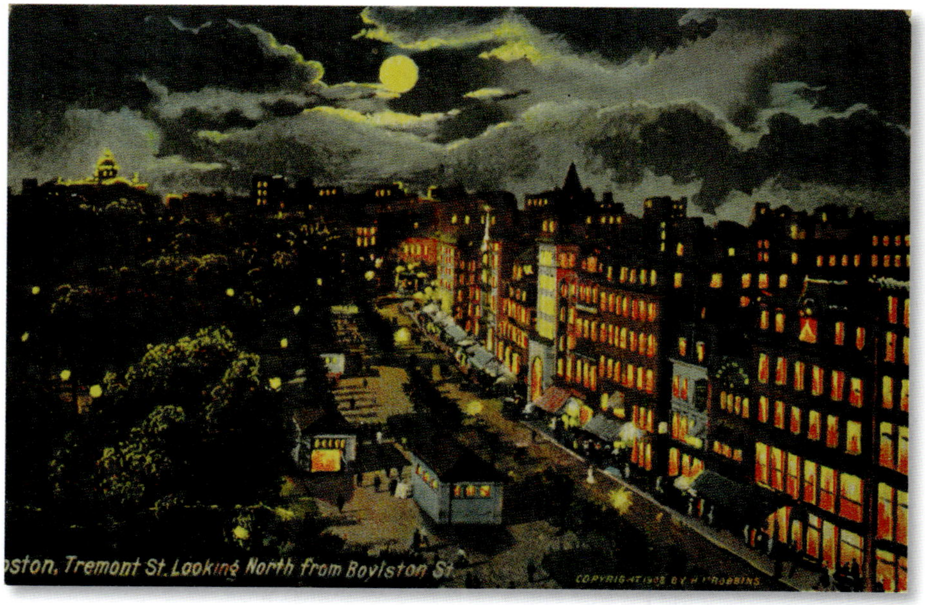

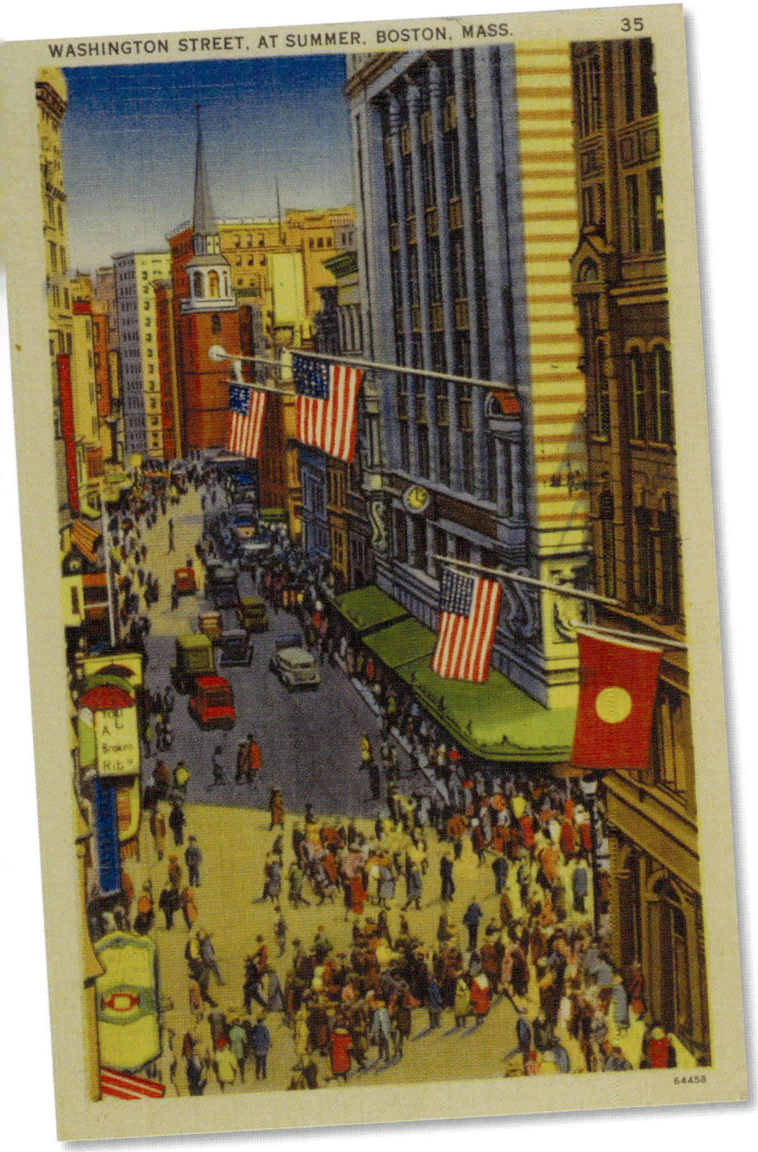

In this image, can be seen the flags of Filene's and Jordan Marsh, two of Boston's finest department stores.

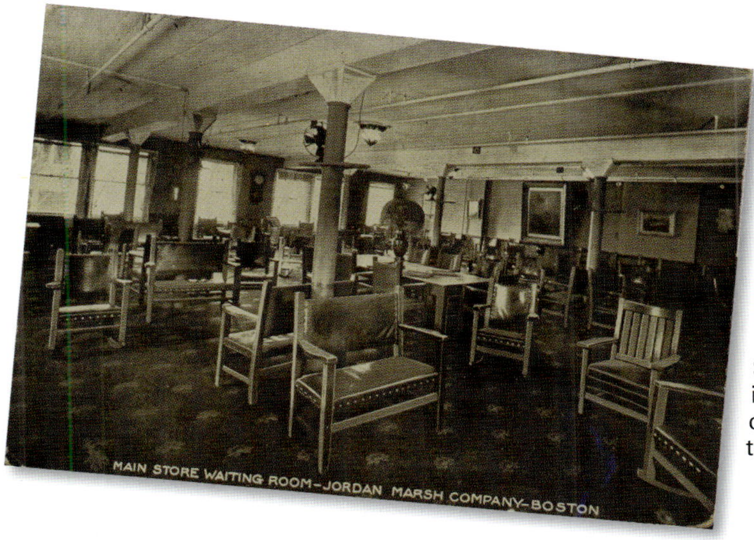

Jordan Marsh Company was a Boston institution. Arriving in town with about $1 in his pocket, Ben Jordan from Maine went to work for Boston's largest dry goods firm so he could learn the business. In 1851, Jordan and a cohort opened Jordan Marsh Company at 129 Milk Street with $5000 in capital. Macy's bought it later. Waiting rooms in those days certainly differ from those of today!

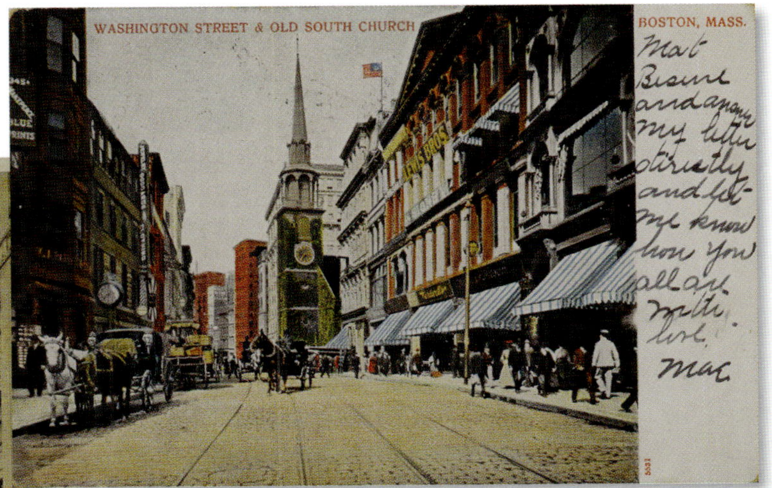

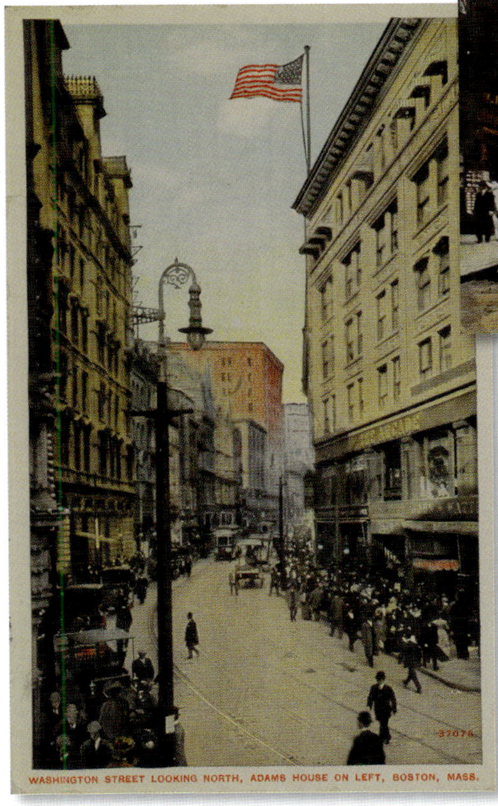

Boston was originally a hilly peninsula, connected to the mainland only by a thin strip of land, known as Boston Neck. In the early nineteenth century, many of the more affluent merchants lived on it. Today, Washington Street runs along the route of the Neck.

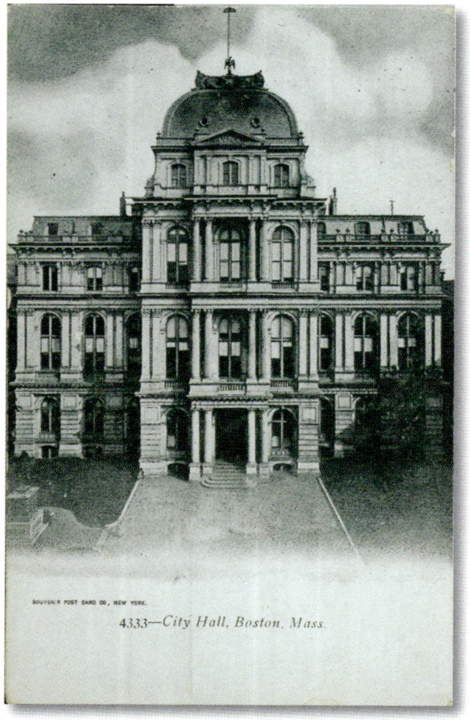

Built in 1862-1865, Boston's Old City Hall (School Street) was the third city hall and one of the first American buildings constructed in the French Second Empire style. The mansard roof, ornamented columns, and projecting granite bay characterize this style. When the Government Center was erected in 1968, this building was retired from public service and converted into a restaurant and first-class office space. The American Institute of Architects acclaimed this then-new concept of rehabilitating public buildings for new uses.

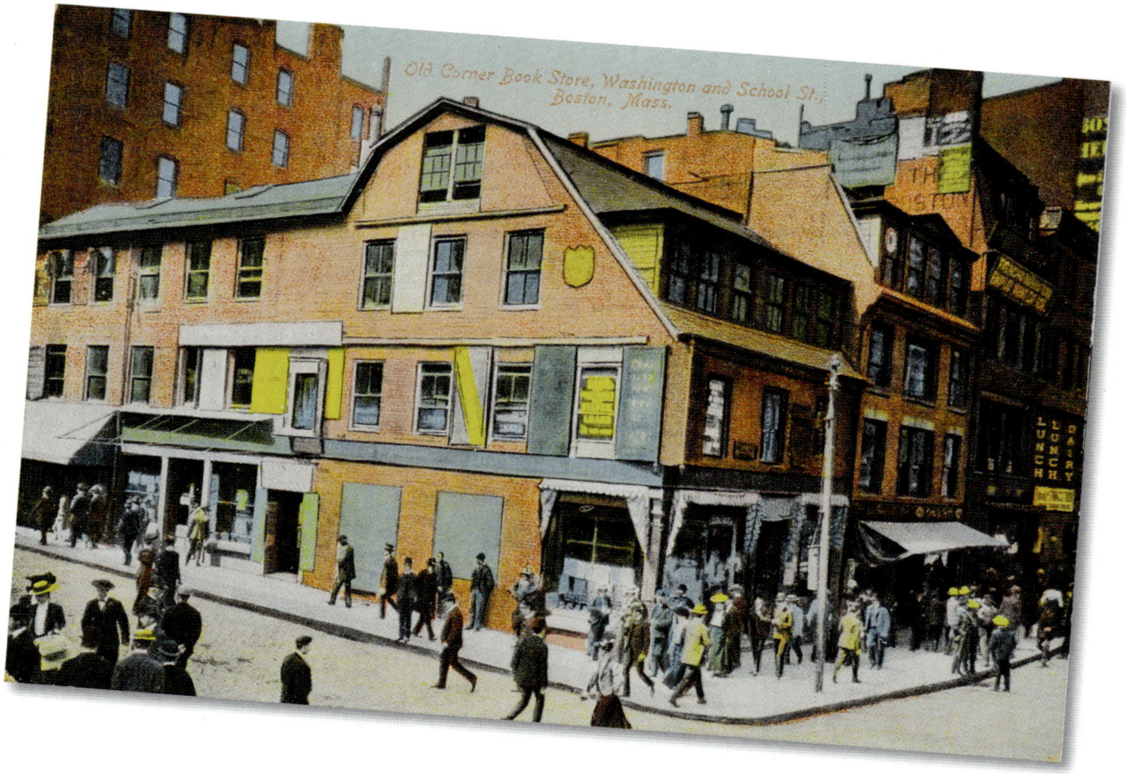

The former site of the red brick Old Corner Bookstore was on School and Washington Streets. Originally an apothecary shop owned Thomas Crease in 1718, it gained international renown from 1829 to 1903, when it housed a series of bookselling and publishing firms. One of the most famous editors was Jamie Fields, whose firm, William D. Ticknor, believed in paying authors. Fields published Whittier, Longfellow, Hawthorne, Thoreau, and Stowe. In 1869, he assumed editorship of the *Atlantic Monthly*, the nation's leading periodical. Later, the Old Corner Bookstore was moved to its present location.

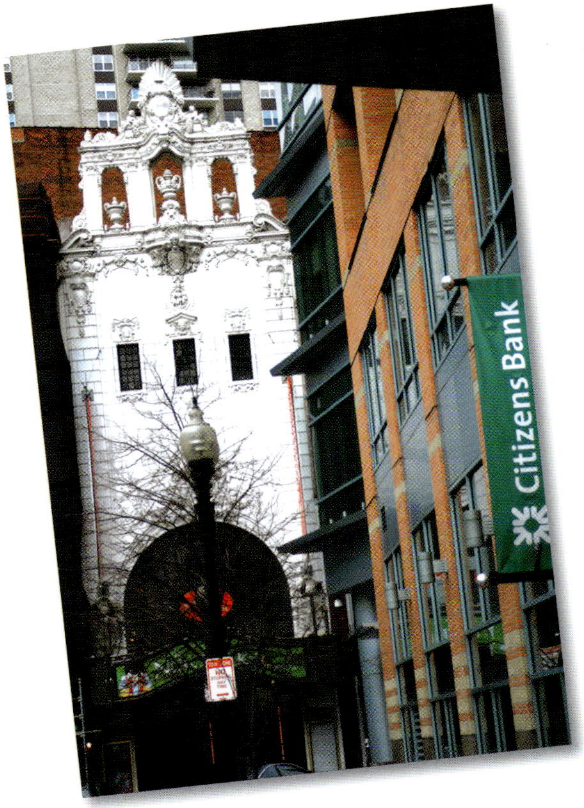

Boston's current Opera House (538 Washington Street) was renovated in 2004. Formerly, an old movie and vaudeville theater, it was opened in 1928.

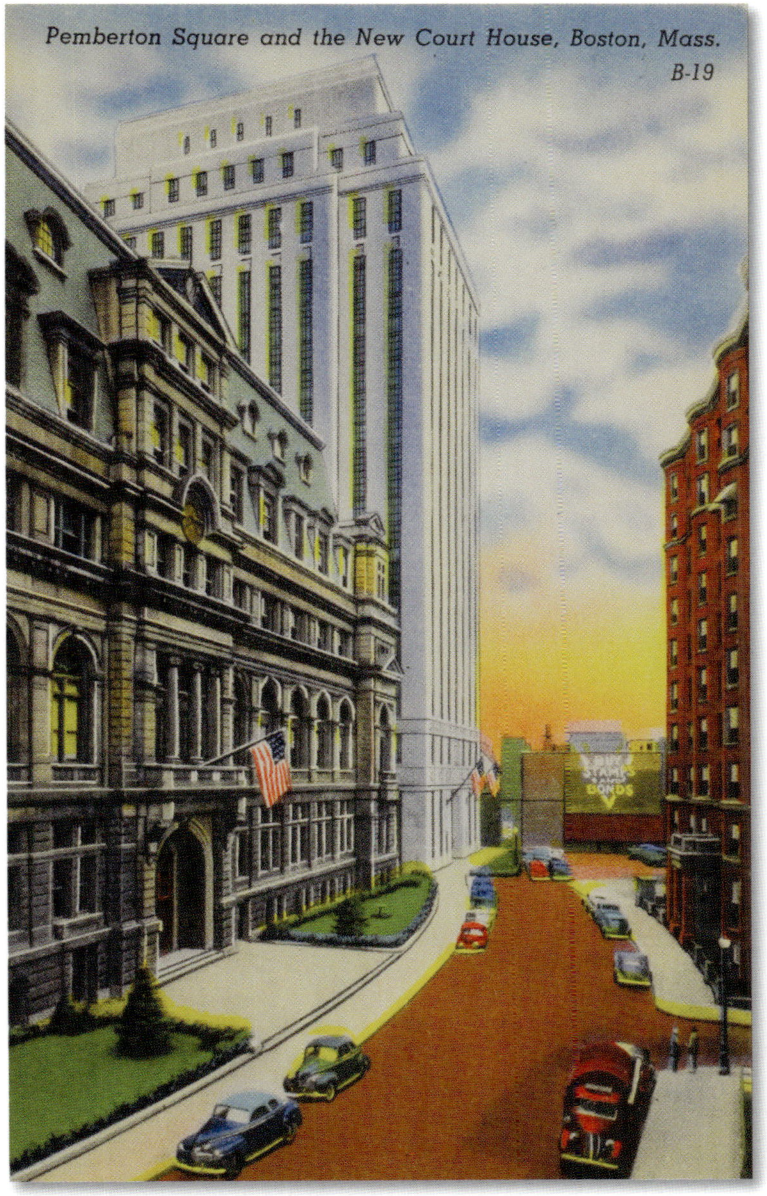

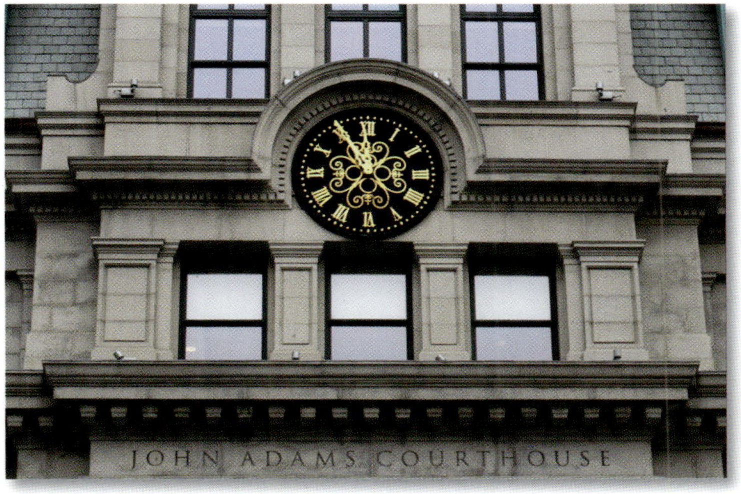

The John Adams Courthouse (One Pemberton Square) is a historic nineteenth century building designed in neo-classical style by Boston's first city architect, George Clough. The Massachusetts Supreme Judicial Court, the Appeals Court, and the Social Law Library are housed there. The John Adams Courthouse offers a variety of free educational opportunities for educators and students to learn about the judicial branch of government, John Adams, and the Massachusetts Constitution.

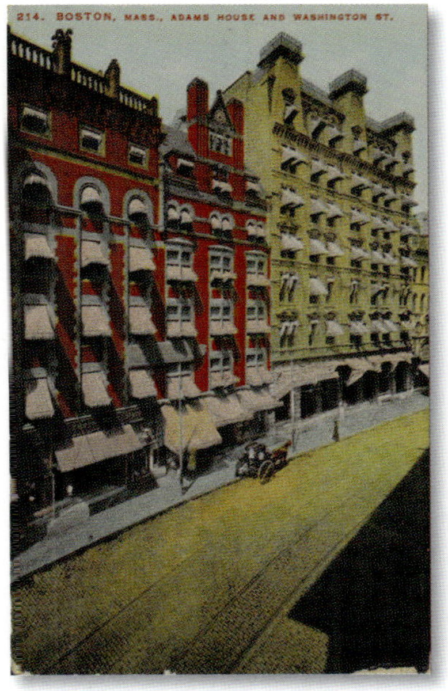

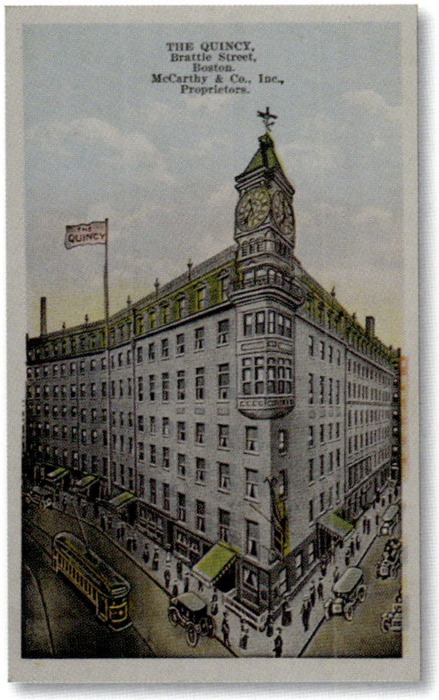

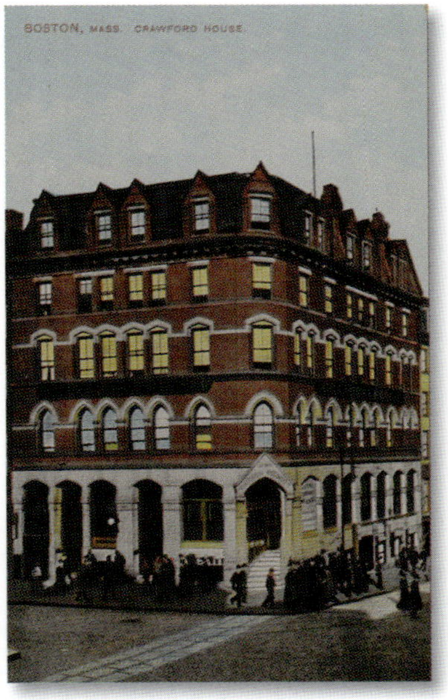

Pemberton Square used to be Cotton Hill, which blocked the town's westward spread for many decades. In the beginning of the nineteenth century, the magnificent elms on its summit were familiar landmarks to any ship approaching the harbor. The hill was leveled in 1835. Today, it is the site of the courthouse, which maintains one of the oldest national collections of deeds, wills, and records. When it was opened, Chief Justice Holmes showed his father, Dr. Oliver Wendell Holmes, around.

During the nineteenth century, more and more travelers attracted by Boston's growing economy traveled to the city. Lodging and dining houses proliferated throughout town, many bearing patriotic names, like the Adams House or, the Shawmut, and the Revere House. Lodging in Boston became so refined that even ladies were ably accommodated.

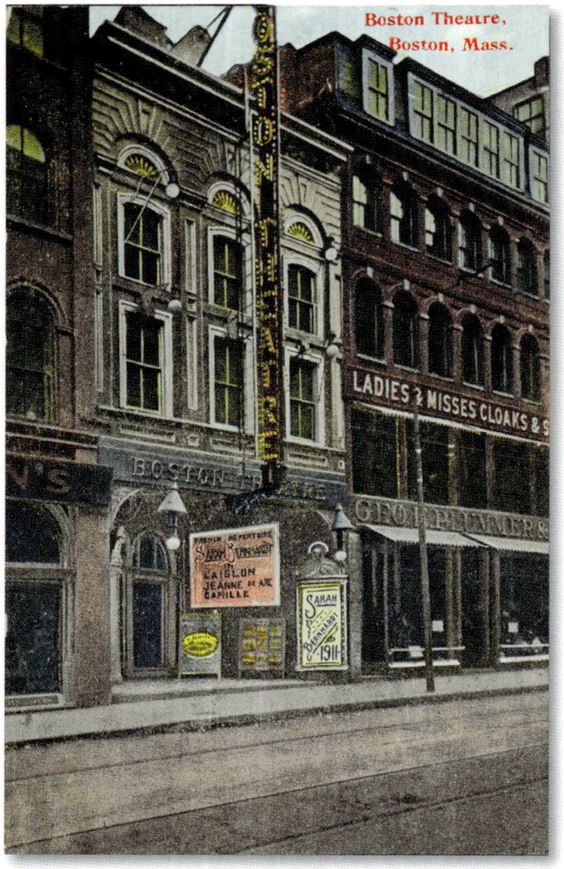

By 1793, Boston had opened its first theater – its Puritanical days were long gone. By the next century, Boston had become one of the primary locations for trying out new plays and possessed many elegant theaters. Many famous plays (e.g., Tennessee Williams' *A Streetcar Named Desire* and Gershwin's *Porgy and Bess*) premiered in Boston.

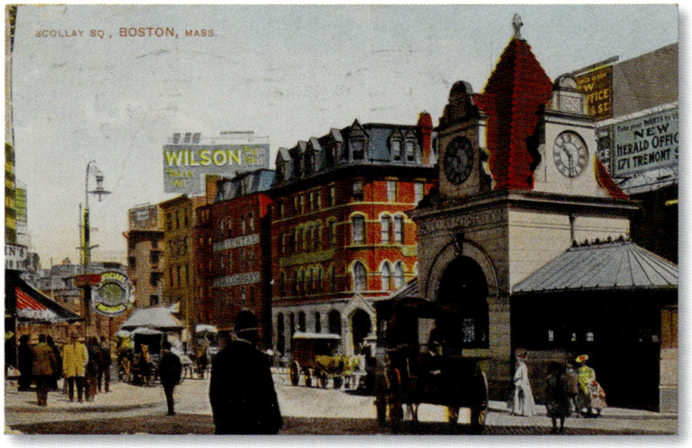

Scollay Square is renown for its exciting nightlife. It offered pawnshops, bars, burlesque theaters, and shooting galleries. Some early abolitionist activities took place here, while many of its buildings played a role in the Underground Railroad.

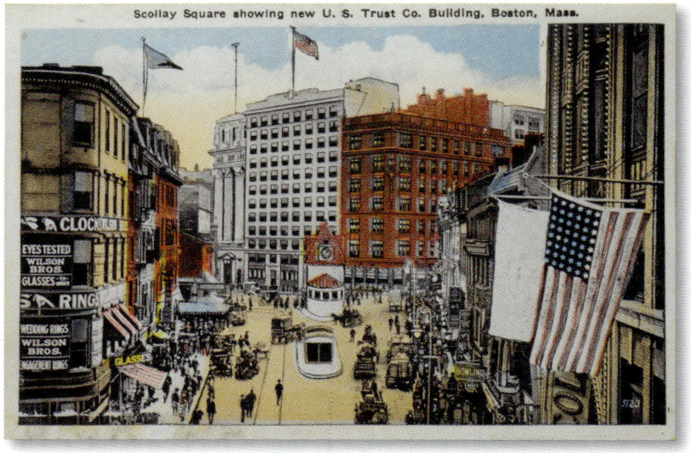

In the early 1960s, city officials replaced the narrow streets and decaying buildings of Scollay Square with an approximately 10-acre plaza known as Government Center. The center of it is the massive Boston City Hall, considered by some to be an architectural masterpiece.

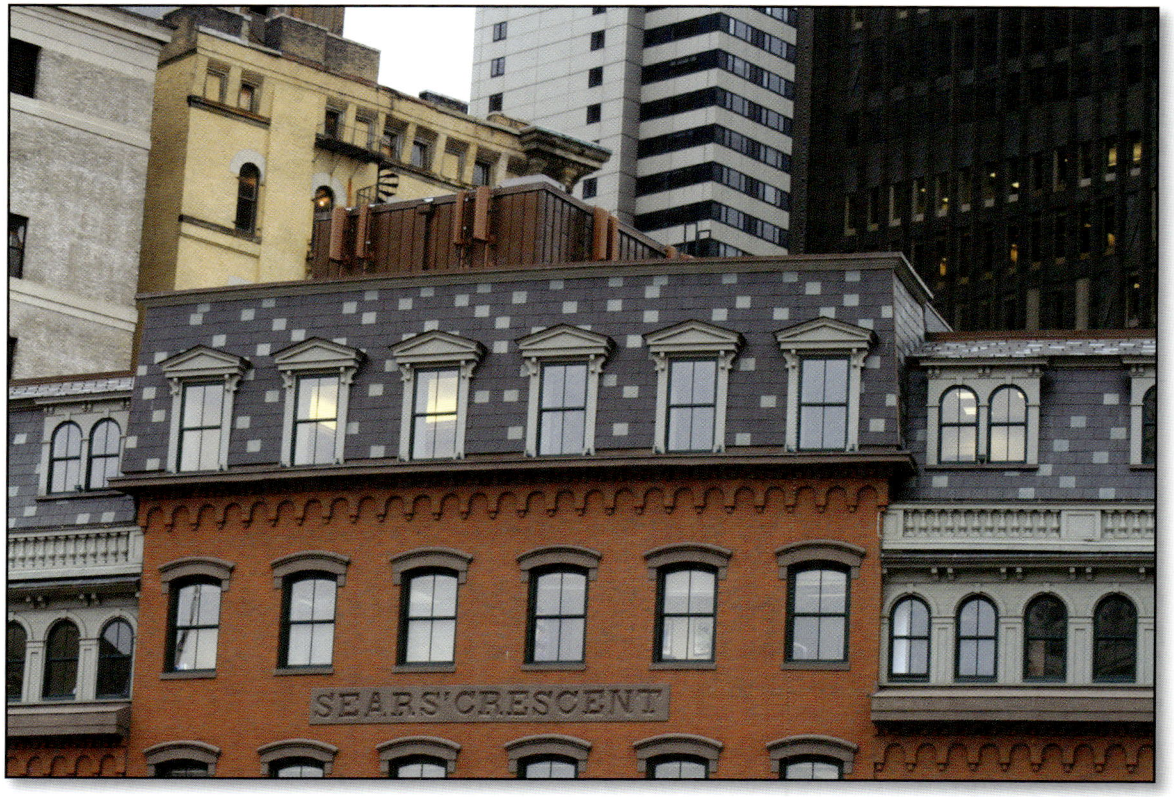

Named for its curved facade, the Sears Crescent Building, located at 100 City Hall Plaza, is one of Boston's most historic office buildings. At one point, it graced the main street of the Cornhill District. Constructed in 1816, it was remodeled in mid century and some fine Italianate detailing was added. *Courtesy of D. Peter Lund*

Chapter 8

The Fenway Area

Samuel Eliot Morison pointed out that in Boston, when a family acquires wealth, it does not continue to seek it or build monuments to its name, but invests its energies and often its money in art, music, and literature.

Initially, The Fenway was considered a quiet residential area for Boston's growing middle class. In his 1881 plan, Frederick Law Olmstead designed a winding Riverway with forest-covered hills and wooded sloping banks and controlled the flow of the Muddy River. Known as the "emerald necklace" today, Olmstead's park system began with the Back Bay Fens, beginning where Commonwealth Avenue ends.

Once the streetcar line was extended into the area, it began to grow. By 1892, people could live in the Fenway and work in Boston. By the beginning of the twentieth century, the Back Bay Fens or the Fenway had attracted many Bostonians who built handsome neo-Georgian red brick townhouses.

Boston's Fenway also became home to the city's premier cultural organizations such as the Museum of Fine Arts, The Boston Symphony Orchestra, and The Boston Opera Company.

First Church of Christ, Scientist

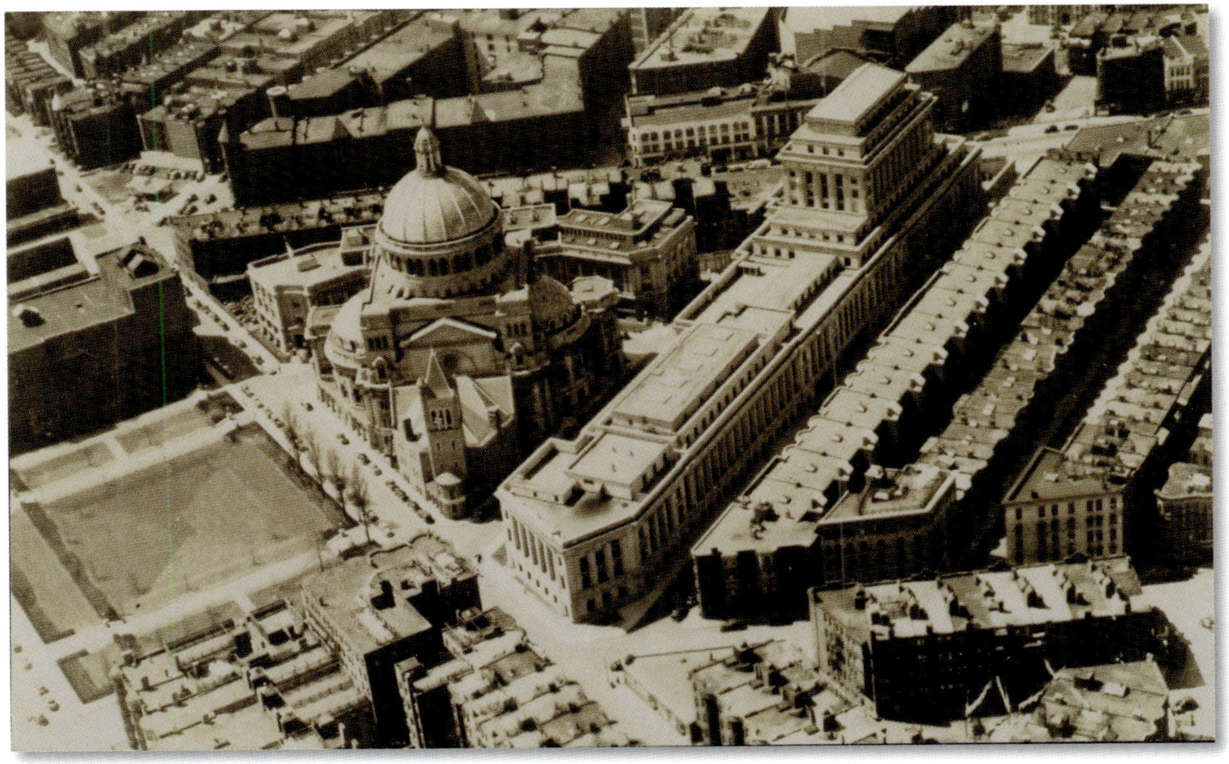

The world headquarters of the First Church of Christ, Scientist, is located on fourteen acres at the intersection of Huntington and Massachusetts Avenues.

In 1879, Mary Baker Eddy organized this religious body, which is also known as Christian Science. Her creed emphasizes the efficacy of prayer in healing and spiritual regeneration. In 1894, Brigham & Spofford designed the granite "Mother Church" with its impressive dome.

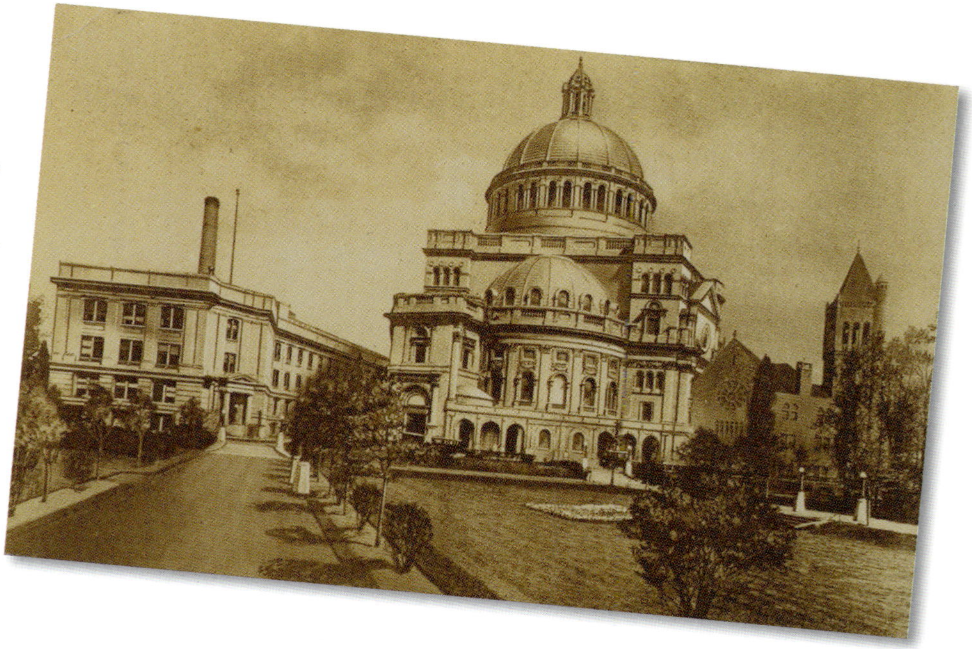

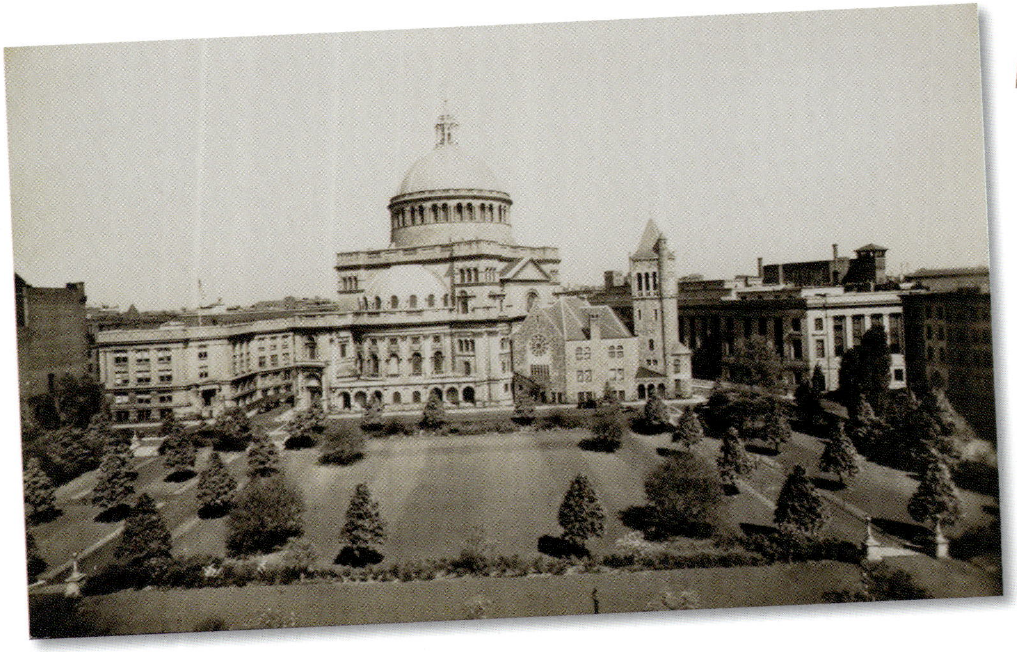

Dominating the intersection, the 220-foot, classically inspired, Byzantine church was dedicated in 1906.

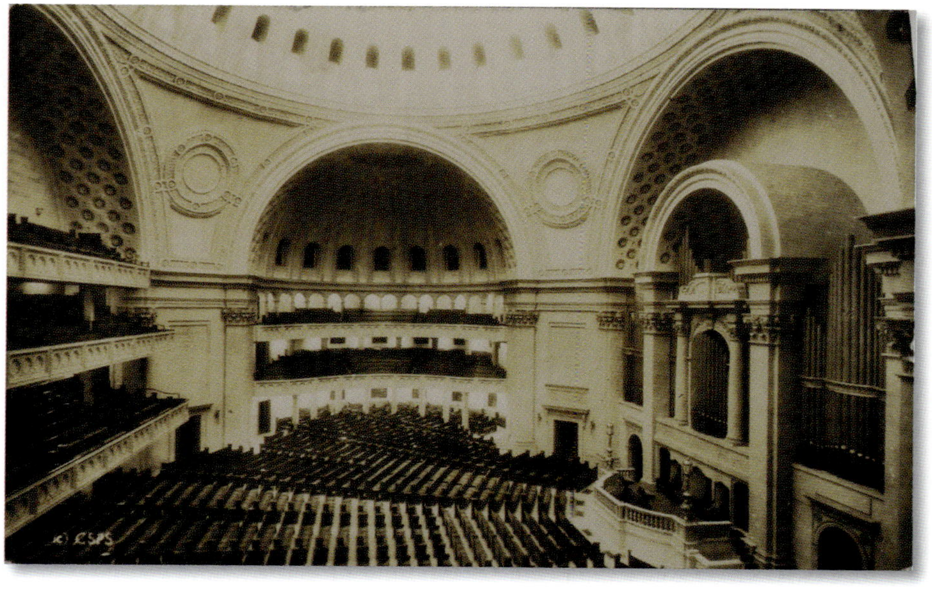

The Boston-based Aeolian-Skinner Company manufactured the hemisphere's largest pipe organ for the church.

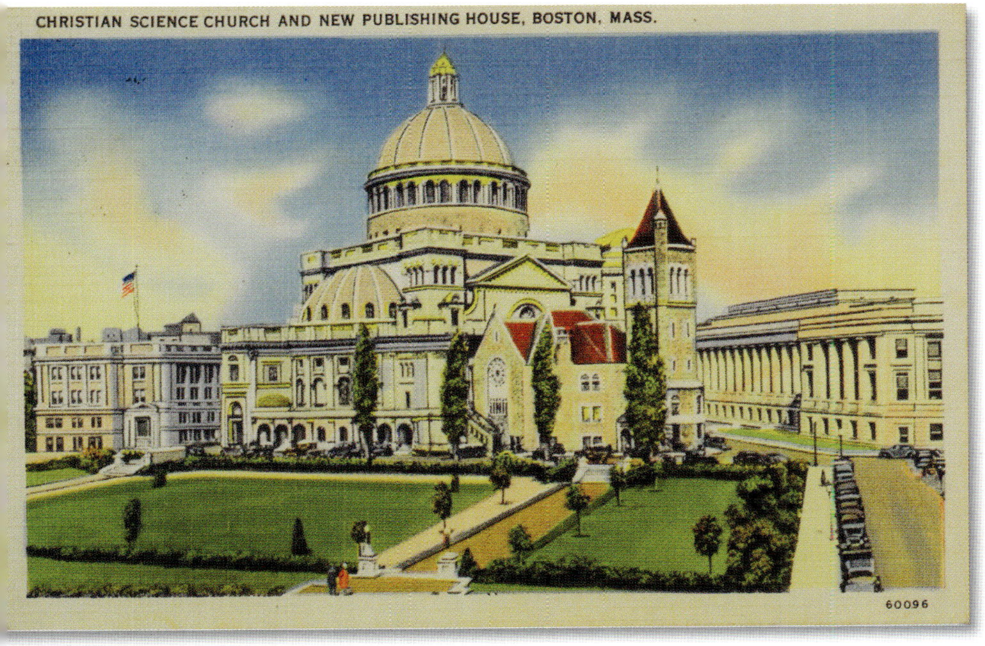

In 1973, architect I.M. Pei redesigned the Christian Science complex to include a freestanding, poured concrete, administration building and a reflecting pool that extends along Huntington Avenue. His monumental, tree-lined plaza wed the twenty-two acres belonging to the Society into a cohesive urban design.

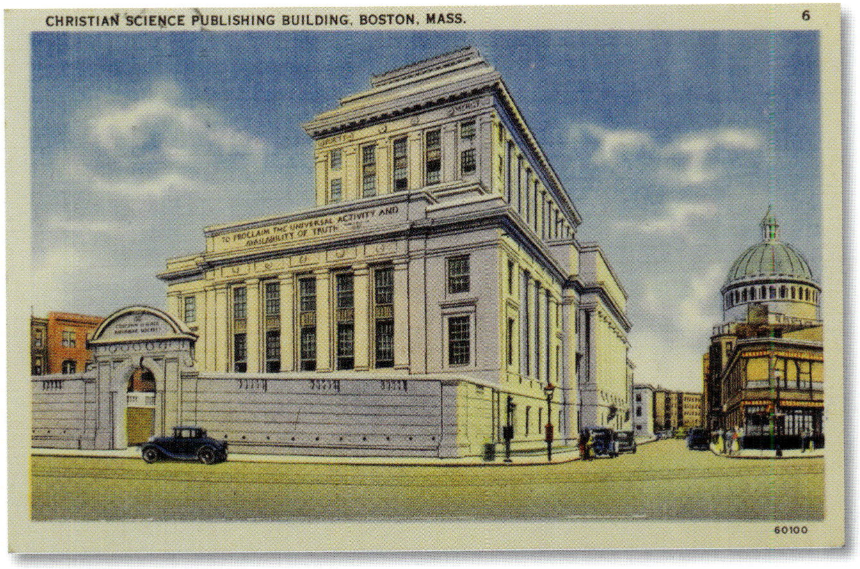

On the Massachusetts Avenue side of the complex is the Christian Science Publishing Society building, dating from 1908.

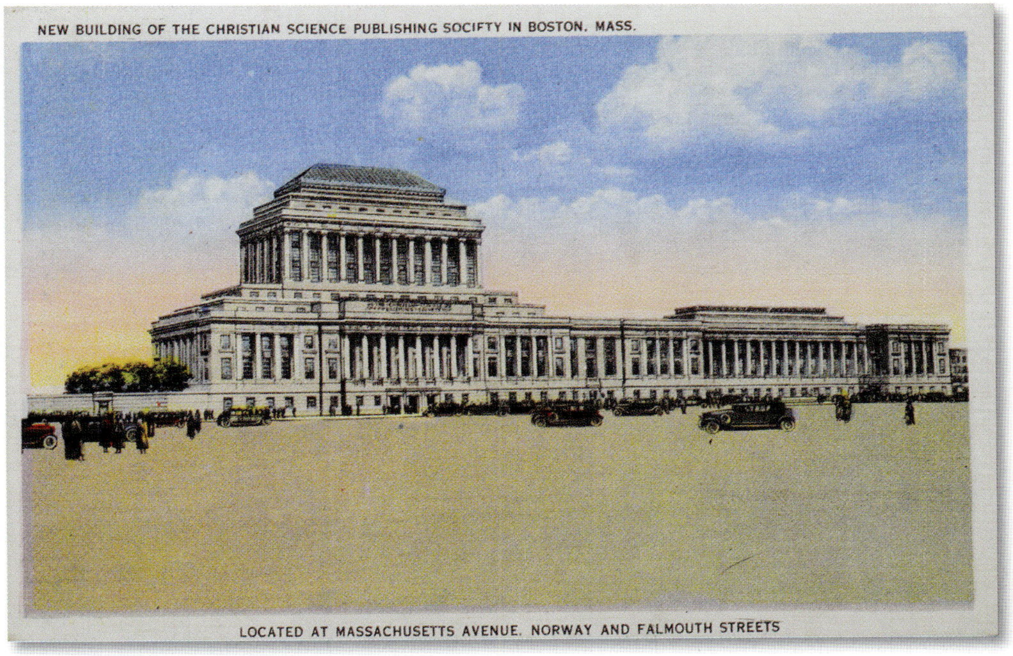

In 1908, when she was eighty-seven years old, Mary Baker Eddy founded the newspaper, the *Christian Science Monitor*, which is read throughout the world.

Within the complex stands the two-story stained glass globe of the world known as the Mapparium. Opened in 1935, it represents the worldwide activities of the church. Visitors can actually walk through the center of the globe, viewing the world from its interior. Of course, the land areas are those from the early 1930s!

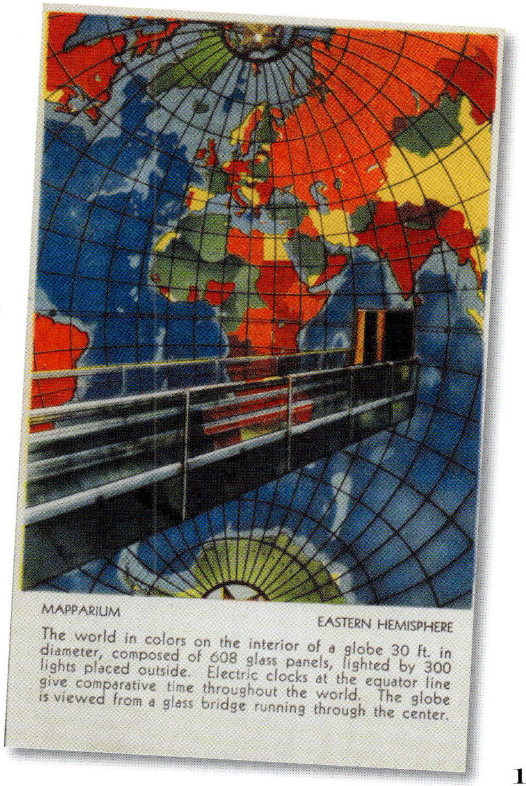

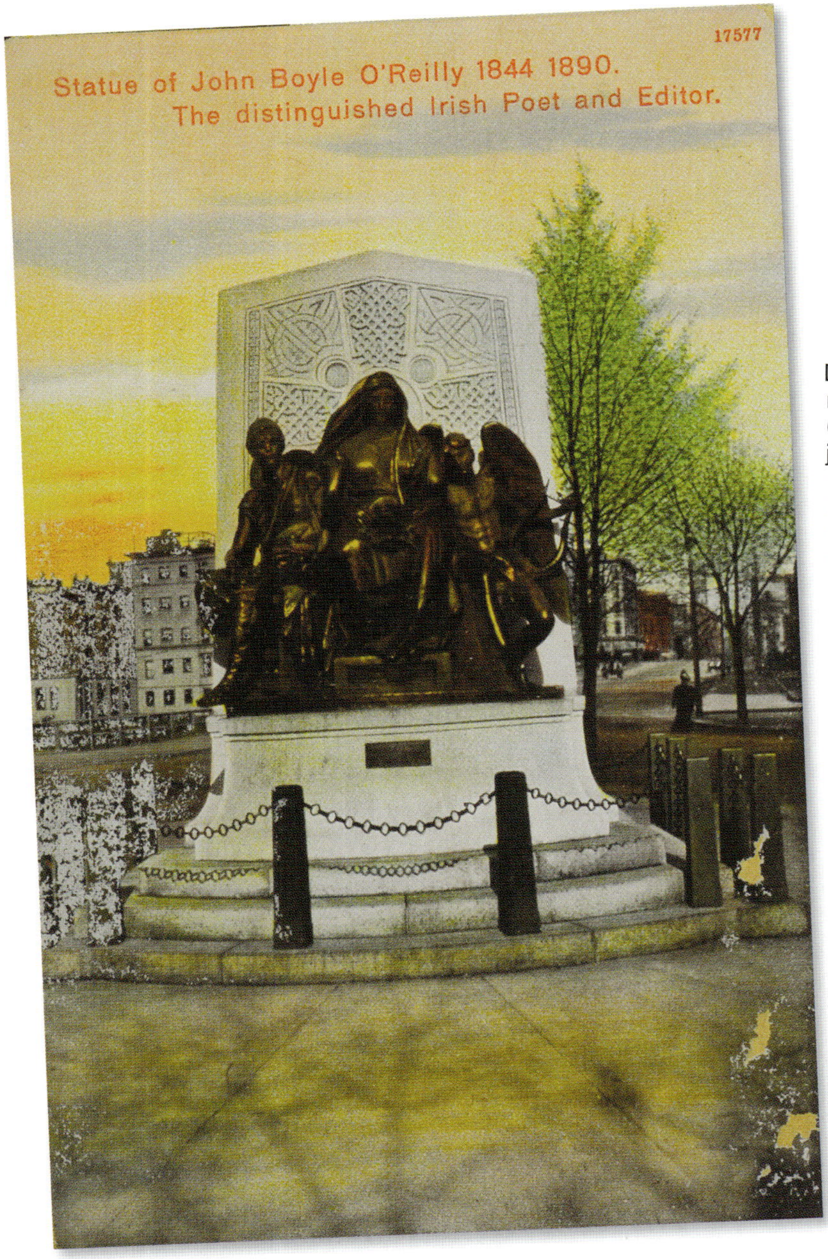

Designed in a Beaux Arts style, the Hotel Minerva was built in the early twentieth century opposite the First Church of Christ, Scientist. The Midtown Motor Inn replaced its lovely double swell-bay facade and Ionic-pilastered entrances in the 1960s.

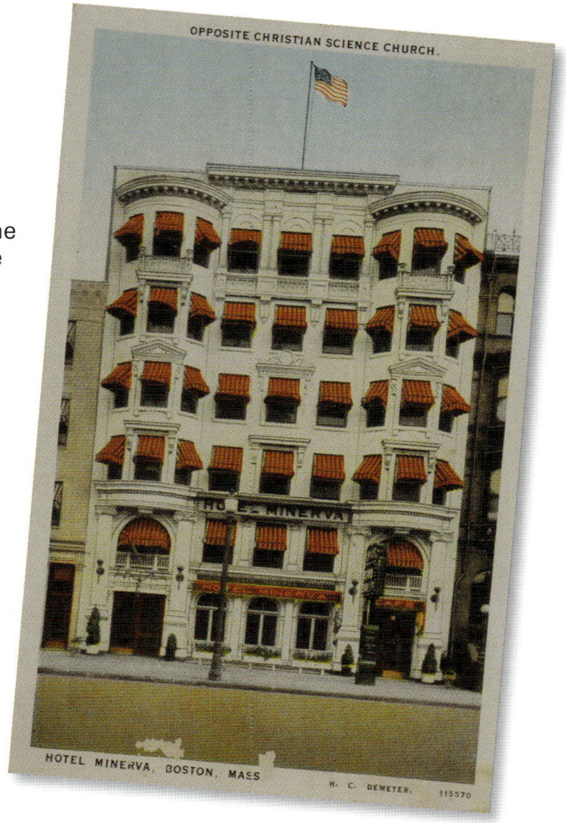

Daniel Chester French sculpted this monument to John Boyle O'Reilly (1844-1890), Irish revolutionary, poet, journalist, and immigrant. A member of the Fenian movement, O'Reilly was banished to Australia but made his way to America in 1869. Here, he became the editor of the *Pilot,* Boston's leading Catholic newspaper. This bronze statue with the inscription "Poet, Patriot, Orator" was erected in 1896 at the Boylston Street entrance to the Fenway.

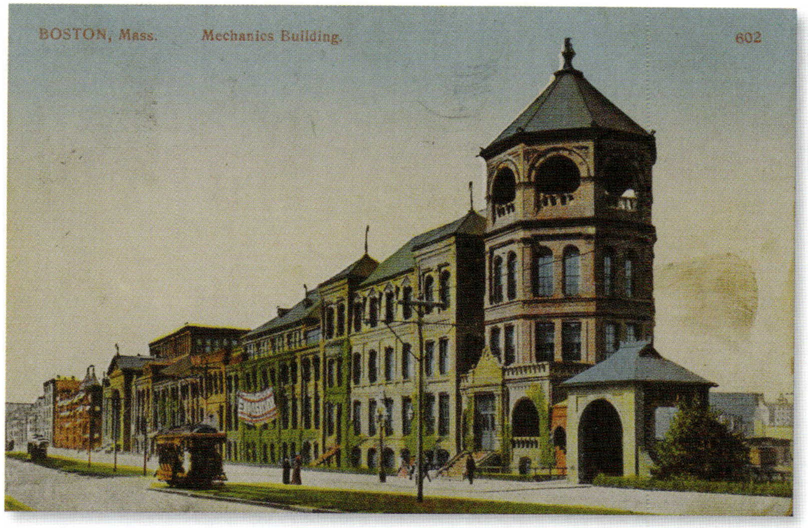

The Massachusetts Charitable Mechanics' Association Building on Huntington Avenue has been demolished. Known as "Mechanics Hall, " the sprawling red brick building was designed by William Gibbons Preston. Its auditorium served as a meeting hall and convention center.

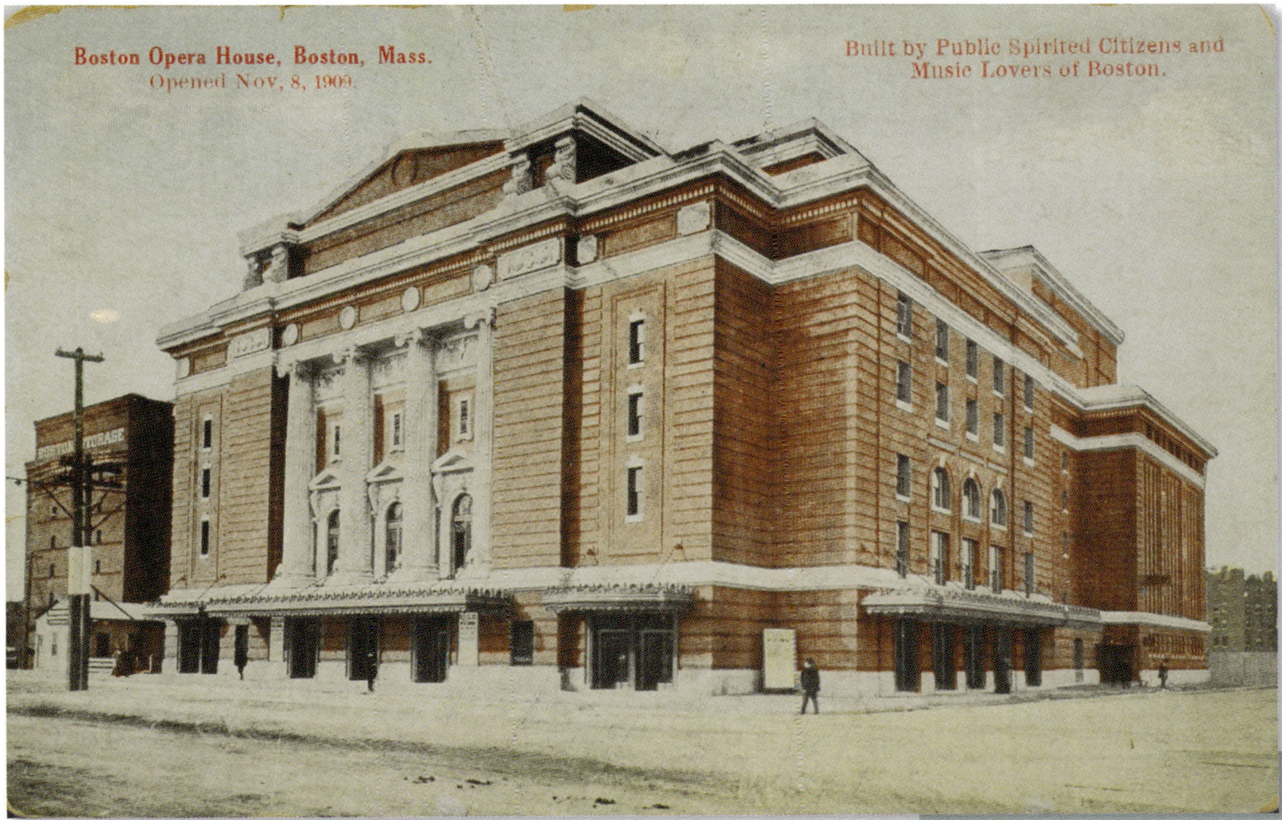

Eben Jordan erected the brick and stone Opera House with a pilastered facade near Symphony Hall. It was torn down in 1958.
The Boston Symphony Orchestra (BSO) housed at 301 Massachusetts Avenue owes its founding in 1881 to Henry Lee Higginson, who imported European musicians. For many years, Higginson made up symphony deficits. Designed by McKim, Mead, and White, the Huntington Avenue hall, opened in 1900. The nearly acoustically perfect hall ranks among the three best in the world. The niches with their Greek and Roman statues and the pierced detail of the balconies aid the hall's acoustics as well as its aesthetics.

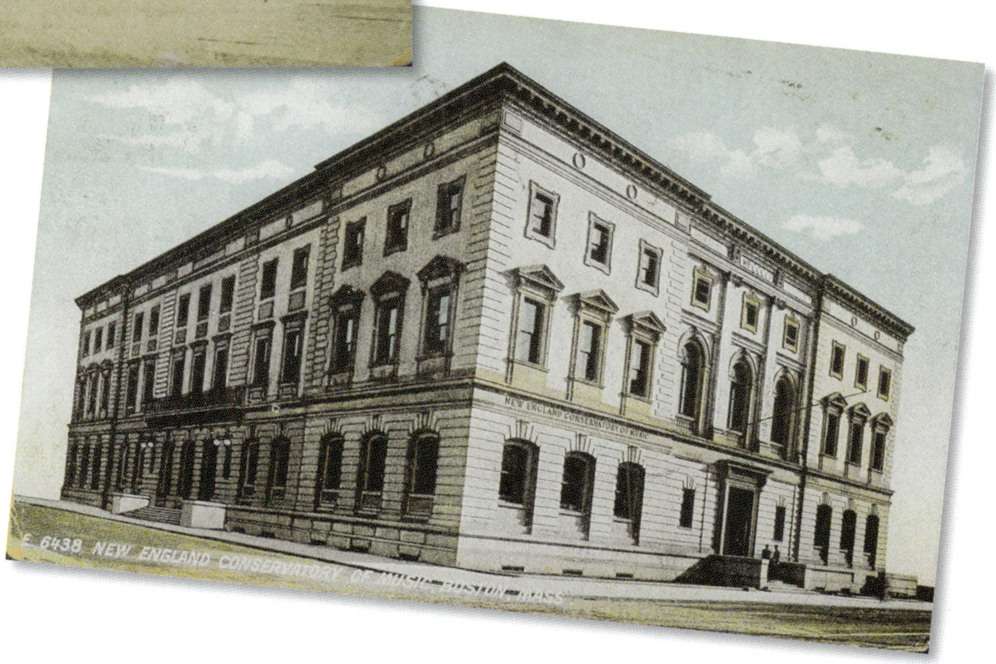

Established in 1867, New England Conservatory of Music became one of the country's foremost music schools. Designed by Wheelwright & Haven, the conservatory includes Jordan Hall, which is named after the donor, Eben Jordan of department store fame.

Education

Some sixty colleges and universities are in the greater Boston area. The total number of students attending them increases each year. Today, Boston's Fenway is the site for the Art Institute of Boston, the Boston Conservatory, the New England Conservatory, Emmanuel College, the Massachusetts College of Art, College of Pharmacy and Health Sciences, Harvard School of Dental Medicine and School of Public Health, the Museum School, the New England School of Photography, Northeastern University, Simmons College, Wentworth Institute of Technology, and Wheelock College.

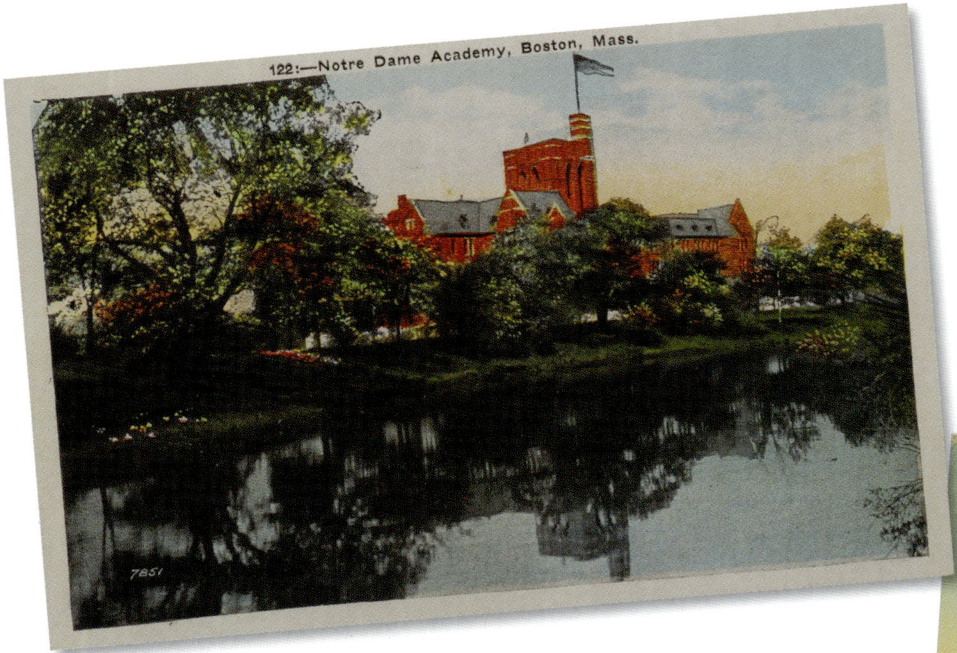

Notre Dame Academy, sponsored by the Sisters of Notre Dame de Nemours, is the oldest Catholic day school for girls in New England. Opened in 1853, it moved, in 1916, to 400 The Fenway; by 1919, it shared that location with the new Emmanuel College. As the college grew, the Academy moved once again, to Granby Street.

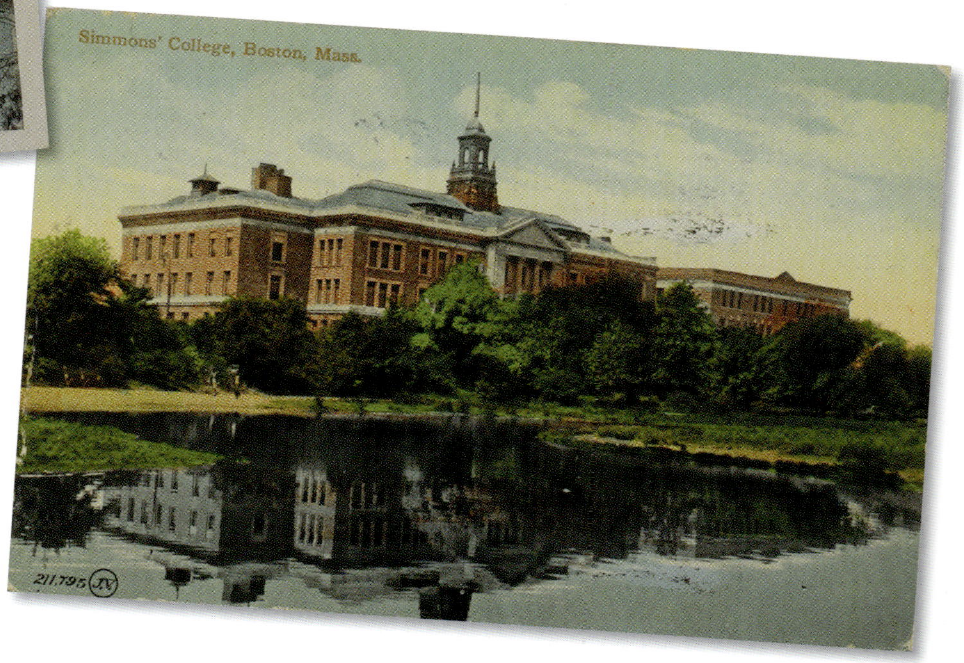

Founded in 1899, Simmons College provided instruction for women in those areas of art, science, and industry that would help its students become independent. Designed by Peabody & Stearns, the school was named after its benefactor, John Simmons, a wealthy Boston retailer.

MEDICINE

Medicine is a major industry in Boston. First family Yankees founded many of the hospitals, and family members still sit on their boards. Today, many patients come to Boston to avail themselves of its formidable array of medical facilities. The Fenway attracted famous medical establishments such as Children's Hospital, Beth Israel Deaconess Medical Center, and the Harvard School of Medicine. The area, which also includes Brigham and Women's Hospital, Dana-Farber Cancer Institute, and Joslin Diabetes Center, is known as the Longwood Medical Area.

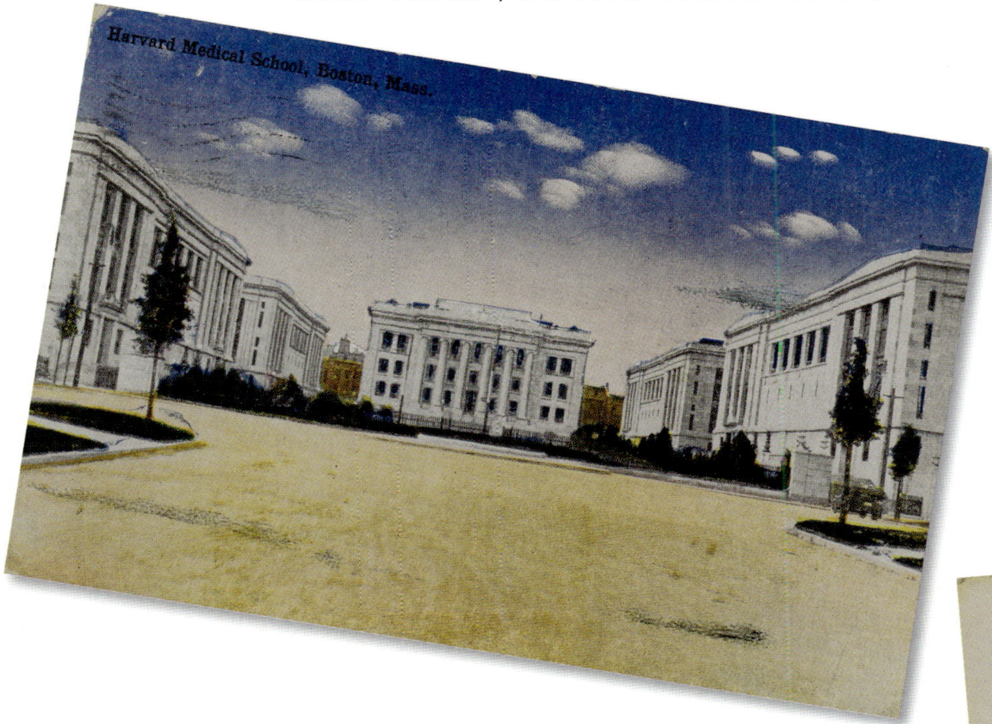

The first of Harvard's professional schools, the Harvard Medical School was founded in 1782. It began with a staff of Harvard alumni who had participated in forming the American Army's Hospital Department at the outbreak of the Revolutionary War. In 1906, the Medical School's new campus on Longwood Avenue in Boston was opened. The Fenway at that time was open farm and marshland. The combination of the new medical school and the empty land drew other hospitals to the area. Built in 1906 by architects, Shepley, Rutan and Coolidge, these formal, white marble buildings are identical externally, except for the four-story portico on the administrative building. They are still used for classrooms, research laboratories, and administrative offices.

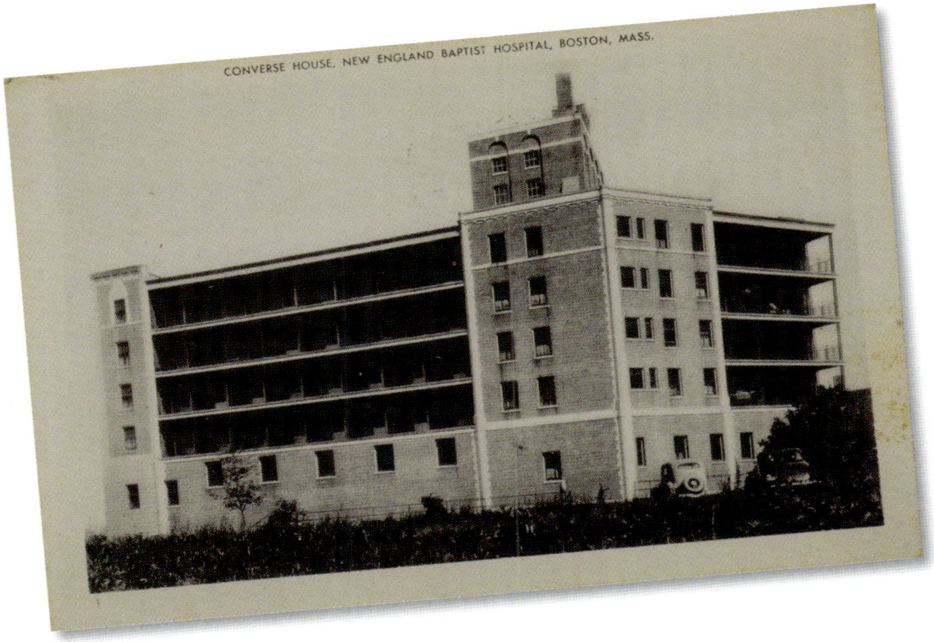

Established in 1893, New England Baptist Hospital is a 141-bed adult medical/surgical hospital, located in the Mission Hill neighborhood of Boston, with specialty services in musculoskeletal care, sports medicine, occupational medicine, and cardiology.

Boston Museum of Fine Arts

Huntington Avenue was laid out, one hundred feet wide, in 1872. When the Boston Museum of Fine Arts (MFA) moved to the Fenway (465 Huntington Avenue), it acquired twelve acres, which provided ample room for it to continue to house famous collections. One of the more important national art museums, its extensive holdings and ongoing exhibits attract millions of visitors each year.

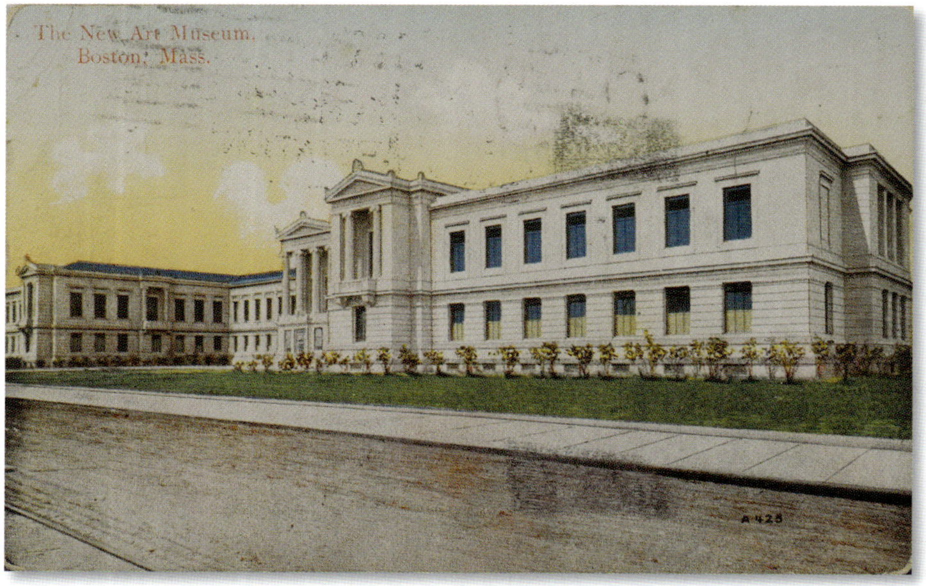

Designed by Architect Guy Lowell, the monumental Classical Revival building was built in 1911-1915. Throughout the twentieth century, the museum acquired many notable pieces of art.

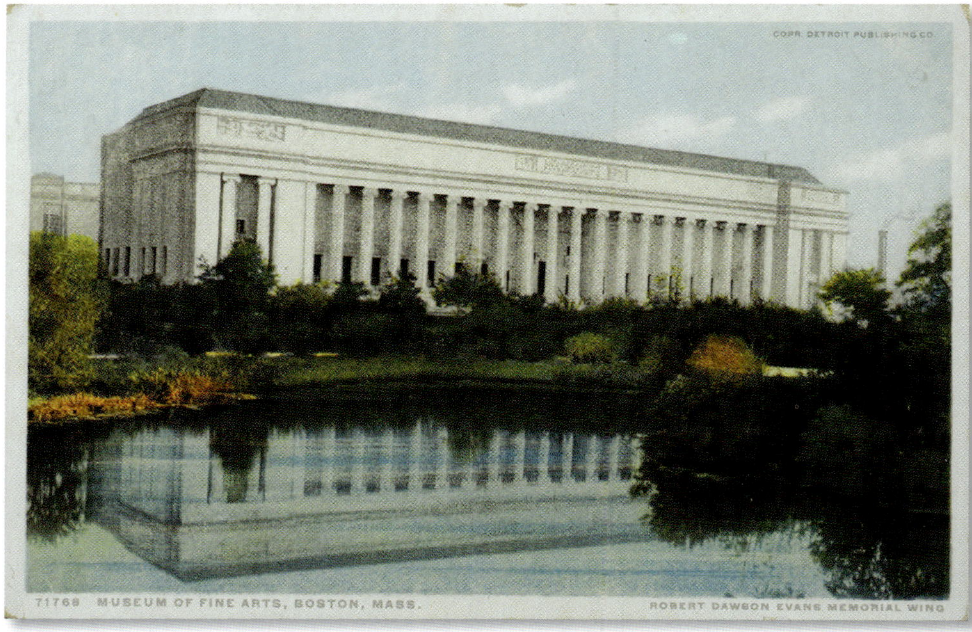

The Boston Museum of Fine Arts Evans Memorial Wing, also designed by Guy Lowell, enlarged the museum in 1915. Its elegant granite facade has a colonnade of Ionic columns flanked by bay projections. In 1925-1928, the Decorative Arts Wing was built.

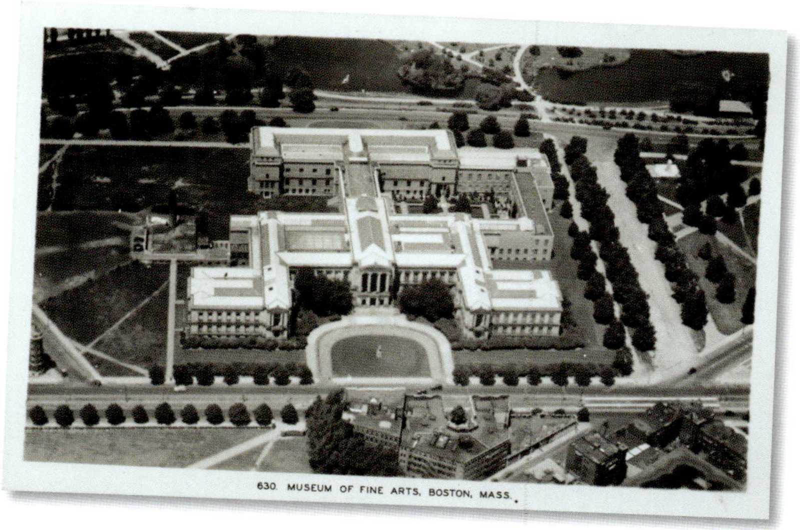

The museum has greatly expanded since this aerial view was taken. In 2007, it began a significant expansion, which includes a new American Wing and a glass-enclosed family courtyard.

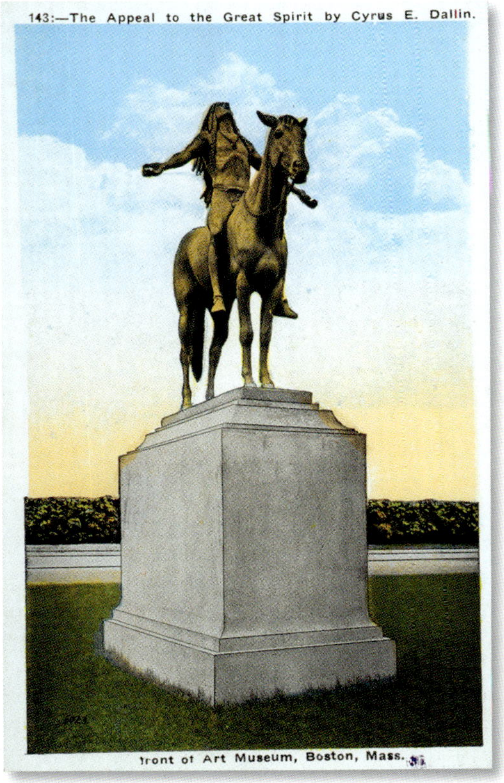

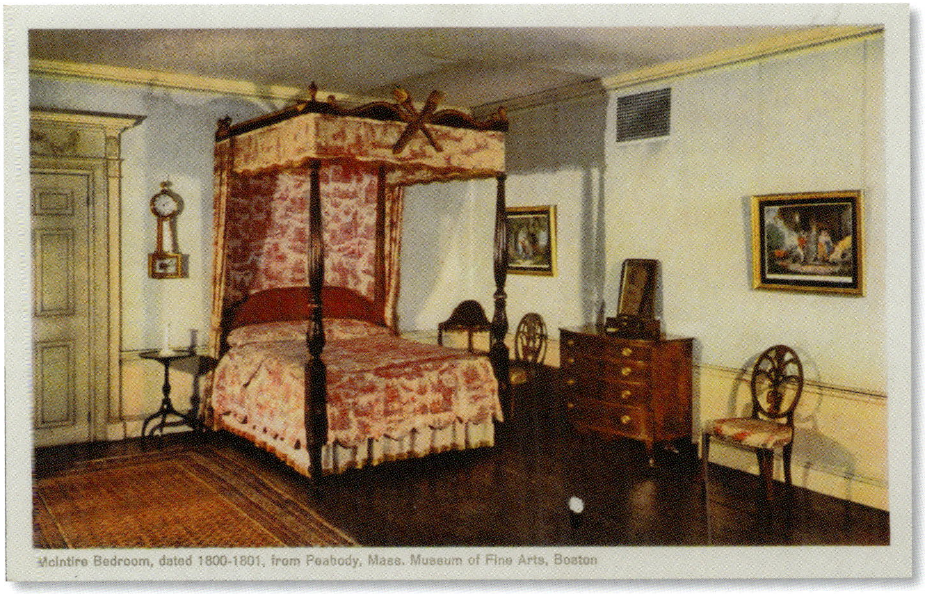

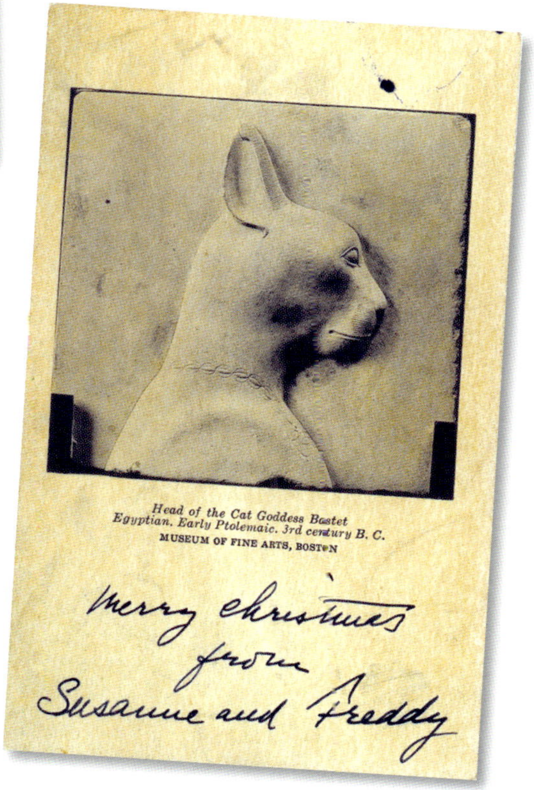

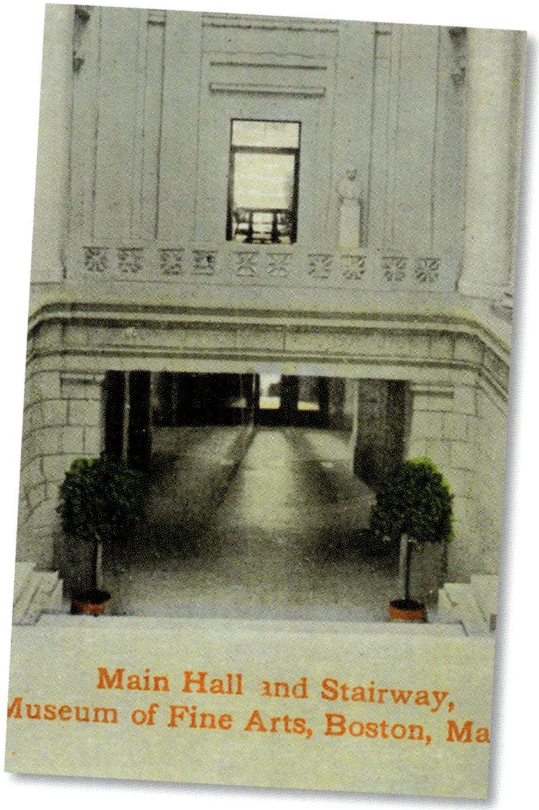

With approximately 450,000 objects in its collections, the Boston Museum of Fine Arts always has something new on view. It also offers an ongoing schedule of special exhibits and daily activities, including gallery talks, films, concerts, artist lectures, and family programs.

Isabella Stewart Gardner Museum

In Boston they ask, "How much does he know?" In New York, "How much is he worth?" In Philadelphia, "Who were his parents?"
–Mark Twain (Samuel Langhorne Clemens)

The daughter of a New York dry goods merchant, Isabella Stewart married John "Jack" Lowell Gardner, a grandson of one of the shipping magnates. In a society where the ultimate public activities – especially for a married woman – required decorum, which she didn't seem to possess, Isabella soon became well known. She had a pet lion, she drank beer, and she attended the Boston Symphony wearing a headband emblazoned with "Oh, you Red Sox." She spent money on Paris fashions and wore her diamonds on gold wire springs waving six inches above her hair. She was too much for proper Boston women!

Her only child died at age one. Shortly after her husband died in 1898, she suffered a nervous breakdown and the doctors told her to take up a hobby. In 1907, Isabella Stewart Gardner bought a fantastic Italian palazzo and had it shipped to Boston in pieces. She erected it at 280 Fenway, providing Bostonians and tourists with a world-class museum housing the works of old masters as well as modern artists. Boston women had to pay attention then!

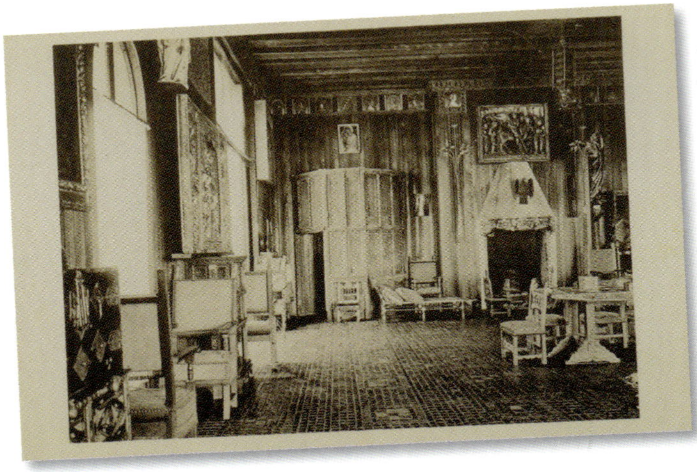

The interior is a four-story Venetian palace. Mrs. Gardner lived on its fourth floor until her death in 1924.

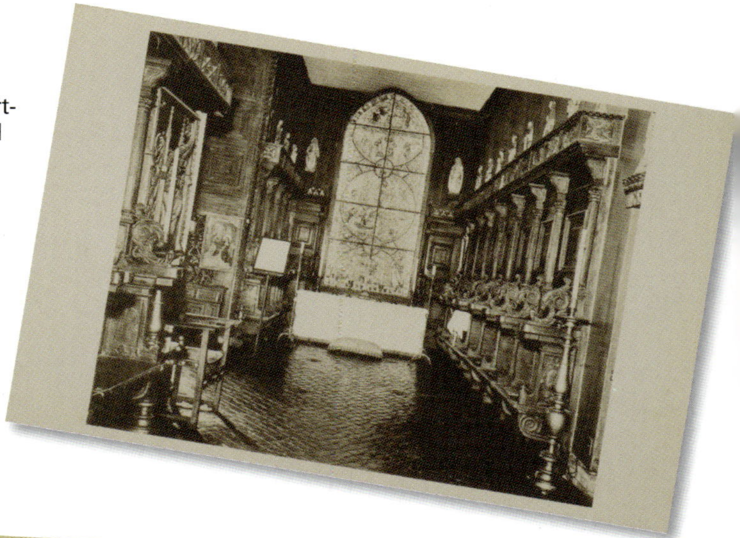

She knew which artists to sponsor and which paintings to buy.

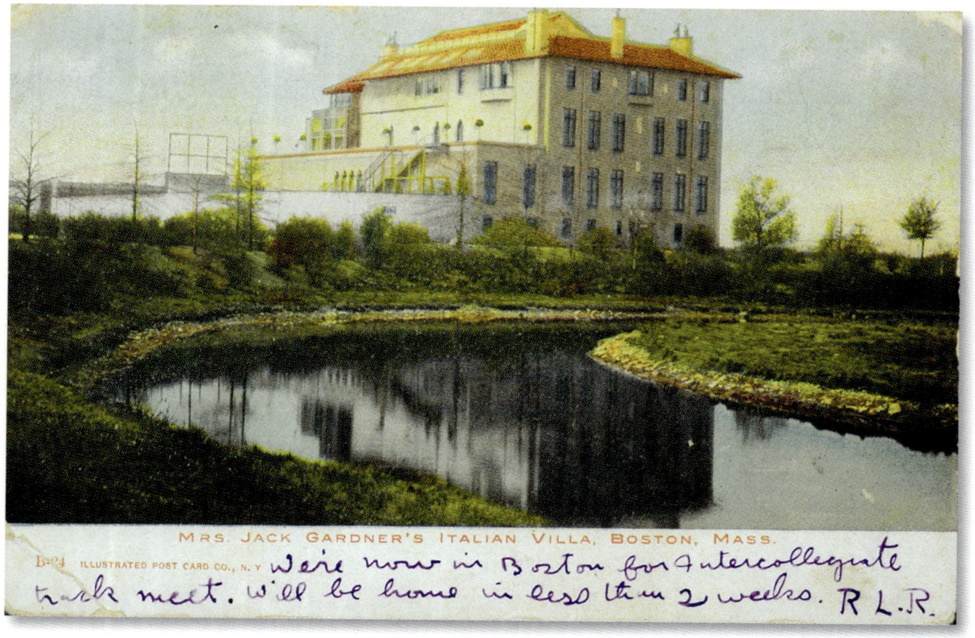

The exterior of the building is plain.

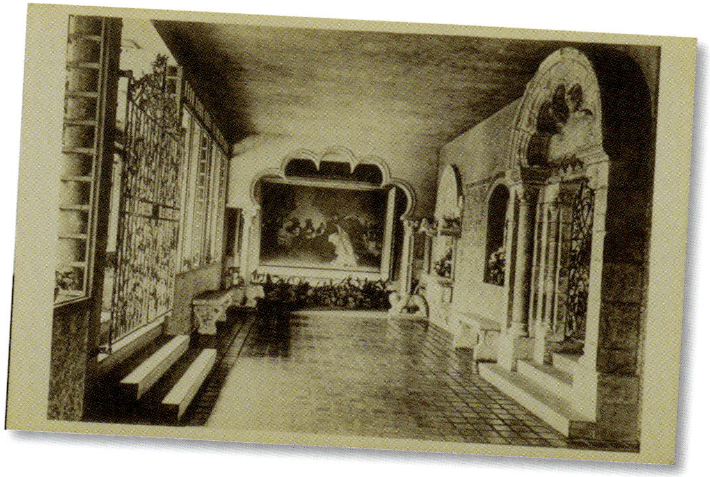

The museum collections contain 2,500 paintings, which include works by Rembrandt, Michelangelo, and Degas, sculptures, tapestries, and rare books.

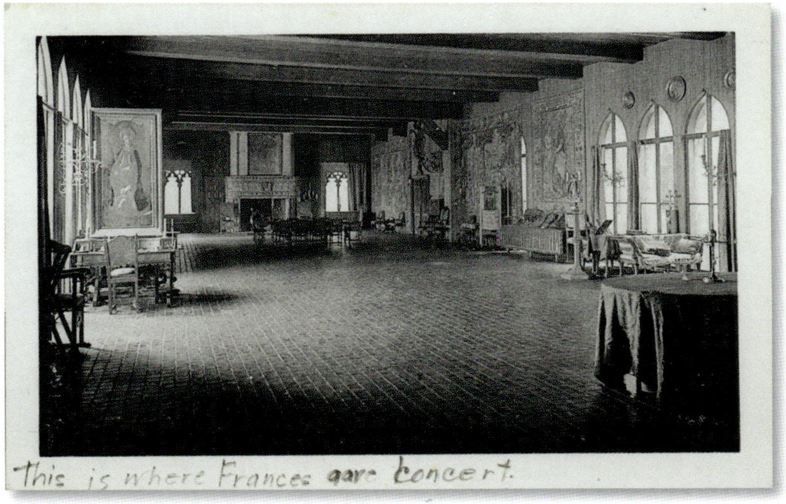

As stated in her will, her palace is a "museum for the education and enjoyment of the public forever."

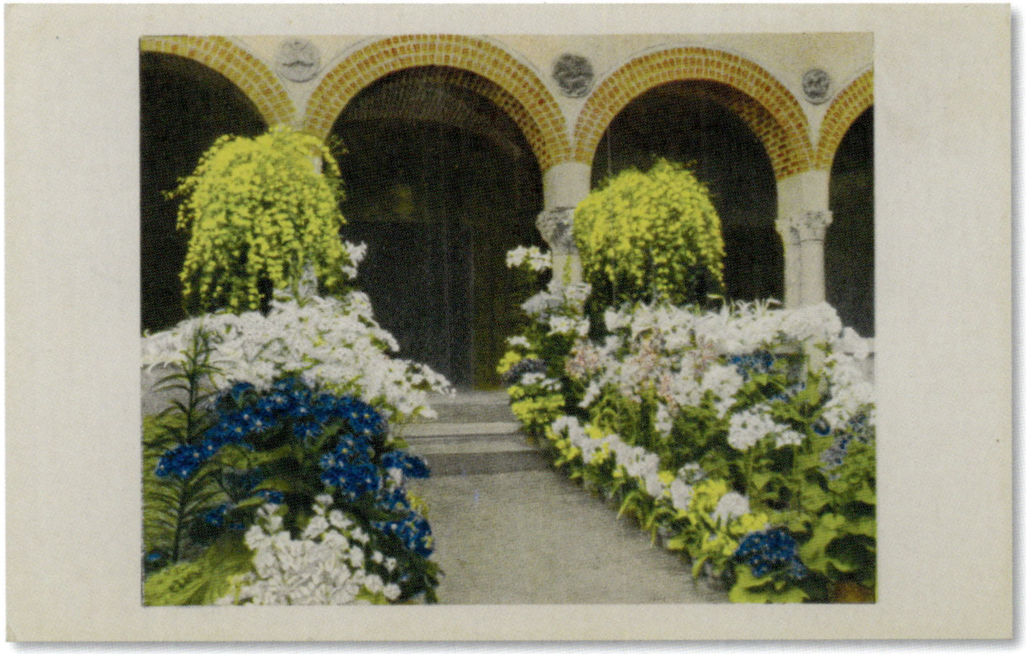

The central courtyard is full of colorful statues and fountains. To commemorate Gardner's birthday each April, the museum hangs nasturtiums dangling eight feet from the balconies.

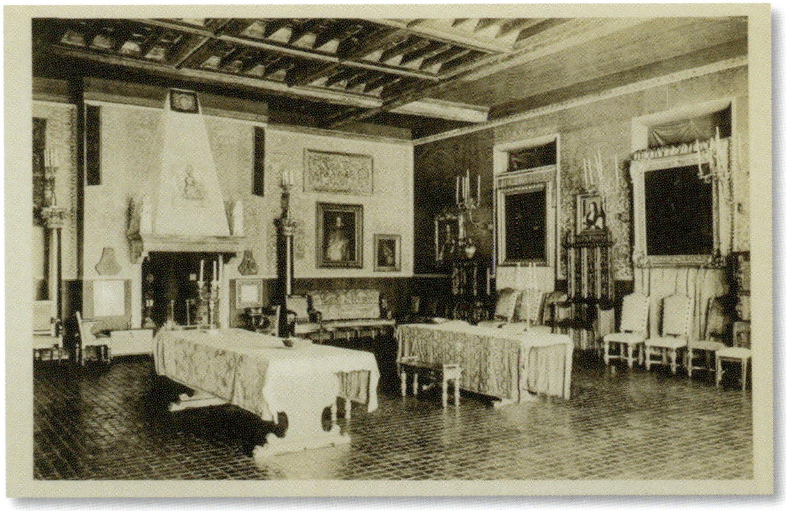

Rooms displaying great works of art surround the four-story high great courtyard at the palace's center.

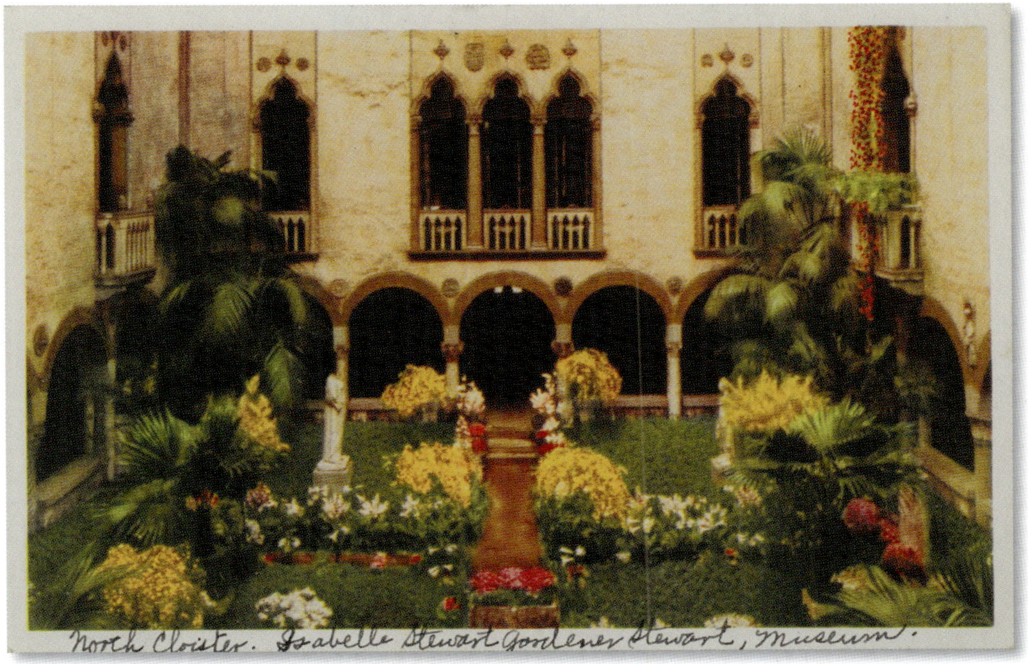

To this day, people are wide eyed when they see the courtyard with its vivid display of seasonal flowers centered among the treasure-filled rooms.

Chapter 9

Charlestown

But sea power has never led to despotism. The nations that have enjoyed sea power even for a brief period – Athens, Scandinavia, the Netherlands, England, the United States – are those that have preserved freedom for themselves and have given it to others. Of the despotism to which unrestrained military power leads we have plenty of examples from Alexander to Mao.
–Samuel Eliot Morison, *The Oxford History of the American People*

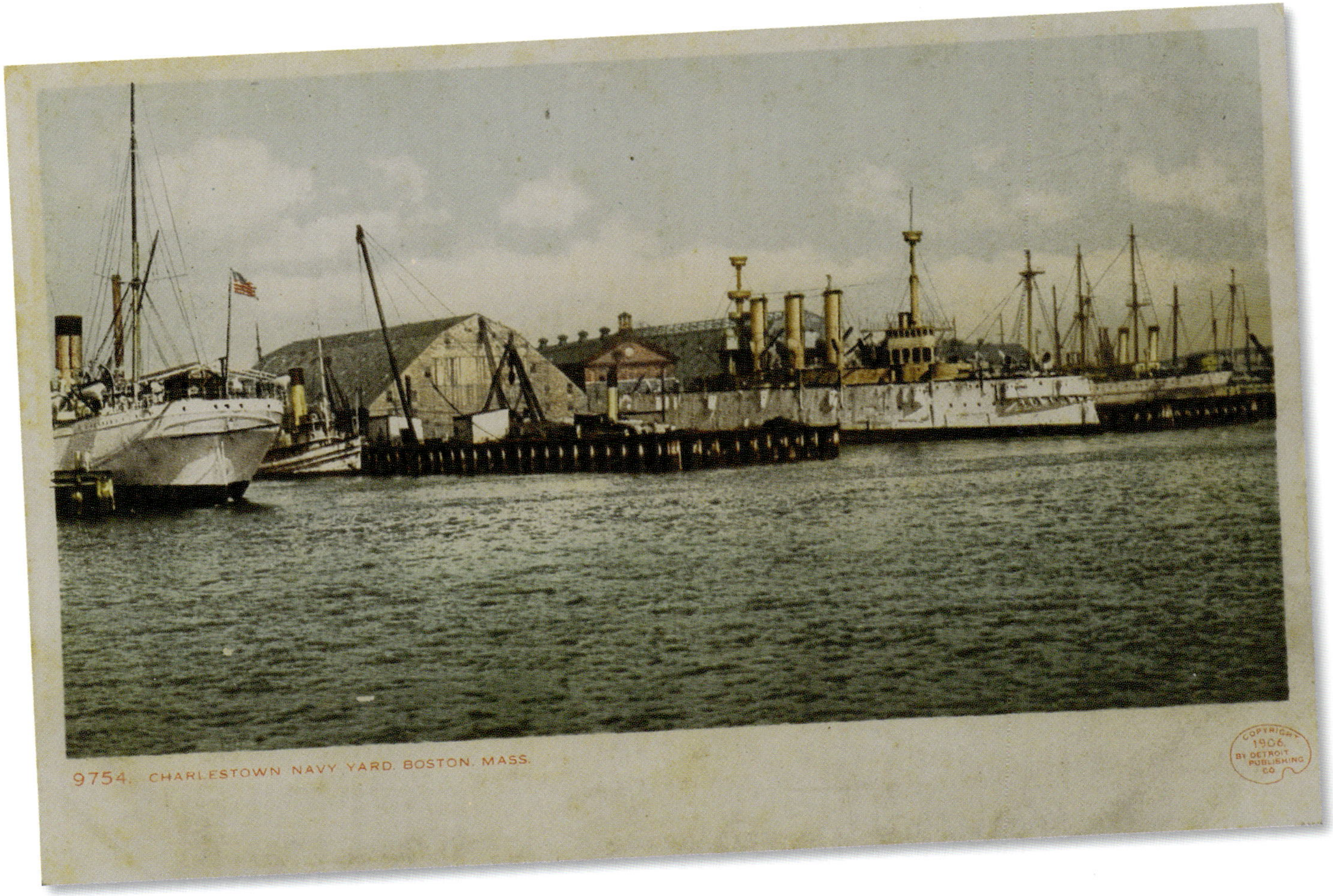

Boston has the largest harbor in New England. From its inception, the port was crowded with brigs, sloops, and later the square riggers and clippers tied up at its many wharves. Brick warehouses held the expanding trade with the East Indies, China, and the American coast. Whaling and cod fishing also became lucrative industries.

Old Ironsides

Old Ironsides
Ay, tear her tattered ensign down!
Long has it waved on high,
And many an eye has danced to see
That banner in the sky;
Beneath it rung the battle shout,
And burst the cannon's roar; --
The meteor of the ocean air
Shall sweep the clouds no more.
–Oliver Wendell Holmes, September 14, 1830

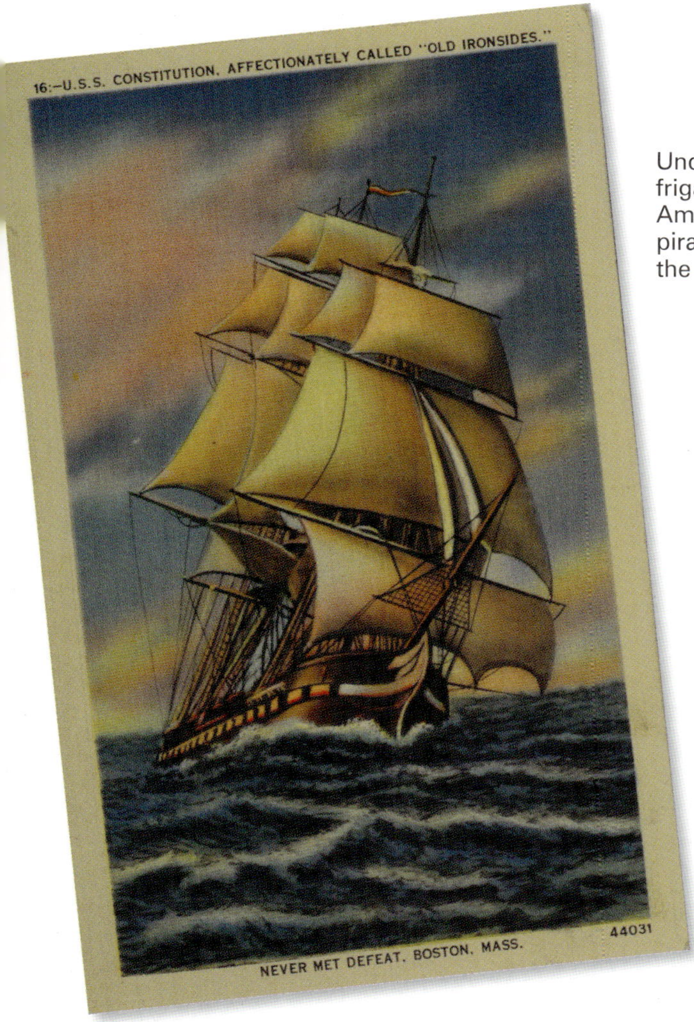

Edmund Hartt at Hartt's Ship Yard built the three-masted, heavy frigate, known as the *USS Constitution*, from approximately 2000 live oaks. She displaced 2,000 tons—about the same as a World War II destroyer. The hull was fitted with copper sheathing produced by Paul Revere. Launched on October 21, 1797, she is the oldest commissioned warship afloat in the world. Her reputation and her nickname "Old Ironsides" are a result of her sinking the British frigates *Guerriere* and *Java* in the War of 1812 and in a single battle capturing two sloops of war. British sailors are said to have coined the name because cannon balls bounced off her hull.

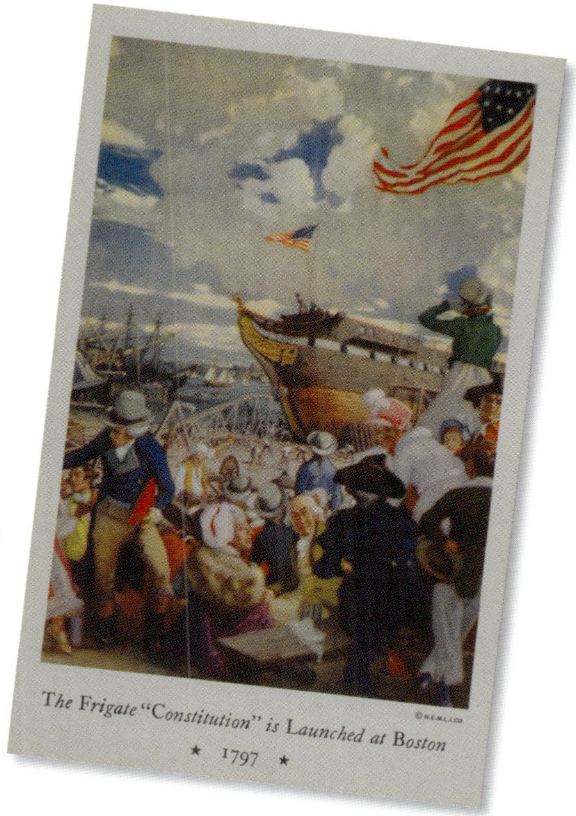

Under President George Washington, six frigates were constructed to protect the American merchant fleet from the Barbary pirates. Designed by Joshua Humphreys, the ships were built in six different cities.

In 1830, she was considered unfit for service. Then Oliver Wendell Holmes at age 21 wrote a poem that funded her overhaul.

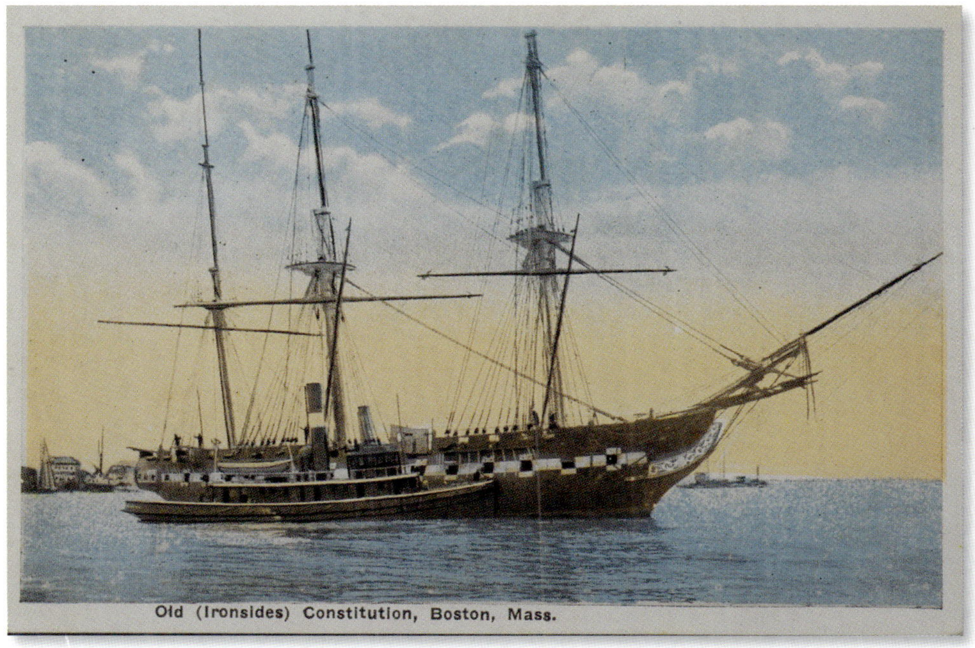

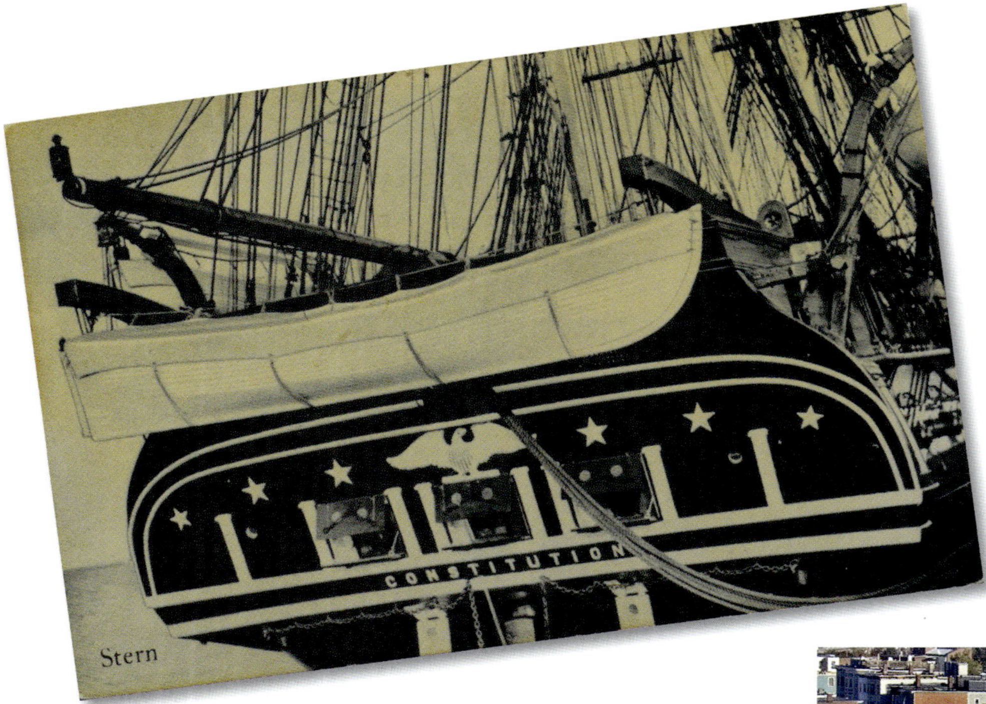

Placed back in commission, she served as a flagship in the Mediterranean and the Pacific; training ship for the Naval Academy, receiving ship, and barracks. She even circumnavigated the globe.
Today, her mission is to promote the Navy to millions of visitors each year. Her 55-sailor crew participates in ceremonies, educational programs, and special events while keeping the ship open to visitors year-round and providing free tours.

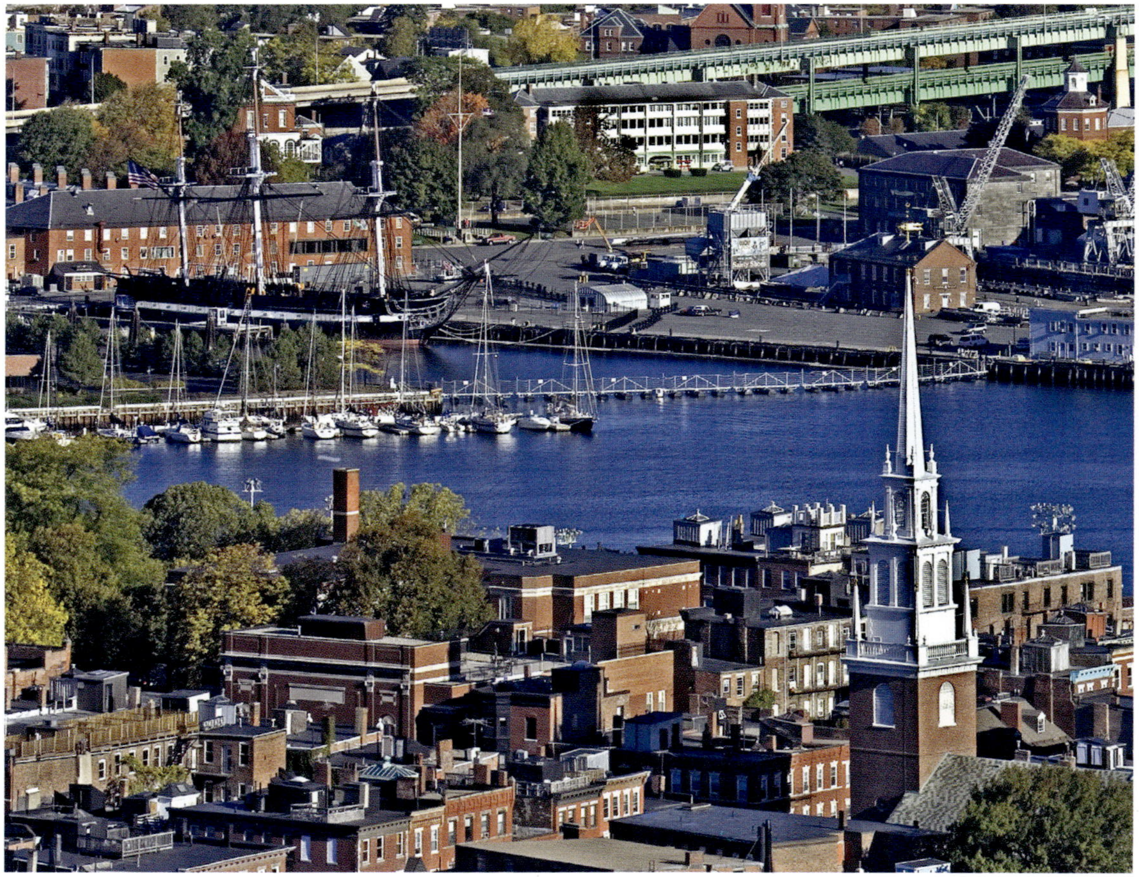

Old North Church is in the right front. Across the harbor is Old Ironsides in the former Boston Navy Yard. *Courtesy of Paul E. Doherty*

Boston Naval Shipyard

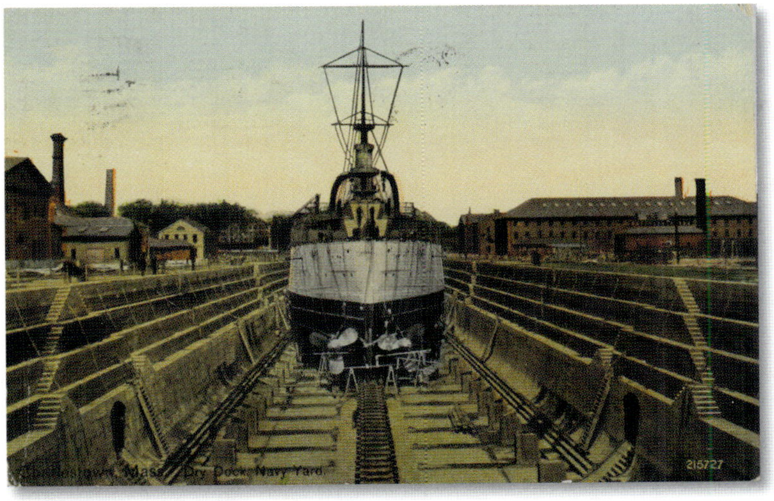

Boston was known for shipbuilding. The Charlestown Navy Yard, or Boston Navy Yard, or Boston Naval Shipyard was established to build warships. The 30-acre Boston Navy Yard built the first US ship of the line, *USS Independence*, and slowly evolved to meet the needs of a changing navy. Before the Civil War, the Boston Navy Yard had a superior dry dock built to accommodate the *Constitution*, a great rope-walk, and all the necessary shipbuilding facilities. In this image, a ship is on the ways.

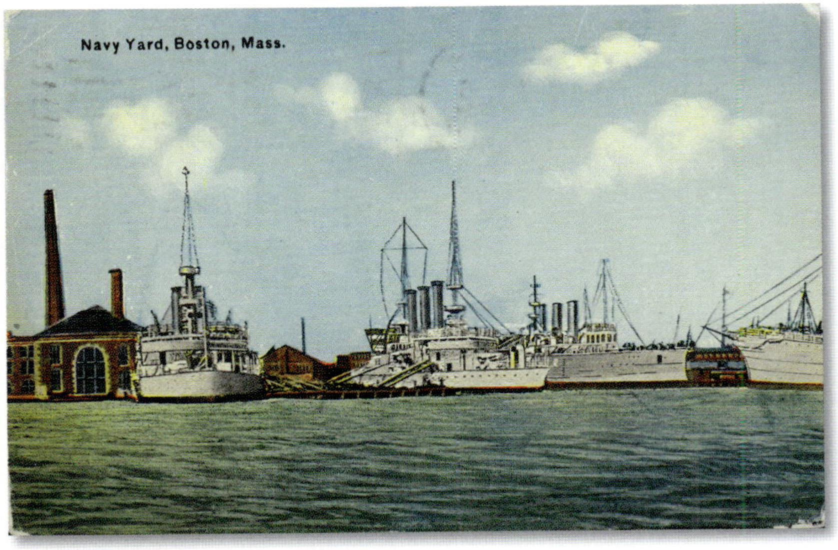

Established in 1801, the yard was officially closed after the Vietnam War ended in July 1974, and the property became part of the Boston National Historical Park.
The yard continues to support the *USS Constitution* and *USS Cassin Young,* which are berthed here as representatives of the vessels that have served the United States.

Bunker Hill

Located on a peninsula in Boston Harbor at the confluence of the Mystic and Charles Rivers, Charlestown has two hills: Bunker and Breed's. During the Colonial period, it was a busy seaport until the Revolutionary War occurred. The British burned it to the ground during the Battle of Bunker Hill.

Grandmothers Story of Bunker Hill (as she saw it from the belfry)
'Tis like stirring living embers when, at eighty, one remembers
All the achings and the quakings of "the times that tried men's souls"; ...
To you the words are ashes, but to me they're burning coals.
I had heard the muskets' rattle of the April running battle;
Lord Percy's hunted soldiers, I can see their red coats still;
But a deadly chill comes o'er me, as the day looms up before me,
When a thousand men lay bleeding on the slopes of Bunker's Hill....
–Oliver Wendell Holmes

Said to be that nation's first public obelisk, the soaring granite Bunker Hill monument is an important part of the Boston skyline. On June 17, 1775, the first major battle of the American Revolutionary War took place here. Although the more highly trained and better-equipped British army won, the colonists repelled two major assaults and inflicted great casualties until their powder ran out. Although it is called the Battle of Bunker Hill, the battle really occurred on Breed's Hill.
The Marquis de Lafayette laid the cornerstone in 1825 for the 220-foot granite monument designed by Solomon Willard. The stones were transported on our country's first railroad, constructed specifically for that purpose.

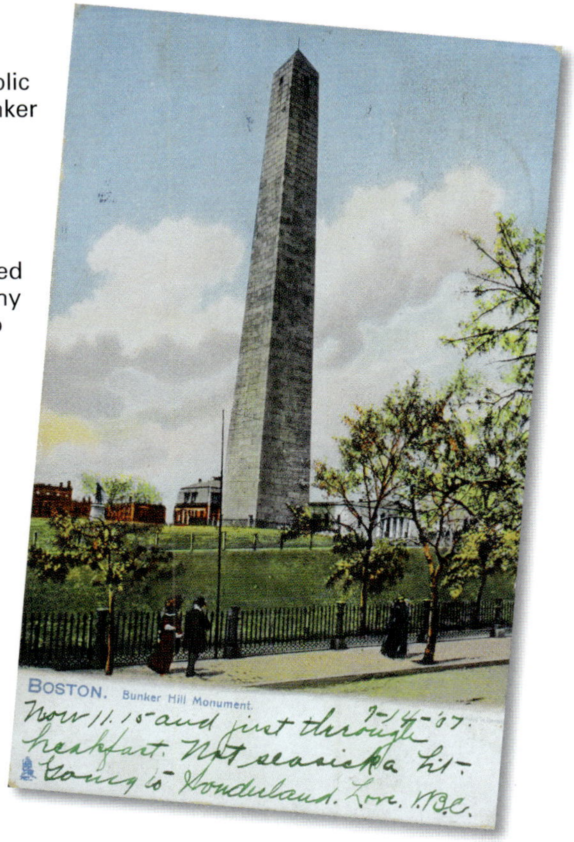

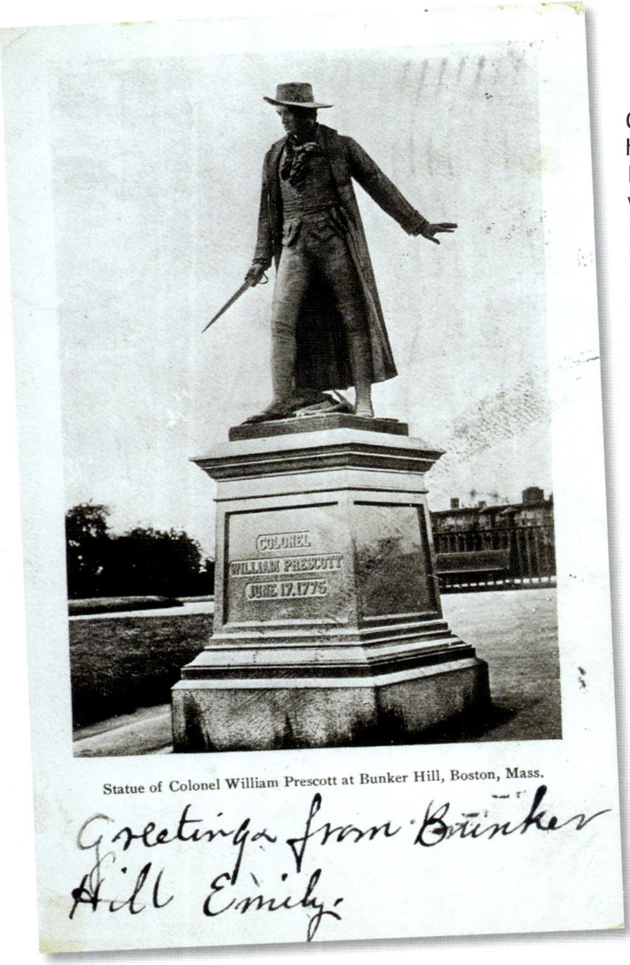

Colonel William Prescott and his men defended Breed's Hill. Many believe that it was Prescott who first said, "Don't fire 'til you see the whites of their eyes," during this battle between the ill-equipped colonial forces and the British Army. William Storey sculpted the bronze monument.

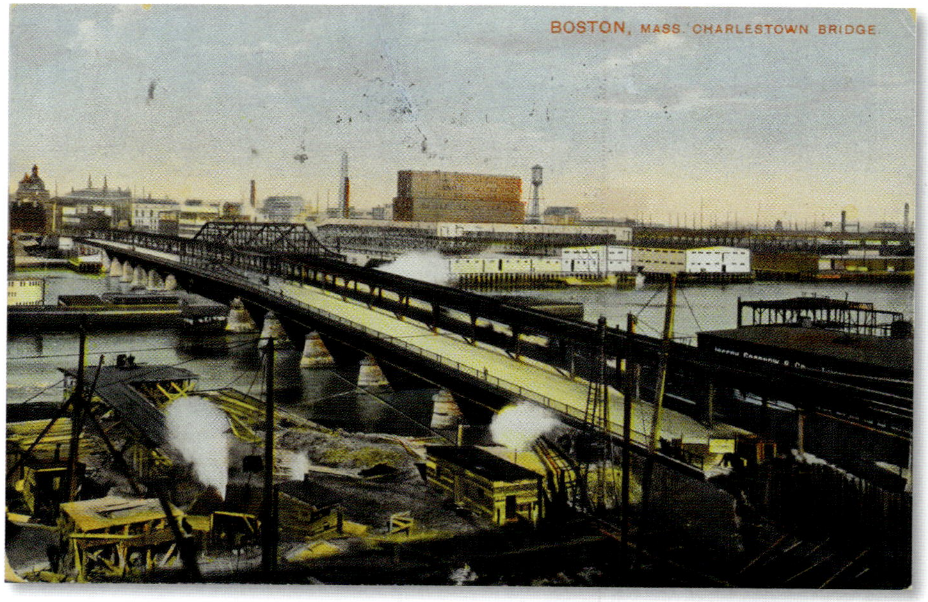

After the war, it rebuilt, and many eighteenth and nineteenth century houses remain standing today

Charlestown was demolished during the battle because the British ships fired on the town.

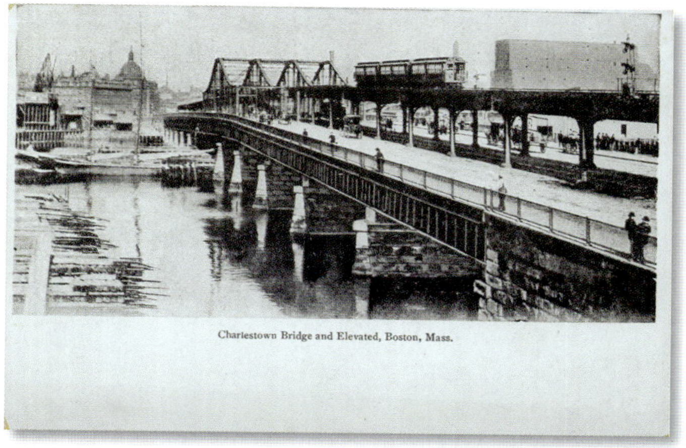

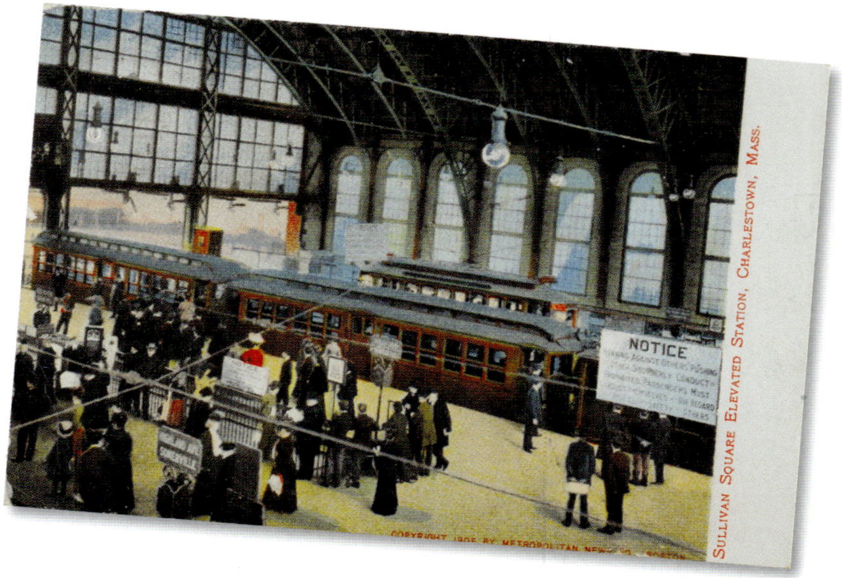

In 1874, attracted by the many services offered by Boston, Charlestown joined the City of Boston as one of its many neighborhoods.

Chapter 10

The Charles River and Scenic Green Spaces

Boston is an oasis in the desert, a place where the larger proportion of people are loving, rational and happy. –Julia Ward Howe

Captain John Smith named the small, meandering river the Charles in honor of King Charles I of England. John Winthrop and his Puritans sited Boston on its back bay. Up the stream was Cambridge. Today, the Charles is the most densely populated river basin in New England. It is dotted with sailboats, kayaks, and racing sculls. The paths along the riverbank are filled with walkers, joggers, and cyclists. During the summer, the Boston Pops and others play in the Hatch Shell.

During the seventeenth century, many settlers found homes on the banks of the Charles. The upstream settlers came to terms with the wilderness and sold their wares downstream. The downstream settlers became artisans and shopkeepers. The settlers soon learned how to harness the river's energy. Francis Cabot Lowell built America's first factory in Waltham in 1814. During the nineteenth century, the Charles River powered many mills and factories, and it was one of the most industrialized areas in the United States. By the twentieth century, twenty dams had been built across the river.

Today, twenty parks, such as the Charles River Esplanade with the Hatch Shell and natural areas along nineteen miles of shoreline, make this river a beautiful place to visit. During the early part of the twentieth century, the Charles River basin was designed to provide city dwellers access to the water and its recreational opportunities. James Jackson Storrow led the damming of the river's mouth at today's Museum of Science, which stabilized the water level from Boston to Watertown and eliminated the mud flats. Subsequently, Storrow's widow donated funds to create along the Esplanade a more generously landscaped park, now known as the Storrow Memorial Embankment. In the 1950s, Storrow Drive was built along the edge of the Esplanade, and the Esplanade was enlarged on the waterside of the new highway.

A river seems a magic thing. A magic, moving, living part of the very earth itself—for it is from the soil, both from its depth and from its surface, that a river has its beginning. –Laura Gilpin

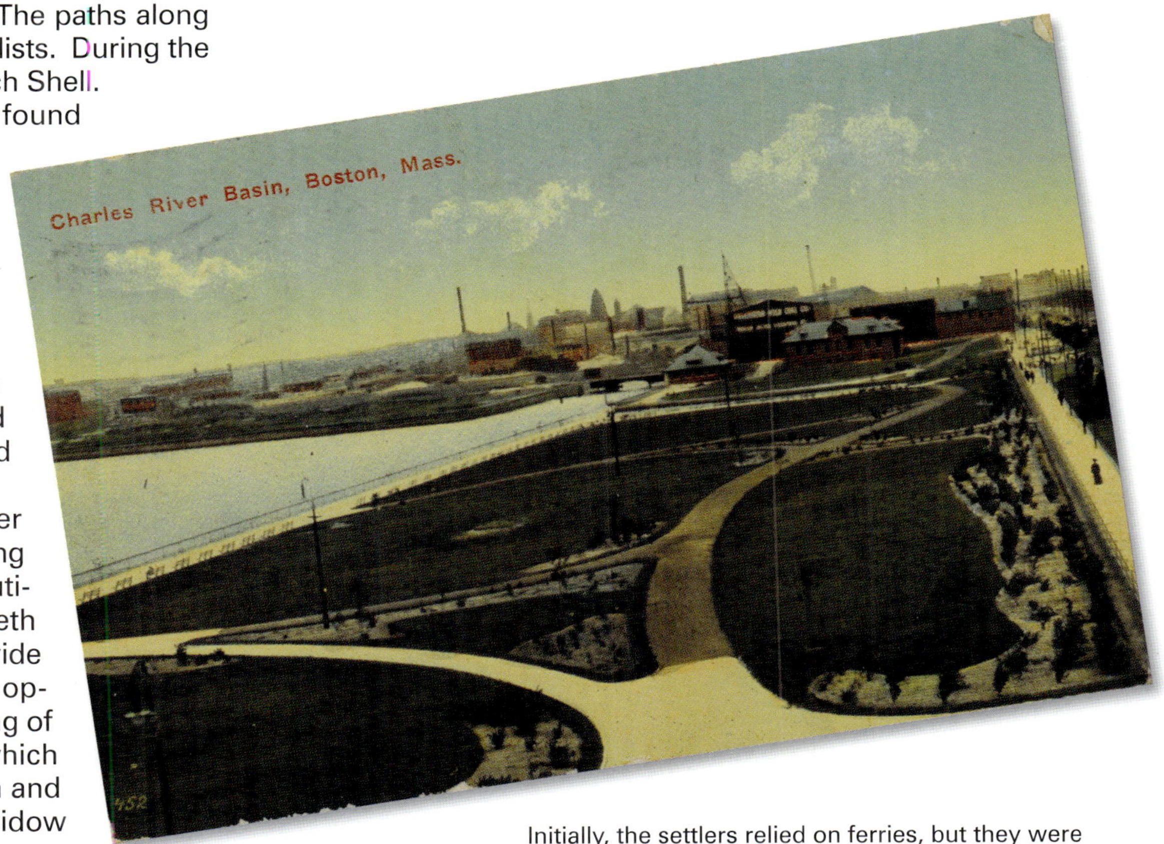

Initially, the settlers relied on ferries, but they were weather dependent. Subsequent bridges, roads, and canals such as the West Boston Bridge facilitated Cambridge's industrial growth.

Completed in 1891, the Harvard Bridge (also known locally as the "M.I.T. Bridge" or the "Mass. Ave. Bridge") carries Massachusetts Avenue (Route 2A) from Back Bay, Boston, to the Cambridge flats, the ultimate site of M.I.T. The longest bridge over the Charles River, it is also the oldest.

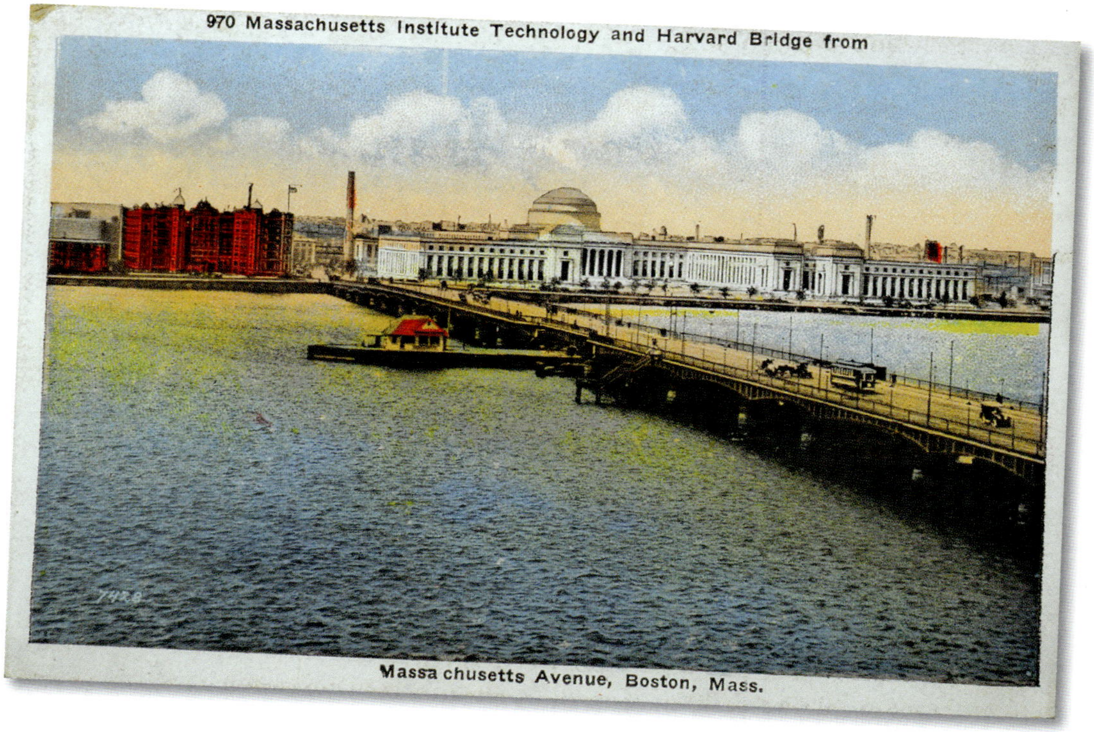

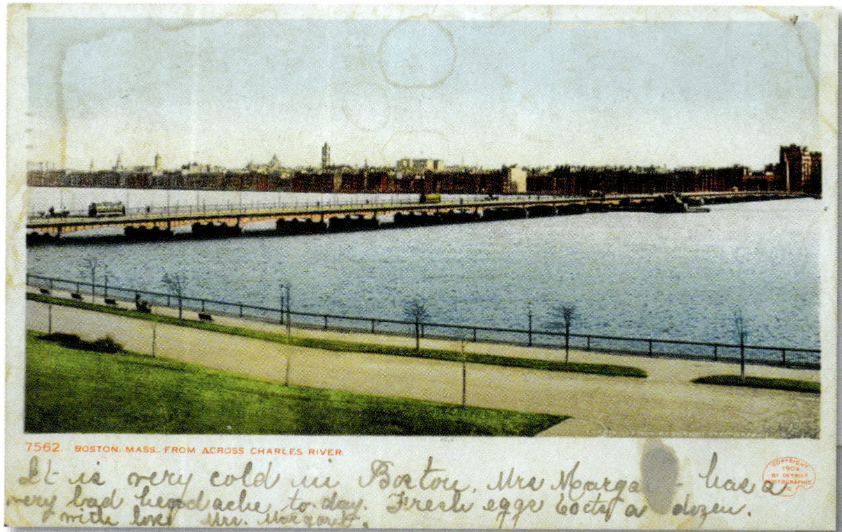

In 1958, members of the Lambda Chi Alpha fraternity are said to have measured the bridge by carrying or dragging the shortest pledge, Oliver Smoot, end over end across to Boston. Interestingly, Oliver Reed Smoot, Jr. was Chairman of the American National Standards Institute (ANSI) from 2001 to 2002 and President of the International Organization for Standardization (ISO) from 2003 to 2004.Twice each year, fraternity members paint length markers at 10-smoot intervals to remind pedestrians that the bridge is 364.4 smoots and one ear long. Given that Mr. Smoot is 170 cm tall, measuring the bridge from the zero smoot mark yields a bridge length of about 619 m. Other sources give the length of the bridge as approximately 660 m.

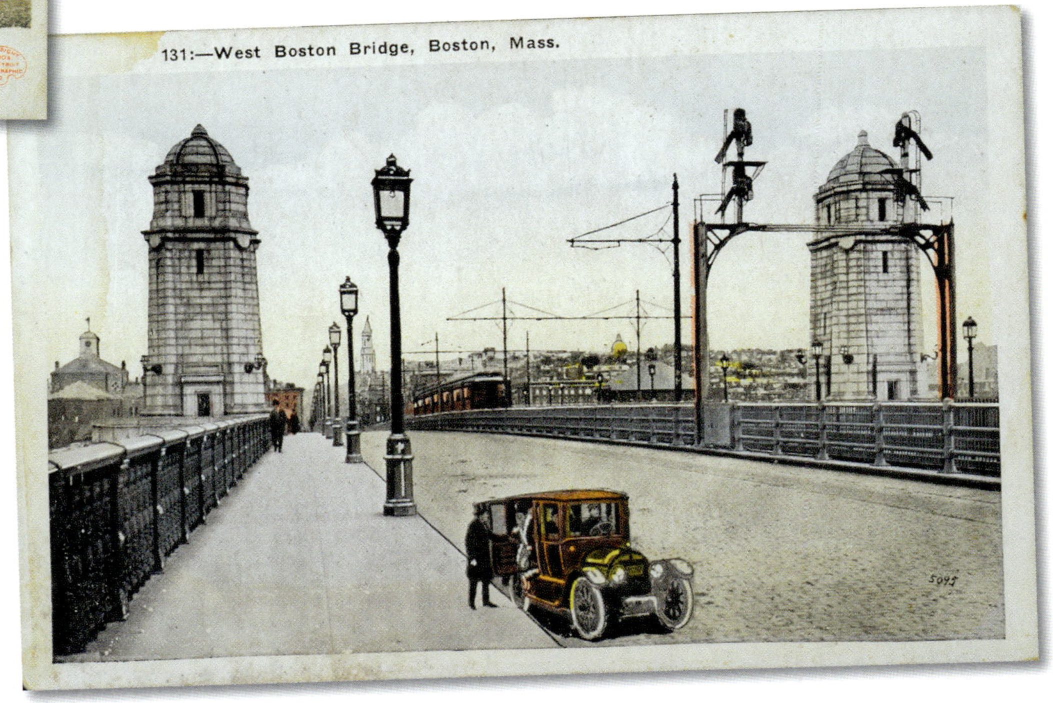

The original West Boston Bridge, connecting Cambridge with Boston, was opened on November 23, 1793. During Longfellow's courtship of his second wife, Fanny Appleton, he frequently walked from Harvard Square to her home on Beacon Hill, crossing the Charles River via the West Boston Bridge.

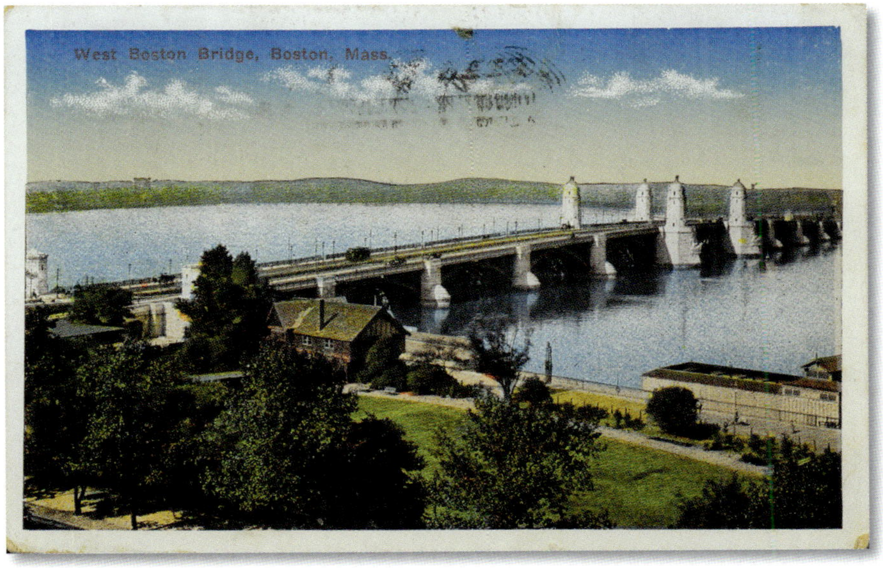

In 1906, a new bridge was built on the site of the original West Boston Bridge. It was renamed the Longfellow Bridge, but it is often referred to as the Salt and Pepper Shaker Bridge because the towers on the main piers resemble salt and pepper shakers. The 1893 Columbian Exposition inspired Architect Edmund M. Wheelwright's design, which was intended to rival the great European bridges with their towers and stonework.

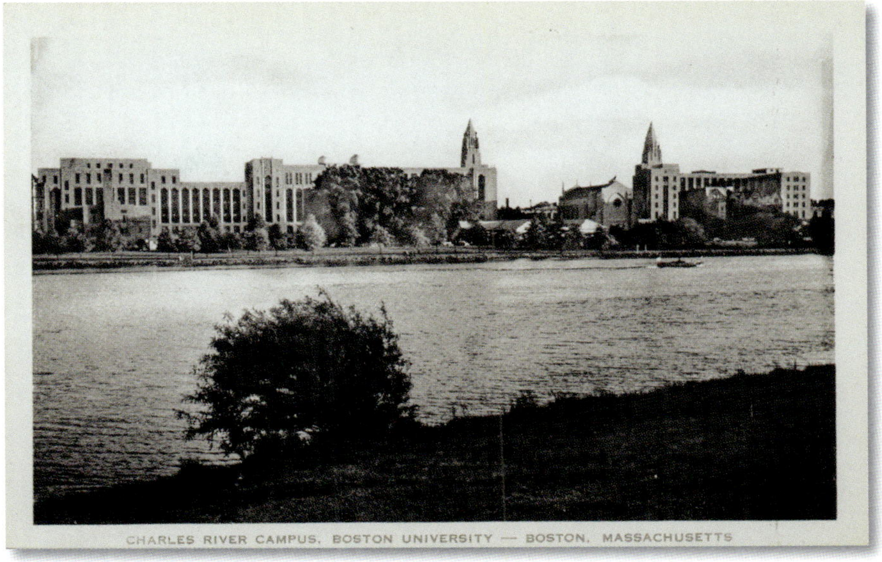

Lee Claflin, Jacob Sleeper, and Isaac Rich, three successful Methodist businessmen with abolitionist ideals, established Boston University in 1869. They envisioned an inclusive university that engaged in service to the City of Boston. Boston University has always admitted students of both sexes and every race and religion. It proudly points out that Martin Luther King, Jr. is one of its alumni.

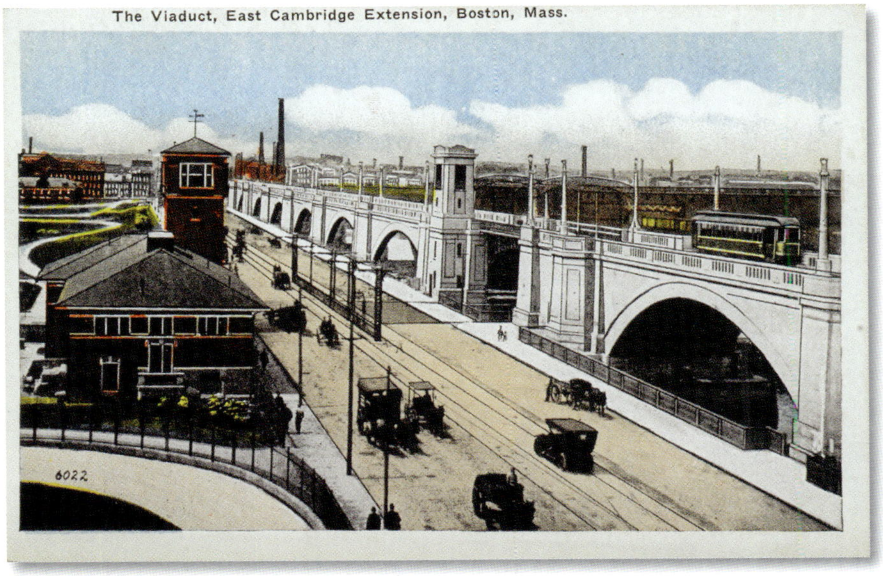

The East Cambridge viaduct was constructed from 1907-1912.

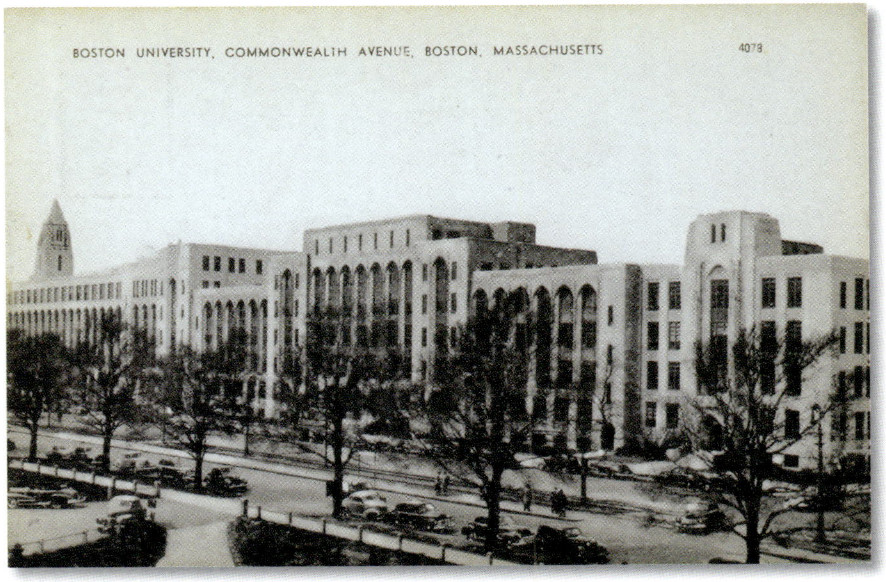

The Gothic-styled university is situated between Commonwealth Avenue and the Charles.

Today, the Charles River Esplanade is a scenic green space, attracting thousands of city dwellers annually. Its banks offer bicyclists, joggers, and walkers an attractive site for exercising, having a picnic, or just napping in the sun. Boston's enjoyment of the river goes back several centuries. In 1860, the city council resolved to support six floating bathhouses (Haglund, p. 73) as part of the growing concern for public health in the city's tenement neighborhoods. By 1898, the city managed thirteen floating bathhouses. Students were boating on the Charles before the Civil War.

The Charles has become a part of the American culture. It is featured in songs, movies (*Eternal Sunshine of the Spotless Mind*, *The River Wild*) and novels (Quentin in Faulkner's *Sound and Fury* drowns himself in the Charles). The Charles River is an icon for Boston.

Down by the River...
Down by the banks of the River Charles
(Oh, that's what's happenin' baby)
That's where you'll find me
Along with lovers, muggers, and thieves.
(Ahh, but they're cool people.)
"Dirty Water" by the Standells

He saw the narrow, twisted, age-browned streets of Boston, then, with their sultry fragrance of fresh-roasted coffee, the sight of the man-swarm passing in its million-footed weft, the distant drone and murmur of the great mysterious city all about him, the shining water of the Basin, and the murmur of the harbor and its ships, the promise of glory and of a thousand secret, lovely and mysterious women that were waiting somewhere in the city's web.
Thomas Wolfe, *Of Time and the River*

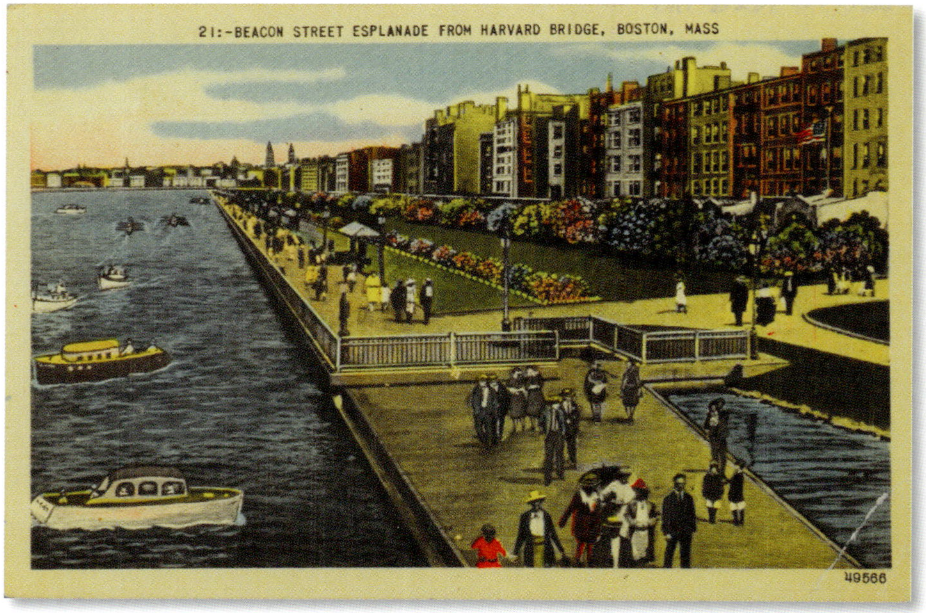

Site of Boston Pop's annual Fourth of July gala, the Esplanade runs along the southern bank of the Charles River from Charles Circle to the Boston University Bridge. This famous river park was once an area of mud flats. The nineteen-mile park on both sides of the river evolved in stages. Part of Boston's Emerald Necklace, this area of manicured lawns, gardens, and children's playgrounds offers scenery, exercise, and free concerts.

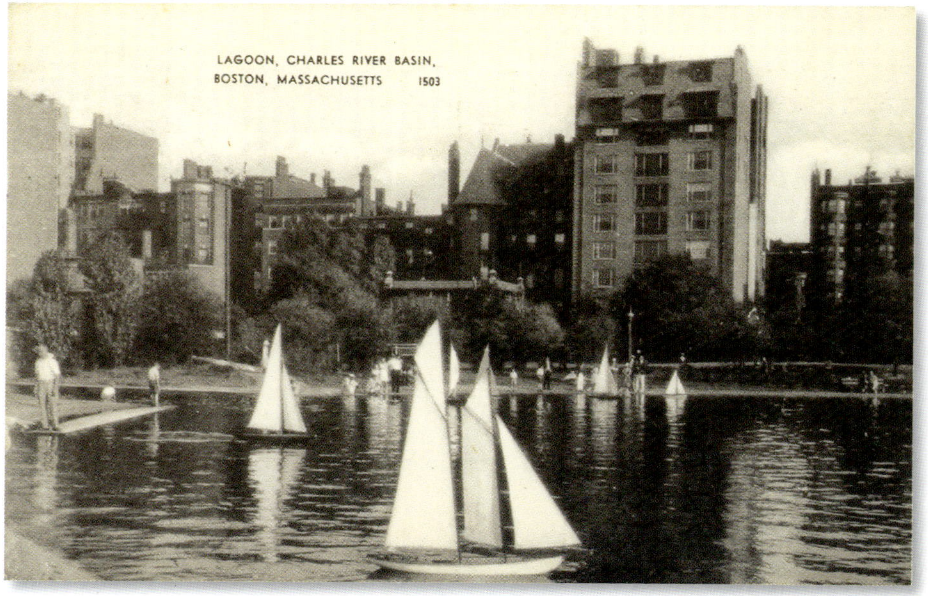

The focal point of the Back Bay area was a new lagoon that created a quiet shallow area used for sailing of model boats in summer and ice-skating in winter. Bridges at either end provided pedestrian access to the breakwater that formed the lagoon.

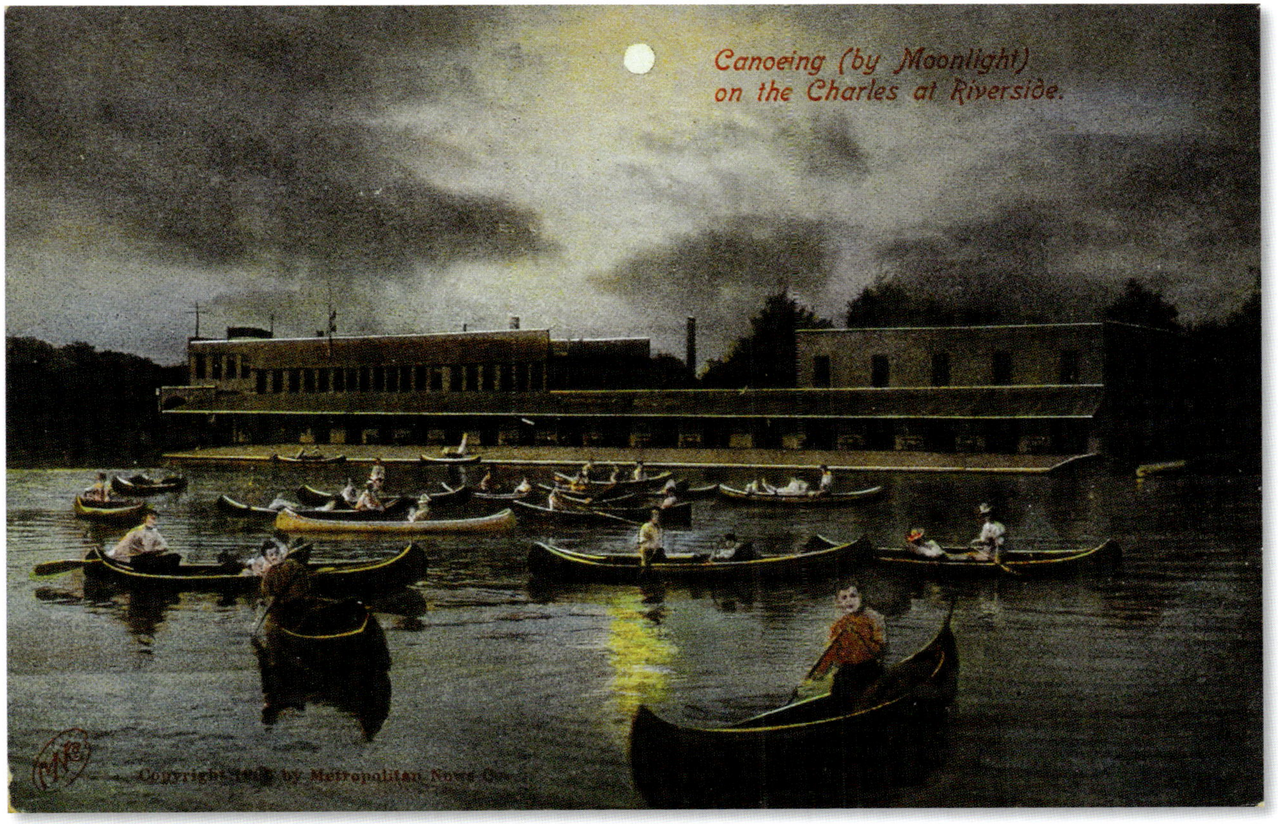

Views on the Charles River.

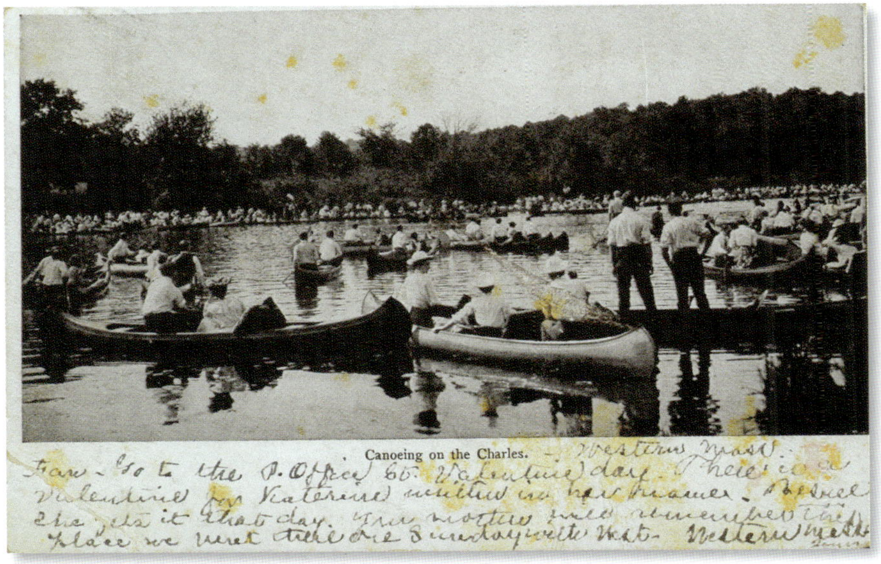

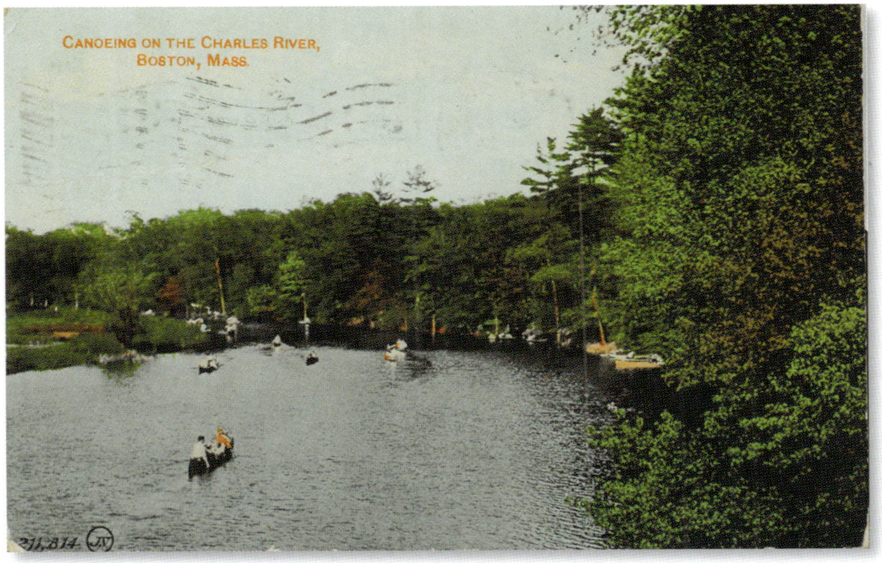

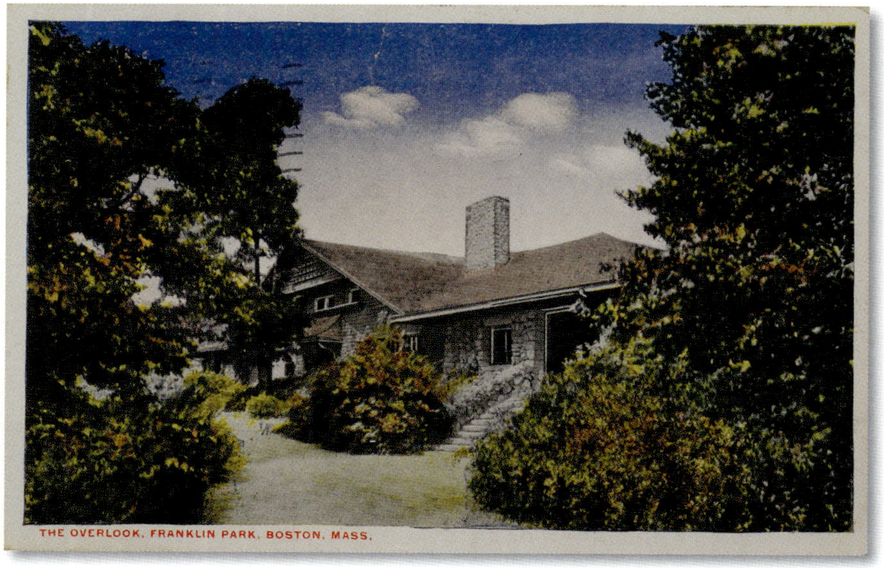

Located in the Jamaica Plain and Roxbury neighborhoods, the 527-acre Franklin Park is the largest and last component of Olmstead's Emerald Necklace.

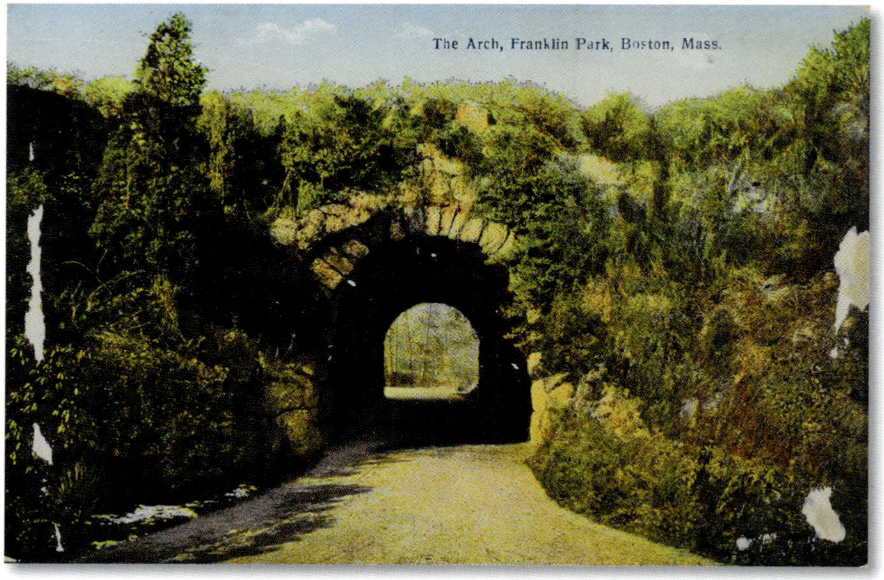

In 1887 the park commission requested that he interconnect those parks and design a continuous line of parkland, stretching from the Boston Common to West Roxbury.

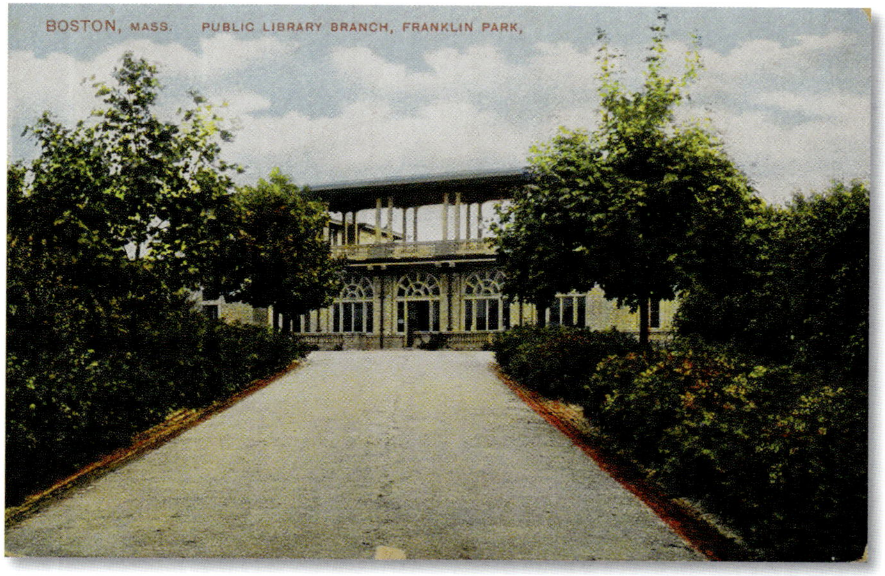

During the 1870s, Frederick Law Olmsted had already designed two major park projects in Boston, the Arnold Arboretum and the Back Bay Fens.

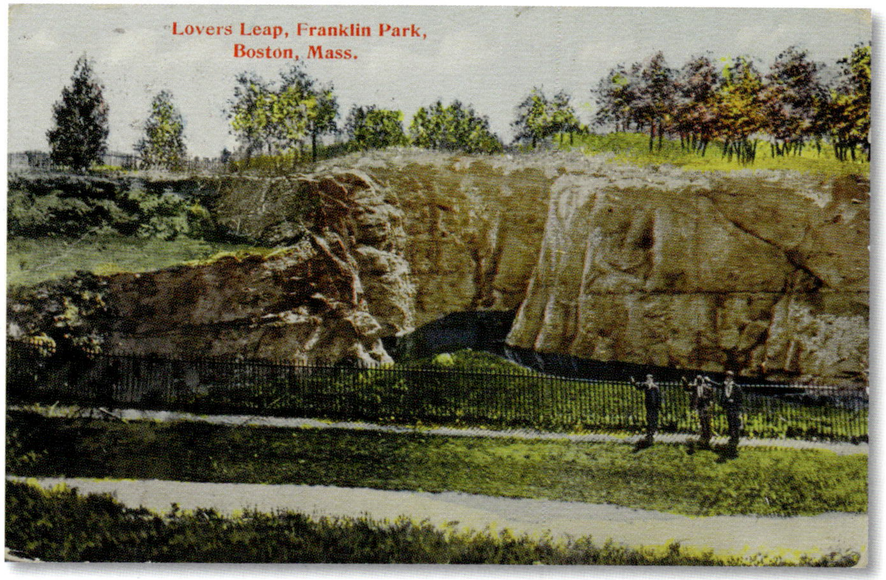

The result of this vision was the 1,100-acre chain of parks in Boston and Brookline, Massachusetts.

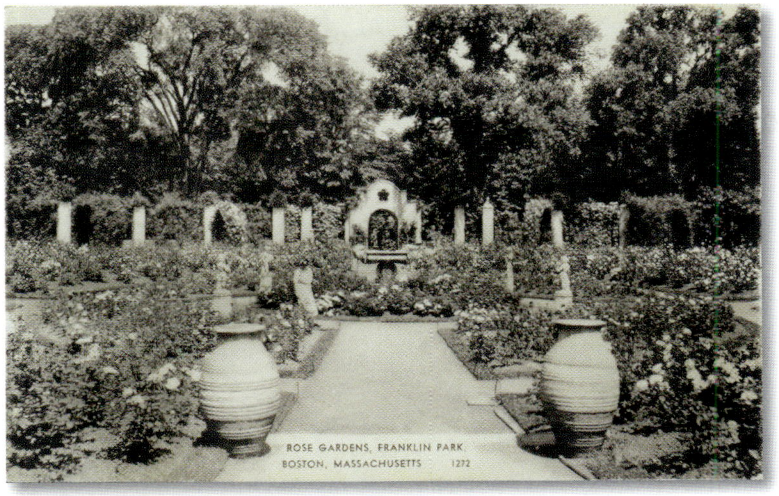

Called the Emerald Necklace, the entire scheme comprised The Boston Public Garden, the Common, Commonwealth Avenue, the Back Bay Fens, the Riverway, Olmsted Park, Jamaica Park, Arnold Arboretum, and Franklin Park. They are strung together through a series of parkways and waterways.

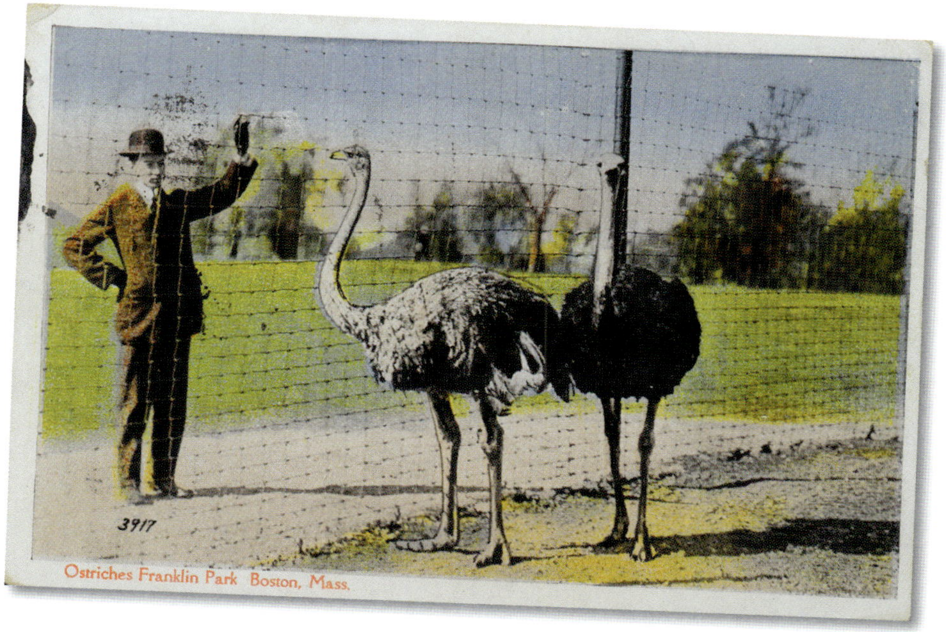

Franklin Park Zoo is located within park grounds.

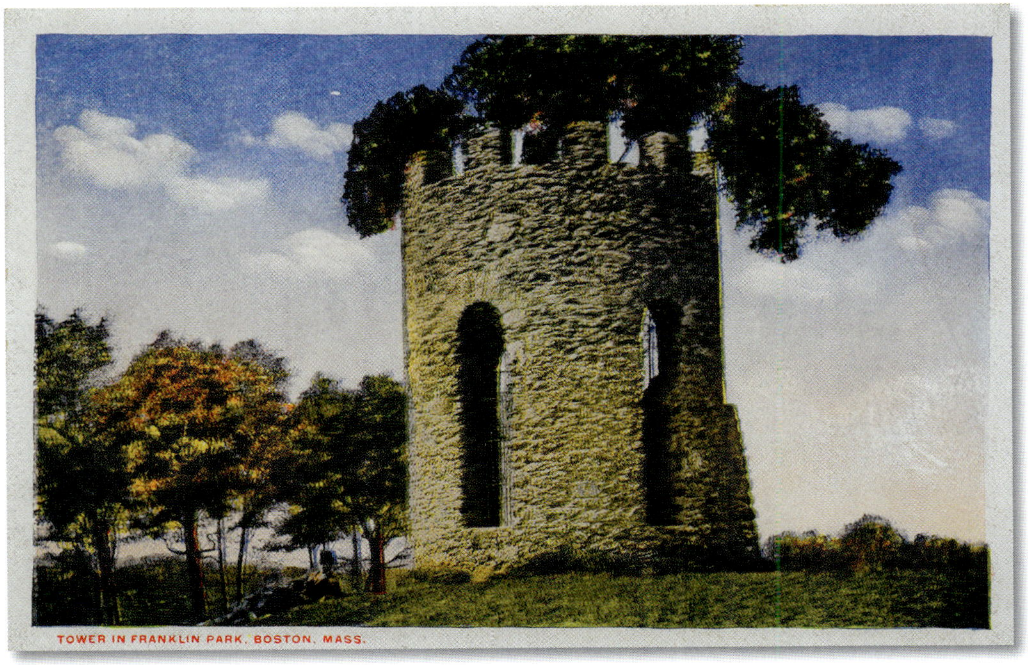

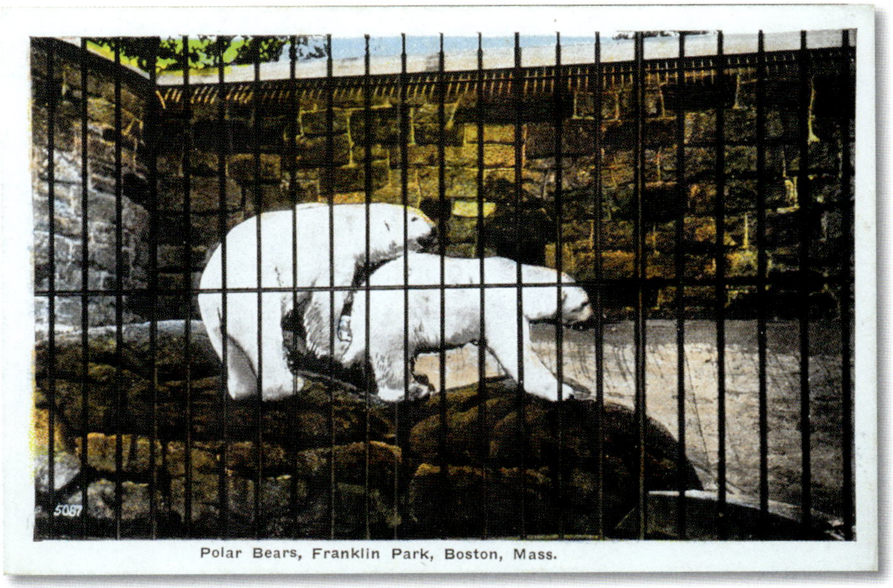

The 72-acre site zoo has such exotic animals as western lowland gorillas, a white tiger, and a herd of Grevy's zebra.

Although often neglected in the past, Franklin Park is considered the "crown jewel" of Olmsted's work in Greater Boston.

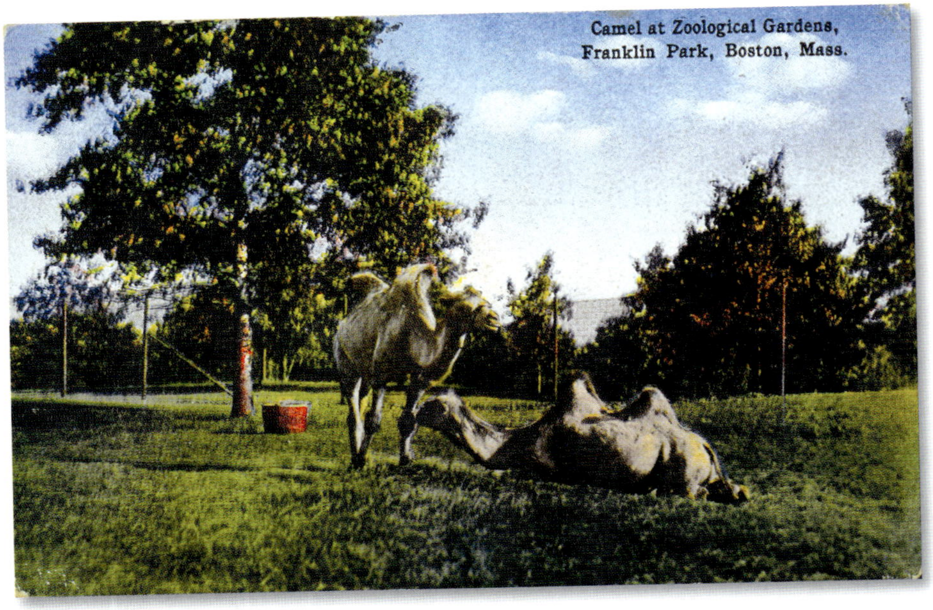

Franklin Park Zoo is one of the oldest zoos in North America and is the largest zoo in New England.

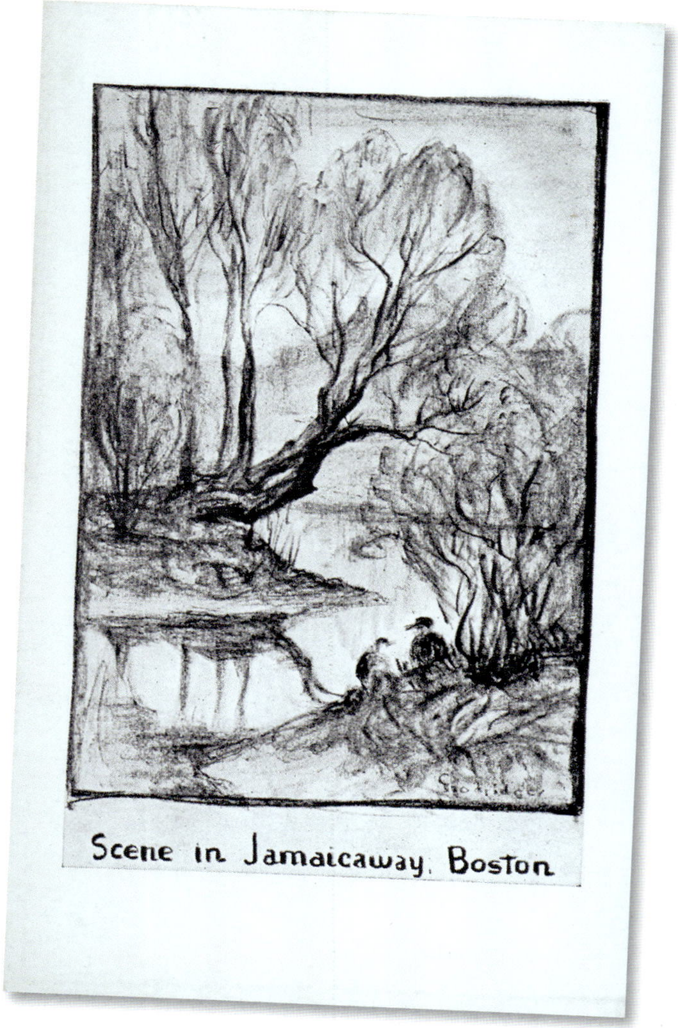

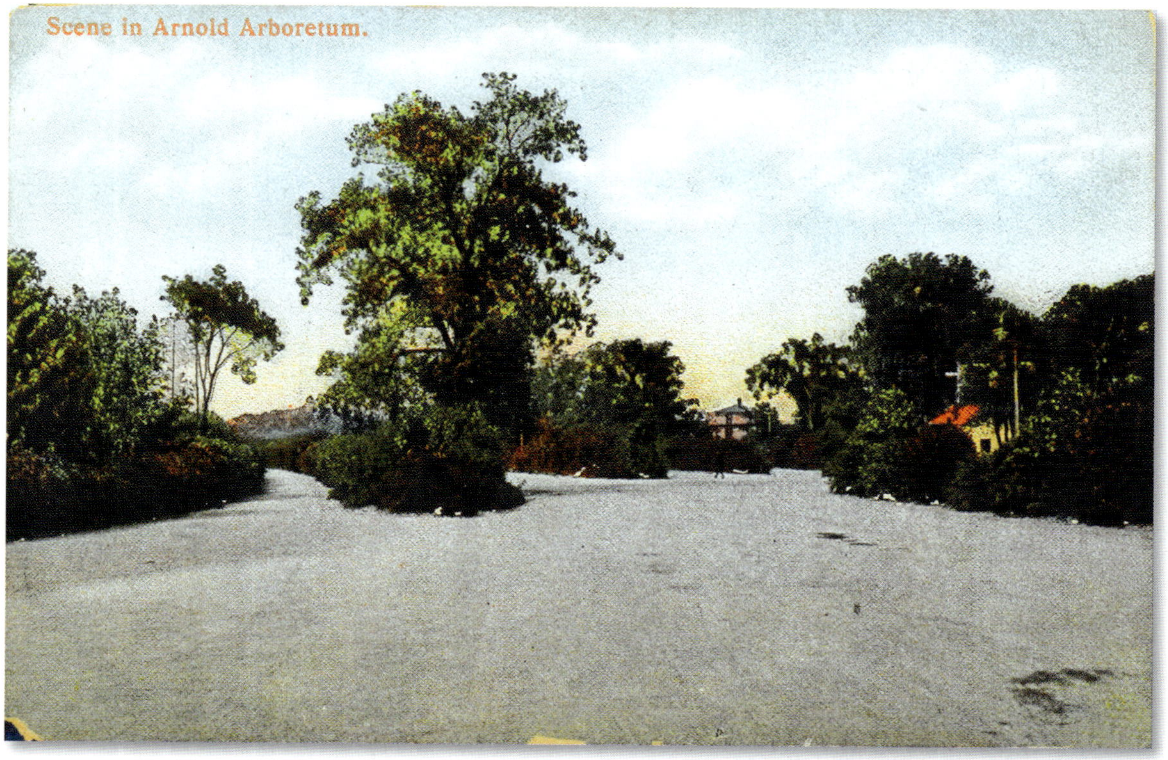

Designed by Frederick Law Olmsted, the Jamaicaway connects the Riverway in the north with the Arborway in the south. A four-lane undivided parkway, it passes many architecturally interesting houses.

A National Historic Landmark, the Arnold Arboretum is a 265-acre botanical garden containing over 14,000 woody plants, flowers, and trees. The nation's oldest university botanical garden, it is beautifully landscaped and open from sunrise to sunset at no cost.

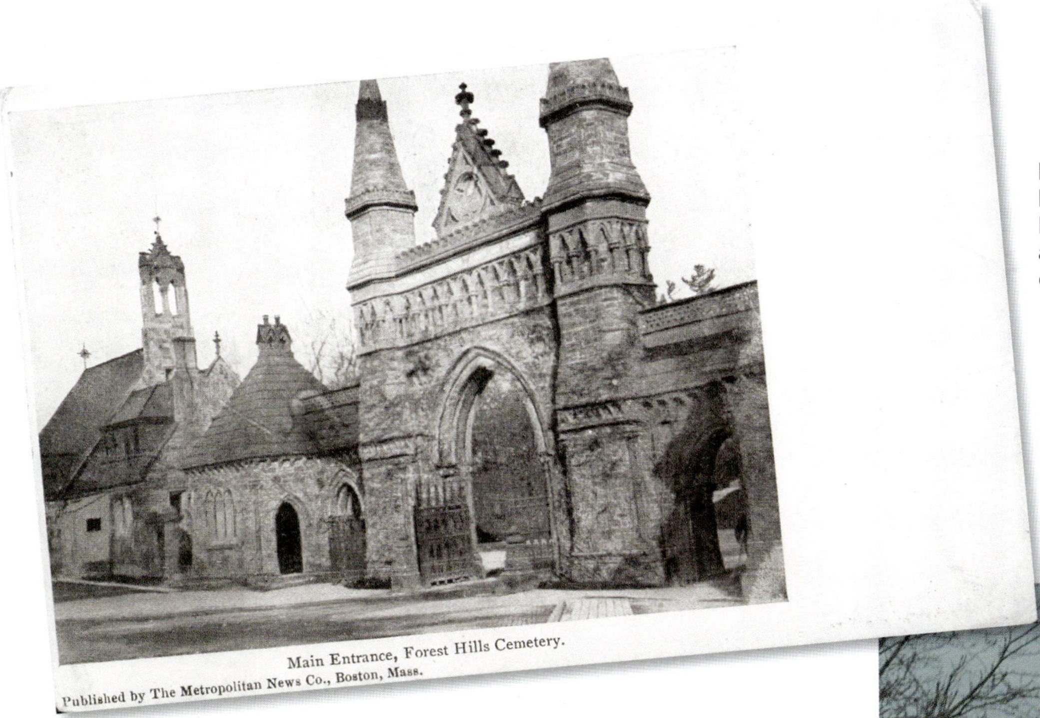

Between Arnold Arboretum and Franklin Park, Forest Hills is a lovely rural garden cemetery. Its 250 acres offer the public a tranquil sanctuary just minutes away from the hubbub of downtown Boston.

London has Big Ben, Paris has the Eiffel Tower, Boston has the CITGO sign.

The 60 by 60 foot CITGO sign has been a part of the Boston skyline since 1965. It has appeared in TV shows and movies, been in newspapers and magazines; withstood hurricanes and potential demolition. The people of Boston love it so much that they came to the sign's rescue in 1983 when Citgo decided to take it down.

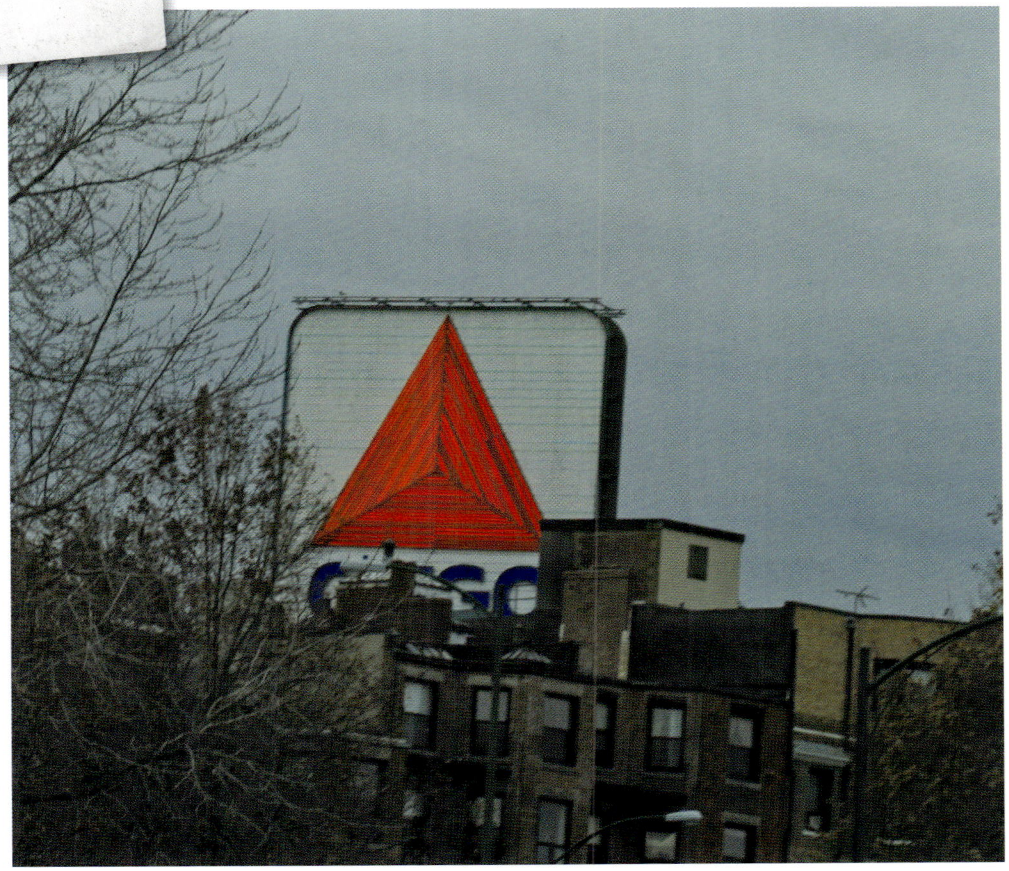

BIBLIOGRAPHY

Amory, Cleveland. *The Proper Bostonians.* New York, New York: E.P. Dutton & Co. 1947

Andros, Howard S. *Buildings and Landmarks of Old Boston.* Hanover, New Hampshire: University Press of New England. 2001

Atwood, Rhea Hollis. *Boston's French Secrets.* Bennington, Vermont: Images from the past. 2004

Bacon, Edwin (ed.). *Boston Illustrated*, Cambridge, Massachusetts: The Riverside Press, 1886

Beebe, Lucius Morris. *Boston and the Boston Legend*, New York, New York: D. Appleton-Century Company. 1935

Bunting, W.H. *Portrait of a Port Boston 1852-1914*. Cambridge, Massachusetts: The Belknap Press. 1971

Chamberlain, Allen. *Beacon Hill.* Boston, Massachusetts: The Riverside Press. 1925

Cushing, George M. *Great Buildings of Boston.* New York, New York: Dover Publications, Inc. 1898

Haglund, Karl. *Inventing the Charles River.* Cambridge, Massachusetts. The MIT Press. 2003

Harris, John. *Historic Walks in Old Boston*. Chester, Connecticut: Globe Pequot Press. 1993

Holmes, Oliver Wendell. *The Poetical Works Of Oliver Wendell Holmes*. Boston, Massachusetts: Houghton Mifflin Company. 1975

Howe, Julia W. "Social Boston Past and Present." *Harper's Bazaar.* Vol. XIIII, No 2, Feb., 2009

Kilham, Walter Harrington. *Boston after Bulfinch.* Cambridge, Massachusetts: Harvard University Press. 1946

Kreiger, Alex and David Cobb with Amy Turner (ed). *Mapping Boston*: Cambridge, Massachusetts: The MIT Press. 1999

Lodge, Henry Cabot. *Boston*. London, England: Longman's Green, and Co. 1899

Morris, Jerry. *The Boston Globe Guide to Boston*. Old Saybrook, Connecticut: Globe Pequot Press. 1989

Morison, Samuel Eliot. *Builders of the Bay Colony.* Boston, Massachusetts: Houghton Mifflin Company. 1930

Petronella, Mary Melvin (ed.) *Victorian Boston Today*. Boston, Massachusetts: Northeastern University Press. 2004

Ross, Marjorie Drake. *The Book of Boston the Colonial Period*. New York, New York: Hastings House Publishers. 1960

____________. *The Book of Boston the Federal Period*. New York, New York: Hastings House Publishers. 1961

____________. *The Book of Boston the Victorian Period*. New York, New York: Hastings House Publishers. 1964

Sammarco, Anthony Mitchell. *Boston's Fenway*. Charleston, South Carolina: Arcadia Publishing. 2002

State Street Trust Company. *Boston's Growth*. Boston, Massachusetts: Waltham Advertising and Publishing Company. 1910

Suffolk Savings Bank for Seamen and Others. Boston, Massachusetts: Walton Advertising and Printing Company. 1933

Thwing, Annie Haven. *The Crooked & Narrow Streets of the Town of Boston*: *1630-1822*. Detroit, Michigan: Singing Tree Press. 1970

Thoreau, Henry David. *The Writings of Henry David Thoreau, vol. 4*, p. 268, Boston, Massachusetts: Houghton Mifflin. 1906

Toll, Ian W. *Six Frigates.* New York, New York: W.W. Norton & Company. 2006

Vanderwarker, Peter. *Boston Then and Now*. New York, New York: Dover Publications, Inc. 1982

Whitehill, Walter Muir. *Destroyed Boston Buildings.* Massachusetts Historical Society, 1965

Whitehill, Walter and Kotker, Norman, *A Pictorial History Massachusetts*. New York, New York: Charles Scribner's Sons. 1976

Index